THE SPEECHMAKING PROCESS

RAYMOND S. ROSS

Wayne State University

Allyn and Bacon

Boston • London • Toronto • Sydney • Tokyo • Singapore

Business Agent, Ross Enterprises: Ricky Ross
Vice President, Editor in Chief: Paul Smith
Editorial Assistant: Kathy Rubino
Marketing Manager: Karon Bowers
Editorial Production Service: Chestnut Hill Enterprises, Inc.
Manufacturing Buyer: Suzanne Lareau
Cover Administrator: Suzanne Harbison

Internet: www.abacon.com
America Online: keyword: College Online

Library of Congress Cataloging-in-Publication Data

Ross, Raymond Samuel
    The speechmaking process / Raymond S. Ross. — 11th ed.
        p.   cm.
    Rev. ed. of: Speech communication. 10th ed. 1995.
    Includes bibliographical references and index.
    ISBN 0-205-27304-1
    1. Oral communication.   2. Public speaking.   I. Ross, Raymond
Samuel Speech communication.   II. Title.
P95.R675   1997
808.5´ 1—dc21   97-16476
                                                           CIP

Printed in the United States of America
10   9   8   7   6   5   4   3   2   1   02   01   00   99   98   97

CONTENTS

PREFACE

Good communicators are also almost always knowledgeable in the critical areas of the communication process, perception, language, logical thinking, and presentation. *The Speechmaking Process* addresses all of these important areas and relates them eclectically to effective and responsible public speaking.

The most important educational goals of this book are:

1. To help students become effective critical thinkers, language users, organizers, and ethical purveyors of informative and persuasive messages.
2. To help students learn that receivers are coactive participants in the communication process who affectively, cognitively, and/or behaviorally respond to messages.
3. To help students understand that meaning is heavily dependent on one's experience and the realities their social constructions allow.
4. To help students transfer the communication fundamentals learned from public speaking to all other forms of communication.

The more pragmatic objectives are implicit in Cicero's five essentials of public speaking:

1. Determining exactly what one intends to say, and to whom it will be said.
2. Arranging the materials in a proper order with good judgment.
3. Selecting well-chosen words and carefully phrased sentences.
4. Fixing the speech in mind (practice).
5. Delivering it with dignity and grace.

Relevant theory and pragmatic student needs have guided the content decision for most of this book. Its basic pedagogical assumption is that students are better served by a "theory and practice" approach than by one that is all practice. The theory is necessary to power and steer the practice. Its obvious eclecticism is, I think, better informed than earlier editions. (I've had more time to read.) However, this edition is clearly influenced by the popular interactionist and social construction views of today as well as by the relevant behavioral/cognitive theories of yesterday and today. Its rhetorical roots are also evident in its treatment of ethics, models, and practice. These generalizations from theory to practice, whether cast as rules or laws, have been simplified to facilitate understanding and application. Speaking experience governed by theory, principle, and professional criticism should promote sound communication habits whatever the setting.

I'm pleased that "critical thinking" scholars also identify as essential the practical skills taught in the chapters of this book: organizing, outlining, information gathering, goal setting, analysis, reasoning, and effective delivery. The theory chapters plus classroom applications are designed to lead to still richer thinking, language, and speaking skills.

My recent experience in teaching at our new state-of-the-art University Center in Traverse City, Michigan has brought me up-to-speed on computer-assisted everything, especially research, graphics, and visual aids.

These matters are also improved by the counsel and efforts of Professors Jack Kay of Wayne State University and Timothy Borchers of Moorhead State University. Their excellent appendix, "Researching through the Internet," is also the result of their cutting edge research and application experience in these matters.

I would also like to thank the reviewers of the eleventh edition: Diane O. Casagrande, West Chester University; Kay M. Robinson, Bemidji State University; W. Robert Sampson, University of Wisconsin at Eau Claire; David E. Majewski, Richard Bland College; Jim Fatka, Montcalm Community College. In a time of name changes, this edition has been retitled *The Speechmaking Process* (formerly *Speech Communication*). This better reflects its purpose and the course it seeks. Most of the "Speech" associations and journals have also recently changed titles. Reviewers also pointed out that all serious, competing public speaking books have now dropped speech communication from their titles. Reviewers also suggested a leaner, simpler format and package. I have tried to oblige.

I don't usually thank vice-presidents of large publishing houses for much. This time I commend Joe Opiela of Allyn & Bacon for taking over in mid-book when our regular editor went on to bigger things. I am much impressed and much obliged. The current editor, Paul Smith, is determined to make this edition the most successful ever. What more can I ask!

Mark, my professor son and sometimes co-author, keeps me current, honest, and motivated. The charming Ricky, my spousal business agent and personal editor, adds to my *douceur de vivre* and makes the effort worthwhile.

RSR

P.S. Please ask my publisher or your sales representative about ancillaries and the *Instructor's Manual.*

1

PUBLIC SPEAKING AND COMMUNICATION

CHAPTER OUTLINE

THE IMPORTANCE OF PUBLIC SPEAKING IN SOCIETY

Why study public speaking? A dozen or more occupations have a direct interest in public speaking. The "people professions"—law, teaching, public relations, advertising, health care, management, criminal justice, sales—could just as well be called the "communication professions."

It's always a shame when a guy with great talent can't tell the board or a committee what's in his head.

The most important thing I learned in school was how to communicate.

Lee Iacocca

On the 1992 election—

I just wasn't a good enough communicator.

George Bush

Take all the speech and communication courses you can because the world turns on communication.

J. H. McConnel, CEO, Worthington Industries

It has been estimated that there are over 3,000 speaking platforms on any given day in Los Angeles alone, 30,000 in Chicago, and 50,000 in New York. These include Rotary Clubs, universities, women's groups, church groups, and conventions. In today's golden age of the lecture business, Notre Dame former football coach Lou Holtz and motivational speaker Tony Robbins command fees of $20,000 to $75,000 per appearance. Ralph Nader earns $800,000 a year speaking. Who says talk is cheap?

Approximately 60,000 conventions or major meetings are held each year in hundreds of cities across America. Many of these gatherings include intelligent, entertaining, or humorous paid presentations. Add to this, unpaid speeches (for example, over 3,000 program participants at the yearly National Communication Association convention), and the numbers grow quickly. Do real people ever give speeches?

A survey of the speaking habits of 478 New York adults revealed that (1) between 55 percent and 63 percent of these adults gave at least one speech in the past two years to ten or more people, with 71 percent of these speakers giving at least four speeches during that time; (2) people are more likely to give job-related speeches, and these speeches are the informative and persuasive type; and (3) people with more education and income give speeches the most frequently. Knowing this last connection, a person who wants a high-income job would be wise to get a good education and prepare to speak well. Obviously this is a skill you may need.

Still think it isn't important? In a Michigan poll, 500 adults were asked: "What most influences your decisions about political candidates?" The respondents put party affiliation first, *speaking ability* second, appearance or good looks third, age fourth, race or ethnic background fifth, and the person's sex last. One would hope that honesty, issues, and intelligence might have been mentioned more often . . . but speaking ability is clearly critical.

> Skill in utilizing the spoken word provides one of the major means of maximizing the rewards obtained from the environment and of minimizing the punishments.
>
> *Gerry Miller*

Are students any good at this important oral skill? Dr. David Adamany, a university president, thinks not:

> It has become increasingly clear that students are significantly deficient in their ability to make oral presentations. Yet this skill has become steadily more important in a world which requires collaboration between specialists in widely varying fields and in which communications technology—by telephone, television and audiovisual tapes—implicates the ability to make effective oral presentations. Contrary to some journalistic assertions, a technological age heightens the need for human collaboration—and thus for effective oral communication—rather than diminishing it. . . . I ask the commission to consider how the university might improve the ability of students to make oral presentations, which is certainly one of the basic skills required of most educated persons.
>
> *David Adamany, President, Wayne State University*

The University of Colorado faculty and students across the curriculum agree. Survey data make clear that both groups feel that students are deficient in the following:

1. Expressing ideas clearly
2. Organizing messages
3. Expressing ideas concisely
4. Using evidence
5. Use of speaking voice
6. Anxiety control
7. Listening effectively[1]

There is hope that we are correcting the problem.

> On higher education—
>
> "79% require speech communication in Gen Ed."
>
> *SPECTRA, April, 1995*

The national call for students to improve their critical thinking relates directly to the concepts covered in this text. ". . . we are teaching far more than a set of skills to use to affect others. We are also teaching structures for thinking."[2] The interaction between how we speak and how we think is a compelling reason for learning and applying the lessons in your public speaking course.

Many researchers show that you can improve your speech skills significantly by taking a speech course. Moreover, testimonials by successful individuals have affirmed the value of speech training, and research has indicated its usefulness to you in better understanding your other university courses.

Modern technology often makes speech preparation and critical thinking unusually important. In one case reported by New York state occupational education czar Willard Daggert, a speech was in IBM hard copy transcripts within 90 seconds of its completion—*and simultaneously translated into four different languages*. We'll have more to say about critical thinking in the chapters that follow.

THE COMMUNICATION PROCESS

Meaning

For many social theorists communication is primarily concerned with *meaning*. Meaning for them becomes a social construction based primarily on our life experiences, our perceptions of reality, and our language habits. For *social-construction* theorists all objective reality is entirely dependent on our thinking habits and our communication abilities.[3]

> Human action is critically dependent on the cognitive processing of information, that is, on the world as cognized rather that the world as it is.
>
> *Professor K. J. Gergen*

This is not to say that there is not any "true" or "real" reality in the world—just that our abilities to discern it are heavily biased by our experience, our attitudes, and our language and thinking habits. The question "What is reality?" is not a new one. In a dictionary sense the answer is, "a person, entity, or event that is actual or true," or "that which exists objectively and in fact."

In philosophy reality (realism) can mean "the doctrine that universal principles are more real than objects as sensed," or "the doctrine that the objects of perception exist independently of the perceiver."

A better question might be "Where is reality?" In the final analysis a person's individual reality, however accurate or inaccurate, is still one's individual perception of reality. The same can be said of society and its definable subgroups. One's concept and understanding of the interaction of (1) "real" reality, (2) individual perception of reality, and (3) society's perception of reality can affect our ability to be objective, rational, and realistic.

Some people perceive reality better than others. They make more accurate social constructions of what they see and hear. The bias of communication professors is that these people do better because they are more knowledgeable in the critical areas of communication, perception, language, and logical thinking.

This book addresses all four of these areas and hopefully relates them clearly to the pragmatic dimensions of public speaking. Language and critical thinking will be covered in detail in Chapters 2 and 12.

Perception

The perception process is really another way of looking at the communication process and how we discern or assign meanings to messages. The theory here is that we hypothesize about messages which we then accept or reject on the basis of personal constructs based on prior learning and experience.

Have you ever been on a train that was stopped next to other trains in a railroad terminal? Have you then felt, seen, and heard all the signs indicating movement, only to find it was the other trains that were moving? Perhaps you discovered this by noticing that the other trains were gone, or by fixing your gaze on something you *knew* was not moving, such as the ceiling of the station, a roof support, or the ground.

The point of this is that perception is essentially two things: (1) the *sensation* caused by the stimulation of a sense organ and (2) the *interpretation* of that sensation. In our study of speech we are concerned mainly with the interpretation. As was stated earlier, it is through our knowledge and experience that we interpret or attach meaning to a symbol.

Our *mood* (or *set*), or readiness to perceive a stimulus in a certain way, affects our ability to perceive and to accept a stimulus. The consciousness defends itself by apparently refusing to accept certain messages. On the other hand, we may wish so much to hear something that, regardless of the actual message, we hear, interpret, and attach meaning to it according to what we *wish* to hear. One of the great barriers to good communication is our tendency to hear what we wish to hear, see what we wish to see, and believe what we wish to believe.

A closely related perceptual and communication problem arises from our normal tendency toward **completeness.**

KNOCK KNOCK
WH   TH   ?

Figure 1.1

In communications that appear to be only partially complete, we often fill in the unsaid part or complete the pattern. If we do not have a sense of completeness about something, we often feel upset, ill at ease, confused, and unhappy about it. This tendency can be important in motivating people. Perhaps you have had a teacher who communicates just enough knowledge in a stimulating way to motivate you to do further reading and research so that you can complete or close the pattern. A problem arises when we close incomplete communication patterns in ways not intended by the speaker, or when we become frustrated by a lack of details. It is easier to see Figure 1.1 as a *complete* triangle and to see its companion as eight strange marks—or can you fill in the missing information and find the hammer? Who's there?

Sometimes our habits and previous experiences cause us to leave things out. Read the three messages in Figure 1.2 quickly. Many people see nothing unusual about these messages, even after two or three readings. The good, rapid readers seem to have the most trouble. Why should this be so? A group of second and third graders had no trouble finding the double words in each message. To a certain extent, we perceive what our habits, our emotions, and our prior knowledge and experience let us perceive. A good reader has learned to skim and to ignore nonessential words. The beginning reader sees one word at a time.

Test your perceptual ability in Figure 1.3. Do you see anything familiar or identifiable? Do you see a message?

You should see a word in white on a partial black field. Your experience is usually just the opposite of this pattern; here the area *between* the letters is black instead of the letters themselves. Even after you see the message, it may escape you momentarily as your long-standing habits and previous patterns of experience assert themselves.

As was noted above, your *mental set*—that is, your readiness to interpret a message in a certain way—has a lot to do with what you "see." Look for a duck in Figure 1.4. You should find one quickly because a duck is what you are looking for. Keep studying the duck. You should also find another animal. Did you get the message?

A group of professional photographers found it almost impossible to "see" the photograph in Figure 1.5. What do you see?

Don't proceed until you see a cow looking right at you! If you haven't seen it by now, you may actually become annoyed, particularly if you've asked for help and your friends see the cow immediately. Communication is like that. We don't do our best when we begin to feel awkward, stupid, or left out.

Figure 1.2

Figure 1.3

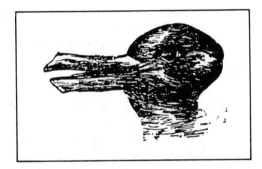

Figure 1.4

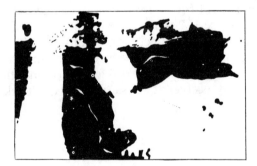

Figure 1.5

How are you doing with LEFTY and the rabbit? Have you lost them? When experiences are new to us, we may understand or "see" one moment and "not see" the next.

The same person does not always perceive the same object exactly the same way every time he or she observes it. It is no wonder that other observers do not always agree on what they see.

Carl Rogers explains that every individual exists in a continually changing world of experience of which he or she is the center. Whether this world is called the ***phenomenal field*** or the ***experiential field,*** humans exist in a sea of experiences, both conscious and unconscious.

Communication Models

The word ***model*** generally refers to a representation of a thing or a process. We have relatively little trouble producing a model of a physical object. We can learn much about the physical behavior of trains, boats, and airplanes by building models of them. However, when we attempt to make models of more abstract things—things that are difficult to measure physically—we often oversimplify to the point of poor or dangerous representation, or we may simply be unable to agree on exactly what it is we are modeling.

The advantages of using a model are evident. The model gives you a different, closer look. It provides a frame of reference, suggests informational gaps, underlines the problem of abstraction, and expresses a problem in symbolic language when there is some advantage in using figures or symbols. Of course there are some drawbacks to using models, such as oversimplification and other dangers inherent in gross abstraction.

We may use words, numbers, symbols, and pictures to illustrate models of things, theories, or processes. In geometry we accept the theorem that the square of the hypotenuse of a right triangle is equal to the sum of the squares of the legs. This statement is a form of ***verbal model.*** If we draw a picture of this theorem (Figure 1.6), we have a ***verbal-pictorial model.*** Communication experts have used mostly verbal-pictorial models in trying to give us a closer and more scientific look at the communication process.

The Schramm Models (Figure 1.7) make clear the importance of common experience. Speakers and audiences need some commonality of language, culture, training, and so on if there is to be any real communication. Schramm helps us better understand the mutual influence notion whereby a participant can be both sender and receiver at the same time. Feedback makes

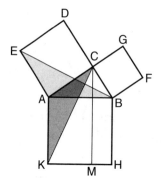

Figure 1.6 The square of the hypotenuse of a right triangle is equal to the sum of the squares of the legs, or AKHB = ACDE + BFGC.

an audience a sender and a speaker the receiver. It is also clear that your "signal" is more effective if placed in the overlapping fields of experience.

The transactional model (Figure 1.8) attempts to illustrate the following definition of communication:

> A transactional process of skillfully sharing, selecting, and sorting ideas, symbols, and signs in such a way as to help listeners elicit from their own minds a meaning or construction similar to that intended by the speaker.

By *transactional* we mean that this is a socially derived process involving an unending activity that reciprocally affects or influences both parties. That is, we are capable of being both sender and receiver at the same time. We are, one might say, *transceivers*.[4]

The frame of the model shows the world in which this communication takes place. It suggests the importance of *situation, mood, context,* and *psychological climate.* The *situation* could range from a speech to a simple exchange of information. **Mood** refers to feelings of the moment. At different times your

Figure 1.7 Three Schramm Models. From Wilbur Schramm, "How Communication Works," in *The Process and Effects of Mass Communication,* ed. Wilbur Schramm (Urbana, Ill.: University of Illinois Press, 1955), pp. 4–8.

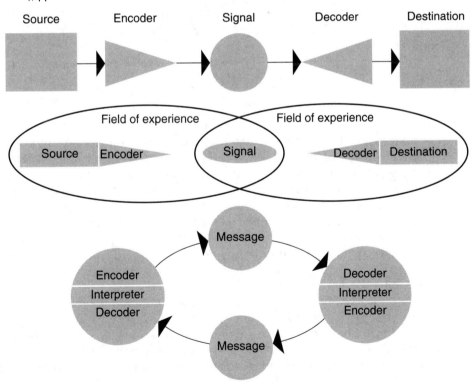

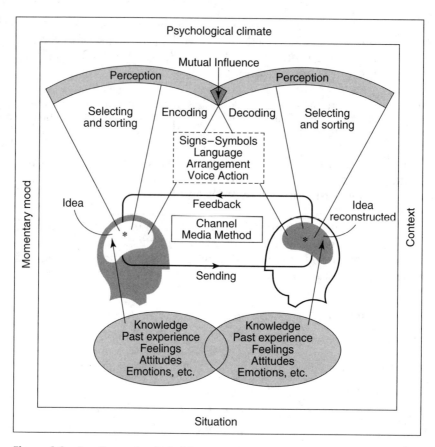

Figure 1.8   Ross Transactional Model

mood might be happy, angry, tense, and so on. Your mood can greatly affect what you say or hear and how you say or hear something. **Context** is the framework of other words or ideas into which yours fit. If you are talking about paper, note how the word changes in these contexts: The paper was late today (newspaper). The paper is crooked (wallpaper). It is an A paper (homework). *Psychological climate* is a lot like weather or physical climate. Just as our weather might be bitterly cold, so too might the psychological mood of a classroom or a speech occasion. An unhappy, impersonal (cold) speaker typically hinders rather than helps communication. Sometimes climate is the most important part of a speaker's message.

Let's assume we have a message (which might be referred to as an ***idea*** or ***concept*** or ***meaning***) that we wish to convey to another person. Our brain now sorts through our storehouse of knowledge, experience, feelings, and previous training to select and refine the precise meaning we are seeking to communicate. Before we transmit this meaning, we ***encode*** it; we put it into signs and symbols that we commonly think of as ***language.*** (Gesture, facial expression, and tone of voice may also be considered signs, symbols, or codes.)

The way in which the message is coded, the medium or channel chosen for its transmission, and the skill with which it is transmitted influence the meaning it will have for the receiver. Assuming that the medium for this illustration is simply the air between the speaker and the listener, we now have the encoded message, its transmission, and its reception by the other person. The listener then ***decodes*** the signal, or at least attempts to decode it. The listener sorts out, selects, and elicits meanings from his or her storehouse of knowledge, experience, and training until there has been constructed in his or her mind a notion of the images and ideas contained in the mind of the sender. However, if the signal is in a code with which the listener is not familiar, such as a foreign language, not much communication of any kind will take place.

To the extent that the listener's notions or constructions are similar to the sender's images and ideas, we have usually achieved satisfactory communication. The idea, concept, or meaning in the mind of the listener is therefore very dependent upon the knowledge and experience he or she can apply to the code. The value of knowing your listeners now becomes evident. Because all of this sharing implies intention, perhaps one *can* "not communicate"—at least where poor speechmaking is involved. The *thoughts* you are trying to communicate and provoke are the principal energizers of the speechmaking process. They are the fuel that makes a serious communication possible. However, like a car with a full gas tank, it will not go far if the subsystems fail or if the fuel was watered down in the first place.

Let's assume that the speaker in Figure 1.8 is a woman who wishes to communicate a message (a thought or an idea) to an audience. The idea is represented by the star inside her brain.

Let's suppose the idea is an abstract one, such as *love*. Within this woman's 12 billion brain cells are stored her knowledge and past experiences, her feelings, attitudes, emotions, and many more things that make her the person she is. The brain, with a storage capacity able to accept ten new facts every second, can hold information equivalent to 100 trillion different words. Our sender now sorts through and selects from this vast storehouse of knowledge and past experience, choosing items that help her define and refine what she is trying to say. She has to have a basis upon which to perform this operation, a program if you will. We can think of the brain in some ways as a system computer. The forebrain, for example, becomes a kind of input regulator into which we feed the program. This woman's program had better include at least three questions, or she is already in trouble. These are: (1) What do I have stored under *love?* (2) What do I know about the audience? and (3) What do I have filed for this particular situation and context? You can almost visualize the program in action: assessing, accepting, rejecting, cross-referencing,

'hesizing both the information in the storehouse and in the system—
selecting and sorting the appropriate knowledge, past experience,
⌄o on. In this complex process the brain actually burns electrical power.
⌐1. A. Johnson comments wryly:

> "The human brain, deep in thought, consumes about 14 watts of power. It gives some insight into world politics to consider that when three heads of state meet at the summit their combined brain power is that of a 40-watt light bulb, scarcely sufficient for reading the lines, to say nothing of reading between them."
>
> Horton A. Johnson, *Perspectives in Biology and Medicine*

Although there is some confusion among scholars as to exactly how and when the encoding takes place, it is useful, if only for instructional purposes, to think of it as a *sequence*. Our sender must next choose her codes and should apply a program similar to the one used in sorting ideas.

The speaker now delivers the message. Let us assume that there is no unusual distraction or noise in the system, and that the sensory access of the audience is adequate. Assuming the audience is listening, the message is received; the auditory and other sensations experienced by the listeners are only the first part of human perception. The more critical part is the interpretation of those sensations, all part of the decoding of the signs, symbols, and language of the speaker. The listeners sort through their knowledge, experiences, attitudes, and so forth and select those meanings that will allow the creation of a message concerning love. To the extent that this reconstruction or response is similar to the sender's intended message, we hopefully have meaningful communication. This reconstructed idea, then, is largely dependent upon common knowledge, fields of experience, language, and some understanding of the communication process.

The term *feedback* in the model requires a moment of important consideration. It is necessary if our model is to be transactional and interactional. In engineering terms interactional feedback also refers to some of the transmitted energy or signal being returned to the source. The automatic pilot used in airplanes is an example of self-correcting machinery that uses feedback. The analogy between this kind of feedback and the feedback used in human communication appears to break down a bit when we consider the kind of electronic feedback all of us have observed in public-address systems or recorders, in which a reentry of some of the sound from the speaker to the microphone causes a howl or loud noise. However, human communication is also vulnerable to disruptive feedback, heckling, loud argument, and fear. When severe enough, one may suffer encoding difficulties or even anger to the point of ending the transaction. Of course, some people just don't listen well, and some speakers don't allow for feedback! (See Figure 1.9.)

For most speech purposes we usually think of feedback as useful in a self-correcting sense. As our transmitted signal is "bounced off" our receivers, it feeds back information that allows us to correct and refine our signal. A

Figure 1.9   Making a point. Drawings by David John McKee, by permission of *The Times Education-al Supplement* (London). Published in the United States by *The Saturday Review.*

quizzical look, a frown, a yawn, the sound of our own voice—any of these may cause us to reevaluate and recode our signals. On the other hand, speech fright to the point of forgetting can be compared to the intense feedback of the pub-lic-address system type, which momentarily, but completely, shorts out the sending device, and the whole system goes down. For now, let us think of feedback as part of the transactional process that we should make work for us.

Obviously not every member of an audience will decode, reconstruct, and respond in the same way (Figure 1.8). This is another reminder that audi-ence analysis is critical to message input. Recall also that the ***encoder*** and ***decoder*** can perform their functions only in terms of their own fields of experience. There must be some shared experience *common* to both in order for the communication to even begin to convey the intended message. The decoding of a message by the receiver starts that person's process of encoding. The roles of encoder and decoder, speaker and audience, are interchangeable. Thus each person in the communication process is to some extent an encoder, decoder, and interpreter.

SPEAKER INTEGRITY

Being Communicationally Sensitive

A persuasive appeal (as we shall learn in Chapter 11) is only as good as its "fit" or match to a given audience. Ironically, unethical persuaders have usually learned this lesson well. The patent medicine salesperson takes care to avoid the medically informed or quickly fails. Honest salespersons can fail just as readily if insensitive to their audiences and become unintentionally unethical by selling a product or idea to unknowns who will injure themselves or others. The bartender is interested in your age; the handgun seller in your permit; the doctor in your medical history, and so on. For any of these people not to care about these matters is clearly an ethical matter.

Communication sensitivity involves effectively and ethically matching the message we are sending to the requirements of the receivers, the situation, and the context. It is a measure of a speaker's willingness to consider carefully the psychological environment before encoding messages. It is the ability to judge public and interpersonal encounters accurately and to sense when to be rhetorically sensitive and when to be rhetorically assertive.

For a speaker to use complicated statistics to impress a sophisticated audience is one thing; to use them as a deceptive strategy on an unsophisticated audience is unethical. To use inflated statistics to raise consciousness or because the cause is just is also unethical. This fact is often overlooked by politicians and even spokespeople for very worthy causes.

We learned earlier that a given message does not mean the same thing to all people and that perceptions and understandings vary with contexts and situations. Without some consideration of the receivers, we stand a good chance of confusing or unintentionally deceiving our receivers. A child may decode a message quite differently from that of a mature adult. How a particular person will interpret a particular message is also an ethical consideration.

Culpable Ignorance

Most moral, professional, and legal codes carefully consider *intent* in passing judgments. However, our legal systems are harsh on people who are expected to "know better" and to "behave better." Witness the large number of medical and legal malpractice suits or our treatment of political, religious, and even sports figures who stray. Trained, educated speakers have special ethical obligations beyond intent. Listeners, like patients and clients, also have responsibilities to society and to themselves.

The role or status of a speaker enters into ethical evaluations of that speaker. A qualified person serving in a leadership role has special ethical obligations. We expect our political and religious leaders and our professional people to be responsible, regardless of intent. A doctor convicted of malpractice rarely intended to do harm. An incompetent teacher may have good intentions. We hold such people ethically responsible, even though their intent may have been good. As one jokester put it, "Congress has the Ten Commandments bottled up in the ethics committee." They had better "unbottle" them since our laws accommodate these premises, not just for political leaders and professionals, but for all public figures as well. Senators, representatives, and other public figures have less protection from libel and slander than does the average citizen. (They do, of course, have their protective immunities.)

All of us have some ethical obligations beyond intent. Many people have been hurt by those who "meant well." All of us have an obligation to get our facts straight before sending messages that might capriciously misinform or injure the receiver. Moralists call this **culpable ignorance,** that is, ignorance that comes from carelessness and thus deserves blame.[5]

Affording Clues and Choice

The following postulates are offered as guidance. If there is such a thing as a covering law, it would be that speakers are ethically responsible for the strategies employed, inferred, or attributed.

It is unethical for a speaker to simply conceal his or her real purpose, the organization represented, or to pretend to speak objectively when really an advocate of only one point of view. This postulate or rule is obvious in some contexts but not as clear in others: a man posing as a minister to bilk a senior citizen of her money; a Marxist pretending to be a capitalist. These are unethical if the concealment or deception is *total* (that is, if there is no real clue), whether the concealed entity be purpose, organization, or point of view. But what of legitimate strategy? Perhaps rhetorically one should not be too quick to shout out one's point of view or purpose. To do so might prohibit any kind of a hearing. The emerging theorem is that you are rhetorically ethical as long as your concealment is not total or is not delayed until it has no chance of being heard.

As process-oriented receivers we should be on guard and perhaps expect some overstatement when listening to a person with an obvious ax to grind—a politician, salesperson, or promoter. If that person is within the law (no false claims, or statistics, slander, and so on) and does not falsely or totally conceal the purpose or the organization represented, he or she is probably meeting this ethical postulate.

Honest clues protect the receiver's fundamental right of choice. Even in social compliance situations, one usually has some choice. When choice is minimal, one usually has some alternatives (the courts, when necessary). The ultimate decision on how to behave, act, interpret, or believe must in some way, however small, be left to the receiver. That choice must be a viable one. "Your money or your life" is no real choice. In a democracy choice is a very special ethical consideration for speakers, especially when their purpose is to persuade.

USE OF EMOTIONAL APPEALS   Appealing to the emotions is not a new ethical question. Plato and Aristotle argued it long ago. Plato counseled that emotional appeals should be avoided because they detract from the truth. Aristotle felt that it was a speaker's moral *purpose,* not his or her art, that made such appeals unethical. The use of emotional arguments when there is *no* evidence to support one's point is for Aristotle (and most modern rhetoricians) unethical. It is also unethical if the emotional argument clearly flies in the face of what the receivers, given time, would find in their own investigations.

In an angry speech one is not always searching for truth. One may not intend to distort unfairly, but it happens. As receivers we should be reminded that humans are emotional as well as rational and that free citizens have a right to sound off and frequently do. Our ethical tolerance should include a healthy discounting of legitimate emotional appeals.

FAIR HEARING   As receivers we have an obligation to seek out clues and choices, to question and clarify, to give a fair hearing once we have committed ourselves to some legitimate interest in an issue. We must make an effort to understand the sender's biases and intent. We should show tolerance. Fair hearing replaces force in a free society. The listener must also help decide what constitutes valid proof and a legitimate appeal to the emotions.

To give fair hearing we must also analyze our range of acceptance. Are we really stuck with a "hard" attitude? Is there some latitude in our position? Giving a fair hearing also means allowing the other person some chance to talk. Ethical communication doesn't outlaw aggressive arguing, but it does outlaw excessive monologuing; it does necessitate giving the sender some chance to make and explain his or her point. Fair hearing also calls for fair fighting. Sandbagging or setting people up for obvious embarrassment borders on unethical (and often illegal) entrapment. Dragging in every superfluous issue in order to deliberately confuse is another violation of ethics.

LIES AND FALSE FACTS   A lie is a statement intended to deceive. "He tells a lie who has one thing in his mind and says something else by words or by any signs whatsoever." To some moral philosophers, the natural end of speech is to communicate with our thoughts, and a lie is evil because it frustrates the very purpose of speech. A speaker is responsible for telling the truth and for the social consequences that result if the truth is not told. This view includes not only our words but all of our nonverbal communication.

Figure 1.10

FALSE PRETENSE   A person posing as a doctor of medicine may do considerable harm through such a charade. Speaking as a qualified economist or engineer while lacking the background to do so is also dangerous and unethical. This is not to say (assuming we are not posing) that we must remain silent on taxes, wage concessions, automotive engineering, and the like. The point is that we should not mislead others about our *qualifications* to expound.

Someone may be a brilliant NBA star but not an expert on foreign policy. This individual has as much right as anyone else to speak his mind, but less so if he's *posing* as an authority or if we've paid thirty dollars to hear him speak about basketball. There are, however, several clues for us here, and so he may be guilty of poor judgment but not unethical communication (unless he was grossly in breach of his contract).

UNSUPPORTED PERSONAL ATTACKS   When a speaker attacks the character of an opponent rather than the issue at hand, that person is guilty of *ad hominem* argument (unless the character of the person *is* the issue). When *ad hominem* is used solely to change the argument from one of issues to one of personalities, as a rule it is considered unethical. Our legal system calls it *slander* if the personal charges are unsupported, and *libel* if the charges are put in writing—clearly serious matters of ethics (and legality) for responsible speakers. It is unethical for a speaker to divert attention from weaknesses in his or her argument by unsupported attacks on an opponent.

Democracy and Demagoguery

A democratic system based on a sound legal system is designed to avoid decay by welcoming free speech and often harsh criticism. It needs that input to adapt to a changing world. However, there is a limit. Free speech turned to license and irresponsible rhetoric is demagoguery. Such speaking injures and threatens the integrity of any speechmaking subsystem; but more, it threatens the social, political, and legal systems of all of us. Articulate demagogues like Hitler and Mussolini have destroyed political systems in large part through deliberately using irresponsible speech. The United States has had its eloquent

Figure 1.11 The Wizard of Id

By permission of Johnny Hart and NAS.

demagogues as well: Huey Long, Joseph McCarthy, Charles Coughlin, and some zealots still on the scene. Their *intent,* then and now, was ostensibly to preserve the system through intemperate criticism or impassioned calls for radical behavior, which in reality threatened the system.

Being honest and fair to the facts are agreed-upon rules for most of us. We must play by the rules and obey the law. The use of outright lies, manu-factured facts, and "dirty tricks" is unethical.

It is also possible to be fair to a legal statute and yet lose sight of one's ethical responsibilities to a larger system. Meeting the letter but not the spir-it of the law is an example.

> "Every wicked man is in a state of ignorance as to what he ought to do and what he should refrain from doing, and it is due to this kind of error that men become unjust and, in general, immoral."
>
> *Aristotle*

SPEAKING WITH CONFIDENCE

You Are Not Alone

After reading national surveys that put speech fright or what psy-chologists call "performance anxiety" as Americans' number one fear with death well down the list, Jerry Seinfeld cracked, "At a funeral you'd be better off in the casket than giving the eulogy."

Figure 1.12 "One of life's terrors for the uninitiated is to be asked to make a speech." (George Plimpton).

© *International Paper Company*

One conclusion of all the surveys and much of the research is that many of you will suffer some form of speech fright of varying intensity. If it is true that misery loves company, then it will be reassuring to know that you are certainly not alone. Even professional performers report startling emotional reactions before public performances.

When I least expect it, my breathing will accelerate; I'll perspire like a professional wrestler . . .

Willard Scott

Boy, if you tell me that 400 people are coming in here to see me perform, I will strategically place buckets in my dressing room because my stomach cannot handle the anxiety.

Patty Duke

After missing a precommencement honoring ceremony because, "I was a nervous wreck," and later at commencement speaking to the crowd, "Boy am I nervous."

Bob Seger

. . . It took about six or seven speeches before I began to loosen up, but the experience wasn't near as bad as I thought it would be.

Chuck Yeager

The only difference between the pros and the novices is that the pros have trained the butterflies to fly in formation.

Edwin Newman

Beginning speech students also consider this a problem. Surveys indicate that 60 to 75 percent of a class may admit that they are bothered by "nervousness in speaking," an expectation that they have more to lose than to gain from speaking. Fourteen to 20 percent may be concerned enough to ask for help in the form of instructor conferences, specific reading assignments, or exercises that help ease speech fright. Most nervousness is typical, if not always normal. Much of it is temporary and based on expectations of anxiety in speaking situations. Most of you will find that the more formal the audience or the situation, the more speech fright there is. If you're new to speechmaking, be advised that the sooner you start facing such nervousness, the more likely you are to overcome it and subsequently do better in your remaining college courses.

Speaking or acting, like sky diving, might be an exhilarating, satisfying behavior for those who know and enjoy what they are doing, but a nightmare for the uninformed. Skills about which we have only limited knowledge frighten us, and in some instances should. Part of speechmaking is frightening; perhaps all of it is for some speakers. It is mostly a skill, partially an art.

It helps to know that audiences do not view your fright as seriously as you do indicating that you do not appear and sound as bad as you feel. There is good evidence that audiences perceive speaker anxiety to be lower than the speakers themselves report.[6] This fact should be reassuring.

Whether or not your fear is readily apparent, the result may be the same. As in other frightening situations, you may feel a dryness in the mouth, a rapid heartbeat, a sinking feeling in the stomach, difficulty with abdominal control, dysfluency, and even agitation.

Once again, evidence indicates that these nonverbal manifestations are evaluated by your classmates as modest and transitory. Your fright nonverbals are not as detrimental as you think they are. Furthermore, your classmates share your same predicament. The situation is no more novel for you than it is for them, and there is no reason to feel conspicuous. Negative thoughts only increase your anxiety. If they persist to the point of panic, research confirms that the quality of your speech behavior will suffer.[7]

For the most part, people with much speech fright do not vary from others in general intelligence, reasoning ability, or the most important aspects of personality. They may vary, however, in education, experience, linguistic ability, self-concept, and social attraction.

While you are pondering these symptoms and aspects of fright, you should realize that speech courses do help with this all-too-common problem. Of course, certain people (and audiences) are sometimes frightening to all of us. This text, course experience, and careful preparation have helped thousands of frightened students. Researchers found that after eight weeks and four speeches, observable anxiety was significantly reduced. Actual speaking experience appears to help students gain confidence. So does oral reading.[8]

To a great extent, we humans are afraid of what we do not understand. Young children may be paralyzed with fear during a severe electrical storm until their mother or father explains what causes the thunder and lightning. Afterwards, the child will experience fear, but not of a paralyzing nature. Loud noises make all of us jump, but knowledge and understanding of what causes the loud noises make it possible for us to stop jumping between noises. Because we are dealing with the symptoms and causes of an emotional reaction, we are better able to control emotion if we know how it operates.

Even the President gets rattled.

In a speech to a joint session of Congress, the teleprompter scrolled the wrong speech. "Wrong speech," he told Vice President Al Gore. "Impossible," Gore replied. "You're not reading it. I'm reading it!" retorted the President. Aid George Stephanopoulos "had no blood in his body," reported DeeDee Meyers, White House spokesperson. The unnerved President was forced to ad-lib for six minutes.

Understanding Emotion

The famous philosopher and psychologist William James provides us with a relatively simple and extremely useful theory of emotion. The gist of the theory is that it is not just the *speaking* that panics us, but also our *aware-*

ness of our reactions to a frightening situation. This awareness *is the real emotion.* James's favorite illustration of this theory was that of coming upon a bear in the woods.

In a nonscientific way, we might say the bear triggers the emotion of fear in us. Not so, for according to James our body reacts almost automatically to the bear. Our natural survival devices take over to prepare us for an emergency. Our muscles tense for better agility; our heartbeat and breathing quicken to provide larger supplies of fuel; our glands secrete fluids to sharpen our senses and give us emergency energy. All of this happens in an instant. Then we become aware of these bodily reactions. We sense our heavy breathing; our muscles tense to the point of trembling; perhaps adrenalin surges into our system. It is this *awareness of our reactions* that frightens us. In other words, the awareness is the emotion. Of course, the bear still has a lot to do with our condition!

The label (fear, anxiety, and so forth) we have learned for this special awareness comes from our past experiences that fit this situation. If we observe other people acting frightened, then our own deductions are strengthened. When the cause of our emotional state is not clear, we may attribute the emotion to any available cue in the environment.

It would be ridiculous to tell you that if you understand clearly all the physiological and psychological reactions described above, you have eliminated the bear. However, this knowledge and understanding will help you *control* what action you take and thereby improve your chance for survival. This is what we mean by emotional or speech fright control, and this is why we use the term *control* rather than *eliminate* when we speak of fear.

In the same manner that our fear of the bear is caused not by the bear itself but by our awareness of our bodily reactions to the bear, in speech fright it is our awareness of our internal and external reactions that provides us with

Figure 1.13

the emotion—or at least heightens the emotion. The speech situation, though obviously less dangerous than the bear, poses a more difficult problem. Nature prepares us for *flight or fight,* so we either flee from the bear or attack it. The speech situation rules out the use of survival tactics, for you can neither attack the audience nor run for the woods. The problem is to drain off some of your excess energy while holding your ground and facing a fear-provoking stimulus (the audience). In your favor, however, there are no recorded instances of an audience eating a speaker!

The point of the bear story is to help you understand the nature of emotion, for understanding and knowledge almost always promote emotional adjustment.

Controlling Speech Fright

OBJECTIFYING   The principle of *objectification* is an intellectualization or pragmatic explanation of what is happening to you. Such explanations take the edge off of emotions. Imagine a great lover who, when kissing his beloved, decided to analyze exactly what he was doing.

A former student, reporting on one of his own objectification experiments, reported, "You know, Doc, it takes all the kick out of it!" By the same reasoning, detailed intellectualization of speech-fright experiences should help take some of the "kick" out of them.

Have you ever asked yourself, "Why do my arms and hands tremble? Why do I have that sinking feeling in my stomach?" The issue is not *whether* you experience these things, but rather *why?* If you do ask why and the answer is, "Because I'm scared to death," you probably only add to the emotion. This is the time to apply the principle of objectification. Remember that the emotion is largely the result of your awareness of your own bodily reactions and that an objective explanation of these reactions will take the edge off your awareness.

The sinking feeling in the stomach that we experience under stress can also be explained in great detail. When faced with a fear-provoking situation, the body calls upon its glandular secretions, notably adrenalin, for emergency energy. These secretions chemically interfere with the digestive system. This process tends to make the stomach contract and produces the sensation typically referred to as a "sinking feeling."

Analyzing these reactions should help you control fright. Emotion loses its intensity under examination and objectification. Face up to your problems and get the facts straight. *It is healthy to talk objectively about your fright.* Instructors are good listeners. Let yours help you talk out your fright. In these ways you will meet your fright on a conscious level, at which you have the most control. If your mouth feels dry, find out why. If your knees shake, find out why. If you feel faint, find out why. The *why* is usually rather mundane and unexciting, but it is extremely logical and objective.

ACTING "AS IF"   Most individuals cannot experience two opposite or different types of emotional reactions at the same time. For example, at the instant when you are boiling mad, you are probably not afraid. (This is not to suggest that you should freely substitute anger for fright.) You may already have observed that when a speaker is really involved in a subject, he or she will tend to be less frightened by the platform situation. This helps explain our almost instinctive actions to ward off fright situations—why, for example, we whistle while walking through a dark alley. We are acting "as if" we are unafraid—perhaps happy, indignant, or angry. Acting "as if" has helped all of us through emotionally charged situations; it is a form of **cognitive restructuring.** For example, try substituting coping statements for negative ones: "They'll probably not even listen" for "I'll appear ridiculous;" "I've really prepared, and I've got something to say" for "They'll think I'm stupid;" or, if you are already into the speech, try "I'm still together—I'm getting by" for "I think I'm going to be sick."

In some cases cognitive restructuring involves a cognitive reorientation of how you view the public speaking situation. Motley and Molloy suggest that speakers who view the situation as requiring a flawless, show-biz type performance will experience more anxiety than those who concentrate primarily on sharing an important message. Indeed, they were able to achieve such an anxiety-reducing reorientation through the use of persuasive written arguments. They call this form of cognitive restructuring "Communication-Orientation Motivation."[9]

Another way of restructuring an anxious negative outlook is to visualize yourself thinking and acting in very positive and successful ways. In its simplest form this kind of *visualization* (VIS) asks you to imagine yourself making a very effective presentation. In one approach, on the day of your speech or before, start thinking positively about all aspects of the speech from the time you get up in the morning until after you've given the speech. Good evidence shows that such positive visualizations or acting "as if" reduce one's anxiety.[10] It is healthy to whistle in the dark; it is often the difference between poise and panic. Of course, actually *working* on your skills, preparation efforts, and rehearsals can also help enhance speech quality *and* your confidence level. The use of combined treatments for anxiety often works better than a single treatment.[11]

Let your emotions work for you when you can. In moments of strain, redirect your attention to other things and bring more tolerable emotions into focus. Try to become so involved in one thing that you are less aware of the other. Psychologists call this process **compensation.** It helps at the moment of truth when you must speak and also aids in visualizing during your preparation.

Your choice of a speech topic may therefore be important to you emotionally as well as rhetorically. If you are excited or can become excited about your subject, you will make theory work for you—a kind of natural and intelligent whistling in the dark. If you can find humor in your task or in your reactions to it, you may have found a very healthy distraction.

One can sometimes cognitively restructure by concentrating on the smiling and pleasant faces in the audience for moral support. Most audiences are, after all, supportive, or at worst disinterested. One professor reported that he started to overcome his speech fright when he began concentrating on the sleeping faces. He may have been substituting anger in this instance, or he may have decided his fear was a little ridiculous if he was talking only to himself.

CHANNELING EXCESS TENSION   We direct our actions most usefully once we break the wall of tension with the first step. Your first problem is to release some of the extra energy that your body dutifully provides. Bodily activity will help you utilize your extra energy or tension.

In a speaking situation you might be concerned about how your activity looks and what it communicates to the audience. The strategy here is very simple. Plan and direct some of your gross bodily movement, visualize in advance—not in a stereotyped way, but nevertheless systematically, complete with options. For example, at the close of your introduction or perhaps at a transition between points, you might plan on moving a step to the side or raising a book or card for emphasis. You have the option of selecting the precise time and action, depending upon how natural it seems and how tense you are.

Another very natural kind of activity is that associated with *visual aids*. If you comment on a picture, demonstrate an object, or write on a blackboard, you have to make perfectly natural movements in the process. This is an excellent way to channel excess energy.[12]

Prespeech physical activity can also help you reduce your tension and relax. A brisk walk has helped many an athlete unwind. Deep breathing and lifting or pressing your chair has been prescribed successfully by speech teachers. A yawn is a natural outlet as long as you do not look *too* relaxed!

Figure 1.14

If the journey from your chair to the speaker's platform is a real torture, *rehearse* this activity in an empty classroom or in measured distances at home. Keep rehearsing it until you sense a monotony in the repetition. Often college debaters inadvertently repeat certain strategies and argument patterns so zealously in practice that they risk becoming stale when presenting the same ideas in debate. Football teams have had similar experiences. The point is that monotonous repetition may help drain off that keyed-up feeling.

A moderate amount of repression of external behavior may also be in order to help you get started. By **repression** we mean a form of mental discipline in which you force yourself to get on with the business at hand. This is by no means a final adjustment, because continued repression would result in extreme fatigue. However, it is neither unusual nor abnormal to use moderate repression of external behavior as a *first step* in adjusting to the speaking situation.

> The only way to get over the fear of public speaking, one successful public speaker says, is "to just do it. You've got to suffer through it."
>
> *Dorothy Fuldheim, news commentator*

HELPING YOUR MEMORY   Beginning speakers are often frightened by just the thought of forgetting their speech. Apparently speech fright becomes a cause of forgetting, and the thought of forgetting causes or reinforces speech fright—a vicious circle.

As in redirecting attention, your topic can be important in helping your memory. The more you know about a subject and the more enthusiastic you are about it, the less likely you are to forget your material. Your attitude toward your subject, your involvement in it, and your eagerness to communicate it are all related to your ability to remember it.

In preparing your speech, the key word for memory protection is *system*. We remember better, we learn better, and we speak better if the material with which we are dealing is arranged systematically. It is easier to remember a list of twenty automobile names grouped according to some system (that is, according to manufacturer, size, horsepower, and so on) than in random order. Have you ever noticed how rapidly you can learn the names of baseball players? Obviously it is because of the system of positions they play; if you do not know the positions, you will be slower at learning the names. Find a natural and constructive way (for you) of ordering your speech materials, and you will find it much easier to remember what comes next.

One of the most effective memory aids is a visual aid. If your speech uses numbers and statistics, a large card with the numbers listed and identified considerably eases the pressure on your memory. As a precaution, a note in your pocket containing testimony, statistics, or other details is also helpful. Just the knowledge that you have such a backup is often worth more than the material on the cards.

Research suggests that the thinking that goes into developing a visual aid will also improve the content and the delivery of your speech.[13]

Despite all the protection you can give your memory, all speakers occasionally experience the frustration of "blanking out." If you have ever watched youngsters delivering memorized poems or salutations at an elementary school convocation, you have heard them forget their lines on occasion. You have probably also noticed that they almost instinctively keep repeating the last line they *do* remember in a frantic effort to rerail their memory. This effort may help, but more often the prompter has a busy day. Word-for-word memorization is really not a very intelligent "system," because the memory cannot relate so many small, unrelated parts. However, the principle of repeating the last thing you do remember is still useful. The practical application is to *review* the material you have just covered.

If your memory fails toward the end of your speech, you can *summarize* the key points you have made. Practical experience indicates that such a technique does help you reawaken your memory. One student who found this suggestion useful formulated her own rule: "When in doubt, summarize."

VISUALIZING REALISTICALLY   We talked earlier of a professor who felt less speech fright when he discovered that most of his class was asleep. With all due respect to student audiences, an honest appraisal of them is that they are not eagerly leaning forward, straining with every muscle to record for all time the wisdom you are about to deliver. Professors know this and so should you. Audiences may on occasion be lively, but more often than not this liveliness is due to the efforts of the speaker. Be objective about your audience. An analysis of speaker evaluations indicates that the audience sympathizes with the speaker. This means that if your audience is listening at all, it is rooting for you.

While the anxiety we experience is heavily conditioned by our individual predispositions to respond and deal with emotion, let us not forget that the specific audience we face or think we face also contributes something—such things as status inequality, dissimilarity, novel or ambiguous circumstances, or unusual formality.[14] Realistic audience appraisal at least allows us to measure and objectively analyze the beast so that we can visualize more positive situations as we prepare.

Research suggests that proper preparation,[15] a clear understanding of your speech assignment, and being adequately informed about the topic you choose can help ameliorate anxiety.[16] Realizing that your speech will probably not be recorded for posterity should also have a calming effect. If every speaker in a class of 25 gives ten speeches, any particular speech is one out of 250. If it is reassuring to be part of the crowd, then relax. Be realistic about your speech goals and their effect upon your audience.

Think of your speech in terms of the communication process discussed earlier, and realize the worthy purpose of speech training. Instead of worrying about the damage your ego may suffer, be afraid of not being able to *motivate* an audience to listen.

Finally, *evaluate your communication role* completely. Take heart from knowing that your speeches will be lost among hundreds of other speeches; your audience is generally sympathetic; your instructor is trained to be alert to your problems. Research in speech has given us reliable methods to help you learn: "All current practices to reduce anxiety were effective."[17] Have faith in hard-earned experience and knowledge. Have faith in the goodness of people. And have faith in yourself.

> If you are able to talk ably on your own subject in a living room or at a dinner table, you will be safe from harm behind a lectern.
>
> *Gerald Gardner*

Summary

Public speaking is a skill you will need. There are over 3,000 speaking platforms on any given day in Los Angeles, 30,000 in Chicago, and 50,000 in New York. More education and more income predict more and more job-related speeches.

Speaking ability is more important than ever in our technological age, yet students are significantly deficient in their ability to make oral presentations. Research shows that a course in public speaking can offset this deficiency.

Communication is largely concerned with meaning. For social construction theorists reality is dependent on our personal perceptions, our language, our thinking habits, and our communication abilities. Reality can be "real" reality, individual perception of it, or society's perception of it. Some people are better at discerning reality than others. We can improve our social constructions of what we see and hear by being knowledgeable about the communication process, perception, language, and logical thinking.

Perception involves how we discern or assign meanings to objects and messages. The theory is that we hypothesize about messages which we then accept or reject on the basis of personal constructs based on prior learning and experience.

The word *model* refers to a representation of a thing or a process. The Schramm communication models clarify the importance of common experience and mutual influence.

Communication is *a transactional process of skillfully sharing, selecting, and sorting ideas, symbols, and signs in such a way as to help listeners elicit from their own minds a meaning or construction similar to that intended by the speaker.*

By *transactional* we mean that the process involves an activity that reciprocally affects or influences both parties. The Ross Transactional Model (Figure 1.8) makes clear the importance of: situation, context, climate, mood, and the notion of feedback. It focuses on how ideas are processed, encoded, and delivered by a speaker and then decoded, intrapersonally reconstructed, and reacted to by receivers.

Responsible speakers and listeners should know that a democratic system based on a sound legal system is designed to avoid decay by welcoming both free speech and harsh criticism. However, free speech turned to license and irresponsible rhetoric is demagoguery. Responsible speakers have an ethical obligation to match their message to the specific audience, context, and situation. A given message does not mean the same thing to all people, and perceptions and understandings vary with contexts and situations. We have an ethical responsibility to analyze our audiences and their circumstances. A qualified person serving in a leadership role has special ethical obligations. All of us have some obligation to get our facts straight before sending messages that might capriciously misinform or injure the receiver. Moralists call this *culpable ignorance*—that is, ignorance usually arising from carelessness and deserving of blame.

A communicator is responsible for telling the truth and for the social consequences that result if the truth is not told. Using outright lies, manufactured facts, and dirty tricks is clearly unethical. Some mental reservations are allowed as long as there are fair and sufficient clues within the special contexts and situations. A strict mental reservation without any clue is a lie in any context. The ultimate decision or choice on how to behave, act, interpret, or believe must in some way, however small, be left to the receiver.

As receivers we have an obligation to give fair hearing once we have committed ourselves to some legitimate interest in an issue. Ethical communications preserve the integrity of the ego, provide the information needed, permit and encourage the expression of thought and feeling, and reveal respect for the person as a person.

Most beginning speech students admit that they are bothered by nervousness. Professional performers report similar feelings of tension. Significantly, though, reports indicate that you do not appear and sound as bad as you feel. Research also indicates that frightened people do not differ from the confident minority in very basic ways, such as intelligence and the important aspects of personality.

An understanding of our bodily reactions to frightening situations helps us control our emotions. Specific suggestions for controlling speech fright include: *objectification,* the intellectualization of what you are experiencing; *acting "as if"* you are not afraid, preparation in which you visualize yourself positively; *channeling excess tension,* directing your actions meaningfully; *helping your memory* through systematic topical arrangement; *visualizing realistically,* being objective about the audience and your assignment and your fears.

Learning Projects

1. Develop your own verbal-pictorial model of the communication process. See student example, Figure 1.15.

2. Apply one of the communication models to a specific incident, event, or interaction. Report (verbally and/or pictorially) the insights or lessons of this exercise. Pay special attention to feedback. (See Figure 1.16.)

3. Using the optical illusions in Chapter 1 or other perceptual abnormalities you may find, test a few people outside class and record what they see. Assess the reasons for any differences and be prepared to share your experiences in class. Is self-image involved?

Figure 1.15   A speaker-analogy model.

From a model by a student at Wayne State University.

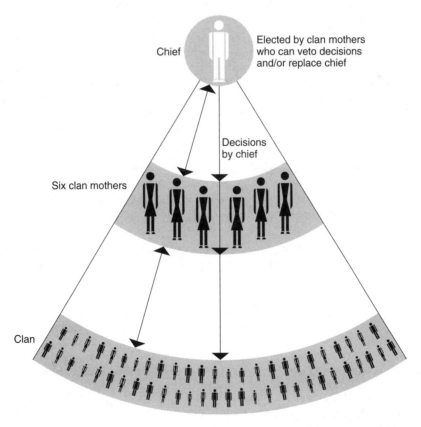

Figure 1.16   Iroquois Indian (Wolf Clan) communication model. From a model by a student at Wayne State University.

4. With a classmate, prepare an eight- to ten-minute dialogue in the form of an interview or role play (for instance, a job interview, a dialogue with an arresting officer, a doctor's appointment, a conversation with a friendly bartender), so as to introduce yourselves to the rest of the class.

5. Communication models often serve very specific purposes—instruction, prediction, research, classification, and so on. Prepare for a class discussion on communication models.

6. Collect two examples of unethical audience–message mismatch (or context or situation manipulation). Prepare to discuss the ethical obligations of a responsible public speaker.

7. Prepare to discuss President Adamany's charge (p. 3) that students are deficient in their ability to make oral presentations.

8. In one to two pages, describe your behavioral reactions to facing an audience. Explain how you might use one or more of the five suggestions for controlling your emotions.

9. Collect one good example of culpable ignorance.

10. Keep a communication log. The communication log is a record and analysis of your personal communication experiences. Minimum standards (for a grade of B on the log) are as follows:

    a. *Number of entries:* Entries should be made on *at least* four days of each week. Date your entries.

    b. *Nature of entries:* Each week, at least one entry should describe something that occurred in class, and at least one entry should be of something that occurred outside class. Some of the entries may be brief (for example, one sentence). Other entries should be much longer in order to demonstrate that you are growing in the ability to understand and analyze the communication problems of both yourself and others. In either case, try to explain why a speech or discussion went well or poorly. Your efforts to explain what occurred are the principal criterion for distinguishing between A and B logs.

    In the first two weeks of the course, you *must* make one entry that describes your strengths and weaknesses in communicating with others and that states what you expect to accomplish in this course. Be specific.

    During the last week, one entry *must* describe again what you think your strengths and weaknesses are and what you think you have accomplished during the term.

    c. *References to the textbook:* The log must show that you have read the text. This requirement can be met by making a *minimum* of ten references to the text in your log entries.

Notes

1. Sherwyn Morreale, Pamela Shockley-Zalabak, and Penny Whitney, "The Center for Excellence in Oral Communication: Integrating Communication across the Curriculum," *Communication Education,* 42, no. 1 (January 1993), 10–21.

2. Patricia R. Palmerton, "Teaching Skills or Teaching Thinking," *Journal of Applied Communication,* 20, no. 3 (August 1992), 335–41.

3. K. J. Gergen, "The Social Construction Movement in Modern Psychology," *American Psychologist,* 40, no. 3 (March 1985), 266–75. Also see J. Yerby, "Family Systems Theory Reconsidered: Integrating Social Construction Theory and Dialectical Process," *Communication Theory,* 5, no. 4 (November 1995), 339–65; M. D. Dixon, "Teaching Social Construction of Reality in the Basic Course" (Paper delivered at the Speech Communication Association convention, San Antonio, Texas, 1995). For the seminal work see P. Berger and T. Luckmann, *The Social Construction of Reality* (Garden City, NY: Doubleday & Co., Inc., 1966).

4. L. Hoffman, "Constructing Realities: An Art of Lenses," *Family Process,* 29 (1990), 1–12.

5. Richard L. Johannesen, *Ethics in Human Communication,* 4th ed. (Prospect Heights, Ill.: Waveland Press, 1997), p. 10.

6. C. R. Sawyer and R. P. Behnke, "Public Speaking Anxiety and the Communication of Emotion," *World Communication,* 25, no. 1 (Winter 1996), 21–30.

7. Mike Allen and John Bourhis, "The Relationship of Communication Apprehension to Communication Behavior: A Meta-Analysis," *Communication Quarterly,* 44, no. 2 (Spring 1996), 214–26.

8. H. M. Rose, A. S. Rancer, and K. C. Crannell, "The Impact of Basic Courses in Oral Interpretation and Public Speaking on Communication Apprehension," *Communication Reports,* 6, no. 1 (Winter 1993), 54–60.

9. Michael T. Motley and Jennifer L. Molloy, "An Efficacy Test of a New Therapy ('Communication-Orientation Motivation') for Public Speaking Anxiety," *Journal of Applied Communication Research,* 22, no. 1 (February 1994), 48–58.

10. Joe Ayres and Theodore S. Hopf, "The Long-Term Effect of Visualization in the Classroom: A Brief Research Report," *Communication Education,* 39, no. 1 (January 1990), 75–78; see also Melanie Booth-Butterfield and Steven Booth-Butterfield, "The Mediating Role of Cognition in the Experience of State Anxiety," *Southern Communication Journal,* 56, no. 1 (Fall 1990) 35–48.

11. Kent E. Menzel and Lori J. Carrell, "The Relationship between Preparation and Performance in Public Speaking," *Communication Education,* 43, no. 2 (January 1994), 17–26. See also R. H. Whitworth and C. Cochran, "Evaluation of Integrated Versus Unitary Treatments for Reducing Public Speaking Anxiety," *Communication Education,* 45, no. 4 (October 1996), 306–14.

12. Joe Ayres, "Using Visual Aids to Reduce Speech Anxiety," *Communication Research Reports,* 8, no. 1 (June 1991), 73–79; Joe Ayres and Tim Hopf, "Visualization: Reducing Speech Anxiety and Enhancing Performance," *Communication Reports,* 5, no. 1 (Winter 1992), 1–10.

13. Menzel and Carrell, "Relationship between Preparation," 17–26.

14. Michael J. Beatty and Matthew H. Friedland, "Public Speaking State Anxiety as a Function of Selected Situational and Predispositional Variables," *Communication Education,* 38, no. 2 (April 1990), 142–47; also see Joe Ayres, "Situational Factors and Audience Anxiety," *Communication Education,* 39, no. 4 (October 1990) 283–91.

15. J. A. Daly, A. L. Vangelisti, and D. J. Weber, "Speech Anxiety Affects How People Prepare Speeches: A Protocol Analysis of the Preparation Processes of Speakers," *Communication Monographs,* 62, no. 4 (December 1995), 383–97.

16. M. Booth-Butterfield and S. Booth-Butterfield, "The Mediating Role of Cognition," 35–48; also see Menzel and Carrell, "Relationship between Preparation," 17–26.

17. Mike Allen, "A Comparison of Self-Report, Observer, and Physiological Assessments of Public Speaking Anxiety Reduction Techniques Using Meta-Analyses," *Communication Studies,* 40, no. 2 (Summer 1989), 137–39.

2

LANGUAGE HABITS

CHAPTER
OUTLINE

IMPORTANCE

The average speaker of English knows between 50,000 and 250,000 words. These words are somehow learned and used with reasonable facility but not always.[1] Sometimes words can be strung together awkwardly. Consider these church bulletins.

---

1. The ladies of the church have cast off clothing of every kind and they may be seen in the church basement on Friday.
2. Thursday at 5:00 P.M. there will be a meeting of the Little Mothers Club. All wishing to become little mothers please see the minister in his study.
3. At the evening service tonight, the sermon topic will be "What is Hell?" Come early and listen to our choir practice.
4. Wednesday the Ladies Liturgy Society will meet. Mrs. Jones will sing, "Put Me in My Little Bed," accompanied by the pastor.

The situation worsens when we learn, thanks to computers, that the 500 most commonly used English words show more than 14,000 recorded dictionary uses. Robert Pula, former Director of the Institute for General Semantics, suggests three main sources of these "same term" differences:

- *lexical*—"same" term, different definition, e.g., *fast* (abstain), *fast* (stuck), *fast* (morally loose), *fast* (quick), etc.
- *contextual*—"same" term, different situation: even if we know "all" of the accepted uses and definitions of a term, we still need sensitivity to context to determine *which* use is intended by a speaker or writer.
- *neurological*—"same" term, different brain—even if a speaker and listener agree on the particular use of a term in a given context, idiosyncratic structural and experiential *differences* of each brain (nervous-system-as-a-whole) will generate to varying degrees, different semantic reactions.[2]

Clearly vocabulary alone is often a sensitive matter and is capable of altering or even short-circuiting meaning. To compound the problem many words *sound* exactly the same but have startlingly different meanings. One student speaker was shocked that his description of *erratic* personalities was decoded by some listeners as *erotic* personalities. And how do "Fat Chance" and "Slim Chance" come to mean the same thing?

The language problem is often worse for the speaker than the writer because the listener has more *concomitant signals* to deal with than the reader. These are the nonverbals that accompany and operate at the same time as the words. Your *voice,* for example, is a wonderfully sensitive instrument with a powerful influence upon the meaning the listener attaches both to your words and to you, the speaker.

The appearance of the speaker—dress, movements, facial expressions, and gestures—are other signals that affect how language is decoded.

Another, less obvious point to be made is that these codes and signals affect one another. Sometimes they work together and strengthen the meaning intended by the speaker. At other times, however, they conflict with one another and distort the intended meaning to the point where the listener is confused, suspicious, or frustrated. Consider the sloppy student presenting a speech on the value of personal neatness, or the professor with a frozen grin discussing the possibility of a student's failing the course. We often act in a way contrary to what we really intend. The cause may be tension, emotional involvement, or poor language and thinking habits.

Where you are often affects your language; "L. A. speak" is for real. Generic names are out, it seems; it's Filofaxes, Reeboks, Ray-Bans. "Valley Talk" is, of course, "totally awesome." In Detroit, slang is in (or was yesterday): finest vines, bull skating, Roscoe, wiggers.

There are also simple slips of the tongue called *bloopers* or *Spoonerisms* (named after Professor Spooner) from which recovery is sometimes impossible. Try the emcee who blooped, "We now have Dr. Christiaan Barnard who will talk about his now famous rear transplant—I mean rare transplant." Or the sports announcer who was laughed out of the booth after stating, "Toronto hockey fans will be glad to learn that their goalie made his first girl ever in the last ten seconds of play" (that's *goal*).

Language as a system is *holistic,* that is, the whole of it is greater than the sum of its parts. Perhaps that explains how Yasin, a student from Kuwait with a good sense of communication but weak, barely adequate English, was able to give a well-received speech on his reaction to American women. However, another foreign student with somewhat better English skills failed miserably. If language is so poor or so inappropriate that it makes simple decoding impossible, then, of course, the entire system goes down.

This is good reason to not only use our language in the best and most appropriate way possible, but also to take every opportunity to improve our language ability. Perhaps this helps explain why some communications fail with one group and work with another. Your code was proper for one set of receivers but perhaps incomprehensible for the rest.

LANGUAGE AND CRITICAL THINKING

Our understandings and perceptions of the world are thought to be inextricably tied to language, particularly its grammar. If this long-standing *Whorf-Sapir hypothesis* is true, then our very thinking is largely governed by this powerful language system.[3]

> . . . .if we lacked the ability to use language we would not be able to even *think* in any meaningful sense.
>
> *John Chaffe, author of Thinking Critically*

Critical thinking involves exercising intelligent, objective, cautious judgment and evaluation of the language we use and of the language we receive and decode from others. More will be said about logical thinking and formal argument in Chapter 12.

Meaning and Abstraction

The heart of the difficulty with language is the confusion of the word with the thing for which it stands. The further we are from this thing—the **referent**—the more problems of meaning arise. If we use the word *dog* while pointing to a Golden Retriever, we are indeed close to a *concrete* referent and the *denotation* or literal meaning is quite clear. If we are talking about someone who is *dog* tired, or perhaps a dirty *dog,* we are seeking a more distant and *abstract* referent. This added meaning usage is called *connotation.*

Meaning is thought to have three elements: a person having thoughts, a symbol (or sign), and a referent.

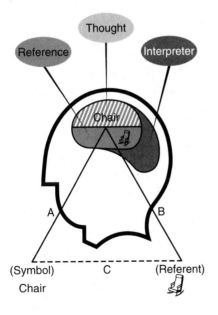

Figure 2.1

When we receive a symbol or sign, it travels to our thought or refer-ence center. We then consult our storehouse of experience to find the thing or referent to which the symbol refers. Line A in Figure 2.1 indicates what a person ideally perceives as a *correct symbol,* in this case the word *chair.* Line B represents the cognitive selecting and sorting of knowledge and experience which ideally represents an *adequate referent.* The broken line C indicates that the *word* chair and a *real* chair are not the same, making very clear the crucial point that the symbol and its referent are not *directly* related. The *word is not the thing!* You cannot *sit* on the word *chair!*

Clear communication calls for a referent, a reference, and a symbol. This concept leads us to the subject of misuse of abstractions. ***Abstracting*** is a process of thinking in which we selectively leave out details about concrete or real things. We have learned previously that perception has at least two ele-ments, (1) sensation and (2) interpretation of this sensation. This interpreta-tion is controlled by our individual knowledge, experience, and emotional set. For this reason, as well as because of the limitations of our language sys-tem, all language contains an element of abstraction.

In abstracting, we go beyond the specific fact or thing that is usually observable or demonstrable. For example, if one were giving a speech on "fly-ing machines," one could be talking about balloons, gliders, blimps, heli-copters, and airplanes. A speech on "airplanes" would be more specific (or less abstract). "Fighter aircraft" narrows the topic even more. "World War I Jenny" is quite specific. Think of abstracting as a stepladder with the most specific item on the first rung and the most general on the third or fourth (Figure 2.2).

Figure 2.2 Abstraction stepladder.

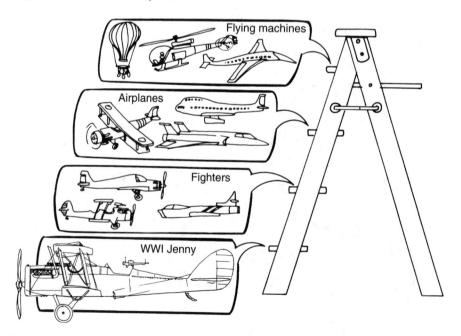

As we move from lower- to higher-order abstractions, we tend to consider fewer and fewer details of the specific, original object.

Another way of looking at abstraction is to consider firsthand observations as facts, but as facts that may never be described completely. If we move away from firsthand descriptions, we will be in a different order of abstraction—*inference.* Most simply, an inference goes *beyond* what is observed. If an ambulance is in your driveway when you return home, you may conclude, "One of my family has been seriously hurt." This is an inference. You must go into the house to see if it is valid. Upon entering your house, you may find a close friend telling your healthy family about his new business venture of converting station wagons into ambulances. When we are in the realm of inference, then, we are dealing with *probability* rather than with *certainty.*

Classifying Concepts and Things

Recall that the 500 most commonly used English words have more than 14,000 dictionary definitions. The problem is that there are an infinite number of things and concepts, each worthy of its own label. In short, if we did not use a limited number of words to represent an infinite number of things, we could hardly reason or communicate at all.

For example, if each *individual* chair in the world had its own label, we would have to have dictionaries of chairs. Even with the general classifying word *chair,* we have developed a large vocabulary of chair words—for example, Windsor, Hitchcock, stuffed, swivel, rocking (Figure 2.3). Despite our useful and necessary dictionaries, no word has real meaning except in the particular **context** in which it is used. The meaning of a word is never quite the same from one occasion to another, although the variation in meaning may not always be great. Word meanings change when we take words for granted and think of them as *actual* things rather than as what they really are—*representations* of things. A good speaker must always ask, "What does *this* word mean to *this* audience in *this* situation, in *this* context, as used by *this* speaker at *this* time?" (see Figure 2.4)

Figure 2.3

Figure 2.4

The propositional nature of language can be a word problem in some language systems. Even absurd statements can be grammatically correct. Try these!

Red is Green	Tony: "What color is the sky?" Cleo: "Blue." Tony: "Wrong!"

Because of the propositional nature of language, we may become too literal and too rigid in our evaluation of words. These characteristics often lead to poor thinking and misunderstanding.

When we arrange words into the context of a sentence—that is, when we create *syntax*—we are really fitting generalizations together. The meaning of an English sentence is determined not by its words alone, but by the whole arrangement and sequence of the words. In one sense, the communication pattern of a sentence is the systematic exclusion of meanings the listener might attach which are *not* intended by the speaker. In short, the sentence may define meanings *not* intended.

A distortion of this process has been called "doublespeak," often used to soften bad news, shift blame, or, if completely unethical, to cover up the truth. Firing of workers has been referred to as: "Consolidating operations," "derecruitment," "rationalizing marketing efforts," even "career change opportunities." All so-called doublespeak is not unethical. Some is really a more tactful way of explaining harsh realities. Tact versus forthrightness can make for difficult language choices for ethical speakers.

The particular character you give your language usage is important to your messages. The most characteristic language pattern of schizophrenics is an apparent confusion between words and things. Because objective abstraction is difficult for schizophrenics, they tend to be extremely one-sided and opinionated. The sobering thought in discussing abnormal language habits is that we all exhibit these habits to some degree. It behooves us to be aware of our language patterns lest we, too, represent a one-value world of words without referents.

Almost any speech course, whatever its context, puts a high premium on language habits. The instructor will criticize you diligently, knowing that proper language habits will make it easier for you to adjust to the linguistic demands of life in college and after.

MEANING MANAGEMENT

Specificity and Accuracy in Language

> Any simple-minded person can come up with an obvious idea in a simple, straightforward way; only a true scholar can come up with an obvious idea in a complex, incomprehensible way.
>
> *Ronald F. Reid, Rhetorician*

Were Confucius alive today, he might well be pained by our fascination with slang and jargon. He once said, "The first step in finding out the truth is to call things by their right names." **Jargon,** or specialized language, can confuse or even stop communication. Try this gem from the Department of Housing and Urban Development.

> Action-oriented orchestration of innovative inputs, generated by escalation of meaningful indigenous decision-making dialogue, focusing on multi-linked problem-complexes, can maximize the vital thrust toward a non-alienated and viable urban infrastructure.

Confusion about what language means is often very frustrating. Note the speech given at a freshmen orientation session:

At this university, education for the undergraduate has as purposes the fostering of the intellectual and personal growth of the individual student. The student, ultimately responsible for his or her own development in both of these areas, must be an active participant in framing his or her own education. A central aspect of this development is the relationship of the student with professors and fellow students and with the material they approach together. Structures, rules, and regulations of the university should facilitate these relationships and should provide the student with the maximum opportunity to formulate and achieve his or her educational objectives.

"KISS," said one student (*keep it simple, stupid*) and translated as follows:

> THE TRANSLATION:
> There are no course distribution requirements. If you make mistakes in choosing courses, you have only yourself to blame. Ask the advice of your professors and peers if you would like help in choosing your courses.

Consider that Lincoln's Gettysburg address contained only 272 words and that 196 of them were of one syllable. There are only 297 words in the Ten Commandments and 300 in the entire Declaration of Independence—a good lesson for long-winded speakers.

The confusion isn't always caused by windy jargon. Sometimes our desire to be specific is not always conditioned by critical thinking and careful preparation. Here are the exact words of a witness in an arbitration case. See if you can figure them out.

> Now, there is two obligations on them here in the plan, and I think one is more controlling over the other, and that is to do what they said they were going to do, and if they can't do what they said they were going to do in the manner in which they said they were going to do it, I don't feel that they are relieved from the obligation of doing what they said they were going to do, even if it had to be done in a manner other than what they said they were going to do, in as much as doing what they said they were going to do is consistent with their obligation under the agreement to do what they said they were going to do, and anything else would be inconsistent.

> Some people have a way with words. Some no have way.
>
> *Steve Martin*

Accurate word choice is a must for speakers to be effective. A debater of religion who really does not know the difference between atheism and agnosticism is apt to raise confusion to a still higher level. Atheism denies the existence of God. Agnostics merely claim not to know if God exists, a critical difference if critical thinking is to occur.

Naming things or people can make a difference. Remember "Who" is on first!? Try this one.

There were four people named Everybody, Somebody, Anybody, and Nobody. There was an important job to be done and Everybody was sure that Somebody would do it. Anybody could have done it, but Nobody did it.

Somebody got angry about that, because it was Everybody's job. Everybody thought Anybody could do it, but Nobody realized that Everybody wouldn't do it. It ended up that Everybody blamed Somebody when Nobody did what Anybody could have.

Sometimes language inaccuracy seems deliberate. Why else would the military refer to a bullet hole as a "ballistically induced aperture in the subcutaneous environment" or a parachute as an "aerodynamic personnel decelerator"?

Perhaps there are some times when obfuscation (to make obscure) is justified. When Daniel Patrick Moynihan was the White House domestic advisor, he got stuck with making the dedicatory remarks on receipt of *Isis,* a modern art sculpture made of welded steel discards (that's junk) donated by the Scrap Iron and Steel Institute. His spoof (?) is a classic.

As chairman of the board of the Hirshhorn Museum and Sculpture Garden it falls to me to accept this splendid gift from the Institute of Scrap Iron and Steel, and I recall that on the occasion that Margaret Fuller declared, "I accept the universe," Carlyle remarked that she had better.

Isis achieves an aesthetic transubstantiation of that which is at once elusive yet ineluctable in the modern sensibility.

Transcending socialist realism with an unequaled abstractionist range, Mr. di Suvero brings to the theme of recycling both the hard-edge reality of the modern world and the transcendent fecundity of the universe itself; a lasting assertion both of the fleetingness of the living, and the permanence of life; a consummation before which we stand in consistorial witness.

It will be with us a long time.[4]

Figure 2.5 *B.C.*

By permission of Johnny Hart and Creators Syndicate, Inc.

Principles and Rules

OVERSTATEMENT AND OVERGENERALIZATION   One of the most widespread "thinking" faults of student speakers is ***false generalization.*** This is the problem of selectively leaving out details and concluding after only a superficial examination that a thing is true beyond any shadow of a doubt. For example, if upon driving into Detroit for the first time you (1) witnessed a serious accident, (2) observed a truck exceeding the speed limit, and (3) had your fender dented at a busy intersection, you might be tempted to draw some strong conclusions and speak in strong language about Detroit drivers. However, you would have to examine comparative safety records, driver education programs, and driver insurance rates before participating in any intelligent discussion about Detroit drivers. Even then, you might want to hedge your generalizations by noting that Detroit has more cars per person than any other city in the world.

The irony and tyranny of overgeneralization is that it is usually not intended. It seems so obvious that all Detroit drivers are crazy! That all male politicians are sexist! That all whites are racist! All Democrats are *not* alike, *nor* are all Republicans alike. We should think in terms of, if not actually index or catalogue, Democrat 1, Democrat 2, Democrat 3, and so on. It is a safeguard against taking stereotypes seriously and failing to appreciate individual differences. Fifty-five miles per hour may mean 62 in Illinois, but when you cross into Wisconsin on highway 41 you are greeted by the sign in Figure 2.6.

With the ***either/or response*** type of overgeneralization, one's language habits conceal differences of degree. The absolute ruler and the demagogue use this device regularly. All of us in moments of frustration or desperation seem to revert to "They're all no good," "You're either for me or against me," or "You'll never understand." When we routinely use words such as *all, nobody, everybody,* and *never,* we are guilty of a false-to-fact use of language. The speaker guilty of these exaggerations runs risks of creating resentment, particularly among sophisticated audiences.

An extremely irritating form of the either/or response is what we might call *arrogant dismissal.* "That's ridiculous!" "Out of the question!" "Nonsense!"

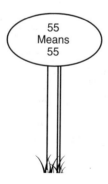

Figure 2.6

Figure 2.7

The responder clearly indicates that the discussion is over; the speaker and the topic are dismissed as stupid. Individuals who consistently engage in this kind of behavior are considered by some psychologists to have serious adjustment problems. Simplistic language such as that above usually reflects simplistic thinking or a high degree of emotional involvement.

When a person speaks from firsthand experience in a sincere and friendly voice without being aware of faulty abstracting or generalizing, that person is creating a serious problem. The communication problems of generalization are complicated, frustrating, and often dangerous. Once you understand this clearly, you have already solved much of the practical problem, for it is when you are *aware* of abstracting and generalizing that you begin to restrain your own overstatement and reckless generalization. A practical way of using this awareness is to qualify your statements with great care.

> He can compress the most words into the smallest ideas of any man I ever met.
> *Abraham Lincoln*

Speakers carry an ethical responsibility proportionate to their reputation. Perhaps this is why sophisticated persons with high ethical standards are often accused of qualifying or explaining things to the point of vagueness. This tendency raises the ethical question of how much you can qualify before you completely dodge your obligations and responsibilities.

Helpful Rules

1. *The index rule* reminds us to beware of stereotypes and other forms of overgeneralization. We should think in terms of actually indexing or cataloguing Christian 1 (Catholic), Christian 2 (Lutheran), Christian 3 (Methodist), Christian 4 (Baptist), and so on. Then there are liberal and conservative indexes to be considered as well, some within the previous index. The index rule is a warning against taking stereotypes seriously and failing to appreciate individual differences.

2. *The "is" problem* is related to the principle of nonidentity. The map is not the territory as anyone who has ever been misled by an old map can readily tell you. The injunction to "call a spade a spade" is profoundly misleading because it implies that we call it a spade because that's what it is. Language and thought are not identical. Words are not the things signified (the *referents*). Dictionaries give only the meanings that people have given to words.

3. *The et cetera rule* is related to the principle of "nonallness." In a sense, this rule also refers to the awareness of abstracting—an awareness that we are leaving something out. One cannot say everything on a given matter; there is always more to be said. Thus the good speaker leaves listeners with the impression that he or she has not attempted to say the last word on a subject.

4. *Dating your language.* Often the specific date of an event significantly affects the meaning a listener will attach to it. "At last the Japanese people have taken the actions that will restore their rightful dignity." Certainly, we would attach different meanings to this hypothetical statement by the Emperor of Japan according to whether it was uttered on

> January 7, 1925 (no special significance)
> December 7, 1941 (Pearl Harbor)
> September 2, 1945 (surrender of Japan)
> *July 1, 1968 (return of Okinawa)
> January 1, 1998 (?)

A favorite exam question of one psychology professor was, "What are Thorndike's laws of learning?" This question is challenging because Thorndike changed his mind about some of his laws of learning and made this clear in his most recent writings. The student who had read only his early writings would inevitably give the wrong answer.

5. *Discerning presymbolic language.* It should be evident by this time that it is impossible for a person to "say exactly what one means." Much of our language behavior is **presymbolic**—that is, it may function even without recognizable speech, or perhaps with symbols approaching an **idiom** (an accepted expression with a meaning different from the literal). A grunt from my office partner at 8:00 A.M. means, "Good morning, it's good to see you." When you pass a friend on the street and she says, "Hi," how does this really differ from "How are you?" Does "Nice day" mean just that and no more?

When language is used in a presymbolic sense, we have to look beyond the words to obtain the real meaning intended. In our efforts to become alert, critical listeners, we must take care not to become so literal that we mistake tact and social grace for foolishness, hypocrisy, or stupidity. Much of what we refer to as "small talk" is in part presymbolic language. In order to become an objective and honest sender or receiver, we must strive to distinguish presymbolic from symbolic language.

COLORFUL LANGUAGE

Vividness

Make your language bright and colorful as well as meaningful. Our drama major makes his menus interesting yet clear and, for most of us, humorous. (See Figure 2.8.)

Consider this passage from Ecclesiastes:

> I returned and saw under the sun, that the race is not to the swift, nor the battle to the strong, neither yet bread to the wise, nor yet riches to men of understanding, nor yet favor to men of skill; but time and chance happeneth to them all. (9:11)

"SOME KID WHO'S MAJORING IN DRAMATICS AT STATE, DOES THE MENUS ! "

Figure 2.8   *Cliff Wirth, cartoonist,* The Detroit News.

Now consider George Orwell's less colorful, more pedantic translation of the passage from Ecclesiastes found in his essay "Politics and the English Language."

> Objective consideration of contemporary phenomena compels the conclusion that success or failure in competitive activities exhibits no tendency to be commensurate with innate capacity, but that a considerable element of the unpredictable must invariably be taken into account.

If we are not prudent, our attempts at vividness can easily turn maudlin, showy, or even destructive. Note the internecine warfare between the saints as found in the sports pages.

ST. MARY BLITZED BY ALLEN PARK CABRINI

ST. ANDREW RIPS BISHOP BORGESS

HAMTRAMCK IMMACULATE CONCEPTION FLATTENS DEARBORN DIVINE CHILD

Imagery is a form of vividness that employs figures of speech to produce mental pictures in the mind's eye of the listener.

Words, strain,
crack, and sometime
break, under the burden.

T. S. Eliot

Mental pictures, images, or word pictures are typically accessed through sensory recollections. One can almost *hear* (auditory) "a voice that would fracture glass," or *see* (visual) "a flash of blinding insight," or *feel* (tactual, touch) "the cold, north wind icing its way through the pines," or *smell* (olfactory) "the foul, whiskey-soaked breath of the bully." You probably wouldn't sell much *sushi* if you described it as "cold caked sour rice soaked in vinegary liquid covered with raw dead fish." For some it may not be much better as "rice dressed with vinegar, shaped into small cakes, and topped with garnishes of raw fish" (*taste*, gustatory). "The queasy, faintish, life-weary feelings of a young soldier too long on the battlefield" stimulates *internal feelings* (organic). "The fatigue ridden, paralytic numbness of legs on a march too far . . ." produces a mental picture of *muscle strain* (kinesthetic).

The French have a way with imagery when they are upset. Here is French writer Jean Cau describing the EuroDisney theme park near Paris:

> It is a horror made of cardboard, plastic and appalling colors, a construction of hardened chewing-gum and idiotic folklore taken straight out of comic books written for obese Americans.

On a higher note, consider the beautiful close of General Douglas MacArthur's speech after accepting an award for service to the nation:

> . . . the soldier, above all other people, prays for peace, for he must suffer and bear the deepest wounds and scars of war. But always in our ears ring the ominous words of Plato, that wisest of all philosophers, "Only the dead have seen the end of war."
>
> The shadows are lengthening for me. The twilight is here. My days of old have vanished tone and tint; they have gone glimmering through the dreams of things that were. Their memory is one of wondrous beauty, watered by tears, and coaxed and caressed by the smiles of yesterday.
>
> I listen vainly, but with thirsty ear, for the witching melody of faint bugles blowing reveille, of far drums beating the long roll. In my dreams I hear again the crash of guns, the rattle of musketry, the strange, mournful mutter of the battlefield.
>
> But in the evening of my memory, always I come back to West Point. Always there echoes and re-echoes Duty-Honor-Country.[5]

One of the most vivid and moving speeches of our time was delivered to some 200,000 people from the steps of the Lincoln Memorial in Washington, D.C. on August 28, 1963 by Martin Luther King. Consider these selected paragraphs from the speech, "I Have a Dream."[6]

> I have a dream that one day this nation will rise up and live out the true meaning of its creed, "We hold these truths to be self-evident, that all men are created equal."
>
> I have a dream that one day every valley shall be exalted, every hill and mountain shall be made low, the rough places will be made plane and the crooked places will be made straight, and the glory of the Lord shall be revealed, and all flesh shall see it together.
>
> So let freedom ring from the prodigious hilltops of New Hampshire. Let freedom ring from the mighty mountains of New York. Let freedom ring from the heightening Alleghenies of Pennsylvania!
>
> Let freedom ring from the snowcapped Rockies of Colorado! Let freedom ring from the curvaceous slopes of California!
>
> But not only that. Let freedom ring from Stone Mountain of Georgia!
>
> Let freedom ring from Lookout Mountain of Tennessee!
>
> Let freedom ring from every hill and molehill of Mississippi. From every mountainside, let freedom ring.
>
> And when this happens, when we allow freedom to ring—when we let it ring from every village and every hamlet, from every state and every city—we will

be able to speed up that day when all of God's children, black men and white men, Jews and Gentiles, Protestants and Catholics, will be able to join hands and sing in the words of the old Negro spiritual, "Free at last! Free at last! Thank God almighty, we are free at last!"

Figures of Speech

> That crook is drowning in money.

Figures of speech are metaphorical statements that can add vividness, spunk, and delight to your message. But, they can create confusion if used in excess. Twenty-five major types have been identified. Some examples follow:

- *Metaphor:* implied comparison.
  "Fiery temper, thirsty sword."
  "She's a pussycat."
- *Metonymy:* substituting the name of an item associated with a larger concept for the concept.
  "Sword" for war.
  "Brass" for military officers.
- *Synecdoche:* the use of a part for the whole or the whole for a part or parts.
  "All hands on deck."
  "She wears a jewelry store."
- *Hyperbole:* exaggeration.
  "His arms dangled a mile out of his coatsleeves!"
- *Prosopopoeia:* having the dead speak.
  "If Washington were here, he would say . . ."
- *Paradox:* a seemingly self-contradictory or absurd statement.
  "We'll teach these natives democracy even if we have to shoot every last one of them."
- *Catachresis:* somewhat abusive phraseology, involving the use of an incompatible word.
  "He threatened me a good turn."
  "I am not guilty of such virtues."
- *Euphemism:* a mild, inoffensive substitute for a "bad" word.
  "Grandpa passed away."
  "Pleasingly plump."
- *Onomatopoeia:* words that imitate the sounds to which they refer.
  "Buzz," "snarl," "tintinnabulation."
- *Oxymoron:* use of incongruous details.
  "Cruel kindness."
  "Make haste slowly."

- *Alliteration:* the use of words beginning with the same letter.
  "Over stock and stone."
  "Through thick and thin."
- *Simile:* comparison with "like" or "as."
  "The present administration is bobbing around like a cork in a stormy sea."

There is clearly more to language than denotative meaning. When arranged with elegance and style, words can connote strength, grace, and all manner of meanings beyond the dictionary. Vivid messages are also more persuasive than those presented in a less colorful manner.

APPROPRIATENESS

"Politically Correct" Language

"Shooting from the lip" has killed or injured the careers of many public figures. Insensitivity goes beyond language, of course, but some word and language choices are really self-destructive.

Marge Schott

Cincinnati Reds' owner suspended from baseball for making racial slurs against African Americans, Jews, and Asians.

Ross Perot

Unknowingly offended an African-American audience by repeatedly referring to them as "You people."

Edward Derwinski

Veterans Affairs Secretary who referred to illegal Hispanic immigrants as "wetbacks."

Evan Mecham

This Arizona governor, who was impeached, defended use of the derogatory word "pickaninny" in a textbook, said Japanese "got round eyes" when talking about golfing, and told Jews they live in a "great Christian nation" where "Jesus Christ is the lord of the land."

In *Dangerous English,* a guidebook written for foreign visitors to the United States, Elizabeth Claire defines her topic as ". . . words that may be embarrassing for the speaker to say, or cause the listener to feel insulted, to become angry, or to judge the speaker in a negative way."[7] She cautions foreign visitors that "some words for racial or national groups are so dangerous they have caused violence and even murder." Sad perhaps, but true—there are words speakers should probably never use, foreign or domestic.

ETHNIC/RACIAL NAMING   "What do I call you?" Mark asked his new friend, Mr. Chippewa. "Chip," replied Mr. Chippewa. "No," said Mark. "I mean, do you prefer *Indian* or *Native American?*" "I can live with either, but the younger folk prefer *Native American.*" Good advice for speakers. Go with the preferred or stick with Mr. Chippewa.

Meeting News had one of their consultants talk to a variety of people from varied backgrounds to see what kind of naming was most appropriate. Here is what she found.[8]

Native American: Native American is more widely accepted than Indian.

Hispanic: Responses varied. Many people in Texas were comfortable with Mexican American while others felt Hispanic was the only correct term. On the West Coast, Latino is common. The vote from the experts: If in doubt, ask. If you can't ask, use Hispanic.

African American: There appeared to be great confusion among professionals whether to use black or African American. An administrator with Project Family in Little Rock, Ark., visited Africa and prefers African American. She likes the connection and heritage the term represents. Yet, many who prefer the term black resent African American.

Asian American: Asian American is usually appropriate. However, in order to recognize individuals from Guam or other Pacific Islands, many use the term Asian-Pacific Islander. The term Oriental is still used, but it is becoming less acceptable. Too many different ethnic backgrounds fall under its umbrella.

Figure 2.9   Diversity in the United States.

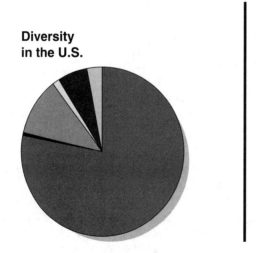

Diversity in the U.S.

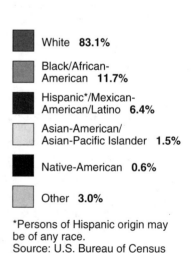

White **83.1%**

Black/African-American **11.7%**

Hispanic*/Mexican-American/Latino **6.4%**

Asian-American/Asian-Pacific Islander **1.5%**

Native-American **0.6%**

Other **3.0%**

*Persons of Hispanic origin may be of any race.
Source: U.S. Bureau of Census

Knowing what is offensive is not always an easy matter. Cultures are changing rapidly and their linguistic preferences are sometimes in flux. If you're going to ask someone about these preferences, ask "What is your heritage?" not "What do I call you?"

The term "Oriental" becomes less acceptable even as I write this. "Black" was offensive to 59 percent of those surveyed in 1964.[9] By 1973 63 percent preferred to be called "Blacks."[10] "Blood," short for *Blood Brother* is used by *African Americans* to refer to other *African Americans*. Are you insensitive if you use the word "Negro?" Does it matter who uses it? In the 1964 study "Negro" offended only 15 percent of "Blacks." Within-race designations is one context where these sensitivities do not always hold—what to do? Perhaps the best answer came from one perceptive student who asked to be addressed and treated as a "person" and to be identified as different only when absolutely necessary.

Overlapping all previous categories of appropriate language is the question of gender-specific or sexist language.

Sexist Language

In 1990 the Sacramento, California city officials considered the term "manhole" too sexist for utility holes in their streets and adopted the term "maintenance hole" to replace "manhole" on official maps and documents.

Gender research proceeds at a near explosive rate, some contradictory, some not. Social roles, especially female, are changing rapidly and with these changes come changes in social orientations and the communication patterns they govern. Sex roles and gender are not the same notion. Some females are quite masculine, some males are quite feminine. Some people combine the roles and are described as androgynous.[11]

In the area of sexist language, both research and experience have provided stable data, suggestions, and important rules. Speakers should be aware of the following:[12]

GENDERED PRONOUNS   Modern audiences are very much aware of the *"he," "she," "he/she," "she/he"* problem and expect speakers to know when they may or may not use gender-specific pronouns. For the moment a Catholic priest may be referred to as "him" but not so for a minister who may be a woman. Gender-specific activities may be referred to in masculine terms. So far, football is male, basketball is not. Mother is female, father is male, but much of what was once gender specific is no longer so. When in doubt *speak in the plural.* "They" can refer to males or females; "their" or "theirs" to the possessive form "his" or "her" (or "hers"); "them" to the objective form "him" and "her." Perhaps one day grammarians will provide us with a generic personal pronoun, but until they do speakers must beware of the masculine pronouns.[13]

> Does HuMan become Huperson? What about the SON in person? What this country needs is a good 5 cent neuter pronoun . . .
>
> *Columnist Matt Roush*

GENDER INFLECTIONS   We speak here of the changes in form that *words* undergo, not of voice. "Fireman" is an inappropriate gendered inflection unless one is talking about a specific male person. Even here one is better advised to use "firefighter" and avoid all risks. It's also easier for a speaker to say, "Attention firefighters" than "Attention firemen and firewomen." How about "Fellow firefighters?" "Fellow" is pretty much a neutral noun, but don't count on it . . .

Other gendered nouns that speakers may trip on abound—"mailman," "policeman," "chairman." Try "mailcarrier," "police officer," "chairperson" (or "chair"). "Person" can also desex many of these male-gendered occupational designations.

SEXIST ANECDOTES   These are explanations, illustrations, jokes, and "humorous" comments that foster stereotypes or social roles based on gender. This kind of inappropriate discrimination is mostly directed against women. However, this type of inappropriateness can be directed at any group.

> A Secretary of Agriculture was forced to resign when, in a "joke," he said blacks, whom he called "colored," wanted three things. In obscene, derogatory terms, he described alleged preferences for dress, sex, and bathroom habits.
>
> A celebrity lost her job promoting Florida oranges when in an effort to defeat a gay rights ordinance in Miami she said that letting children be exposed to homosexuals was close to feeding them garbage.

One professional comedian with a large collections of Polish, "women" and gay jokes decided to improve his image by changing all his ethnic, sexist, and gay designations to Ecuadorians. The insulted groups figured it out and he's been banned in Ecuador.

Verbal Obscenity

This is also part of the modern scene. Words can hurt us. Shockingly obscene words have a way of affecting the rationality of both those who use them and those to whom they are addressed.

The riots at the 1968 Democratic National Convention in Chicago entailed much obscenity and counter-obscenity. John Bowers and Donovan Ochs maintain that "the tactic that probably prompted the 'police riot,' the violent suppression witnessed by millions on television, was the use of obscenity."[14]

The ancient rhetoricians stated without qualification that profanity should be rejected as a legitimate rhetorical strategy. J. Dan Rothwell, however, suggests that

> Despite centuries of negative criticism, verbal obscenity has become a more frequent rhetorical device. It is successful in creating attention, in discrediting an enemy, in provoking violence, in fostering identification, and in providing catharsis. Its effects are governed by a variety of circumstances which need to be understood more fully. It has precipitated a police riot, brutal beatings, and even death. Hoping it will go away will not make it so.[15]

Vulgar words and phrases are unfortunately being used more frequently. The younger generation seems to have fewer hang-ups with such terms than do older folk. As with any other words, whatever power they have is lost if a person uses them all of the time on any topic. Our mass media still forbids most of them and they are almost always bad news for public speakers.

Research also indicates some shifting of beliefs regarding appropriate language for males and females. However, this same research did find that speakers using obscene phrases were rated lower in "socio-intellectual status" and "aesthetic quality."

Modern research also tells us that using profanity generally has a detrimental effect on the credibility of the speaker. Suitable language is a necessary part of human social behavior. Some people are seriously offended on a religious basis, others on a social basis.

Language Overstatement

An antiunion student speaker opened one of his speeches with the words: "Unions are ruining this country. I am going to prove to you that these Bolsheviks are entirely corrupt and more dangerous than terrorists." This language was enough for his opponents to throw up an emotional communication barrier, and as a result he was not very persuasive. The most interesting part of this story is that the promanagement listeners were most critical of the speech. Even when a sophisticated audience agrees with your point of view, it can be offended by extreme overstatement and overgeneralization, for these are indications of immaturity or emotional insecurity.

When strong attitudes intrude, strong, intense language and word choice often follow. "Guardians of the peace" is a much more positive, less intense description of the police force than "brass-hatted pigs." Language does not stand alone. The audience and the situation should help decide the potency of your language. If you're not potent enough, you may lose audience interest. If you're too potent you may lose them altogether. When strong ". . . ist" words intrude in your communication ("sexist," "racist," "elitist," etc.), such charges not only precipitate conflict, but also make it difficult to find resolution. In plain English, you may get more than you bargained for!

A highly polarized audience (in your favor) may welcome intense language of even bizarre proportions, but beware of such behavior should you try the same language on a more neutral or sophisticated audience. To add to your problems, language that is appropriate one day may be a disaster the next. Some topics, audiences, or speakers seem to be more language tolerant, yet ignorance is seldom excused and insensitive language is mostly perceived as bias. A long look at the total situation and audience you're facing can save you much chagrin and embarrassment later on.

Ode to Sensitivity

Knowing what is appropriate and politically correct in every speaking situation is often a frustrating, but an absolutely necessary effort if we are to be effective and sensitive speakers.[16]

Using politically correct language does not mean that we must abandon our beliefs or positions on socially sensitive subjects. It is fair to use appropriate naming when the discussion or speech concerns *gays* in the military, radical feminism, inner city African Americans, Native-American casinos, and so on.

The meaning of any speech is also in the mind of the listener—it is an *interactive* process. You must choose your language so it helps your listeners sort and select from their word representations something approximating your purpose.

Is there room for humor regarding PC? Is this sexist? Does the situation matter?

> Remember way back when women had such names as Patience and Prudence . . .

Considerable controversy exists in these matters, and even the academic debates have become polarized and extreme in their arguments.[17]

That speakers may sometimes feel threatened by unreasonable demands for political correctness is a serious matter. Columnist Charles Osgood addresses this problem in a lighter and less threatening way.

AN ODE TO BEING SENSITIVE

Today folks are so sensitive about what's said or sung that one must always watch one's step, and also watch one's tongue. One's career can be ruined and one's life completely wrecked, if one says something that is not politically correct.

Beware of anything that smacks of sexism or racism, of lookism or ageism, of timeism or placeism. There are so many isms it will drive you up the wall. and it's terribly important that you recognize them all.

To say that someone "failed" is much too negative, you see.

What you want to say is that they have "achieved deficiency."

If you're opposed to "otherness," that's called "assimilationism." If you question Mr. Darwin, they'll accuse you of "creationism." There's heightism and fatism, and good old isolationism. Don't complain or you are guilty of "anti-ismizationism."

Nobody is disabled, "handi-capable's" what's said, and you're "terminally inconvenienced" now instead of simply dead. To say that someone "failed" is much too negative, you see. What you want to say is that they have "achieved deficiency."

You do not want to be "centrist," either anthropo or eu. So never say you want to see the "Middle Eastern" bureau. For by now you should have noticed at the very, very least that's considered eurocentric now. There is no "middle east."

You are not supposed to ever give anyone a "test." A "needs assessment" is the term that's now considered best. If you're drunk, you are "sobriety deprived" we can report, and "vertically challenged" if you're too tall or too short.

The active voice is much preferred by Messrs. Strunk and White, but the PC crowd is not so sure politically that's right . . . To say how you see something is nowhere near as keen as saying what the subject of discussion is now "seen as."

By whom, in this construction, you do not have to say, so sometimes you can get completely off the hook that way. A fact which in too many ways exploiters have exploited, so both the active and the passive voice should be avoided.

Which doesn't leave you room for saying what you want to say, but the way things are, most likely you are better off that way. If all this seems quite strange to you, it's just as I have feared, and you better get that handbook by Chris Cerf and Henry Beard.[18]

Reprinted by permission: Tribune Media Services

Summary

The average speaker of English knows between 50,000 and 250,000 words. The 500 most commonly used words have more than 14,000 uses. These same-term differences may be described as lexical, contextual, and neurological. A listener has more concomitant signals to deal with than a reader. Voice, for example, has a powerful influence upon meaning. A speaker's appearance and gestures are other concomitant signals that affect the listeners.

Language as a system is holistic—the whole of it is greater than the sum of its parts. Language that is appropriate one day may be a disaster the next. Our understandings and perceptions of the world are thought to be inextricably tied to language and particularly to its grammar. If this long-standing *Whorf-Sapir Hypothesis* is true, then critical thinking is governed by this powerful language system.

Abstraction is that process of thinking in which we selectively omit details about concrete or real things. The heart of the difficulty with language is the confusion of the word with the thing for which it stands. The further we are from the referent, the more problems of meaning that arise. Short speeches may foster overgeneralization, and this is why short speeches often call for more preparation than long ones do.

Denotation refers to literal meaning; connotation refers to added, more abstract meaning. Meaning has three elements: a person having thoughts, a symbol (or sign), and a referent.

A word is a kind of symbol. A word is a generally accepted representation of a thing. There are obviously more things and concepts in the world than there are words, so a word may be thought of as a representation or generalization with a meaning in accordance with its context. A speaker should ask, "What does *this* word mean to *this* audience in *this* situation, in *this* context, as used by *this* speaker at *this* time?" A good sentence systematically excludes meanings the listener might attach that are not intended by the speaker—in short, it qualifies by defining meanings *not* intended. A perversion of this process has been called "doublespeak."

The propositional nature of language can be a problem in some language systems. If we become too literal and rigid, logic and language habits may be impaired and misunderstanding may result.

Specificity and accuracy in language behooves us to eliminate as much jargon as possible, to date events, and to make accurate word choices.

Helpful rules include: indexing, "is," "et cetera," dating your language, and discerning presymbolic language. Colorful language includes vividness and imagery.

Vividness suggests that there is more to language than denotative meaning. When arranged with elegance and style, words can connote strength, grace, and all manner of meanings not in the dictionary. Imagery refers to vivid figures of speech that produce mental pictures in the mind's eye of listeners. Figures of speech include metaphor, hyperbole, euphemism, simile, and others.

Language does not stand alone. The audience should help decide the specificity and intensity of your language. Insensitive language is mostly perceived as bias. "Shooting from the lip" has injured the careers of many public figures.

Language which is not "politically correct" has been described as dangerous English . . . words that may be embarrassing for the speaker to say, or cause the listener to be insulted, to become angry, or to judge the speaker in a negative way.

Ethnic/racial naming advice includes: Use the currently preferred designations (e.g. African American, Hispanic, Asian American) and make sure that naming is relevant and necessary.

Research and experience in the area of sexist language provide important rules for speakers. These rules include the use of gendered nouns and pronouns, gender inflections, and sexist anecdotes.

Shockingly obscene words have a way of affecting rationality of both those who use them and those to whom they are addressed. Profanity generally has a detrimental effect on the credibility of the speaker.

Knowing what is appropriate and politically correct in every speaking situation is often a frustrating but absolutely necessary effort if you are to be an effective and sensitive speaker.

Critical thinking involves exercising intelligent, objective, cautious judgment and evaluation of the language we use and of the language we receive and decode from others. One of the most widespread thinking faults is overstatement and overgeneralization.

Language habits reflect your personality. Seriously maladjusted individuals can often be identified by their language habits.

That speakers may sometimes feel threatened by unreasonable demands for political correctness is a serious matter. See "Ode" on pages 54–55.

Learning Projects

1. Collect two examples of context confusion that caused language to mean different things to different individuals.

2. List five words or short language segments that annoy you (almost regardless of context), and try to explain why.

3. Find an advertisement or commercial that you feel is racially, sexually, or culturally debasing (linguistically), and explain your choice.

4. Discuss the following examples of language breakdown, and try to recall instances of breakdown that you experienced.

> There is a story that the Japanese verb "mokusatsu" was responsible for the loosing of American atom bombs on Hiroshima and Nagasaki. The verb can mean either "no comment" or "to kill with silence" and was used in the Japanese newspaper accounts of the Japanese government's reaction to the American demand for unconditional and immediate surrender. By the time reports reached the Allied authorities, the second meaning was accepted, so it seemed that Premier Suzuki had rejected the ultimatum as "unworthy of notice." What he actually said, so the story goes, was that his government had decided to postpone action and withhold comment pending clarification of the demand for surrender.

> DERBY, England—(UPI)—The men who referee women's soccer games have had enough. The ladies' language is too much for them.
>
> "The trouble is that some of the ladies do not behave like ladies," said Frank Hardwood, secretary of the 354-member Derby District Referees Society. "The language can be quite startling."
>
> He said the society is going to train women to referee women's matches from now on.

5. Find an example of false or overgeneralized language. Was it intended? Explain your thinking about it.

6. Reconstruct an example of an *arrogant dismissal.* How might a speaker have better addressed the issue?

7. Create a denotative and a connotative example for the following words: dog, cat, louse, pig, blimp, monkey, and one of your own choosing.

8. Find a higher or lower abstraction for the following words: P-51 Mustang, rocking chair, automobile, patriotism, Hispanic, Muslim, and one of your own choosing.

9. Find an example of a word choice mistake causing problems (e.g. Catholic, catholic). Explain.

10. Translate the short speech by Senator Moynihan on page 41. What was his real message? Messages?

11. Rewrite the negative imagery used by Frenchman Jean Cau ((page 47) regarding EuroDisney, this time with a positive set of mental pictures.

12. Create figures of speech which illustrate: metaphor, hyperbole, simile, oxymoron, and paradox.

13. Find an example of "shooting from the lip" (e.g. Marge Schott) and explain what happened.

14. React to the politically correct suggestions for naming people racially or ethnically. How do you prefer to be named (e.g. German American, Jew, Yankee, and so forth)?

15. Find three examples showing improper use of masculine pronouns (he/she, she/he, and so forth).

16. Find three examples of improper gender inflections (mailman, fireman, and so forth).

17. When is language profane or verbally obscene? Explain your criteria.

18. Do a close reading of Charles Osgood's "Ode to Being Sensitive." What is the real message (messages) here? Prepare to discuss.

Notes

1. Paula J. Schwanenflugel, ed., *The Psychology of Word Meanings* (Hillsdale, NJ: Erlbaum, 1991).
2. Robert P. Pula, "A General Semantics Glossary (Part VI)," *ETC.*, 50, no. 4 (Winter 1993–94), 493.
3. B. L. Whorf, *Language, Thought, and Reality* (New York: John Wiley & Sons, 1957). See also John A. Lucy, *Grammatical Categories and Cognition: A Case Study of the Linguistic Relativity Hypothesis* (Cambridge, England: Cambridge University Press, 1992); Janet Yerby, "Family Systems Theory Reconsidered: Integrating Social Construction Theory and Dialectical Process," *Communication Theory*, 5, no. 4 (November 1995), 339–65.
4. William Safire, *Lend Me Your Ears* (New York: W. W. Norton & Co., 1992), p. 208.
5. Douglas MacArthur, "Duty, Honor, Country," speech delivered at West Point Military Academy, May 12, 1962.
6. Martin Luther King, Jr., "I Have a Dream," speech delivered in Washington, D.C., August 28, 1963.
7. Elizabeth Claire, *Dangerous English* (Dundee, IL: Delta Systems Co., Inc., 1990), p. 1.
8. *Meeting News*, March, 1993, p. 23.
9. G. A. Maddox and R. S. Ross, "Strong Words," *Childhood Education*, 45 (January 1969), 260–64.
10. R. S. Ross, *Speech Communication, 4th ed.* (Englewood Cliffs, N.J.: Prentice Hall, 1977), p. 72.

11. For a broader discussion of gender and communication, see: J. C. Pearson, L. H. Turner, W. Todd-Mancillas, *Gender and Communication* (Dubuque, Iowa: W. C. Brown, 1991); also H. Giles and R. L. Street, "Communication Characteristics and Behavior," in M. L. Knapp and G. R. Miller, eds., *Handbook of Interpersonal Communication* (Beverly Hills, Calif.: Sage), 1985; also see B. Bate, *Communication and the Sexes* (New York: Harper & Row, 1988); for a radical feminist view, see Cheris Krarrarae and Paula A. Treichler, *A Feminist Dictionary* (London, England: Pandora Press, 1985).

12. For more on gender issues in the classroom, see *Communication Education,* 40, no. 1 (January 1991).

13. For a radical feminist view see Julia Penelope, *Speaking Freely: Unlearning the Lies of the Fathers' Tongues* (New York: Pergamon Press, 1990).

14. John Bowers and Donovan Ochs, *The Rhetoric of Agitation and Control* (Reading, Mass.: Addison-Wesley, 1971, 1991), p. 70.

15. Dan Rothwell, "Verbal Obscenity: Time for Second Thoughts," *Western Speech,* 35, no. 4 (1971), 242.

16. See Michael Burgoon and William Baily, "PC at Last! PC at Last! Thank God Almighty, We Are PC at Last," *Journal of Communication,* 42, no. 2 (Spring 1992), 95–104; also see Barbara J. O'Keefe, "Sense and Sensitivity," *Journal of Communication,* 42, no. 2 (Spring 1992), 123–30.

17. Richard Bello, "A Burkeian Analysis of the 'Political Correctness' Confrontation in Higher Education," *The Southern Communication Journal,* 61, no. 3 (Spring 1996), 243–52.

18. Charles Osgood, "An Ode to Being Sensitive." Reprinted by permission: Tribune Media Services. Also see Henry Beard and Christopher Cerf, *The Official Politically Correct Dictionary and Handbook* (New York: Random House, 1992, 1993.)

3

CRITICAL LISTENING

CHAPTER
OUTLINE

HOW LISTENING WORKS

"What you are speaks so loudly I cannot hear what you are saying."

"While the right to talk may be the beginning of freedom, the necessity of listening is what makes the right important."

Walter Lippmann

First listen, my friend, and then you may shriek and bluster."

Aristophanes

"Hearing is one of the body's five senses. But listening is an art."

Frank Tyger

"While ostensibly listening, most of us are inwardly preparing a statement to stun the company when we get the floor."

Stuart Chase

Courage. There is hope! We have evidence that listening can be improved through understanding the process. Listening training improved the listening ability of elementary students. College students improved their listening comprehension through a program first designed for industry. Oral reading seems to help. There is even evidence that improving our listening skills may improve our reading skills.

Good listening habits are important. Fifty-nine percent of the Fortune 500 service corporations provide listening training to their personnel. Clearly they view listening as important.[1]

We Assume a Style

We listen for different reasons—because we feel we have to; because we're enjoying ourselves; because we want to learn something; and because we want to argue with what is being said.

Listening experts have described types or styles of listening as active, supportive, analytic, people-centered, time-oriented, critical, appreciative, even therapeutic.[2]

Four composites of these types that are most useful to speaker/audience situations may be described as:

reluctant
appreciative
critical
aggressive styles

RELUCTANT   This is the style we assume when we feel or think we had better listen, even if what is being said is distasteful. This would include classes you don't like, sermons you've heard before, situations you would just as soon avoid but cannot. Motivation, to say the least, is low. We must work at getting out of this style or find ways to be better listeners within the reluctant style.

APPRECIATIVE   Listeners assuming the appreciative style are generally more responsive, more discerning, and more interested in the topic than reluctant types. For example, during classes that you enjoy or speeches you find stimulating, attention comes more readily because you feel that time spent is rewarding or that the information will be of use to you. Motivation is not a problem, but you may still not be an effective listener (1) if you are so appreciative that you are not thinking objectively, (2) if it is difficult to hear the speaker, or (3) if your listening skills are poor.

CRITICAL   Here critical thinking skills are fairly but firmly applied to what you are hearing whether you are pro, con, or neutral on the topic. It is a democratic but questioning, responsive mind-set. If need be, you generate your own interest and motivation to listen. If listeners have adequate access to the message, possess most of the necessary listening skills, and maintain their motivation to listen, they are on their way to becoming ideal listeners.

AGGRESSIVE   This is more of an opinionated, watchdog style than that used by the *critical* listener described earlier. It frequently appears when faced with high-pressure persuasion for products, political issues, or value systems. This style tends to prompt intrapersonal responses in the form of argument rehearsals which, if unremitting, lead to ineffective listening. One's biases intrude to the point of disruptive interpretations of what is being said. One should strive to achieve an objective, *appreciative* style when called for or an evenhanded, *critical* listening style rather than the less rewarding *reluctant* and *aggressive* styles.

We will have more to say about critical thinking and listening shortly. First a description of the psychological mechanisms involved in the listening process.

A Process Model

Listening is much more than paying attention and hearing. Our memory as well as all of our senses may be called on to make "sense" of a speaker's oral signals in a wide range of settings.[3] The verbal messages often take on quite different or sharper meaning as we observe the nonverbals that don't involve hearing (voice does, of course) such as the eyes, gestures, body movements, and clothing.

As we learned in Chapter 1, "making sense" has to do with how we assign meaning, that is, how we socially construct what we think we are hearing or seeing.

Listening, like other kinds of perceptual activity, goes through a similar process: (1) sensation, (2) interpretation of the sensory inputs, and (3) response. The response is both internal (intrapersonal) and external (feedback). The speaker's message, as well as inputs from the environment (Figure 3.1), affect and in turn are affected by all steps in the process. External responses (feedback) go through a similar process as they return to the speaker.

SENSATION   This phase of the listening process depends heavily on hearing. However, all of our senses operate in most speaker/audience situations. Some sensory barriers are reasonably obvious. If someone is operating a jackhammer or beating a drum, you may lose the verbal signal because of sheer noise. College students frequently are given audiometric screenings (hearing tests), and some are found to have hearing losses of which they were unaware. You have learned that you hear poorly when you are tired. *Sensory distraction* could be competing noises, other verbal messages, or distraction by the other senses. A really foul smell, temperature extremes, an attractive face— any of these can disrupt or interrupt sensory inputs and, therefore, what we hear. Consider the first-grade teacher who has just put on the 35th pair of boots when the last child says, "These aren't my boots. They ———." "Oh no, no, no," interrupts the teacher as she removes the boots counting audibly to ten. The child finishes her sentence. "——— they are my sister's. I couldn't find mine this morning."

A certain amount of mindlessness may be involved at this phase. New information is not heard or truly processed. Prior experiences are stereotypically reenacted.

Figure 3.1   Listening process

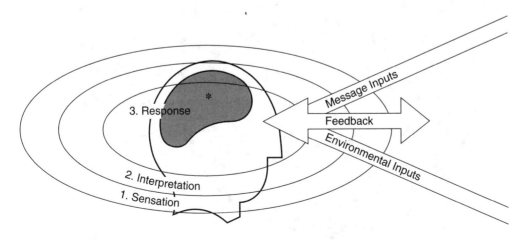

Think of phase one as mostly *auditory* sensation to which all other senses and distractions may contribute. Assume you have overcome the barriers and are willing to remain attentive; you are finally *auding* (or hearing) but may not be seriously listening.

Your first sensory experience in phase one often has a lot to do with the listening style you unconsciously choose and thereby the interpretation (phase two) that follows.

INTERPRETATION   After adequate sensory access, good message interpretation depends mostly on intrapersonal inputs. Your knowledge, past experience, beliefs, attitudes, emotional blocks, and so forth come to bear on what you've heard. Critical decoding has begun. A listener's motivations, intelligence, cognitive complexity, and attitudes will greatly affect what meaning a listener will attribute to the sensory inputs.

These factors serve as filters which often unconsciously affect the interpretations of what we hear. Consider some of the following in Figure 3.2.

What does it all mean? If you understand anything the speaker is trying to say, *what* do you understand? At this point you are interpreting. Here you draw upon all of your inputs and your skills at managing attributions of meaning.

Listen carefully. Opportunity often speaks imprecisely.

Figure 3.2   Listening filters

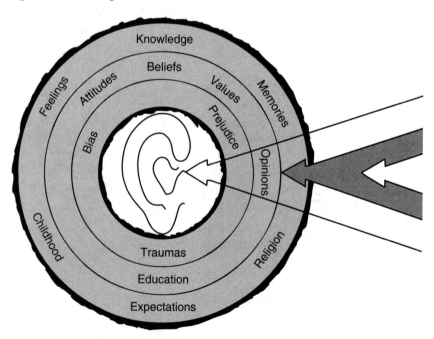

Is the intense speaker to whom you're listening telling the truth? Is he or she perhaps under special external pressure? Is there free choice or does the subject or the speaker's role dictate all or part of the behavior? Does the hostage speak true treason or is there a gun at his family's head?

Attribution theory deals with how and what we infer about the behaviors, attitudes, and intentions we observe or know, or think we know, in others and in ourselves. The *discounting effect* is an important part of attribution theory. A given cause should be discounted if other plausible causes are also present. One suggestion is to withhold evaluation and response and hear the person out. Another suggestion is to consider how these meanings relate or covary.

The *covariation principle* suggests that we often misattribute meanings and causes because we tend to work backward from behavior to inferences about causes and often overlook the other critical influences that covary. If we are listening in an aggressive style and the situation calls for an appreciative style, we are apt to take things more literally than we should. The appropriate style or mind-set would cause us to discount some of what we heard.

RESPONSE   *Internal* responses deal with the final results of your perceptual and attributional efforts during the interpretation phase. This is an ongoing process. One does not have to be at the message end to respond. These internal responses may signal understanding or confusion, approval or disapproval, and so on. It is the start of vigilant critical thinking which leads to external response.

> . . . helping a student unlock his or her thoughts for others, the communication teacher also unlocks a potentially demanding citizen, a citizen with the mental agility to listen between others' lines when they speak and to remember her or his own bottom line when responding to them.[4]
>
> *Roderick P. Hart*

External responses are the overt manifestation of those internal signals—*feedback*. They can be both verbal and nonverbal. They can help an alert speaker adjust his or her message. They can also confuse and occasionally unnerve a speaker. Good listening habits include providing fair, but also forthright feedback.

LISTENING IMPROVEMENT AREAS

Three specific areas where we can pragmatically improve our listening behavior are *motivation, access,* and *skills*. These take place in a sea of knowledge and beliefs which affect our thinking habits and may therefore seriously affect our listening behavior. First the specific areas.

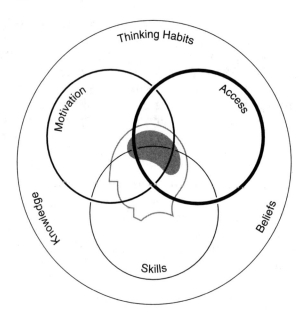

Figure 3.3 Listening improvement areas

Consider three students all clearly confused after a lecture on primitive art.

John: "I really don't dig this stuff, bore—ing!"
Hamza: "Good, but I no understand too much."
Ruth: "Okay, I guess, but my notes are meaningless."

John's listening barrier is a lack of *motivation.* Assuming Hamza has interest and motivation, his problem is *access:* specifically, a language barrier. Ruth has primarily a *skill* problem. She has interest and access, but her ability to organize what she's heard (note-taking) is poor.

1. Improving Motivation to Listen

Rudolph, a theater major and a reluctant listener, falls asleep in his chemistry class. His interest is zero. Why is he taking chemistry? Because it meets the science requirement and is the only class that fits his play rehearsal schedule. Not much motivation here; perhaps Rudy is a lost cause. But wait— concentrate on what motivation there is. Rudy needs to meet a science requirement. This class allows him his first love, namely, acting, and if he fails the course he could lose it all. In short, he has sought motivation in a larger system of interest.

Although it is unlikely that Rudy will ever develop a consuming interest in chemistry, perhaps he can somehow relate the class to his theater interests.

"Maybe I'll play a mad chemist in a Broadway play." "I'll have a better feel for *Arsenic and Old Lace*." "Perhaps I can *act* like a chemistry major for one term." Perhaps discretion is the better part of valor and Rudy will quietly withdraw and take a different course at another time.

In review, to improve motivation to listen: (1) look for motivation (positive or negative) in a larger area of interests; (2) relate the topic at hand to your own selfish interests; and (3) translate the problem to an intellectual challenge: "I'll figure out this turkey subject!"

Rudy should also carefully read the material on improving listening skills which follows shortly.

2. Improving Listening Access

If the listening channel is blocked by physical noise, fatigue, or even a hearing deficiency, there are some obvious ways to improve things: Eliminate or move away from the noise, get some rest, move closer to the speaker, and see a hearing specialist. In short, clear the channel of pragmatic problems.

Some clues indicating when access is diminished by hearing loss follow:

1. Voices sound muffled.
2. Male voices seem clearer than female voices.
3. People assert that you're not listening.
4. You frequently ask people to repeat themselves.

When the problem is language, as in our foreign student Hamza's case, the answer is not as easy. Assuming Hamza's reading of English is not equally deficient, he can start there. He should also seek out those campus support groups that work to improve language proficiency. The language block is not restricted to foreign students. Chemistry has a language and a vocabulary of its own as Rudy discovered. To clear the channel of such barriers one must work on the jargon and vocabulary to gain access to what's being said. Reading is thought to be related to good listening probably because it adds to our vocabulary, thereby giving us more meaningful access.

In review, we can improve our *access* to listening by: (1) managing or eliminating noise, (2) avoiding fatigue, (3) accommodating our hearing deficiencies, and (4) learning relevant language and vocabulary especially through reading.

3. Improving Listening Skills

The skills area overlaps the areas of motivation and access. The following material should also help your efforts in those areas.

NOTE-TAKING   Recall that Ruth was confused after the lecture on primitive art. She was *motivated* to listen, she had reasonable *access,* but her note-taking skills not only failed in function but actually contributed to the cause of the confusion. Skillful note-taking helps one concentrate on what's important as well as serving as an intelligent, brief record of what you've heard.

Ruth's first mistake was trying to take down too much material. That effort lasted about one minute, and she was hopelessly behind. In her panic she switched styles and went to a partial sentence, abbreviated word style. When that failed her notes became almost gibberish and her listening efficiency dropped to a frustrating zero. Here are Ruth's notes on the lecture. What Ruth was trying to take notes on follows.

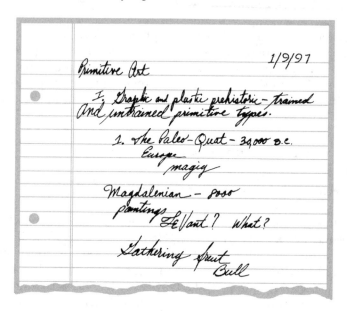

In general primitive art is about the graphic and plastic arts of prehistoric cultures; the term is loosely applied to the art of tribal cultures, of untrained artists in our own culture, as well as of trained artists cultivating a self-consciously primitive style; these last are more properly termed primitivistic.

Paleolithic or Quaternary art dates back to about 30,000 B.C. The hunting peoples of Ice Age Europe made paintings of their game animals, including many now extinct. This initial chapter of human art was concentrated in Western Europe, although manifestations have appeared in Central Europe, which remained free of ice during the Quaternary Era, and in Russia and Siberia. Women's and children's handprints next to the drawings indicate this early rupestrian, or cave, art may have been art for decorative purposes, rather than based on magic as originally assumed.

The Magdalenian period, during which the peak of this art was reached, was followed by the Mesolithic period between 8,000 and 4,000 B.C., when another cycle of particularly beautiful art was created in the mountains of the Spanish Levant. Its development resembles a last echo of the great art of the Paleolithic. It appears to have been the work of hunting people who even at that late date lived a life similar to that of the Paleolithic age, despite development of agriculture and herding in the fertile valleys and the coastal slopes of the Levant. These Levant artists were the first to make use of composition. Although simple, their works are full of movement; they had already begun to realize the problems of perspective. Moreover, the principal subject of their art was the people themselves rather than the animals they hunted. Thus in the rock shelters of the Spanish Levant we see paintings of people hunting, fighting, preparing weapons, dancing, and gathering fruit.

Ruth's note-taking would have been far less frustrating and her listening much improved if she had listened for ideas and facts, that is, main points and supporting data. Her notes would make more sense for review if subpoints were indented in a consistent manner. System is the secret. Be consistent in form, note key words—not everything you hear—and identify supporting evidence.

Here are the notes of a more skillful notetaker and better listener.

```
                                    1/9/97
    Primitive Art

    graphic and plastic forms
       prehistoric
       modern (untrained)
       modern (primitiristic)

    Paleolithic - 30,000 B.C.
       Ice-age Europe
       animal pics
       decorative (not magic)

    Magdal. - Mesolithic - 8000-4000 B.C.
       Span. LeVant (?)
       Compos. and persp.
       First pics of people
```

Of course, not all speakers are well organized, and nothing is more frustrating than trying to organize the unorganizable. It is sometimes advisable to first attempt to figure out what scheme a speaker is using and then adjust your note-taking accordingly.

MANAGING DISTRACTIONS   Distractions range from the physical that deny us listening access (noise, smell, vocabulary, etc.) to the intrapersonal that distort our ability to listen objectively. Some intrapersonal distractions may be: (1) a speaker whose personality, appearance, or manner upsets you enough to disrupt good listening; (2) language that you consider substandard, inappropriate, or obscene; (3) topical opposition that reaches a disruptive emotional level; (4) misinformation and erroneous beliefs.[5]

> "I find it especially difficult to converse with philosophers. They're so busy trying to cut you up that they often don't take the time to listen."
>
> *Thomas S. Kuhn*

Training advice is hard to come by; even the listening experts resort to rules and admonishments in these matters. The assumption is that many people will manage distractions better if their bad habits are simply called to their attention. Are you guilty of any of these?

1. *Overly criticizing the speaker.* Try to disregard a person's appearance or speech mannerisms when they offer you an excuse for not listening to the message.

2. *Avoiding new and challenging topics.* Some topics are difficult and complex, and insisting that they are too complicated is a way of avoiding them.

3. *Calling the topic stupid or uninteresting.* This is a great way to duck listening. Work hard at relating the topic to something you do like or do find interesting.

4. *Prejudging.* Jumping to the conclusion that you understand the speaker's meaning before it is fully expressed. Worse yet, it often means preparing and rehearsing answers to questions or points before fully understanding them.

5. *Reacting emotionally.* If you hear something that challenges your most deeply rooted prejudices, you become overstimulated. You mentally plan a rebuttal to what you hear, or you develop questions designed to embarrass the speaker. Emotionally loaded words distract you.

6. *Seeking distractions.* Looking out the window for something, anything, that might be more interesting; concentrating on another person who excites you; day-dreaming or actually causing distraction.

7. *Faking attention.* You only pretend to listen, and your act gets pretty good. You smile, nod, blink, and so forth; you may even fool the speaker. That is why this bad habit is so cruel. You may be fooling (and cheating) both yourself and the speaker.

The Sperry Corporation program is concerned mainly with improving listening skills. The company and their listening consultant, Dr. Lyman Steil, have developed ten keys or rules to effective listening shown in Table 3.1.

Table 3.1 10 Keys to Effective Listening

KEYS TO EFFECTIVE LISTENING	THE BAD LISTENER	THE GOOD LISTENER
1. Find areas of interest	Tunes out dry subjects	Opportunizes; asks "What's in it for me?"
2. Judge content, not delivery	Tunes out if delivery is poor	Judges content; skips over delivery errors
3. Hold your fire	Tends to enter into argument	Doesn't judge until comprehension complete
4. Listen for ideas	Listens for facts	Listens for central themes
5. Be flexible	Takes intensive notes using only one system	Takes fewer notes. Uses 4–5 different systems, depending on speaker
6. Work at listening	Shows no energy output; fakes attention	Works hard, exhibits active body state
7. Resist distractions	Is easily distracted	Fights or avoids distractions, tolerates bad habits, knows how to concentrate
8. Exercise your mind	Resists difficult expository material; seeks light, recreational material	Uses heavier material as exercise for the mind
9. Keep your mind open	Reacts to emotional words	Interprets color words; does not get hung up on them
10. Capitalize on fact that thought is faster than speech	Tends to daydream with slow speakers	Challenges, anticipates, mentally summarizes, weighs the evidence, listens between the lines to tone of voice

Source: "Your Personal Listening Profile," p. 9. © Sperry Corporation.

All speakers are entitled to *some* listening effort and rule concordance by their audience. In the case of a required course that is notoriously dull and taught by an even duller teacher, you may dramatically discover your own listening responsibilities when you fail the midsemester examination!

> One of the best ways to persuade others is with your ears—by listening to them.
>
> *Dean Rusk*

CRITICAL THINKING AND LISTENING

A 1982 poll of high school students revealed that more than 25 percent actually believed that the moon landing never occurred and was a matter of propaganda, fake photography, or CIA conspiracy. In 1993 David Koresh and the

Branch Davidian cult believed that he was the Lamb mentioned in the Book of Revelations and that he could bring about the end of the world . . .

According to the late Carl Sagan, 1994 surveys indicate that 25 to 50 percent of adult United States citizens don't know the earth goes around the sun once a year. Are we just not listening or just not thinking?

> Mountains of evidence—both in the form of statistical studies and personal testimonies—establish that the American people are suffering from a new and perhaps unprecedented form of mental incapacitation for which I have coined the word *dumbth*.
>
> *Steve Allen*

The state of California has had it with *dumbth* and has instituted a *critical thinking* requirement in its schools. The executive order states:

> Instruction in *critical thinking* is designed to achieve an understanding of the relationship of language to logic, which would lead to the ability to analyze, criticize, and advocate ideas, to reason inductively and deductively, and to reach factual or judgmental conclusions based on sound inferences drawn from unambiguous statements of knowledge or belief. The minimal competence to be expected at the successful conclusion of instruction in critical thinking should be the ability to distinguish fact from judgment, belief from knowledge, and skills in elementary inductive and deductive processes, including an understanding of the formal and informal fallacies of language and thought.

In many ways the most difficult audience a speaker can engage is not a *dumbth* one or even a hostile one, but rather one that holds uninformed, erroneous beliefs, has little mind for facts, and prefers not to even think about reassessing them. "Don't confuse me with the facts; I'm happy with what I think." It's a laid-back refusal to engage in any serious thinking or listening effort.

What can we as *listeners* do to avoid these problems? Obviously we should strive to be better informed. We should also review how we know what we know or think we know. We should learn to suspend our laid-back demeanor long enough to hear what the "wordspinners" are saying. We are frequently wrong. Aristotle thought that male babies were conceived in a strong north wind!

> It ain't so much the things we don't know that get us into trouble. It's the things we know that just ain't so.
>
> *Artemus Ward*

Critical thinking should be defined as *exercising intelligent, objective, cautious judgment and evaluation.* I say *should* because in some contexts "critical" means harsh, caustic, unfavorable evaluation and communication. While this acrimonious approach may be successful in some influence situations, its habitual, unconstrained use often leads to censorious or captious thinking — that is, a proneness to seek out irrelevant issues and to raise objections based on narrow prejudices. However, as long as we apply the positive, more scientific meaning of *critical* to our thinking and strive to give events and ideas meaning through fair hearing and logical analysis, we're off to a good start.

Assuming we are not suffering complete "dumbth," what can we do to improve the critical evaluations of messages we attend to? All of the chapters offer partial answers to that question, but here are some general areas for improving your thinking and listening habits.

> . . . perhaps we are the only existing species capable of sustained logical thought, such thought does not come easy to us. Very few of us ever get very good at it—to most it remains difficult and even alien.
>
> *Leon Festinger*

Interpretations of Chance Events

We hear satanic messages in garbled music. We make bets on the chanciest of data. We find acceptable prediction in astrology. Consider that 58 percent of college students agree that astrological predictions are valid.

A predisposition exists in all of us to seek order and meaning in even the most random of data. That is not all bad. It may lead to the solving of a crime or the discovery of a new star. However, to see order in chance events when there is none becomes a real thinking trap. See if the events or data are indeed representative or ordered in some way. Even the basketball fans "hot-hand" theory is invalid and has been proven so statistically.[6] Watch for invalid predictions or arguments based on chance events or random data. Poor thinking is often the result of our normal tendency to seek order in all things. And we sometimes mistakenly find it because we have not taken a really critical look at the data.

Secondhand Information

"A reporter told me, based on reputable sources . . ." We're really talking third-hand here. The further away we get from direct experience, the shakier the facts become. This is an ever-present problem since most of the messages we receive are indeed based on secondhand information. I must, for example, rely on Professors Gilovich, Bartlett, Allport, and Postman[7] for what I am relaying to you regarding the following concepts of *sharpening* and *leveling*. What a relayer had been found to do is (1) *sharpen* or emphasize the gist of the message, and (2) *level* or de-emphasize less essential details. To complicate matters even more, the actor in all of us often leads to story enhancement which may further distort the original message. If you have ever played the game of passing along a message orally to see how much distortion takes place by the time it reaches the last person at your party, you have a good idea of what this critical thinking suggestion is all about.

Wishful Thinking

While listening to the campaign manager touting your favorite political candidate, you may overvalue the argument and overestimate your candidate's chance of winning. Most post-debate (Dole–Clinton) evaluations revealed that supporters all thought *their* candidate won the debate.

There is nothing wrong with being an optimist or even engaging a considered bias as long as you can be objective. It's healthy to be skeptical but not close-minded.

If an assembly of like-minded people want desperately to have their wishes fulfilled, an emergent group mentality may completely destroy critical thinking. Why else did 912 cult members commit mass suicide at Jonestown in 1978?

When our pre-existing beliefs are extremely strong, we may blindly accept new information and direction if it is consistent with those beliefs. New information that contradicts those beliefs is ignored or flatly rejected. The tendency to see and hear what we may desperately want to see and hear is a major threat to critical thinking and listening.

Over a century ago in George Eliot's book *Felix Holt,* the Reverend Rufus Lyon counseled the hot-tempered hero as follows: "Therefore I pray for a listening spirit, which is a great mark of grace. . . . The scornful nostril and the high head gather not the odors that lie on the track of truth."

Ask yourself:

1. How biased or impartial am I on this topic?
2. Are the sources cited credible to detractors?
3. Are the arguments exaggerated?
4. Is the evidence relevant and adequate?
5. Are emotion and desire overwhelming critical thinking?

The topics of support, reasoning, and argument will be discussed in detail in subsequent chapters.

"Conventional Wisdom" and "Wise Sayings"

Some people still agree with Francis Bacon that warts can be cured by rubbing them with bacon. Most architects still avoid numbering the 13th floor because many people believe it's bad luck to be housed there.

Conventional wisdom is not always helpful and is frequently fraught with unwarranted assumptions. Critical thinkers need to know also that logical, scientific thinking may start with first premises or assumptions that are false and go unchallenged. It is therefore possible to be logical and yet dead wrong. Critical thinking involves examining first or major premises and challenging them when necessary.

A group of British engineers concluded that coupling a diesel engine with a locomotive was scientifically impossible. After observing a test model in operation in Detroit, they shook their heads and said, "How could we have been so wrong?" Boss Kettering, the president of General Motors Corporation, replied astutely, "You weren't wrong. You just didn't start out right."

"Wise" sayings or proverbs are also part of some unwise actions. Critical thinkers usually have the good sense to apply them either humorously or after the fact—that is, to support actions or decisions already taken. L. J. Peter of "Peter Principle" fame demonstrates the contradictions in this kind of conventional wisdom.

1. Look before you leap.
   He who hesitates is lost.

2. You can't teach an old dog new tricks.
   It's never too late to learn.

3. Where there's a will, there's a way.
   Time and tide wait for no man.

4. Out of sight, out of mind.
   Absence makes the heart grow fonder.

5. Two heads are better than one.
   If you want something done right, do it yourself.

6. Never look a gift horse in the mouth.
   All that glitters is not gold.

7. You can't tell a book by its cover.
   Clothes make the man.

8. Many hands make light work.
   Too many cooks spoil the broth.

9. Better safe than sorry.
   Nothing ventured, nothing gained.

Steve Allen points out that some old sayings are really dangerous: " 'All's fair in love and war.' Really? No civilized society has ever thought so, even though unspeakable atrocities and savagery are all too characteristic of the behavior of humans engaged in war. As for love, there is no moral code in the world that sanctions the commission of any act—rape, adultery, incest, kidnapping, child abandonment, and so forth—simply because the committer is, or perceives himself to be, seized by the emotion of passionate love."[8]

Language Confusion

> "Language will have maximum usefulness when it properly corresponds to what it is supposed to represent."
>
> *Irving J. Lee*

During the World War II "Blitz" in Great Britain, people wounded during the bombing were rushed to the nearest aid station where they were given first echelon treatment and then relayed to field hospitals. The War Department called these stations "evacuation hospitals." Harsh criticism of these temporary treatment stations followed because of their "unhospital-like" treatment of patients. When the name was changed to "evacuation posts," the criticism stopped.

Our perceptions of and our thinking about events and things are in large part at the mercy of our language. It becomes very clear that critical thinking suffers if we are not extremely careful about how we decode (and encode) language.

> Language is a wonderful thing. It can be used to express thoughts, to conceal thoughts, but, more often, to replace thinking.
>
> *Kelly Fordyce*

How one manages language is a large part of speaking, listening, and critical thinking. That is why an entire chapter was devoted to "Language Habits" (Chapter 2).

SPEAKER RESPONSIBILITIES

Listening is a difficult process even under the most favorable conditions. One reason for this is that *we think much faster than we talk*. The average rate of speech for most Americans is about 125 words per minute. However, we can listen to speech at more than 300 words per minute without a significant loss in comprehension. This is not to say that speakers should sound like a machine gun, but too slow a rate does give listeners more free time to distract themselves.

As speakers, we are also responsible to a large extent for both attentive hearing and objective listening. An audience that is inattentive and half-asleep may not be *hearing* very efficiently because our voice or delivery pattern is dull and monotonous, or because our topic is poorly organized, poorly explained, or both. The audience may not be *listening* for the same reasons. In trying to promote critical listening, the speaker has an ethical responsibility to avoid language confusion, reckless overgeneralizations ("They're all yuppies," "fascists," "commies," and so forth), irrelevant arguments and unrepresentative evidence, and to avoid attacking personalities.

A capable speaker needs to consider the total communication process (Figure 1.8) in trying to elicit good listening habits. Remind yourself that communication is a coactive, two-way process. Watch closely for feedback signs. Listeners usually let you know, one way or another, if you are not being understood or have been tuned out.

Summary

Good listening does not guarantee success, but *poor* listening will stand in the way of its attainment.

We listen for different reasons and assume different styles of listening: reluctant, appreciative, critical, and aggressive.

Listening is a three-phase process: (1) sensation, (2) interpretation, and (3) response. Responses can be (a) internal or intrapersonal, or (b) external or feedback. The process is affected by environmental inputs as well as the speaker's message and also produces feedback. Interpretation is improved by better understanding perception and attribution theory.

Basic areas for listening improvement are: motivation, access, and skills. These three are interactional and interdependent. To improve *motivation* one can (1) look for motivation in a larger area of interests, (2) relate the topic at hand to one's own selfish interests, and (3) translate the problem to an intellectual challenge.

Improving listening *access* can be accomplished by (1) managing or eliminating noise, (2) avoiding fatigue, (3) accommodating our hearing deficiencies, and (4) learning relevant language and vocabulary, especially through reading.

We can improve our listening skills by learning the skills of key word note-taking and of managing distractions.

Note-taking should concentrate on ideas, main points, subpoints, facts, and evidence. Notes should be recorded in a consistent, systematic, brief manner and form.

Major listener distractions range from the physical (for example, noise) to the intrapersonal. They include (1) the speaker's appearance or manner, (2) the speaker's language, (3) topical opposition to the point of emotional disruption, and (4) misinformation and erroneous beliefs.

Bad habits that distract us from efficient listening include: (1) overly criticizing the speaker, (2) avoiding new and challenging topics, (3) calling the topic stupid or uninteresting, (4) prejudging, (5) reacting emotionally, (6) seeking distractions, and (7) faking attention.

> The Sperry Corporation listening program offers ten "Keys" or rules for good listeners to follow: (1) find areas of interest, (2) judge content not delivery, (3) hold your fire, (4) listen for ideas, (5) be flexible, (6) work at listening, (7) resist distractions, (8) exercise your mind, (9) keep an open mind, and (10) utilize the difference between thought and speech speed.
>
> Critical thinking is exercising intelligent, objective, cautious judgment and evaluation. Areas for improving critical thinking and listening are: (1) interpretations of chance events, (2) secondhand information, (3) wishful thinking, (4) conventional wisdom and wise sayings, and (5) language confusion.
>
> Responsible speakers promote objective listening by avoiding language confusion, overgeneralization, irrelevant arguments, and personality attacks. Good speakers are alert to feedback and help audiences listen by adapting their speech material, mood, and mode of delivery to the total speechmaking situation in which they find themselves.

Learning Projects

1. Create a seven- or eight-word message and whisper it to one class member, who in turn whispers it to the next person. Have the last class member repeat the message aloud and compare it with the original. Discuss the results.

2. Apply "Listening Styles" to a specific communication incident you have observed or were part of and evaluate the listening behavior. Report verbally and/or pictorially what lessons this exercise yielded. Pay special attention also to the bad listening habits.

3. Apply a "critical thinking" analysis to an incident you were part of in terms of:

   Interpretations of chance events

   Secondhand information

   Wishful thinking

   Conventional wisdom and wise sayings

   Language confusion

   Prepare to report in class.

4. Try really listening to a speaker the next time you have an opportunity. Report in 100 words or less what you have learned about your listening habits.

5. Think of a specific person who you feel is a bad listener. Discuss in terms of the bad listener habits described in this chapter.

6. Prepare to discuss the "Listening Process" in terms of an episode in which you were a part.

7. Think of your least liked course and explain how you might improve your motivation to listen to its content.

8. Describe a real or hypothetical situation in which sensory access might have been improved. Explain how.

9. Inventory your listening skills (per suggestions in this chapter) and describe how you might improve them.

Notes

1. Andrew D. Wolvin and Carolyn Gwynn Coakley, "A Survey of the Status of Listening Training in Some Fortune 500 Corporations," *Communication Education,* 40, no. 2 (April 1991), 152–64.

2. Andrew Wolvin and Carolyn Gwynn Coakley, *Listening,* 5th ed. (Dubuque, Iowa: Brown & Benchmark Publishers, 1996), pp. 151–54. Also see J. B. Weaver and M. D. Kirtley, "Listening Styles and Empathy," *Southern Communication Journal,* 60, no. 2 (Winter 1995), 131–40.

3. For more on memory and verbal recall, see L. T. Thornos and T. R. Levine, "Disentangling Listening and Verbal Recall: Related by Separate Constructs," *Human Communication Research,* 21, no. 1 (September 1994), 103–27.

4. Roderick P. Hart, "Why Communication? Why Education? Toward a Politics of Teaching," *Communication Education,* 42, no. 2 (April 1993), 103.

5. For more on these matters see Thomas Gilovich, *How We Know What Isn't So* (New York: The Free Press, 1991).

6. Ibid., pp. 11–12.

7. Ibid., p. 91.

8. Steve Allen, *Dumbth* (Buffalo, New York: Prometheus Books, 1991), p. 156.

4

AUDIENCE CONSIDERATIONS

CHAPTER
OUTLINE

(Phone rings) "Hello. Joe Dakota here."

"Joe, this is your old coach, Vince Gipper, from Bay View High School."

"Hi Coach. What can I do for you?"

"Joe, Bay View is having a convocation on teamwork. As our only all-state alumnus and now a university student, we'd like you to say a few words. It's next Monday."

"Sounds interesting Coach. What time?"

"Seven thirty. Will you do it?"

"Sure, sounds like fun. See you Monday."

Joe is already in big trouble! He knows nothing about the total setting: the program, his role in it, the physical arrangements, and nothing about the audience. On Monday Joe arrives promptly at 7:30 in the Bay View gym, of course. Another mistake because the program is in the auditorium and is ready to start. Joe left no time to accommodate last minute program changes or problems.

Joe guessed wrong about almost everything. It wasn't in the gym. It wasn't high school students. "Who are these people? What is Professor Brainy doing here? Why didn't Coach tell me what I was getting into?!"

It turns out that Coach Gipper was calling as a member of the local Chamber of Commerce, who were using the high school auditorium for their program on "Teamwork in the Workplace." Coach was also at fault, of course, but Joe should have asked for more details and considered the setting and the people in the audience. It was a long, awkward evening for Joe Dakota.

Unlike Joe, we most often know the general type of audience we will meet (for example, business people, teachers, hospital volunteers). In your classroom speeches you will get to know the specific audience. The speeches of self-introduction give you a marvelous opportunity to gain insights into your specific audience, which can make a real difference. Suppose in planning your "Role of a Manager" speech you discovered that your audience was composed of management majors instead of freshmen liberal arts students. You might want to revise your purpose and your speech as follows: "To review the five managerial functions of planning, organizing, controlling, coordinating, and communicating to an audience of management majors," or perhaps concentrate on just one function. Unless you felt very well-informed or had unusual credibility, you might even choose to change topics.

What follow are insights and suggestions on how to better understand the setting and how to describe an audience demographically and psychologically. The advice extends beyond the classroom since you will be giving speeches and reports in other classes and programs and beyond.

CONSIDERING THE SETTING

The Occasion

Joe Dakota forgot to ask about the *program* and its *purpose.* With only very general answers to these questions, he could have pursued more specific questions. "Why have I been chosen to speak?" Are you a second or a third choice? Are you being paid? Is this a special meeting called for the specific purpose of hearing you? Did the audience pay for this experience? Were they forced to come? Is this one of a series of programs? Are you the headline attraction, or are there other events or speakers on the program? If there are other speakers, when, in what order, and for how long will each person speak? How large is the audience? Will there be an open forum?

The time at which the speech is scheduled is often a critical factor. Occasionally, A.M. and P.M. have been incorrectly assumed. The concept of "company time" versus "our time" often applies, and speakers might regulate not only the content but the length of their speech accordingly. It has been observed that industrial and business audiences often are more generous when they are listening on company time. Remember to arrive early (even for a classroom speech) or you may wind up like Joe Dakota.

Assuming you understand the time, place, and speech length, you are ready to ask about the physical setting and arrangements.

Physical Arrangements

Physical arrangements include seating configuration, type of room, lighting, sound system, and so forth and are an important part of adapting to the setting. The pulpit in a church adds something to the minister's message. In like manner the raised dais in the House of Representatives imparts extra authority to the Speaker's words. The old Globe Theatre was no ordinary house. What we do with lighting, music, and pomp is also part of the physical setting and ritual. The same message uttered in a church, a restaurant, and a fraternity house might be sacrilege in the first, rudeness in the second, and understatement in the third. People have different expectations in different settings as well as in different situations.

The *proximity* of the speaker to the audience is also thought to be important. If you are on an elevated platform far removed from the first row of the audience, your style of delivery should be different from the style you would use if you were close to the group.

The *seating arrangement* of the audience also affects how listeners react to persuasion and influence. Logical, factual persuasion is probably more effective when listeners are separated, and emotional appeals are probably more successful when listeners are close together.

The noise level of the room is often a problem, as are the lighting and ventilation. Many of these circumstances can be controlled, or at least improved, if you consider them early enough.

If you'll be using a PA system, it may have an important effect on the way you use your visual aids. Most microphones fade if you move more than two feet away from them. It's a good idea to check such things *before* you speak.

The effectiveness of visual aids is closely related to environmental factors. The size of the visual aid should be appropriate to the size of the room and the size of the audience. A chart big enough for a group of twenty-five may be hopelessly small for a group of several hundred. A series of slides may be useless if the room will not darken, and a tape recording may not be heard in a room filled with echoes.

Seating arrangement, closeness, and the like are clearly an important aspect of the setting. Advance information on the physical setup can save you a lot of surprises. Consider some of the configurations in Figure 4.1; their identifying names are usually derived from their appearance: herringbone, T, U, and so forth.

Ritual and Protocol Orientation

In somewhat polarized or formal audiences, the *ritual* and associated *protocol* may become a critical part of your audience consideration. The Japanese auto worker who does five minutes of company-coordinated calisthenics every morning, sings songs, and cheers his or her second-shift replacement is for the present a different breed from most of the auto workers in Detroit; perhaps California is changing. . . .

We take the rituals of our social clubs, veterans' organizations, temples, and churches in stride. However, speakers should be cautious and pragmatic about the rituals of their audiences. The old public-speaking adage against using foul language is a useful one, especially when ritual is part of the occasion.

If possible, you should know the special rules, habits, rituals, and practices you are likely to encounter. For example, organizations such as the Kiwanis, Rotary, Lions, Eagles, and Elks clubs have relatively standard meeting formats. Many of these same organizations have certain "fun" rituals, which, though great sport if you are warned in advance, can be a nightmare if you are unaware. A speaker was once fined a dollar before saying his first word because he was wearing a red necktie! Dress codes are often part of the protocol. See that you are not under- or overdressed. Know your audience so well that you can take language, ritual, and protocol into account in your preparation. If you are the youngest person in the room, don't dwell on it.

Often part of the ritual and protocol is the inevitable *speech of introduction.* (If you are the introducer, read Chapter 13 now.) A bad speech of introduction can make life very difficult for the speaker. Seldom do introducers mean any harm. Quite the contrary! If they give a lengthy speech, it is meant to be complimentary. They may even be so enthusiastic about your subject that they give part of your speech for you.

The chairperson or introducer almost always asks the speaker for help with the introduction, and the novice or incautious speaker almost always answers with a blush and says, "Oh, it doesn't really matter." But it *does* matter,

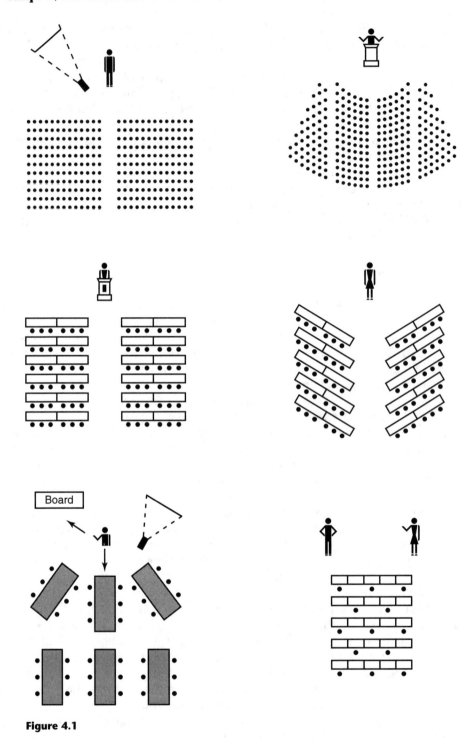

Figure 4.1

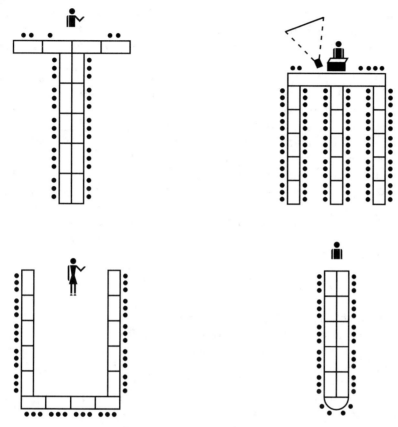

Figure 4.1   *(Continued)*

so *do* give them help. They will appreciate it, and you will reduce your risks at the same time. On one occasion a speaker was asked to give a ten-minute critique of a championship debate. The university's public relations department had sent a standard release to the person chairing the debate; this consisted of about four pages of biographical material, including a listing of every award the speaker had received and every publication with which he had been associated. You can guess what happened. The well-intentioned chairman read *every* word, and took ten embarrassing minutes to do it, before introducing the speaker.

DEMOGRAPHICS

The average American is a 32.7-year-old married white woman living in a mortgaged suburban three-bedroom home heated by natural gas. She's also a myth. The family has been dramatically redefined by delayed marriage, deferred childbirth, and divorce. One in four children born is being reared by a single parent; six in ten mothers with four children are in the labor force; three in a hundred households conform to the family made up of a working husband, his wife, and their two children.

If you're planning a speech for the public school students of New York city, consider that nearly 15 percent of them are not proficient in English and speak a different native language—including 90,000 who speak primarily Spanish, 13,000 who speak Chinese, 7,000 who speak Haitian Creole, 5,000 who speak Russian, and 500 who speak Farsi.[1] Clearly this is a demographic (or census analysis) to be wrestled with, helpful but not controlling since each school and each class may vary considerably. If you are campaigning for mayor or school superintendent, these demographics take on a different significance.

Demography refers to the study of groups in terms of their common vital statistics. Demographic classroom audience description is typically a statistical averaging of your classmates' ages (e.g., 18–22), their education (e.g., twelfth grade), their politics (e.g., 90 percent Republican), and more or less common characteristics. Not all elements will be relevant to your particular speech, of course, but others obviously will be.

For example, you might want to adjust your speech promoting abortion quite carefully if you knew that your audience was 90 percent Catholic. On the other hand, most demographics are conditioned by other demographics. The education of a group often alters the inferences we might make from their age or gender. The point being that one should look at relevant demographics in concert and as interacting descriptive measures.

In psychological studies of social relationships, it was found that we assess people first in terms of *cultural* information, second in terms of *sociological* information (social groups, roles, and so forth), and third in terms of *psychological* information. The latter is the most personal and most specific. Your audience demographic analysis might profit from similar ordering of assessments. Some demographics or general descriptive measures you might consider follow.

ETHNIC-CULTURAL IDENTITY   Almost all audiences in America are becoming more diverse and are proud of it. There are many different racial, ethnic, and cultural groups, each with very special customs, attitudes, language, and behavior patterns. In addition to the larger African-American and Hispanic-American groups, you will meet classmates of other cultural identities including Asian, Arab, Native American, European, and African. Estimates indicate that by the year 2000, Blacks, Latinos, and Asians may constitute a majority of the nation's children. Gender is viewed quite differently by some groups; crime and punishment standards vary; they often reflect quite different political philosophies. Consider your language choices very carefully. Ross Perot lost ground in the 1992 presidential election when he used the words "you people" with an African-American audience. Do your homework on this measure, and be prepared to be wrong.

RELIGION   Five Pentecostal students walked out of a class when the speaker used a "d . . ." and a "h . . ." in his speech. One mostly Catholic class tuned out a pro-choice speaker. In one case a Jew and an Arab student shouted at each other until the professor told them they needed a good Christian attitude. Class dismissed! Find out if your audience is fundamentalist Christian, Orthodox Jew, Muslim, and so forth or some combination. One's religion does not, of course, predict one's attitude or behavior on each and every social issue, but speakers are well-advised to carefully consider religious orientations when they are central and closely related to their topic.

GROUP MEMBERSHIPS   If the Alpha Kappas or the Delta Sigma Rhos dominate your class, find out about them. The same is true of other groups that offer insights into attitudes you may encounter—Young Republicans, Young Democrats, the debate team, varsity basketball players, National Rifle Association, Vietnam veterans, National Organization for Women, Hillel Foundation, ROTC, Arab-American club, and many others. Even more "average" audiences are often highly polarized if they all have some special interest in common. A small community with a winning high school basketball team may unceremoniously ignore a guest speaker who is unaware of this special interest. Sometimes these interests are temporary, but a speaker will do well to seek out and become familiar with any special interests about which the audience expects him or her to know something.

GENDER   An audience of twenty men may, on a given subject, differ considerably in outlook from an audience of twenty women. Likewise, an audience of ten men and ten women may be different from either of the homogeneous audiences. An audience of nineteen men and one woman may cause a male speaker to alter many of his remarks and examples, not necessarily because of the one woman, but because of the expectations of the nineteen men that the speaker will be conscious of the one woman. Language is a special case. Many modern men are unintentionally sexist in their use of pronouns, and some women's groups are unforgiving. See Chapter 2, "Language Habits."

AGE   It is obvious that an audience of ten-year-olds will call for considerably different preparation by the speaker than will a group of forty-year-olds, even if the subject is Little League baseball. Even a few children in an otherwise all-adult audience sometimes present a problem. Even if you choose (or are advised) to ignore them, you can assume that the audience will not; rather, they will establish norms of appropriateness and understanding based on the presence of the youngsters. Some language is less well received when even a single child is present. In one study young people experienced greater pressure to comply with the persuasion of seventy-year-old speakers and they expected more direct, forceful language from them.[2] But then, all seventy-year-olds, like all twenty-year-olds, are not alike!

EDUCATION   A person's education is the sum of that person's learning. Do not confuse schooling with education for schooling is no guarantee of an education. There are many uneducated college graduates. Nevertheless, formal schooling is in many cases a faster and more systematic way of acquiring knowledge than are the other ways. Your language and vocabulary should be adapted to your audience's educational level and previous schooling. Moreover, an audience with a highly technical education will require a different approach than will one with a religious or a liberal arts background. Better educated people usually know more about current events and have a wider range of interests. Hopefully, they are more tolerant of change and differences of opinion. But don't count on it. Much depends on the issues and their values orientation.

VALUES

Values are powerful life-guides of right and wrong, good and evil. They are related to some of the demographics discussed earlier. Values are systems or frameworks that hold our various beliefs and attitudes together. The more you know about these central audience orientations, the easier and better your message adaptation should be. This knowledge can help you choose appropriate illustrations, arguments, and forms of support. Considering a given audience's special values orientation allows you to anticipate controversies and sensitivities. A "Nationalizing the Coal Industry" speech given to an audience fiercely holding a "free-enterprise" value orientation would take some special adaptation. Not to know that your audience had such a prominent value orientation could make for a difficult experience. Or try an audience that heavily values "Right-to-Life." Your speech on planning parenthood may need some special adaptation.

Some benchwork value orientations have been suggested by many sociologists, psychologists, and communicologists. One way of applying values analyses is to think of these benchmarks as lenses through which you will analyze your audience. Perhaps your wide-angle lens can give you a view of their largest, most global, most general notions or *ultimate values*. See Figure 4.2.

These large value systems hold our various beliefs and attitudes together. For example, *equality, orderliness,* and *freedom* might include the following:

- *Equality.* Belief in equal opportunity for all, civil liberties, legal rights, responsible citizenship.
- *Orderliness.* Law, control, and predictability; rational, pragmatic behaviors.
- *Freedom.* Desire for an absence of necessity, coercion, or constraint—often a desire for moral self-determination.

Your normal lens might pick up more specific value systems, what have been called ***everyday values.*** See Figure 4.3.

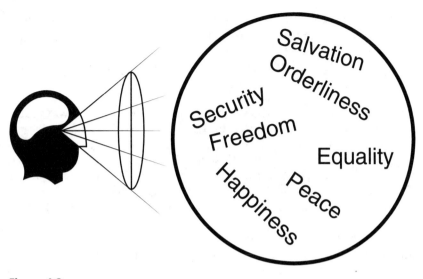

Figure 4.2

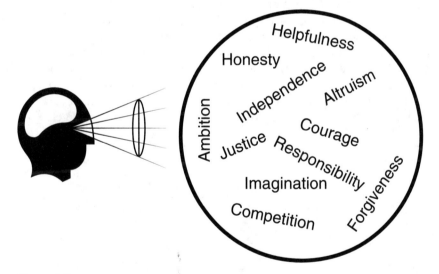

Figure 4.3

These terms capture slightly more specific value systems and suggest still more attitudes and beliefs. For example:

- *Ambition.* Willingness to compete, a desire to achieve occupational success and personal achievement.
- *Independence.* A strong belief in individualism, dignity, and integrity; a resistance to strong authority, which is often construed as exploitation.
- *Altruism.* Unselfish regard for or devotion to the welfare of others; charitableness and generosity.

A close-up lens should help describe even more of these everyday value systems—perhaps those that are most closely related to the specific purpose of your speech. See Figure 4.4.

The following three everyday values might lead to these kinds of inferential analyses:

- *Work ethic.* Belief that one should earn one's own way; hard work is the only way to achieve anything, laziness is evil.
- *Patriotism.* Two types: (A) "Semper Fidelis," those always faithful to the American way; (B) those loyal to our national institutions so long as they don't contradict the larger values (see Figure 4.2).
- *Moral orientation.* Usually a strong belief in an organized religion; a strong, lawlike notion of ethics and human behavior; honesty.

These lenses can be of real assistance in your audience analysis, but they only help classify or categorize the information you find, and they are only as good as your information. Don't overlook the obvious sources of such information. *Ask* about the group; check its literature, from bylaws to newsletters. The library, Chamber of Commerce, and friendly members are other sources of information. A helpful chairperson can also assist you in getting a handle on the group's prominent values. Keep your analysis fresh even as you speak. Audiences don't change their basic value systems frivolously, but they do make different interpretations where related attitudes and beliefs are concerned. A 1976 survey suggested that Americans most valued security and self-fulfillment. By 1990 they were more concerned with a sense of accomplishment and warm relationships with others. People change!

Figure 4.4

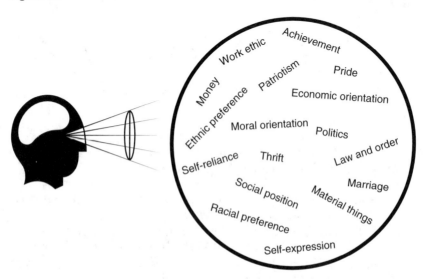

> The only man who behaves sensibly is my tailor; he takes my measure anew each time he sees me, whilst all the rest go on with their old measurements and expect them to fit me.
>
> *George Bernard Shaw*

One final warning: We are assuming a certain amount of audience homogeneity in this discussion, which is obviously not the case with all audiences. It is a good idea to take a second look.

Be realistic in your analysis as you plan your speech message. You can't win 'em all! Current events change things . . . happy or sad moods can't always be anticipated . . . some attitudes under some circumstances become almost totally inflexible.

TOPIC ORIENTATION

Your speech topic should be chosen with your own interests in mind, but you should also be considering audience interests at the same time. To adapt your topic successfully to your audience, getting answers to the following questions would be very helpful:

1. How important is the subject to the audience?
   Very important
   Casual interest
   Not very important
2. What does the audience know about the subject?
   A great deal
   They've heard of it . . .
   Very little
3. How do they know what they know?
   Available facts
   Opinions and sentiments
   Biased sources
4. What is the audience attitude toward the subject?
   Positive
   Neutral
   Negative
   Mixed
   Polarized (positive and negative)
   What percentage of the above?
5. How do they assess my topical credibility?

Answers to these questions are not always easy to find. In your classroom speeches you can often sound out a few students or refer back to your notes on the speeches of introduction. In the real world, such as Joe Dakota faced, Coach Gipper might have been able to answer most of these questions. Joe could have also asked other members of the local Chamber of Commerce. Look also for newsletters, annual reports, and other documents that a specific group might have generated.

You may be asked to do a brief, formal audience survey for one of your classroom speeches. The first four questions in the box above can easily be converted to an oral or written survey. For example, suppose you were considering a topic supporting "Human Organ Donating."

Keep your survey simple and brief or it may be ignored. Allow for some open-ended comments (as shown). One comment offered on a survey similar to this one was, "I wouldn't be in class today without a donor transplant." The speaker made good use of this information by pursuing an interview that provided vital testimony and a great attention step.

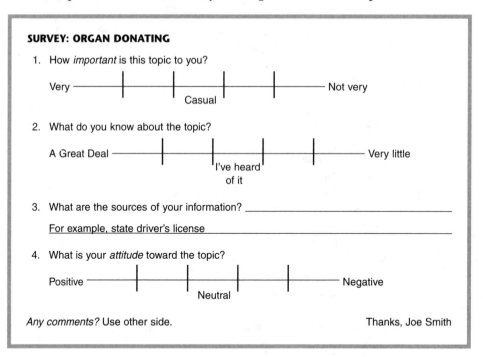

SURVEY: ORGAN DONATING

1. How *important* is this topic to you?

   Very ————————————————— Not very
                    Casual

2. What do you know about the topic?

   A Great Deal ————————————— Very little
              I've heard
              of it

3. What are the sources of your information? _____

   For example, state driver's license _____

4. What is your *attitude* toward the topic?

   Positive ————————————————— Negative
                  Neutral

Any comments? Use other side.   Thanks, Joe Smith

STIMULATION EFFECTS

In speech-communication training the emphasis is generally on passive audiences. However, the modern speaker also meets active, expressive, even aggressive collections of people. In recent times we have seen demonstrations, panics, riots, and other types of collective behavior that challenge long-standing rhetorical advice. If *crowd* is the most general term for a collection of people, then *mob* better describes these aggressive groups, leaving the word *audience* for the more restrained and often prearranged groups. See Figure 4.5.

Another way of visualizing these different types of crowds is to supply an arbitrary universe—say, fifty persons—and targets of behavior (Figure 4.6). The bull's eye in each target represents the most *focused* behavior.

Most research and theorizing assumes relatively passive audiences; we can understand standard audiences by looking at what happens in more stimulated groups. Some ten years ago, eleven young Cincinnatians were stampeded to death in a tragic mob insanity while waiting for a rock concert. Some randomly collected comments by psychologists try to explain:

> A blurring suggestibility occurs.
> The sense of self is lost.
> The mob becomes your identity.
> . . . regressive, irresponsible behavior.
> Peer pressure is contagious.
> A loss of restraint.
> Guilt is lost in anonymity.

When a crowd becomes a mob, as in a panic, we see people at their worst. Early social psychologists Gustave Le Bon and E. D. Martin suggest that when a crowd is focused into a mob, a *psychological law of mental unity* comes into play. The participants become a sort of *collective mind* or crowd mentality, and conscious personality is lost. Each person thinks and behaves quite

Figure 4.5 Varieties of crowds.

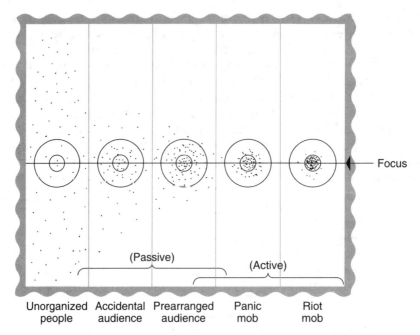

Figure 4.6   Targets of collective behavior.

differently from the way he or she would if acting alone. It is as if our animal nature, or id, were unleashed, and we indulge ourselves in a kind of temporary insanity by all going crazy together. For Martin and Le Bon alike, the mob lurks under the skin of us all. In this view, mobs may be weapons of revenge. They are always uncompromising in their demands, and in no way do they respect individual dignity. Even their achievements are less a testament to their leadership than a consequence of their unbridled fury.

For Le Bon, Martin, and others, the mob is a group in which people's normal reactions become secondary to unconscious desires and motivations. The major mechanisms leading to a state of collective mind or mob mentality appear to be ***anonymity, contagion,*** and ***suggestibility.*** One who is lost in the press of the mob loses much of his or her sense of responsibility. This anonymity produces an inflated feeling of power. It is a kind of high-speed, infectious mayhem.[3] A heightened state of suggestibility leads to hasty, thoughtless, and rash action. Many of our restraining emotions are lost. Fear is often gone in battle; pity in a riot or a lynching (Figure 4.7).

A complete concept of collective mind includes, of course, the ethical and legal issues of sanity and guilt or innocence. We can argue that stupidity, suggestibility, and irrationality exist in individuals as much as in mobs, and that individuals vary in their degree of participation in mob action. We can also argue that mobs simply supply a form of *social facilitation.* Individuals' desires are stimulated merely by the sight and sound of others making similar movements.

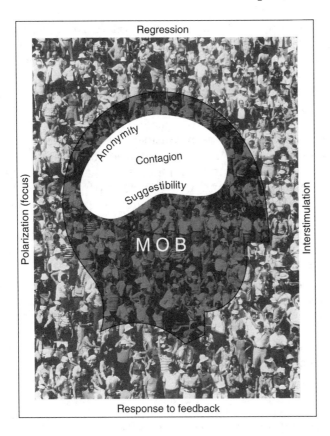

Regression

Polarization (focus)

Anonymity

Contagion

Suggestibility

MOB

Interstimulation

Response to feedback

Figure 4.7   *Photo by United Nations/John Isaac.*

PATTERNS OF AUDIENCE INTERACTION

In a typical audience there is far less emotionality and irrationality than in a mob; the "group mind" is nowhere near as evident. Mobs may regress to adolescence or violence—audiences, rarely. Nevertheless, similar motivational forces are present even in very casually organized audiences. More formal audiences—such as classes of students, church groups, and lecture gatherings, which are intentionally and purposefully organized—are motivated by more readily identifiable forces.

Audiences, like mobs, can vary considerably in size. The small group is special enough to be considered separately in Chapter 14; here we are concerned with relatively formal, intentional audiences of roughly twenty or more persons. We are concerned mainly with audiences that are present physically. When you are dealing with vast, unseen audiences, as in the mass media, you are for the most part beyond interpersonal influence and must utilize a more sociological and political analysis. Nevertheless, much of what follows will also apply to the mass media audience.

Most of what was said in Chapter 1 applies here. An audience model obviously has a larger potential for collective stimulation and its consequences, and the problems of physical setting and feedback are more important. The analysis of audiences by types becomes an averaging process, and we must realize that such generalizing inevitably fits some members of the audience poorly and others perhaps not at all. Accordingly, the model in Figure 4.8 places some of the members outside of the general audience concept.

The audience has frequently been considered as a statistical concept—a means of assembling a large amount of information about individuals into manageable form (average age, income, nationality, education, and so forth). Audiences have also been classified into many general types, such as organized-unorganized, unified, heterogeneous, apathetic, hostile, polarized, and bipolar. More will be said about types of audiences shortly.

In general, the audience we are talking about is a fairly formal collection of individuals who assemble for a specific purpose. Patterns of interaction are reasonably predictable in such groups, if one is given enough information. Three of these patterns are polarization, interstimulation, and feedback-response.

Polarization describes unusually homogeneous audience attitudes. When two relatively homogeneous but opposing factions are present in an audience, the audience is referred to as ***bipolar.*** Debates often attract bipolar audiences. ***Interstimulation*** refers to some of the volatile behavior characteristic of mobs and more specifically to the concept of social facilitation.

Figure 4.8

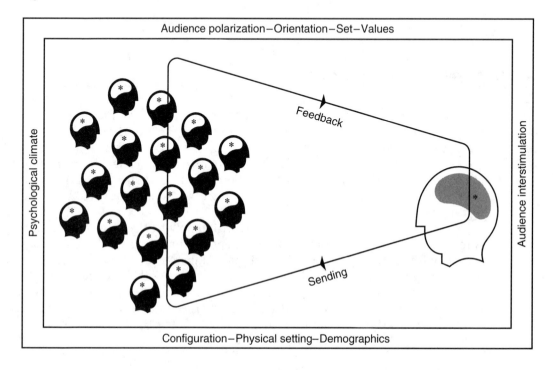

It includes ritual, suggestions, and the reinforcement we receive from similar behavior occurring at the same time. When all of those around us are angry, we are apt to be angry; when all are happy, we are apt to be happy. ***Feedback-response*** is a *positive* response to the efforts of the speaker; a *negative* response is quite another matter. If the speaker is strongly reinforced by positive feedback, he or she may become closely identified with some ideal. With strong interstimulation, this identification may lead to exceptional, if only temporary, polarization among the speaker's listeners—an enviable situation as long as the persuader can control it and live with the results over a period of time. An aroused audience, we remember, is only a few steps removed from a mob.

The classic categorization of audiences was made by H. L. Hollingworth, who suggested five types: (1) pedestrian, (2) discussion-passive, (3) selected, (4) concerted, and (5) organized audiences. Hollingworth's categories make sense not only for dyadic and small-group situations but also for more formal settings. Hollingworth used the term ***orientation,*** by which he meant "the establishment of a pattern of attention, when the group is considered, or a set and direction of interest, when we consider the individuals comprising the group."[4] See Figure 4.9.

The ***pedestrian audience*** is a temporary audience, such as a group of pedestrians on a busy street corner. No common ties or lines of communication bind the members of the audience to the speaker. The first step, that of *catching attention,* is crucial. How far the process goes beyond that varies with the purpose of the speaker.

Figure 4.9   Hollingworth's categories of audiences and tasks.

From H. L. Hollingworth, *The Psychology of the Audience* (New York: American Book Co., 1935, 1977), p. 21.

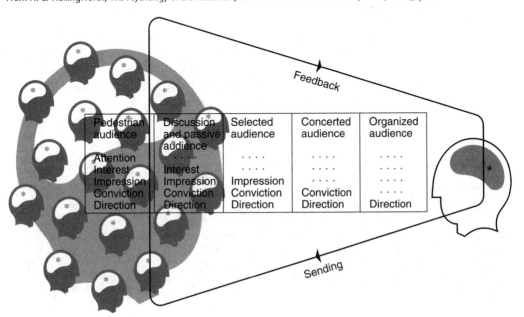

The ***discussion group*** or ***passive audience*** is one whose attention is already secured or guaranteed by rules of order. The persuader's initial problem is more likely to be the second step, that of *holding attention* or interest. Again, how long the persuader can do so depends upon the occasion or the success of the persuader.

The ***selected audience*** is one whose members are assembled for some common purpose, but not all are sympathetic to one another or to the speaker's point of view. Impression, persuasion, and direction characterize the speaker's undertaking here.

The ***concerted audience*** is one whose members assemble with a common, active purpose in mind, with sympathetic interest in a mutual enterprise, but with no clear division of labor or rigid organization of authority. A sense of conviction and delegation of authority are the speaker's chief responsibilities.

The ***organized audience*** is a group with a rigid division of labor and authority supported by specific common purposes and interests. The tasks of members are well learned, having already been assigned by the leader. The persuader only issues instructions, because the audience is already persuaded.

Before appearing in front of the audience, according to Hollingworth, the speaker ought to secure as full a knowledge as possible of the mode and degree of the audience's orientation. The speaker must be prepared to shift tactics if first reactions show that the initial judgment was wrong.

According to Hollingworth, the five fundamental tasks of a persuader are ***attention, interest, impression, conviction,*** and ***direction.*** From these we can gain a better picture of what distinctions Hollingworth saw among the five types of audiences. In Figure 4.9 we have listed these five tasks under the types of audiences to which they are most relevant. For instance, the principal tasks of a person speaking before a concerted audience are to instill conviction and to delegate authority.

According to Hollingworth, the craving for an audience is one of humanity's fundamental needs. One of the most significant characteristics of individuals is indicated by the type of audience that most readily motivates their thought and conduct. There is often a striking conflict between our craving for an audience and our fear of it. We probably seek a certain amount of confrontation and at the same time resist it.

Summary

Considering the setting includes learning about the occasion, the purpose and specifics of the program, the physical arrangements, and the rituals and protocols.

Audience analysis should include seating arrangements. These configurations have names derived from their appearance: herringbone, T, E, U, etc.

Demography refers to the study of groups in terms of their common vital statistics.

General audience demographics discussed include age, gender, group memberships, ethnic-cultural identity, religion, and education.

Values are benchmark life-guides that hold our various beliefs and attitudes together. These benchmarks serve as lenses through which one can analyze audiences. The most global values are called *ultimate;* more specific values are called *everyday.*

Useful questions for topical orientation are: (1) How important is the subject to them? (2) What do they know about it? (3) How do they know? (4) What is their attitude toward it? and (5) How do they assess my topical credibility?

Crowd is the most general term for a collection of people; *mob* describes aggressive groups; *audience* describes more restrained groups. The major mechanisms leading to mob mentality are anonymity, contagion, and suggestibility.

When an audience is hyperinterstimulated, normal reactions become secondary to unconscious or repressed desires and motivations. To cope with this problem, carefully consider your audience, your topic, and your language.

An audience may be considered as a statistical concept: average age, income, nationality, education, etc. Three patterns of audience interaction are *polarization, interstimulation,* and *feedback-response.* Hollingworth described five types of audiences: (1) pedestrian, (2) discussion/passive, (3) selected, (4) concerted, and (5) organized. The five fundamental tasks of a persuader are: attention, interest, impression, conviction, and direction.

Learning Projects

1. Describe two speech situations: (1) where the setting (occasion and physical arrangements) interfered with a speaker's attempt to communicate; (2) where the setting enhanced a speaker's efforts.

2. Attend the meeting of a relatively ritualized group (for example, a church service, an award ceremony, a graduation, or a funeral service), and write a short report on the influence of ritual and protocol on communication.

3. Describe a real or hypothetical situation in which a specific knowledge of demographics would have been, or was, clearly relevant.

4. Do a two- to three-page value description of a group with whom you are acquainted. Use the lens analogy and make predictions about their attitudes and beliefs. Prepare to report in class.

5. Prepare and circulate an audience "topical orientation" survey on a subject you are considering for a speech. Collate and summarize the data, and explain how it might affect your speech preparation and audience adaptation.

6. Observe live or televised groups of people until you find clear-cut examples of (1) a mob and (2) an audience. Describe each in a page or less.

7. Describe in one page an audience situation that approached the "crowd [mob] mentality" description of E. D. Martin.

8. Remain near the center of an active group (for instance, a demonstration, revival meeting, athletic event, fight, or political rally) until you feel a sense of interstimulation (anonymity, contagion, suggestibility) or collective mind. Write the most detailed account possible of how you felt, what impulses came over you, what seemed to cause these impulses, and how you might have avoided them.

Notes

1. Sam Roberts, *Who We Are* (New York: Times Books/Random House, 1994).
2. James Price Dillard, Karen Henwood, Howard Giles, Nikolas Coupland, and Justine Coupland, "Compliance Gaining Young and Old: Beliefs about Influence in Different Age Groups," *Communication Reports,* 3, no. 2 (Summer 1990), 84–91.
3. For more on these matters, see Jaap vanGinneken, *Crowds, Psychology and Politics 1871–1899* (Cambridge, England: Cambridge University Press, 1992).
4. H. L. Hollingworth, *The Psychology of the Audience* (New York: American Book Co., 1935, 1977), p. 21.

5

PREPARING AND RESEARCHING THE SPEECH

CHAPTER OUTLINE

The cornerstones of speech preparation are the speaker's goal or *specific purpose* followed closely by the *central idea*—the major thought upon which the speech evolves. The speaker obviously has a lot to do with these matters, but so does thinking critically about the larger world that may pertain to and constrain the topic. Consider a defense lawyer whose goal in the legal system is clear: defend the client. However, even the rule-bound legal system offers choices: plead innocent, plead guilty, or plea bargain, whatever best defends the client. To make these choices and prepare and plan the defense, our lawyer considers the audience, which, in this case, is the jury, the media, and the public at large. Most of us are stuck with the audiences we get. Lawyers can sometimes alter theirs by dismissing a juror or requesting a change of venue and literally moving the trial environment. The point of this illustration is that a speaker's purpose, however charged, convinced, or predisposed, must also consider the audience simultaneously, a kind of synchronic thinking and preparation.

Practicing the speech preparation suggestions that follow will make you feel more confident, speak more fluently, and generally improve the content and quality of what you say.[1]

SELECTING A TOPIC

The lawyer in the earlier illustration has no trouble finding a speech topic; neither does Green Bay Packer coach Mike Holmgren or aviator Chuck Yeager. Your job, expertise, current interests, timely events, and the occasion will all help dictate what your speech topic will be, often its length, and so on.

In some ways speech class is more difficult simply because you have so much topic freedom. At one university almost all of the students had either full-time or part-time jobs usually related to their major course interest. Topics were abundant: "Marketing at Krogers," "What a Law Clerk Does," "A PR Internship at GM," "My Quality Circle at Ford," "House Husbandry," "Buying a Used Car," "Psychology at McDonald's," "Soul Food," "How Films Are Made," "Auto Body Repairs," "The Peace Corps."

Don't forget your school major or main academic interests. Your school catalog and its course descriptions offer hundreds of topics where you may already have information and interest.

Your personal interests and hobbies are other fertile sources of speech topics: "Working Out," "Pee Wee Hockey," "Umpiring Little League," "Scuba

Diving," "Sailboarding," "Ballooning," "Kite Fighting," "Archery," "Birding," "Falconry," "Dog Training," "Laser Disks."

People who interest you make good topics—an unusual family member, a celebrity you've met, a person you admire: "J.R. Said to Me," "Martin Luther King," "F.D.R.," "David Letterman," "The Lone Ranger," "Waylon Jennings," "Neil Diamond," "Hillary Clinton," "Mayor Dennis Archer," "Eleanor Roosevelt," "Michael Jordan."

Consider processes and events that interest you, the how-to speeches from "Ski Racing" to "Home Cooking," the "I was there" from "Saudi Arabia" to "The World Series."

Problems that are in the news or your environment are worth informing people about in more detail. If you have opinions on these matters, you may have found topics for your persuasive speech: "Acid Rain," "Blockbusting," "Peace," "Child Abuse," "Hand Guns," "Cocaine," "Drunk Drivers," "Teen Violence," "Grade Changes," "Potholes," "Parking," "Teenage Pregnancy," "Political Advertising," "Militias."

Start a speech topic list. Collect interesting information from magazines, newspapers, your other classes, radio, and television. No topic is too simple, too tired, or too old if you make it interesting and tell it well.

Nothing is said that has not been said before.

Terence, 150 B.C.

Topics and titles might be worded identically. If your topic is "Prehistoric People," your title could be the same or it could be "Cave People," "Whence Human," "Early Ancestors," and so on. It is typically inserted at the top of the outline proper.

Topic:	Prehistoric People
General Purpose:	_____
Specific Purpose:	_____
Central Idea:	_____

CAVE PEOPLE

The title of your speech is important for several reasons. First, it forces you to consolidate your thoughts and progress toward a speech purpose. A clever title helps promote interest. "Reach out and touch someone" is more provocative than "Use the phone." Titles should also fit the audience and occasion as well as your central idea. "Objective Exams?" might fit your classmates but sound boring to other groups. Keep titles brief. Long titles turn off many audiences and upset program planners who have to list them in publicity and use them in introductions.

More topical ideas will be suggested as they relate to subsequent chapters. If you're really stuck, see the *Topic Locator* in the Appendix.

STATING YOUR PURPOSE AND CENTRAL IDEA

General Purpose

The insurance agent who comes to your door with policy in hand is interested mainly in selling you a policy. Even though he or she may present an armload of objective and practical *information* that explains the risks of not having insurance and that describes how the policy works, the general purpose is to *persuade*. A speech billed as an "Informative Talk on the Arts" may turn out to be a highly belittling piece of persuasion on abstract painting, even if most of the material is informative and perhaps very entertaining. These examples illustrate the difficulty of intelligently dividing the purposes of speaking into even the apparent ones of *informing, persuading,* and *entertaining*. George Plimpton depicts all of these general purposes in Figure 5.1, plus a special kind of persuasive end—to "inspire."

There is probably no such thing as a purely informative, purely persuasive, or even purely entertaining speech. Even the most overgeneralized, flowery oratory probably presents at least a bit of information. Entertainment ranging from court jesters to comedy players has for ages been the means of subtle and effective persuasion. Some very effective persuasive speeches have sounded like informative talks; some, in fact, have been composed almost wholly of information.

By itself the sheer number of informative, entertaining, or persuasive elements in a speech does not determine the kind of speech or the speaker's purpose. The arrangement of the material, the knowledge possessed by the audience, the speaker's style and voice, the length of the speech, and many more factors also must be considered. Here's a short one! (Figure 5.2)

Figure 5.1

© *International Paper Company*

THE WIZARD OF ID

Figure 5.2 The Wizard of Id.
By permission of Johnny Hart and NAS.

If your instructor asks you to prepare an informative speech for the next class, and you state your purpose as being "to inform the class why it should join the Republican party," you had better be prepared for criticism. The instructor will probably suggest that you save the subject for the persuasive speech assignment and that you then state your purpose more accurately as being "to persuade the class to join the Republican party." You might use as your purpose "to inform the class about the history of the Republican party." The speech then becomes either informative or persuasive, depending upon the treatment and emphasis you use.

Your real purpose can be determined by the primary reaction you want from your audience. Rhetoricians have described these as: enlightening understanding, influencing the will, moving the passions, and pleasing the imagination.[2] These fit the general purposes that follow:

PURPOSE	GOALS
To inform	Clarity
	Interest
	Understanding
To persuade	Belief
	Action
	Stimulation (Inspiration)
To entertain	Interest
	Enjoyment
	Humor

TO INFORM   One of the most frequent purposes of speaking is to inform people of something about which you either have more knowledge or know in a different or more specific way. This is the purpose of the typing teacher who is showing students how to use the keyboard. The instructor lectures primarily to inform. The speaker who would inform has the obligation of making the information or instruction clear and interesting as well as easy for the audience to learn, remember, and apply. To achieve these goals, a speaker should know something of how humans learn.

Briefly, we learn through our previous knowledge and experience, and we do so more easily when the material is arranged in some logical sequence. We remember better because of reinforcement (strengthening the message through repetition), verbal emphasis, organization, effective use of voice, and other techniques. (More on learning in Chapter 10.)

The goals in informative speaking are *clarity, interest,* and *understanding.* One key means to these goals is appropriate *organization of material.*

TO PERSUADE   The general goals of a persuasive speech are to convince people to *believe* something, convince them to *do* something, and *stimulate* them to a higher level of enthusiasm and devotion.

These divisions (belief, action, and stimulation), like the general purposes of speaking, often overlap and are not easily recognized at first. When no immediate action is warranted, the speaker may be attempting to convince or to induce *belief.* This purpose might be illustrated by persuasive speeches such as "Foreign Policy," "The Threat of Fascism," or "Uphold the United Nations." No specific and immediate action or performance is asked of the audience. Rather, the listeners are asked to agree with the speaker and to believe and be convinced. This assumes that the audience does not have the power to act except in some distantly related way. If the audience were the United States Congress, these belief purposes could become action purposes.

When the audience is asked to do something specific immediately following the speech, the purpose is *action.* A speech asking for donations to the Red Cross that ends with the passing of a container for contributions from the audience is an obvious example. Election speeches asking people to vote or to sign petitions are further examples. Most sales talks are action speeches—even though the TV announcer does not really expect you to run out and buy a Ford at 11:30 P.M. The desired action is typically specific and typically available in the very near future.

When a speaker is seeking a higher degree of audience involvement, enthusiasm, or devotion on issues and beliefs that the audience already holds, the purpose is one of *inspiration* or *stimulation.* Examples might be a speech for party unity at a political convention after the nominee has been selected or a football coach at the half—"win this one for the Gipper." In short, the purpose of stimulation is found in those situations in which the speaker is (1) not trying to change any basic attitudes, but rather to strengthen them, (2) not trying to prove anything, but rather to remind the listeners, or (3) not calling for any unusual action, but rather to inspire the listeners to a more enthusiastic fulfillment of the actions to which they are already committed.

TO ENTERTAIN   When your purpose in speaking is to help people escape from reality, and when you sincerely want them to enjoy themselves, your general purpose is to *entertain.* The "fun," after-dinner, or radio-television speeches are the most typical examples. These speeches contain jokes, stories, and a variety of humor, all of which depend upon the experience, skill, and personality of both the speaker and the audience. In a speech designed solely to entertain, the audience should understand that purpose and be encouraged to relax and enjoy themselves. Sometimes people like to hear witty rather than profound speakers. Most of us can learn to be more humorous but some seem blessed. Adlai Stevenson was one of them. "I saw a woman there (Democratic convention) who was eight months pregnant and carrying a sign that said . . .(pause), 'Stevenson's the man.' "

A word of warning is in order for both beginning and experienced speakers. Other things being equal, the speech to entertain is the most difficult kind of speech to give. Probably, and perhaps fortunately, this is the least likely speech you will be asked to present. Even when you try to be entertaining or humorous within more conventional speeches, consider your audience carefully and practice, practice, practice. There is little doubt when a funny story or joke does not succeed. The effect of such failure on the speaker is often demoralizing, and the presentation of the rest of the speech may suffer. Helpful suggestions will be detailed in Chapter 13.

Specific Purpose

After you have decided or been assigned your general purpose and chosen a topic, you are ready to limit your purpose to one specific aspect of the topic. The *specific purpose* attempts to describe precisely what it is that you want your audience to understand, to believe, to feel, or to do. Said another way, the specific purpose is the *outcome, objective,* or *response* that your speech is supposed to achieve. A teacher, for example, prepares lesson plans; the specific purpose is called a learning outcome (a desired objective or response). A geometry teacher has the general purpose of informing (about geometry); the specific purpose or learning outcome for a given class might be to inform the class about the applications of geometry to map and chart reading.

If you are interested in flying, you might start preparing your speech with the general idea (purpose) of informing the class about flying. Obviously, the general subject of flying is far too big a subject for a short speech. You'll want to *restrict* your subject to what you can reasonably cover in the time available. Deciding what to leave out is often the most difficult decision you'll have to make. In many respects a short speech is more difficult to prepare than a long one. President Woodrow Wilson discerned that: "If you want me to talk for ten minutes, I'll come next week. If you want me to talk for an hour, I'll come tonight." Here's how one student restricted the "Flying" topic.

Topic:	Flying
General Purpose:	To inform
Specific Purpose:	To inform the audience about the principle of aerodynamics that allows a wing to "lift."

Perhaps you feel that your particular audience would find aerodynamics too abstract. A more concrete and interesting choice might be:

Topic:	Jennies
General Purpose:	To inform
Specific Purpose:	To inform the audience how weapons were propeller-synchronized in World War I Jenny airplanes.

Because one must always consider the audience, you will probably want to check to see if you have a class comprised of AFROTC students who may already be informed on such topics.

The more exactly you can state what you are trying to say or do, the more systematic and intelligent your preparation and communication will be. In some speeches to persuade, you may not wish to state your purpose to the audience; however, when preparing and outlining your speech, you should always start with a precise statement of your specific purpose.

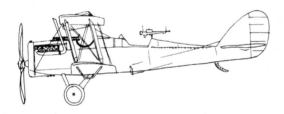

Do not confuse speech topics—"Flying," "Jennies," "Propeller and Weapon Synchronization," "How to Shoot Through a Propeller,"—with a statement of specific purpose. Specific purposes should be full statements, clearly defined, concrete, and limited.

> Don't undertake to tell your audience everything it ever wanted to know about your subject but were afraid to ask.
>
> *Gerald Gardner, Professional Speaker*

A speech entitled "To persuade that rock music is far out" fails (as a statement of specific purpose) on almost all counts. It is unclear, incomplete, and figurative ("far out") instead of concrete. This student wanted to say that rock music has significant social impact. He was trying to persuade the class that rock music brings social problems to light and seriously affects individual and group social behavior. He might better have done the following:

Topic:	Rock Music
General Purpose:	To persuade
Specific Purpose:	To persuade this audience that rock music has significant social impact.

Central Idea

A *central idea* is a mini-outline of what you are going to say. It is an expansion of your specific purpose. In the case of an informative speech, it summarizes the information or main thoughts you are trying to communicate. In a persuasive speech it states the thesis or the claim you are making and suggests the action or belief you wish the audience to adopt. In the rock music example it might look like this:

Topic:	Rock Music
General Purpose:	To persuade
Specific Purpose:	To persuade the audience that rock music has significant social impact.
Central Idea:	Rock music illuminates and reflects societal problems, and its individual and group impact should be viewed objectively.

Suppose you're a management major and choose the topic "Managing Effectively" or "Role of a Manager." What you're really intending to talk about are basic management functions. Your central idea is:

Topic:	The Role of a Manager
General Purpose:	To inform
Specific Purpose:	To inform my audience of five basic management functions.
Central Idea:	Five basic management functions are planning, organizing, directing, coordinating, and controlling.

Here you really have a mini-outline. The five functions become the five major points or body of the speech. A clearly stated central idea is important to speech preparation because it helps you organize your ideas, arrange and outline your speech, and direct your research of relevant speech materials. Like your specific purpose, the central idea should be stated as a full sentence. Use concrete terms and be even more specific.

The best way to be boring is to leave nothing out.

Francois Voltaire

The language and the wording of specific purposes and of central ideas are worth some extra effort because these help you clarify where your speech is going. For example, an informative speech on sailboats might be developed in several ways:

Topic:	Sailboats
General Purpose:	To inform
Specific Purpose:	(different emphases)

1. To explain how wind powers a sailboat.
2. To explain the various classes of sailboats.
3. To describe the Coast Guard sailing regulations.
4. To inform the class about sailboat racing.
5. To offer advice on buying a sailboat.
6. To describe a harrowing sailing experience.
7. To sell your Lightning sailboat. (General purpose changes *to persuade.*)

Central Idea: (varies with specific purpose)

1. Sail power is based on angle to the wind and sail position—close haul, reach, downwind.
2. Sailboat designs are carefully controlled by class to assure fairness in competition—size, weight, sail area, crew, and so forth.
3. Coast Guard regulations for sailboats include safety, right-of-way, signal recognition, and sailor qualification.
4., 5., 6., 7., etc.

When your purpose is clearly to *persuade,* the language of your central idea (thesis or claim) helps direct your audience (and yourself) to the reasons why you are arguing as you are. To say "The proposed bypass around Petosky, Michigan, should be condemned" makes your *purpose* clear but not your *central* reasons *why.* The reasons could be ecological (it destroys wetlands); practical (it won't handle enough traffic); economic (it's too expensive); or political (the mayor owns the land).

GATHERING MATERIALS

Once you have thoroughly considered your topic, specific purpose, and central idea and related them to your audience and the occasion, you are ready to start collecting the materials that will make up the speech. The question now is, "Where do I find these materials?"

Conversation and Interview

An obvious way to gather materials is to talk with people about your topic, to "try it out" on somebody. If the somebody has firsthand or second-hand experience with your topic, you may be in luck. If there are known experts on your topic who are available for consultation on your campus or in your locality, you may be able to turn from conversation to a more formal interview. Before you interview someone, always do some preliminary research, inventory your own knowledge, observe or poll your friends. Then you will be prepared to ask clear and brief questions of your subject. Explain early in the conversation why you want this person's opinion or information. Avoid loaded or biased questions (even though you may have a bias), and try to be objective. Note any sources mentioned. Listen carefully, letting the other person do most of the talking.

Conversations with knowledgeable people can be very valuable. However, any serious interviewing or corresponding should usually follow some reading and observing. The purpose of starting your research early is to help you understand what the important questions are. If, for example, you were going to interview a professor of electrical engineering on the subject of information theory, you would be well advised to browse through one or two of the classic books or articles in the field to obtain maximum value from the interview. The same would be true if you were going to interview a speech professor on such subjects as semantics, psycholinguistics, or debate.

Once you are ready for your interview appointment, be sure you have the right place, day, and time. Briefly review your purpose and listen to the informant. He or she should do most of the talking. Don't argue, and do respect your informant's time. Be on time and stop on time. Say thanks, and find a quiet place to review and rewrite your notes while you can still remember what you heard.

The Library

The largest source of speech materials is your library card catalogue or more likely its computerized version. This source is a vast treasure house of information, so take advantage of it. This is a user-friendly system. It has many Help screens and there are instructions at each terminal. If you haven't used an online library catalog before, you will find it an exciting new way to search for information.

The biggest difference you will note will be the TERM SEARCH capability. In the old card catalog you had a choice of author, subject, or title. Term Search allows you to locate a book through any word in the subject or title.

A library is built for random access, that is, for finding information about a topic that you have already worked on in advance. It is for filling in holes in your previous preparation.

Almost every library has the *Reader's Guide to Periodical Literature*. This source lists magazine articles by author, title, and subject. It is computerized into volumes by year or is found bound in the reference section of the library. You should use it much as you would the computer catalogue. You might also look through *Books in Print,* the *Cumulative Book Index* and its predecessor, *The United States Catalog;* these sources do for books what the *Reader's Guide* does for magazines. The *Book Index* is arranged according to author, title, and subject. See if *The New York Times Index* is online. This is the only complete newspaper index in the United States; it can be a real timesaver. There is also an *Index to the Times of London.*

A good selection of general encyclopedias (such as *Britannica, Americana, New International, World Book)* and special ones (such as the *International Encyclopedia of Communication, International Encyclopedia of the Social Sciences, New Catholic Encyclopedia,* the *Jewish Encyclopedia,* and the *Encyclopedia of Religion and Ethics)* is found in many libraries. Very often, these sources present the best short statement on a given subject to be found anywhere. Encyclopedias are usually kept current by annual supplements called yearbooks; however, they should not be the sole source of your information.

Do not overlook your dictionary. Good ones carry much more than a good vocabulary. Here are some quality desk dictionaries:

- *American Heritage College Dictionary*
- *College Standard Dictionary*
- *The American Heritage Dictionary of the English Language, 3rd ed.*
- *Random House College Dictionary*
- *Webster's New Collegiate Dictionary*
- *Webster's Third New International Dictionary*
- *Webster's New World Dictionary, Revised Edition*

For descriptions of cultural and political events, see *The Official Associated Press Almanac* or *Facts on File;* for geographical topics, see *The Information Please Almanac. The Reader's Digest Almanac* offers facts and household hints and advice. When you need statistics and short statements of factual data, see *The Statesman's Yearbook, The World Almanac and Book of Facts,* and the *Statistical Abstract of the United States* from the U.S. Bureau of the Census. This last source covers social, political, and economic facts of a wide range. Smaller general encyclopedias, such as *Columbia* or *Everyman's,* also contain compact statements and facts. Finally, an atlas can provide political facts as well as detailed maps. Try *The Hammond Citation World Atlas,* the *National Geographic Atlas of the World* or the *Rand-McNally Commercial Atlas and Marketing Guide.* Check the date of publication on all of these sources; the world has changed dramatically in the last few years.

To learn more about famous individuals, you can consult some of the better-known directories and biographical dictionaries, such as *Current Biog-*

raphy, *Who's Who in America, Who's Who in American Education, Who's Who in Engineering, American Men of Science,* and the *Directory of American Scholars.* For information on prominent Americans of the past, see *Who Was Who in America, Dictionary of American Biography, Lippincott's Biographical Dictionary,* and *The National Cyclopedia of American Biography.*

Most professional or trade associations publish journals of their own. Some of these organizations are the American Bar Association, the American Bankers' Association, the American Medical Association, the National Communication Association, the American Psychological Association, and the AFL-CIO. Many of the articles in the journals published by these organizations are indexed by special publications often available on CD-ROM: *Biological and Agricultural Index,* the *Art Index,* the *Index to Legal Periodicals, Index Medicus, Psychological Abstracts, Psychology Books, Encyclopedia of Associations,* and many more.

In addition to the *Statistical Abstract of the United States,* mentioned earlier, other government publications can be excellent sources of speech materials. The *Commerce Yearbook,* the *U.S. Government Manual,* and the *Monthly Labor Review* provide much valuable information. The *Congressional Record* is an especially fruitful source for speech students. It includes a daily report of the House and Senate debates—indexed according to subject, name of bill, and representative or senator—and it has an appendix that lists related articles and speeches from outside of Congress.

Other sources of speech materials are the thousands of organizations that issue pamphlets and reports, often at no cost. You can write directly to these organizations for information; in some cases (for example, Planned Parenthood League, the World Peace Foundation, the American Institute of Banking, and the AFL-CIO), you may receive a speech outline or manuscript in return. If you would like to know the addresses of these or other organizations, refer to *The World Almanac* under the heading, "Associations and Societies in the United States."

If you cannot find enough information in these sources, or if you would like to start out with a printed bibliography on your subject, some libraries provide an index of bibliographies called the *Bibliographic Index.* Online databases such as *ERIC, NEXIS,* and *LEXIS* are also available. Most college and community libraries have a computerized information service, with a search being done for the reader by library personnel. Information searches that would have taken eight hours just a few years ago can now be done in seconds. A fee is charged to the person requesting the search, with the amount depending on the cost per minute of the data base being searched.

Subjects cover the entire range of human thought, from law and medicine to philosophy and current events. Many libraries have installed microcomputers for cardholders to use. Check with your librarian for these sources. More will be said about electronic resources in the section that follows and in Appendix A.

ELECTRONIC RESOURCES

Computerized research can save you time in gathering speech materials. Vast amounts of materials are available. The computer can also help you narrow the list of bibliographies, databases, and articles, but it can become confusing. Many library sources such as the card catalog have been computerized. Other traditional indexes are electronically available in an expanding number of libraries. Perhaps one day electronic resources will replace most books in our libraries. Recently developed fiberoptic cables will be able to transmit the contents of five million books in less than one minute! Stay tuned.[3]

Brief explanations of electronic indexes, commercial servers, and the Internet follow. A more detailed explanation of these resources with an emphasis on the Internet can be found in Appendix A. If your needs for specific help in these matters are urgent, turn now to the excellent Appendix materials written by Professors Jack Kay, Wayne State University and Timothy A. Borchers, Moorhead State University.

ELECTRONIC INDEXES   These indexes list both materials available on electronic servers and in traditional books and periodicals. A number of these indexes are available on laser disc scanners or online databases: newspaper indexes, *Social Science Index, Humanities Index,* and the *Reader's Guide to Periodical Literature.* Find out which electronic indexes are available. Your library may have the index you seek but not own copies of all of the materials you want. Most modern libraries can also offer bibliographic printouts.

COMMERCIAL SERVERS   Prodigy, CompuServe, America Online, and Delphi are designed for home use on PCs. For a fee, subscribers can use e-mail, access online reference materials, news and weather, and even play games.

Other servers like *LEXIS/NEXIS* are more academic, offering full text service on millions of law journals, medical journals, government documents, newspapers, and so forth. You pay by the search or you may have free access through your library's code, if they subscribe to the service.

INTERNET   The Internet is a vast collection of thousands of smaller networks used by people all over the world.[4] As of this writing, it is estimated that 40 million people are connected worldwide.

Information is available on everything from earthquakes and NASA to gardening and dog training. You can communicate with others who share your interests or search libraries all over the world. You will need a Mac or a PC, a modem, a software package, and a subscription server. As a student you may be able to connect to your school's computer which is connected to the Internet. You will be assigned an e-mail address. There are menu-driven databases available such as Archie, Gopher, World Wide Web (WWW), and others.

The art of surfing and navigating this vast sea of information is addressed in Appendix A by two experts who will define this huge resource and explain how to access and find research materials for your speeches. See "Researching through the Internet," Appendix A.

Note-Taking

While you are reading and absorbing all the materials discovered through the sources discussed above, you must consider how to select, sort, evaluate, and finally record the material. You will find that you need an efficient system of taking notes in order not to be overwhelmed by the sheer amount of information available to you. Not remembering exactly what you read or where you read it is frustrating, and if this failure of memory results in a return trip to the library or the Internet, you have lost preparation time as well.

A very general "yes-no" selection of your potential major sources is usually possible after rapid browsing. After this preliminary sorting, you are ready to record the details that are most likely to support your specific purpose and audience analysis. One more suggestion, though, before you begin writing things down. You may wish to revise or add to your specific purpose as a result of your browsing, which may turn up important guidelines for choosing the materials you will use in your speech, selecting the issues you will discuss, or establishing the order in which you will present your topics. In other words, set up *temporary categories* of speech materials, issues to be discussed, and so forth. You can add, omit, or subdivide later as your search becomes more specific. This categorizing will also give you a head start on the organizing and outlining of the speech itself.

Now you are ready to start taking systematic notes. The emphasis is on the word *system.* As long as you have done the rough sorting suggested above and are not taking notes without purpose, you may use any system that works for you. The most common system in library searches is the use of three-by-five or four-by-six file cards. You should write only one subject, source, classification, and note on each card. The big advantage of file cards over a notebook is that you can rearrange the file cards and thus reclassify or subclassify your material very easily. This shuffling of cards becomes very useful when you organize and outline your speech.

```
(Subject) Creativity                        (Classification) Mental
                                                              functions


1. Absorptive - the ability to observe, and to apply attention
2. Retentive - the ability to memorize and to recall
3. Reasoning - the ability to analyze and to judge
4. Creative - the ability to visualize, to foresee, and to
              generate ideas.

SOURCE:  Alex F. Osborn, Applied Imagination
         (New York:  Scribner's, 1973), p. 1.
```

Figure 5.3

```
(Subject) Prehistoric man           (Classification)
                                                    Dinosaurs


" . . . you will often see cartoons showing cave men being
chased by dinosaurs. But this could never have happened.
The physical anthropologists tell us which bones are the
bones of the prehistoric men who lived in caves. The pale-
ontologists tell us which bones are the bones of giant rep-
tiles. The geologists tell us that the humans bones come
from layers of earth that are 50,000 years old, and the
dinosaur bones come from the rocks 150,000,000 years old."

SOURCE: Donald Barr, Primitive Man (New York: Wonder Books,
1987), p. 10.
```

Figure 5.4

The next problem is what to write on the card. If you have found a general source that you may or may not wish to use later, a short summary in your own words would be in order. You will then be better able to decide at a later time whether you wish to reread the source. If you find a statement by an authority that you wish to use, record it *word for word and put quotation marks around it.* Be sure to record the name and qualifications of the authority. In taking down testimony or statistics, make sure you record the date; people change their minds, and so may your sources. If you insert explanations or interpretations of your own, put brackets around these words so that later on you will not confuse your words with those of your sources.

```
(Subject) Problem-Solving            (Classification)
         Systems                              General
                                             Background

Chapter 2 (Reasoning) of this book covers four special readings,
including some special problems. Included are the following:
1.  Reasoning in Humans;  2.  An Exper. Sty. of P. S.;  3.   The
Sol. of Prac. Probs.;  4.  Prob. Sol. Proc. of Col. students.
(Looks impressive)

SOURCE:   T. L. Harris and W. E. Schwahn, The Learning Process
          (New York:  Oxford University Press, 1991), pp. 29-79.
```

Figure 5.5

In your English class you may have been taught a certain system of taking notes for a term paper. Whatever the system, it should be useful here. Whether you use classifications at the top of the card or footnotes at the bottom will depend in part upon your training and preference, as well as upon your specific purpose and subject. Some sample note-taking systems are illustrated in Figures 5.3 through 5.6.

Figure 5.6

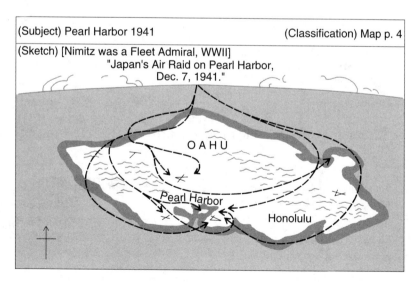

FORMS OF SUPPORT

Illustration or Example

An education major who was a student teacher had as her specific purpose "to inform the class of the basic principles of overcoming discipline problems in the fourth grade." She could have proceeded to discuss "projections of insecurity and overt cognitive intellectualization assistance from an interacting teacher." The class was fortunate because she elected instead to *draw specific examples* from her own experience to illustrate and clarify the complex problems of discipline, and this approach was much more interesting. She opened her speech by describing her experience with George and his habit of putting gum in little girls' hair. She followed this with the story of Richard, who, though a gifted child, took special delight in swearing. Next she explained the psychological reasons for such behavior, the things a teacher should not do, and the proper principles of discipline to apply. In a sense the whole speech was an extended example, and it helped make her point clear. The more detailed and the more vivid the incident, the more interesting it usually is. Very often, verbal illustration can be aided considerably by pictures or actual objects (perhaps a recording of Richard's language).

Similarly the following vivid description clarifies what has happened to calculators in the last thirty years:

> **TEXAS INSTRUMENTS, DALLAS**
>
> TI can put an integrated circuit equivalent to 35,000 radio tubes on a silicon chip 0.24 in. square. In the mid-fifties, a standard computer like the IBM-650 cost $200,000, took five tons of air conditioning to cool, and weighed six thousand pounds. Today, the hand-held TI-60 calculator performs the same functions faster, costs $35, and uses one ten-thousandth of the power. Now that's a little better.

Crime statistics become focused quickly in the following example:

> The National Safety Council reports that an average of 69 persons are murdered each day with handguns. That is more than 25,000 people a year. Every 91 seconds someone is robbed, and every 34 seconds a citizen goes out to start her car and finds it stolen.

If your subject is one with which you have had no firsthand experience, you can often draw your examples from people who do have such experience. An excellent speech on aerial acrobatics was delivered by a student who had never been in an airplane but who used examples and pictures from the experiences of three veteran stunt pilots.

Clarify a point with your own experiences and add personal interest at the same time. One student who had recently survived a DC-10 plane crash opened his speech on "Unsafe Air" with a detailed description of what happened and how he felt.

An illustration or example may also be a hypothetical story (a made-up story that is reasonable and fair to the facts). Such an example usually starts: "Suppose you were . . ." or, "Put yourself in this predicament. . . ." The hypothetical example does not carry the weight of a real or factual illustration, but it does have the advantage of adaptability to the point being made, since you may tell the story as you please. The major problem is an ethical one. Make sure the hypothetical example is never taken for a factual one, and make sure it is consistent with known facts.

Illustration or example is a powerful, efficient way of clarifying and supporting a point. In choosing your illustrations, make sure that they are truly related to the point being made and that they represent the general rule. An example out of context or an example that is an exception to the general rule only confuses in the long run. In addition to being reasonable and fair, your illustrations and examples should contain enough details and excitement to add to the interest of the subject.

Analogy or Comparison

We all spend money on everyday things like postage stamps and cups of coffee. And, we usually buy them without thinking much about what they cost or about the value we get for the price.

But if you take the 32 cents for a postage stamp and the 70 cents for a cup of coffee and apply it to electricity, you will discover some surprising values.

For example, for the price of the stamp you put on a letter, you can run your home stereo system for four hours per day for six days.

And for the price of a 70-cent cup of coffee, you can wash six loads in your dishwasher, or watch your color television for more than 3 ½ hours each night for a week. What you pay for a gallon of milk—about two dollars—can take you even further electrically. Two dollars worth of electricity can dry about 10 loads of clothes in your electric dryer, operate your electric range for about two weeks, or run your refrigerator for five days.

So next time you mail a letter, think of the value electricity gives you for the price of your stamp.

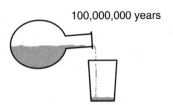

100,000,000 years

Figure 5.7   If molecules of water were poured into a drinking glass at the rate of one per second, it would take 100,000,000 years to fill it.

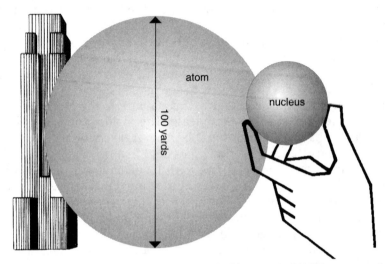

atom

100 yards

nucleus

Figure 5.8   There is so much empty space inside an atom that if the atom could be magnified to a diameter of 100 yards, the nucleus would appear to be only the size of a billiard ball.

Analogy is often the most useful device a teacher or speaker can use in making a point vivid and clear. The nature of an analogy is to *point out similarities* between something already known or understood and something not known (in other words, going from the known to the unknown). If you were trying to explain the microscopic size of a molecule or the gigantic size of our galaxy, the analogies in Figures 5.7 and 5.8 would be both vivid and useful.

At 186,000 miles per second light travels 6,000,000,000,000 miles a year, a distance equal to 240,000,000 trips around the earth. At this rate we could reach the sun in 8 1/2 minutes, the next nearest star in 4 1/2 years. If we started at age 20 and moved at the speed of light, we would be 80 before we reached the star Aldebaran. The really distant stars in our galaxy would take us thousands of years to reach!

Abraham Lincoln made good use of analogy and comparison not only for clarification but also for persuasion. During the Civil War there were those who loudly criticized his method of conducting the war. At that time, a tight-rope walker named Blondin was famous for walking and for riding a two-wheel bicycle on a rope strung across Niagara Falls. In explaining the dangerous position of the nation, Lincoln directed the following analogy at his critics:

Gentlemen, I want you to suppose a case for a moment. Suppose that all the property you were worth was in gold, and you had put it in the hands of Blondin, the famous rope-walker, to carry across the Niagara Falls on a tightrope. Would you shake the rope while he was passing over it, or keep shouting to him, "Blondin, stoop a little more! Go a little faster!" No, I am sure you would not. You would hold your breath as well as your tongue, and keep your hands off until he was safely over. Now the government is in the same situation. It is carrying an immense weight across a stormy ocean. Untold treasures are in its hands. It is doing the best it can. Don't badger it! Just keep still, and it will get you safely over.

Statistics

The use of numbers to help make a point clearer or more specific is not as simple as it may seem. Statistics are frequently used to support a point in a persuasive speech, but they are powerful evidence only if they are (1) *meaningful* to the audience and (2) *related* to the point under consideration. However, when statistics are overly precise and complicated, they may cloud rather than clarify an issue. Have you ever been given directions like these? "You go down Norfolk Street exactly 3.2 miles, turn left on Baker Street and go 2.4 miles to a Y intersection, turn right about 120° onto Charlie Street and go 0.3 miles, then turn right and go 150 yards and you're there." Some details are most helpful, but not these! Even if you were able to keep them straight, you would probably cause an accident by watching your odometer instead of the road. Of course, the other extreme ("You go up Norfolk quite a little piece and then a couple of miles or so on Baker to a kind of wide-angle left turn and then . . .") isn't any better. A "little" piece and a "fur" piece can vary by a good many miles.

MAKE STATISTICS CONCRETE AND INTERESTING   By themselves, statistics are abstract; make them concrete by relating them to known things. To say that Latin America has serious economic problems because the average family income is $650 per year is reasonably clear; to compare this figure with the $39,308 annual family income of the United States, or to show that $650 comes to only $1.78 a day, is clearer.

The confusing and often dull subject of a $2.5 trillion Gross National Product becomes alive when a financial expert explains:

Freshly printed dollar bills stack up 233 to the inch, 2,796 to the foot. The Sears Tower in Chicago is the tallest building in the land at 1,454 feet. At the rate Americans spend money, we consume a stack of dollar bills 200 feet taller than the Sears Tower every *minute* of every hour of every day of the year.

Some students were shocked when an economics major explained that the state budget of $9 billion would buy 3,495 bottles of Stroh's beer for every resident of the state of Michigan—not including the deposit!

Wall Street's Black Monday, October 19, 1987, became more meaningful with the use of these statistics:

The Dow Jones Industrial Average fell 508 pts., or 22.6% (In 1929 it fell only 12.8%.)...

By 10:30 A.M. the number of shares traded was equal to the number traded on a normal day, 140 million...

The total number of shares traded was 604 million...

The value of stocks plunged $500 billion. (Equal to the Gross National Product of France)...

A community library used statistics effectively in seeking (and getting) a tax increase.

BALDWIN PUBLIC LIBRARY IS A GREAT INVESTMENT!

UNLIMITED OPTIONS: SECURE DIVIDENDS

We are in the business of serving people. Our responsibility is to gather books and nonprint materials and make them available to you. If Baldwin's borrowers had purchased individually the books and services they received during the last fiscal year, they would have spent over $4,000,000.00!

For instance:

You borrowed 382,122 books and other items. Buying them at our average price, you would have spent	$3,630,169.00
Newspapers were read on at least 4,680 occasions saving you	936.00
We secured 21,317 for you from our closed stacks. You could have paid one dollar each for them	21,317.00
You viewed 10,534 reels of microfilm and saved	126,408.00
You hung 2,054 art prints in your home or office. You could have spent more than	262,912.00
We secured 1,056 interlibrary loans; some of these books were not available for purchase at any price	10,032.00
We answered 65,423 reference and research questions. Saving you	65,423.00
Twenty-one film programs were presented to about 850 people at the Library. They could have paid more than this at a theater	850.00
At least 3,000 children attended Story Hours	3,000.00
FOR A TOTAL OF	$4,121,037.00
All of these services cost the citizens of Birmingham	$362,558.00

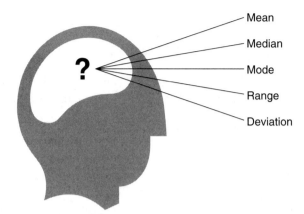

Figure 5.9

USE STATISTICS CORRECTLY   We live by statistics. We accept data on births, deaths, and accidents as facts. However, using statistics as a method bewilders many people. You do not have to be a statistician to realize that the ***mean*** (an average) is not always the most representative measure. To illustrate, let's consider eleven hypothetical educators and their yearly incomes:

Table 5.1

	SALARY		SALARY
Educator A (Administrator)	$60,000	Educator G	$33,000
Educator B (Administrator)	55,000	Educator H	32,000
Educator C	45,000	Educator I	29,500
Educator D	40,500	Educator J	28,000
Educator E	35,500	Educator K	27,000
Educator F	34,000		

The mean income of these eleven educators is $38,136. The problem is obvious: Two educators (the administrators) make the figure unrepresentative, particularly if you are more concerned with teachers than with administrators. Counting halfway down the list of salaries, we find $34,000. This is the *median,* in this case a much more meaningful and representative figure. If we do not include the two administrators, the average income of the teachers is $33,833, and the median is $33,000. You could then figure the amount by which each income differs from the average; the average of these differences is the *average deviation.* If you were to translate these deviations from the average onto a so-called normal distribution, you could then determine the *standard deviation* (also known as *sigma*).

COMBINE STATISTICS WITH OTHER FORMS OF SUPPORT   More and more we live by statistics that predict things. From Unisys's vote predictions to insurance rates, from the number of cancer-causing things in a carton of cigarettes to the average number of cavities in a given group of children, we are in an age of specific, predictive statistics. We have learned to combine statistics with analogies or comparisons to make sense of the astronomical numbers of outer space. We express speed as Mach 1, 2, or 3 instead of miles per hour, and speak of distance in terms of light years.

Statistics can give a speech a sense of precision if you remember to relate the statistics to known things and to make them meaningful and dramatic to the audience. It helps to round your numbers and to use visual aids. The American Cancer Society makes a statistical point with a compelling comparison in Figure 5.10.

Figure 5.10

By permission of the American Cancer Society.

More people have survived cancer than now live in the City of Los Angeles.
We are winning.

Please support the

🐍 AMERICAN CANCER SOCIETY™

IDENTIFY YOUR SOURCES   To hear that 72 percent of the students who enter high school in Detroit do not graduate is a startling statement but easy to dismiss unless you know that the statistic came from the Detroit superintendent of schools. The statistics on teacher incomes might vary considerably if they were drawn from metropolitan Los Angeles or some impoverished, remote area of the country.

Some excellent sources of statistics in general are: the *Statistical Abstract of the United States* from the U.S. Bureau of the Census, *The Statesman's Yearbook, Statistical Reference Index, The World Almanac and Book of Facts,* the *Statistical Yearbook* published by the United Nations, and even the *Guinness Book of World Records.*

Testimony

Like statistics, *testimony* has great use in speeches to persuade but is also valuable for its ability to clarify. In a speech to inform, it may add considerable interest to what might otherwise be straight explanation.

EXPERT AND NONEXPERT TESTIMONY   The idea or statement being supported determines in part who the experts are. If you are trying to prove that the person who crashed into your car ran a red light, the expert is the lone person who was standing on the corner and saw the whole thing. With this kind of nonprofessional testimony, you often need more than one witness. If you are trying to prove that you have observed a bird considered extinct, such as the passenger pigeon, you will need the testimony of a qualified ornithologist. This expert will insist on firsthand observation of the bird in this exceptional case.

Authorities are qualified to give expert testimony by their closeness to a firsthand observation and by their training in observing the phenomenon in question. The authority should be an expert *on the topic under discussion.* You would not ask a maestro to diagnose a problem in an airplane engine!

In most cases you will be using *expert* testimony from people who are recognized authorities or experts in their fields. Their testimony adds interest and credibility to your own thoughts and indicates that you are not alone in your opinions.

One student speaking on "choosing a medical internist" suggested using both kinds of testimony. First, ask friends who have been patients of internists for recommendations; second, ask another physician or medical professional whom you respect and who has made referrals in the past. Of course, a physician who is right for one person may not be right for another. The more your friends' general preferences match your own, the more likely you are to like the physician.

In choosing testimony—expert or ordinary citizen—make sure that it fits or relates to the speechmaking system in which you find yourself. Some "fits" are quite subtle. All Bible testimony is not equal. Some groups put quite different values on it depending whether it is from the Old or the New Testament.

Obviously your expert should be qualified, but in a specific way. Audiences are suspicious of expert testimony when self-interest is obvious. A qualified nuclear physicist who is a member of the Joint Chiefs of Staff may be right in supporting limited nuclear armaments, but his self-interest diminishes his testimony.

QUOTE ACCURATELY AND IN CONTEXT   The shortening or paraphrasing of testimony can be troublesome. One IRS speaker stated, "However undemocratic the new tax law appears to be, we will never achieve true democracy until we embrace and enforce it." The material was paraphrased as "The new tax law appears to be undemocratic." In this case the inaccuracy was deliberate and therefore unethical.

All experts are not equal in all things. You would not ask an aeronautical engineer to testify about heart transplants; you might be equally off target if you asked a gynecologist.

You can observe a lot just by watching.

Yogi Berra

Identify your authorities unless they are fully accepted by all. You may have an excellent quote from John Doe regarding your position on the federal deficit, but if the audience never heard of him you must explain why his testimony is expert. For example, "John Doe is professor of economics at the University of Michigan and a member of the U.S. Tax Commission."

Restatement

Restatement is more than simple repetition. It is saying the same thing in a different and reinforcing way, usually at a later point in the message. This is particularly useful if the material is complex or the vocabulary specialized. For example, restatement provides a better and more dramatic explanation of how many people go through the giant Macy's department store in a single day: "Everyday more people crowd into Macy's New York department store than live in Des Moines, Grand Rapids, or Salt Lake City."

If you reread Chapters 1 through 4 of this book, you will find restatements of the definitions of speech communication, all trying to say the same thing. One definition is a model, another consists of a short paragraph, another may reduce the definition to encoding and decoding. This is an example of restatement for clarification. If the meaning is not clear in one place because of sentence structure or vocabulary or in another because of context, you are given still more choices. If you understood all the definitions at first glance, fine. Assuming that it was not too extended, this repetition should have reinforced the learning.

To restate the value of restatement: It is more than simple repetition. It is saying the same thing in different ways to reinforce learning, and it is particularly useful if the subject is complex or if the vocabulary is specialized or strange to the audience.

Summary

The cornerstones of speech preparation are the speaker's goal or *specific purpose* followed closely by the *central idea* or major thought on which the speech evolves.

When selecting speech topics, consider your job, expertise, interests, hobbies, people, experiences, and problems in the news. A good title helps you consolidate your thoughts and your purpose. General purposes for speaking are: to inform, to persuade, and to entertain. The specific purpose attempts to describe precisely what it is that you want your audience to understand, believe, feel, or do. Your central idea is an expansion of your specific purpose. It is a mini-outline of what you are going to say. When your purpose is clearly to persuade, your central idea (thesis or claim) helps direct you and explain to your audience why you are arguing as you are.

Major ways and aspects of gathering speech materials are: (1) conversation and interview, (2) using the library, (3) electronic resources, and (4) note-taking. Electronic resources described are: indexes, commercial servers, and the Internet. A detailed discussion of these electronic resources, especially the Internet, is found in Appendix A.

Forms of support include: (1) illustration or example, (2) analogy or comparison, (3) statistics, (4) testimony, and (5) restatement. In using the forms of support, especially testimony and statistics: (1) make these concrete and interesting, (2) use them correctly, (3) combine them with other forms of support, and (4) identify your sources. Restatement is more than repetition. It is saying the same thing in different ways to reinforce learning.

Learning Projects

1. From newspapers and magazines, select and clip items that are clearly (a) informative, (b) persuasive, (c) entertaining, or (d) a combination of these, and identify the specific purposes of each item.

2. Analyze any recent speech by a public figure and determine:

   The General Purpose

   The Specific Purpose

   The Central Idea

3. Choose any two of the following topics and write specific purposes appropriate first to informative speeches, then to persuasive speeches.

   The Stock Market

   Nuclear Power

   The U.S. Deficit

   AIDS

   Super Bowls

   Social Security

4. Specific purposes should be: full statements, clearly defined, concrete, and unitary. Assess and critique the following:

   a. To inform my audience about love.

   b. Love is a many-splendored thing.

   c. To persuade my audience to support more AIDS research and to avoid promiscuity.

   d. To inform my audience about punk rock and why it is enjoyable.

5. The wording of a central idea should reflect the general purpose of a speech. Which of the following suggest (1) informative or (2) persuasive speeches? Why?

   a. Hunting of the Canadian harp seal should be stopped on the grounds of cruelty and danger to the species' survival.

   b. Mummification was related to religious beliefs across two distinct cultures: Egyptian and Peruvian Indian.

   c. Passive, sidestream smoking is more dangerous than mainstream, and smoking should be prohibited in all public buildings.

   d. There are four basic influences on the human personality: constitution, group memberships, role, and situation.

6. Try one of these library "fun" projects.

   a. What are your roots? Trace your ancestors. Many libraries specialize in genealogy.

   b. Did George Washington sleep nearby? Or Billy the Kid? Your library's electronic index or collection of local history books can put you on the trail.

   c. Cook a Polynesian feast. Or an ancient Roman banquet. Read how in the library's cookbooks or surf the Internet.

   d. Take up photography. Check the library for consumer reviews of cameras before you buy. Take out books on lighting, composition, or darkroom techniques.

   Or—you name it!

7. Search newspaper editorials and locate three good examples of the use of *forms of support*. Try to find one of each of the following:

   a. statement by authorities

   b. example or illustration

   c. statistics

Notes

1. Kent E. Menzel and Lori J. Carrell, "The Relationship between Preparation and Performance in Public Speaking," *Communication Education,* 43, no. 1 (January 1994), 17–26.

2. William L. Benoit, "Campbell's *The Philosophy of Rhetoric* and the Advancement of Rhetorical Theory: The Integration of Philosophical Antecedents," *Communication Studies,* 41, no. 1 (Spring 1990), 89–100.

3. Joe Elliot and Tim Worsley, eds. *Multi-Media: The Complete Guide* (London: Dorling Kindersly Limited, 1996), p. 161.

4. Allen C. Benson, *The Complete Internet Companion for Librarians* (New York: Neal-Schuman Publishers, 1995). Also see Richard J. Smith and Mark Gibbs, *Navigating the Internet* (Indianapolis: Sams Publishing, 1994); *Communication Education,* 43, no. 2 (April 1994).

6

ORGANIZING THE SPEECH

CHAPTER OUTLINE

The *introduction, body,* and *conclusion* are the basic parts of a speech. Almost all of the serious message organizing goes on in the body. Because the body is the longest and most important part, it is the logical place to begin your critical thinking and planning. Introductions and conclusions are easier to prepare after you have a clear understanding of your message and how you intend to develop it.

ORGANIZING THE BODY OF THE SPEECH

Main Points

LOCATING MAIN POINTS   If you've carefully worded your specific purpose and your central idea or thesis, you have already seen some main points emerge. A well-thought-out central idea often becomes a mini-outline for the body of a speech. Recall the student speech on management functions in Chapter 5 (page 109).

Topic:	The Role of a Manager
General Purpose:	To inform
Specific Purpose:	To inform my audience of five basic management functions.
Central Idea:	Five basic management functions are planning, organizing, directing, coordinating, and controlling.

BODY

Main Points:
    I. The planning function
        A.
        B.
    II. The organizing function
        A.
        B.
        C.
    III. The directing function
        A.
        B.
    IV. The coordinating function
        A.
        B.
    V. The controlling function
        A.
        B.
            1.
            2.

Some main points follow a logical, 1–2–3 order and become evident in your early preparation as well as your central idea.

Topic: Finding a Job
General Purpose: To inform
Specific Purpose: To explain to the class the proper way to find and apply for a job.
Central Idea: Getting a job involves, first, listing employers, then, data preparation, letters, interview preparation, and, last, personal appearance.

BODY

Main Ideas: **I.** Prepare a complete list of prospective employers.
II. Prepare data for an employment application.
III. Prepare three-part letters.
IV. Prepare what you will say in an interview.
V. Plan your dress and grooming.

Speeches to persuade are often more difficult to outline because influence is involved, evidence must be found, and reasons for your viewpoint explained. Look at basic reasons or arguments for your main points. One student sorted out a great many facts and opinions on a controversial topic and settled on two reasons, which then became the two main points.

Topic: Promiscuity
General Purpose: To persuade
Specific Purpose: To persuade the audience that promiscuity has too high a price.
Central Idea: (thesis or claim) Promiscuous persons face new and unusual risks from herpes and AIDS.
Main Points: **I.** Promiscuity has become a major transmitter of genital herpes.
II. Promiscuity has become a major transmitter of AIDS.

RHETORICAL ADVICE

(1) Number of Points.   Classroom speeches are typically short and limited to one central idea. Three to four main points are usually all that can be covered. Should you need more than four or five main points, it will be necessary to cover each one more superficially; as a result, clarity may suffer. Try eliminating some of them on a rank-order of interest or importance; try combining some that may overlap. Eliminating and/or combining, which is the hardest part of speech preparation, is very important because it also directs future research of your topic.

(2) Unity with Central Idea.   This advice, based on a long-standing rhetorical principle, refers to how well your speech organization hangs together and promotes an undivided total effect. As we learned in Chapter 5, we should be able to capture much of the speech in the title, the specific purpose, and the statement of central idea. If you are simply tacking interesting main points to your outline with no clear notion of how or whether they fit the total effect you are hoping to achieve, they should probably be cut. Your speech outline is like the plot of a play. If it gets too tricky, complicated, or strays too far from the point, the audience gives up.

(3) Relatively Equal Merit.   A district attorney arguing a murder case has three main points:

> **I.** Means
> **II.** Opportunity
> **III.** Motive

These points have equal merit relative to her purpose. She must prove all three. However, if the defense concedes *means* and part of *opportunity*, the D.A. will spend more time on *motive*. Equal merit does not necessarily mean equal time or equal emphasis.

If our D.A. adds a fourth point concerning the fact that the accused is an expert marksman, she has then injured her speech organization. "Expert marksman," while important, is not of equal merit with the others. It should be a subpoint under "Means."

Your main points should also be judged on equal merit relative to your purpose. Although you will need to spend a reasonable amount of time on each main point (like the D.A.), it is not necessary to allot equal time and emphasis to each point. A careful assessment of your audience often helps decide time, space, or emphasis.

Suppose your purpose is "To inform the audience about listening." The three points you chose as having equal merit are:

> **I.** Sensory access
> **II.** Motivation
> **III.** Skills

Suppose the audience is composed of healthy, motivated seminarians. Because most of your time and effort will be spent on "Skills," perhaps these three points are not of equal merit. Because merit is relative to purpose, you may need a different purpose to accommodate this audience and this rhetorical advice: "To inform the audience about the skills used by effective listeners."

Wrestling with the question of equal merit not only helps you coordinate your main points, but gives you a good check on your specific purpose and your audience adaptation.

Ordering Main Points

Ordering your main points depends heavily upon the audience and the setting, as well as your purpose. A speech on the U.S. economy depends on the economic sophistication of the audience as well as the latest news from Wall Street. A speech on AIDS might be ordered quite differently for an audience of drug abusers, an audience of homosexuals, an audience of heterosexuals, an audience of physicians, and so on. Nevertheless, several inherently sensible, useful, almost generic methods exist and are used by successful speakers.

CHRONOLOGICAL ORDER   Materials are arranged according to the order in which events took place. In speaking on "Life on Earth," we would probably discuss the following geologic periods chronologically:

Topic:	Life on Earth
General Purpose:	To inform
Specific Purpose:	To inform the audience about the geologic periods of the planet Earth.
Central Idea:	To explain how life developed through six geologic periods, from the Archeozoic to the present.
Main Points:	(chronologically)
	I. The Archeozoic period
	II. The Proterozoic period
	III. The Paleozoic period
	IV. The Mesozoic period
	V. The Cenozoic period
	VI. The Present period

This large topic would have to be severely limited to some specific aspect that cuts across all of the periods, such as changes in life forms. Perhaps the first four could be covered superficially with the emphasis on the Cenozoic period when the mastodons, mammoths, and saber-toothed tigers first appeared. Historical subjects lend themselves readily to this method; so do processes of a sequential (1–2–3) order, such as film developing. Remember, however, that these subjects can be handled in other ways. History is often more interesting and meaningful if discussed topically.

DIFFICULTY ORDER   For some subjects, particularly technical ones, it may help to organize your materials according to order of difficulty, proceeding from the easiest aspect to the most difficult one. In discussing general principles of electricity, you might arrange a series of ideas as shown below.

Topic:	Electricity and Magnetism
General Purpose:	To inform.
Specific Purpose:	To inform the audience about four electromagnetic phenomena.
Central Idea:	To explain that electricity and magnetism are companion physical forces that are responsible for most modern technology.

Main Points: (in order of difficulty)
    I. Electrostatic force between stationary charges
    II. Magnetic force between charges in uniform motion
    III. Electromagnetic induction and varying current
    IV. Electromagnetic radiation and accelerating charges

One electrical engineering student, sensing that her classmates might find all of her main points most difficult, scaled them down as follows:

Figure 6.1

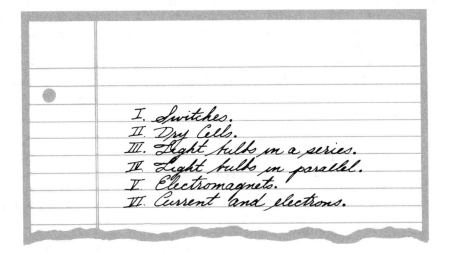

SPATIAL ORDER   This method is particularly useful for certain types of geographic or physical-order subjects. In a speech about the United Nations headquarters in New York, you might first describe each building, then discuss the offices in each building one floor at a time; the ideas are thereby organized spatially. This discussion could also be organized topically if the audience was familiar with the general political structure of the United Nations. In discussing "Nationalism in Africa," you might organize according to geographic location and simply divide the ideas from north to south and east to west. Chronological history might also be a useful method of organizing this speech. A speech on the various peoples of Africa and where they are or are not found could also be ordered and discussed geographically.

              Topic: Different Africans
General Purpose: To inform
Specific Purpose: To inform the class about four regions of differing African peoples.
   Central Idea: To inform the class about the variety of African peoples and four regions where they are found.

Main Points: (arranged spatially)
   I. The Sahara
   II. The Nile Valley
   III. The Great Rift Valley
   IV. The Kalahari Desert

LOGICAL ORDER   This causal-order method uses generally accepted or obvious cause-and-effect relationships, whether we are talking about the fall of the Japanese empire or the building of a house or a boat. When the order is naturally present in the subject or when the association of ideas is evident, it may be convenient to organize your speech materials accordingly. This method differs from the topical method in that the subpoints almost always illustrate or explain to what they are subordinate, unless the audience (for example, experienced boat builders) already knows the logical relationship. If you were talking to boat builders about excessive hull vibration, you might deal first with effects and work back to causes. You must study your audience very thoroughly before using this method. Persuasive speeches often employ the logical method.

Topic: Crack
General Purpose: To persuade
Specific Purpose: To persuade my audience that cocaine is a returning threat to society.
Central Idea: Cocaine is being widely used and is a threat to public health.
Main Points: (causal order)
   I. Cocaine or crack use is accelerating alarmingly.
      A. Statistics on use.
      B. Statistics on reduced cost.
   II. Cocaine use is destroying public health.
      A. Loss of sensory impressions.
      B. Recent evidence that its use leads to stroke.

NEED-PLAN ORDER   Materials are organized according to problems (*needs*) and solutions (*plans*). For example, an affirmative debate team concerned with a resolution on government health programs could divide its material into these two general categories: The first speaker would concentrate on the various needs in the present programs; the second speaker would discuss the various plans and indicate why one is better than the others. The needs could be subdivided into many useful types, such as economic needs, health needs, and social needs.

If the cocaine speech illustrated under the *logical* (cause-effect) method were expanded to the problem of drug use generally, a *need-plan* or problem-solution order might be a better organizational option.

Topic: "H", Crack, Smack, and "Mary Jane" (also the speech title)
General Purpose: To persuade
Specific Purpose: To persuade the audience that a national policy is necessary to control widespread drug use.
Central Idea: The federal government needs a radical new mandatory educational program to stop the flow and use of drugs.
Main Points: (Need-plan order)

Need

   I. The deleterious effects of drug use are out of control.
   A.
   B. } Evidence and argument
   C.

   II. The uninhibited trafficking in illegal drugs is leading to horrendous crime statistics.
   A.
   B. } Evidence and argument

Plan

   III. A federal program of mandatory drug education is necessary.
   A.
   B. } Details of plan
   C.

TOPICAL ORDER   Some topics do not always fit conveniently into the previous ordering systems. These usually can be divided into parts or subtopics of the whole. These then become your main points.

In the topical method, materials are often ordered according to general topics or classifications of knowledge. For example, a history professor might concentrate on the history of religion, war, government, education, or science. The importance of the topic may or may not be such that the presentation of the topic violates historical time. The topical method is a useful way to start breaking down very broad topics, but assess the other, more specific ordering systems before you decide upon this more general one. A broad topic like integration of the races can be looked at in several topical ways—educationally, socially, militarily, economically, and so forth. A city may be described topically in terms of its industry, employment opportunities, recreational facilities, schools, and climate.

Topic: Faltering Integration
General Purpose: To persuade
Specific Purpose: To persuade the audience that racial integration needs to be pursued more aggressively.
Central Idea: Racial integration is uneven across standard societal measures.

Main Points: (topics)

   I. Educational integration is not working.

  II. Economic integration is weak at higher income levels.

 III. Housing integration is mostly unsuccessful.

 IV. Social integration is improving.

  V. Military integration is the most apparent.

A need-plan organization might also be used if you have a plan or a chronological order showing improvement or the lack of it over time.

An audience can be easily confused with the topical method if you mix your main points in terms of function. For example:

        Topic: The Real Zodiac

 General Purpose: To inform

 Specific Purpose: To inform the audience about the latest news on solar system components.

   Central Idea: The solar system is composed of nine planets plus moons, planetoids, comets, meteors, and particles that reflect zodiacal light.

    Main Points: (topical)

       I. 9 planets and 33 moons

      II. 1,600 planetoids or asteroids

     III. Comets and meteors

     IV. Reflectors of zodiacal light

    *V. Space travel

Note that the first four main points are logically consistent, each serving the same function of describing *parts* or components of the solar system. The fifth point, "Space travel," deals not with constituent parts but with another topic (or dimension) completely. This is not to say that a brief anecdote or startling illustration about space travel wouldn't make a good attention-getting *introduction* for such a speech. I suppose one could also organize this speech spatially.

In general, main points should be (1) related in function, (2) unitary (one idea per point), (3) consistent in wording, (4) roughly equal in speech time needed, and (5) ordered to achieve appropriate emphasis.

Cohesion: Connecting Ideas

This includes all efforts at showing that your ideas *cohere,* that is they relate, connect, or hang together in some meaningful way. The principle means are *previews* and *reviews* of main ideas and effective *transitions* between them.

PREVIEWS   You can make clear that your main points are connected by announcing them in advance.

"Today I will explain three reasons why we should support Senator Foghorn:"

1. _____
2. _____
3. _____

This overview of your speech is often a transition between your introduction and the body of your speech. You can then preview each main idea as you come to it.

"My second important reason to support Senator Foghorn is . . ."

REVIEWS   Make your main points more cohesive and better connected by *reviews* or internal summaries of previous main points.

"Now that I've established three needs for change, 1._____, 2._____, and 3._____, let me proceed to ways and means . . ."

TRANSITIONS   These specific language segments connect one idea to another. They are the bridges of words and phrases indicating that you have finished one thought and are moving on to another.

In the case of speeches that follow a fairly clear chronological order, you may need little by way of transitional statement.

"To continue . . ."

"Step two in this process . . ."

"On the third day . . ."

"To sum up . . ."

These are just simple *signs* which hopefully will replace the excess verbalizations often used by inexperienced speakers—"Let's see," "ah," "um," "okay," "so . . ."

You can also use connecting phrases as *signposts* designed to emphasize or indicate a shift in focus.

"More important than my previous points . . ."

"My next argument is crucial . . ."

"Now hear this . . ."

"Most of all . . ."

"In this case . . ."

For lack of a simple connecting word or phrase, these additional situations sometimes provide awkward moments for speakers. The following are some suggestions.

1. *Comparing:* from another point of view, in like manner, in contrast with this.
2. *Citing:* by way of illustration, a case in point is, under this head.
3. *Judging:* this being true, such being the case, under these circumstances.
4. *Excepting:* with this exception, waiving this question, excluding this point.
5. *Opposing:* were this not so, on the contrary, in spite of this.
6. *Conceding:* to be sure, it must be granted, admitting the force of.
7. *Making reference:* in point of, with respect to, as related to.

PLANNING THE INTRODUCTION

Functions

Arousing attention is only one requirement of an introduction. Your introduction should also attempt to establish or strengthen *goodwill* among you, the group you represent, and the audience. In those rare cases in which goodwill is scarce (when you're facing a hostile audience), establishing an atmosphere for a *fair hearing* is perhaps the most you can hope for. For example, statesman Adlai Stevenson used humor to establish rapport with a tough Labor Day audience. "When I was a boy I never had much sympathy for a holiday speaker. He was just a kind of interruption between hot dogs, a fly in the lemonade."

In some situations, a function of the introduction is *orientation.* The speaker must sometimes supply certain background explanations or definitions to help the audience understand the main body of the speech. Certain terms may be unfamiliar, and *not* to define them is to confuse the audience (for example, cybernetics, carcinoma, ROM/RAM, method acting, and organon).

Finally, unless some special strategy of persuasion is involved, the introduction seeks to make your purpose clear; it often previews what will follow in the main body.

In sum, the general functions of an introduction are:

1. to secure *attention*
2. to establish *goodwill* and *credibility*
3. to assure a *fair* hearing
4. to *orient* your audience to the subject
5. to make your *purpose* clear

SECURE ATTENTION   One student with a persuasive speech on chest X-rays secured attention with the following:

There is a subtle killer loose in the room. It killed 40,000 people last year. It likes young people—no one is immune to tuberculosis.

It was topic relevant (X-rays reveal TB), it was audience relevant (young people are most susceptible), and it was startling. How much better than:

A yearly chest X-ray is the best way to avoid TB.

Audiences usually respond to the unique, the strange, the bizarre. One student speaking against terms that stereotype people aroused attention and curiosity with the following:

1. What if this week Dr. Ross asked us to define who we are, or what our roles are? In doing so I wonder how many of us would use such terms as "man," "woman," "female," "male," "husband," "wife," "mother," "father," "masculine," "feminine"? And if so, I wonder how many of us would be stereotyping ourselves?
2. For far too long cliches—such as: "Little boys are made of snakes and snails and puppy dog's tails; and little girls are made of sugar and spice and everything nice"—have represented the image of the male and female in society. Traditionally, males have been depicted as heroic, active, and aggressive, while females pale in the shadow of masculinity.

The title of the student's speech was "A War on Words," which was an attention-getting device in itself when announced by the student chairperson.

Another student speaking on the social impact of rock music opened with audio cassette examples—plenty of attention here.

Statistics make great attention-getters particularly if not commonly known. They are sometimes very poignant when put in question form to a relevant audience. Here are some examples:

Do you know that 72 percent of the freshmen in the Detroit public high schools don't graduate?

Eighty percent of the books written are read by 10 percent of the people.

Fewer than one out of five books published covers expenses.

Quotations are often good openers and attention-getters. Here are some that students have used:

A speech on the future:

I am not afraid of tomorrow for I have seen yesterday, and I love today.
William Allen White (journalist)

A speech on publishing difficulties:

A person who publishes a book willfully appears before the populace with his pants down.
Edna St. Vincent Millay

A speech on human insensitivity:

The young man who has not wept is a savage, and the old man who will not laugh is a fool.

George Santayana

A speech on critical thinking:

For every complex problem there is an easy answer, and it is wrong.

H. L. Mencken

A speech on inexperienced deer hunters:

A little learning is a dangerous thing;

Drink deep, or taste not the Pierian spring;

There shallow draughts intoxicate the brain,

And drinking largely sobers us again.

Alexander Pope

This student not only moved on to a discussion of inadequate training in gun handling, but also, through a play on words, to the problems of drinking and hunting. We'll have more to say about attention and interest factors in Chapter 10, "Speeches to Inform."

ESTABLISH GOODWILL AND CREDIBILITY   Goodwill and credibility are especially important with a controversial subject and a hostile audience. As we shall learn in more detail in Chapter 11, "Speeches to Persuade," some concession to the opposition helps establish goodwill and indicates that you know something about the other side of the argument. So does humor . . . When Jimmy Carter was campaigning for the presidency, he became used to difficult audiences. Upon finally being greeted by a quieter, more contemplative group, he commented: "It certainly is nice to have people waving at me with all five fingers."

In a student speech *against* the repeal of Michigan's container (bottles and cans) law, the speaker opened as follows:

I know that soft drinks cost a dollar a case more in Michigan due to extra handling and storage. I also know that some glassmaking jobs are lost and that some energy is lost because of extra transportation. However, let me tell you about litter reduction and the costs saved there. . . .

Credibility can be established by revealing your experience, training, or any other reason why you are qualified to speak on your chosen topic. Trying to do that without sounding boastful can be a problem.

A speech on scuba diving was opened with a display of equipment and the following words:

> I've only been diving for two years and my deepest dive was only 80 feet to the wreck of the schooner *Kukla*. I'd like to review some basics. . . .

It was clear to all of us (even the divers) that this speaker had credibility and that he wasn't trying to inflate his qualifications.

ASSURE A FAIR HEARING This function is much like securing goodwill and perceptions of credibility. The container-law speech was a good example of an appeal for a fair hearing. Hostile audiences are the main problem particularly if they keep rehearsing arguments to what they *think* you're going to say. The concession suggestion is also a good one here, but sometimes a direct appeal is appropriate.

> I know that most of you are opposed to the by-pass road proposal. I have heard your arguments—it's only American fair play that you hear the other side. I promise to be as objective as I can.

Other methods of securing fair hearing include *appreciation*: "I understand and appreciate your concern—and most of all your willingness to hear both sides"; *personal reference*: "I've lived all of my life in this community and I want only the best for its citizens. . . ."; *humor*: "Your spokesperson just paid me a compliment—I think. He said, 'It must be difficult for you to soar among eagles when you work with turkeys [the road commission].' "

ORIENT YOUR AUDIENCE TO YOUR SUBJECT Sometimes an audience needs to become better acquainted with technical aspects, definitions, diagrams, or terms that you will use in the body of your speech. Review these in the introduction; a visual aid helps too. A speech on the history of firearms made more sense to the audience after the speaker first oriented audience members to the basic nomenclature (names of the parts) of a rifle. He did this by using an exploded diagram, thus giving the audience a vocabulary and a sense of function that greatly assisted understanding.

A brief historical sketch often improves audience orientation. A good example is John F. Kennedy's opening address to a conference on African culture in New York City.

> Some 2,500 years ago the Greek historian Herodotus described Africa south of the Sahara as a land of "horned asses, of dog-faced creatures, the creatures without heads, whom the Libyans declared to have eyes in their breasts, and many other far less fabulous beasts." Apparently when Herodotus found himself short on facts, he didn't hesitate to use imagination—which may be why he is called the first historian.

But we must not be too critical of Herodotus. Until very recently, for most Americans, Africa was Trader Horn, Tarzan, and tom-tom drums. We are only now beginning to discover that Africa, unlike our comic strip stereotypes, is a land of rich variety—of noble and ancient cultures, some primitive, some highly sophisticated; of vital and gifted people, who are only now crossing the threshold into the modern world.

CLARIFY YOUR PURPOSE   If, after a rousing speech introduction, your audience says, "Okay, but what are we talking about?" or "Whadhesay?" we have a dual problem of clarity of purpose and poor orientation. Unless strategy is involved, the introduction should clarify what you are going to discuss and why your audience should listen. The old rule of "Tell 'em what you're going to tell 'em, tell 'em, tell 'em you've told 'em" makes some sense.

A student speaking on music theory started his introduction with a violin demonstration (attention) and ended it with a forthright overview or preview of what was to follow.

I have three points to make that I will relate to playing an instrument: 1. kinds of notes, 2. musical staff, and 3. methods of counting the notes.

Pitfalls

FALSE STARTS

"Before I begin . . ."

"Well, I guess it's time to start . . ."

"Is it all right if I sit down?"

"Before saying anything important . . ."

Statements such as these generally irritate audiences and label you as ineffective.

UNNECESSARY APOLOGIES

"I'm not very good at this . . ."

"I hope you'll pay attention . . ."

"I didn't have much time to prepare . . ."

"I never had a speech course . . ."

"I'm sorry if this sounds complicated . . ."

If any of these apologetic statements are true, the audience will find out soon enough. Don't destroy your credibility before you even get started.

On the other hand, if you are late for the speech, lost your visual aids, or caused the schedule to be rearranged, a brief explanation, if not an apology, is in order.

"I'm late because my ROTC instructor held the class overtime."

"My luggage along with my slides were stolen."

"I apologize to the other speakers and appreciate their accommodating my travel problems."

OVERSTATEMENT   This pitfall includes distortion, imprudence, misrepresentation, and overexaggeration to get attention. Don't promise more than you can deliver.

A social science teacher opened a lecture on nuclear power by asking each student to cut off a lock of hair and deposit it in a metal container. The teacher then burned the hair, which gave off a nauseating stench. This, he explained, was what human flesh smelled like when exposed to nuclear radiation. Next he showed a two-minute film clip of the most grisly pictures of hideously burned people after the atomic bomb raid on Hiroshima. Finally, he snuffed out an ant farm in a fraction of a second by burning up the oxygen with hot magnesium, much, he explained, as people are destroyed in a nuclear explosion.

Attention here all right! But will it help introduce the body of the speech? Not if it is so overpowering that it destroys future concentration or so emotional that it actually turns people off to the point of rejection of the speaker and the speaker's message. Will it assure a fair hearing? Is it a fair hearing? Is it a fair orientation to the subject? Does it confuse the purpose? Is it a case of overkill and misplaced emphasis?

Attention at any price is a mistake. Attention-getting strategies should be relevant to both the topic and the audience, no matter whether it's a joke, a story, an example, or a demonstration. However, some topic-relevant devices are not always audience relevant. One student speaker opened a speech on presidential politics with a joke about one of the more profligate candidates. The story had two four-letter words in it. Half of the audience were members of the Pentecostal Church; more than half of the audience walked out before he got to the message.

Do not be afraid to startle or titillate an audience especially with an important but dull topic. But look for the boomerangs.

Certainly, gaining the listeners' *attention* is an important requirement of the beginning of a speech, but one can overdo as well as underdo attention-gaining devices. The number of attention devices to be used also depends on what attention level the audience has already achieved. In other words, if the listeners are on the edge of their seats and ready to hear what you have to say, a lengthy introduction designed to arouse their attention will be unnecessary.

Model Introductions

The inaugural address of John F. Kennedy, which follows, illustrates most of the functions and requirements of a good introduction.

Attention   My fellow citizens:
We observe today not a victory of party but a celebration of freedom—symbolizing an end as well as a beginning—signifying renewal as well as change. For I have sworn before you and Almighty God the same solemn oath our forebears prescribed nearly a century and three-quarters ago.

Orientation
and Goodwill   The world is very different now. For man holds in his mortal hands the power to abolish all forms of human poverty and to abolish all forms of human life. And, yet, the same revolutionary beliefs for which our forebears fought are still at issue around the globe—the belief that the rights of man come not from the generosity of the state but from the hand of God.

Fair Hearing   We dare not forget today that we are the heirs of that first revolution. Let the word go forth from this time and place, to friend and foe alike, that the torch has been passed to a new generation of Americans—born in this century, tempered by war, disciplined by a cold and bitter peace, proud of our ancient heritage—and unwilling to witness or permit the slow undoing of those human rights to which this nation has always been committed, and to which we are committed today.

Purpose   Let every nation know, whether it wish us well or ill, that we shall pay any price, bear any burden, meet any hardship, support any friend, or oppose any foe in order to assure the survival and success of liberty. This much we pledge—and more.

In still more specific terms, an introduction may utilize appreciation, personal reference, quotations, humor, and related stories or experiences. When the purpose of the speech is relatively obvious and the speaker and subject are well known, a related story, incident, or narrative with built-in attention often reinforces the purpose and gives the audience a fresh orientation. Booker T. Washington's introduction to his classic address at the Atlanta Exposition is a case in point.

Attention   Mr. President and Gentlemen of the Board of Directors and Citizens: One-third of the population of the South is of the Negro race. No enterprise seeking the material, civil, or moral welfare of this section can disregard this element of our population and reach the highest success.

Goodwill   I but convey to you, Mr. President and Directors, the sentiment of the masses of my race when I say that in no way have the value of manhood of the American Negro been more fittingly and generously recognized than by the managers of this magnificent Exposition at every stage of its progress. It is a recognition that will do more to cement the friendship of the two races than any occurrence since the dawn of our freedom.

Fair Hearing   Not only this, but the opportunity here afforded will awaken among us a new era of industrial progress. Ignorant and inexperienced, it is not strange that in the first years of our new life we began at the top instead of at the bottom; that a seat in Congress or the state legislature was more sought than real estate or industrial skill; that the political convention or stump speaking had more attractions than starting a dairy farm or truck garden.

Orientation   A ship lost at sea for many days suddenly sighted a friendly vessel. From the mast of the unfortunate vessel was seen a signal, "Water, water; we die of thirst!" The answer from the friendly vessel at once came back, "Cast down your bucket where you are." And a third and fourth signal for water was answered, "Cast down your bucket where you are." The captain of the distressed vessel, at last heeding the injunction, cast down his bucket, and it came up full of fresh, sparkling water from the mouth of the Amazon River.

Purpose   To those of my race who depend on bettering their condition in a foreign land or who underestimate the importance of cultivating friendly relations with the Southern white man, who is their next door neighbor, I would say: "Cast down your bucket where you are—cast it down in making friends in every manly way of the people of all races by whom we are surrounded.

President Franklin D. Roosevelt also used a story in an introduction to one of the many appeals he made for the purchase of war bonds.

Once upon a time, a few years ago, there was a city in our Middle West which was threatened by a destructive flood in a great river. The water had risen to the top of the banks. Every man, woman, and child in that city was called upon to fill sandbags in order to defend their homes against the rising waters. For many days and nights destruction and death stared them in the face. As a result of the grim, determined community effort, that city still stands. Those people kept the levees above the peak of the flood. All of them joined together in the desperate job that had to be done—businessmen, workers, farmers, and doctors, and preachers—people of all races.

To me that town is a living symbol of what community cooperation can accomplish.

PLANNING THE CONCLUSION

Functions

A good conclusion offers *direction, action, review,* and *reinforcement.* To these we could add *visualization, restatement,* and *summary.* All of these devices intend to rekindle attention and to assist the memory. Aristotle suggested that the major purpose of the conclusion is to help the memory. An attention-getter used here is a good idea just as it was in the introduction.

The conclusion is generally shorter than the introduction. It may, and generally should, include a short summary that reinforces the central idea, thus making it easier to understand. It may provide clearly stated directions if certain actions are part of the speaker's purpose. When your purpose has been inspiration, you may need a more impressive conclusion. Some of the devices suggested in the discussion on introductions (an impressive quotation, incident, or experience) apply here. The three major functions of a good conclusion are:

1. Review the central idea.
2. Reinforce belief or action desired.
3. Impress when appropriate.

REVIEW THE CENTRAL IDEA   "Tell 'em you told 'em." A detailed speech about the dietary laws of the Jewish people, including the biblical and pragmatic reasons behind them, concluded as follows:

   II. In review, an observing Jew may not:
     A. Consume meat that comes from animals that do not possess cloven hoofs and that do not chew their cud.
     B. Consume fish that do not have both scales and fins.
     C. Consume or cook meat and dairy foods together.
     D. Eat any part of a living animal.
     E. Consume blood (hence, koshering).
     F Consume meat from an animal that has not been ritually slaughtered.

In a speech about the future six wonders of the world, where the central idea was to show their useful purposes compared to the ancient seven wonders, this student offered an interesting and detailed review:

CONCLUSION

   I. These new six wonders have useful purposes.
     A. Snowy Mountains Scheme makes Australia's desert lands places of lush vegetation.
     B. Chesapeake Bay Bridge Tunnel enables people to travel more easily from Norfolk to the Delmarva Peninsula.
     C. The Netherlands' Delta Plan secures the land from the damaging storms of the sea.
     D. The New York Narrows Bridge allows traffic to cross the entrance of New York Harbor.
     E. The Mont Blanc Tunnel allows year-round travel through the Alps.
     F. The English Channel Tunnel connects Britain and France by rail transporting passengers and their cars.
   II. These constructions are more wondrous than the ancient ones.
     A. Ancient wonders were noted primarily for art, size, and beauty.
     B. The modern wonders each have all of these plus unchallenged utility.

REINFORCE BELIEF OR ACTION   A speaker can, of course, reinforce by simply reviewing as shown in the illustrations above. However, in persuasive speeches one may also wish to be a little more explicit or manifest. In a speech where the central idea was that nonsmokers have rights and should speak up for them, after a review of actions to be taken, the student concluded as follows:

CONCLUSION

   I.
   II.
   III. There is no reason there can't be places for smoking as well as places not to smoke.
     A. I don't think anyone has ever really died of a "nicotine fit" from not smoking for an hour or two during a class period.

B. You really should stand up for your rights and support movements to designate places to smoke and places not to smoke.
C. So, the next time you're in a car or other enclosed place and someone asks you, "Do you mind if I smoke?" be sure to reply, "Yes, I mind!"

In a speech where the central idea was that latchkey children can survive very nicely if parents will practice specific rules, a student reviewed and reinforced the actions as follows:

CONCLUSION

I. Latchkey children can lead normal lives without fear, drugs, or crime. The proof is standing here in front of you; I was a latchkey child.
II. In review, these are actions to take if you have a child who will have to stay alone.
   A. Teach children to use the phone and lock the doors.
   B. Don't let the child display a key in public.
   C. Instruct children to tell callers that the parent is busy and unable to come to the phone.
   D. Structure activities for the child.
   E. Arrange for the child to spend some afternoons with friends.
   F. Get a pet.
   G. Teach children that independence and resourcefulness are virtues but don't overload the circuits.

IMPRESS WHEN APPROPRIATE   Most classroom speeches other than *special-occasion* assignments don't call for superdramatic, elevated conclusions, but a dramatic or pointed, relevant quotation like those shown in the discussion of introductions usually works well. A very touching speech by a handicapped student on the "Promise of Tomorrow" was concluded using the same quotation with which she had opened her speech.

> I am not afraid of tomorrow for I have seen yesterday, and I love today.
> *William Allen White*

Special-occasion speeches typically do call for a more elevated style of language and a more impressive presentation. A classic inspirational conclusion was provided by Martin Luther King, Jr. in his famous speech in support of civil rights legislation before an estimated 200,000 people. Note that his review is much more than a mere repetition of his main points, and that his purpose is made abundantly clear.

> So let freedom ring—from the prodigious hilltops of New Hampshire, let freedom ring; from the mighty mountains of New York, let freedom ring—from the heightening Alleghenies of Pennsylvania!
>
> Let freedom ring from the snowcapped Rockies of Colorado!
> Let freedom ring from the curvaceous slopes of California!
> But not only that; let freedom ring from Stone Mountain of Georgia!

> Let freedom ring from Lookout Mountain of Tennessee!
> Let freedom ring from every hill and mole hill of Mississippi.
> From every mountainside, let freedom ring,. . .

> When we allow freedom to ring, when we let it ring from every village and every hamlet, from every state and every city, we will be able to speed up that day when all of God's children, black men and white men, Jews and Gentiles, Protestants and Catholics, will be able to join hands and sing in the words of the old Negro spiritual, "Free at last! thank God almighty, we are free at last!"

A presidential inauguration is a very special occasion and the "Ask Not" speech of John Fitzgerald Kennedy made an impression that will be long remembered. The conclusion deserves a piece of marble.

> And so, my fellow Americans, ask not what your country can do for you: Ask what you can do for your country.
> My fellow citizens of the world: Ask not what America will do for you, but what together we can do for the freedom of man.
> Finally, whether you are citizens of America or citizens of the world, ask of us here the same high standards of strength and sacrifice which we ask of you. With a good conscience our only sure reward, with history the final judge of our deeds, let us go forth to lead the land we love, asking His blessings and His help, but knowing that here on earth God's work must truly be our own.

Pitfalls

DEPRECATION OF EFFORT

"I should have had more time to prepare."

"I'm sorry I couldn't say it better."

"I guess there are more important things."

"I'm not an orator, but I hope you got something out of this."

This kind of apology is almost always superfluous and damaging to your credibility. Apologies and qualifiers germane to other issues may sometimes pertain, but should probably have been stated earlier.

OVERAMPLIFICATION   Overamplification refers to a disproportionate expansion of the points already covered in the body of the speech. In its worst example new material is introduced. Main points with their support belong in the body of the speech, not in the conclusion.

PROLONGED CLOSE   Most important, make it clear when you are finished; consider your exit lines carefully. Speakers who do not know when to finish appear awkward and frustrate the audience. The never-ending conclusion leaves you with so many things to tie together that you cannot conclude your speech in any unified manner. The lesson is obvious; prepare your conclusion as carefully as the rest of your speech. Doing so serves as a good check on organic unity. And quit while you're ahead. Don't let an audience hypnotize you so much that you ruin a good speech by an overly long or overly dramatic conclusion.

Summary

The introduction, body, and conclusion are the basic parts of a speech. Main points are found in your central idea and early preparation. In persuasive speeches, look at your basic reasons or arguments for the main points. Rhetorical advice regarding main points includes: (1) limit them to three or four, (2) keep them unified with your central idea, and (3) give each relatively equal merit.

Methods of ordering main points include: (1) chronological, (2) difficulty, (3) spatial, (4) logical, (5) need-plan, and (6) topical. The principal ways of coherently connecting main ideas include: (1) previews, (2) reviews, and (3) transitions.

The functions of the *introduction* part of a speech include: (1) securing attention, (2) establishing goodwill and credibility, (3) assuring a fair hearing, (4) orienting the audience, and (5) clarifying your purpose. Pitfalls to avoid include: (1) false starts, (2) unnecessary apologies, and (3) overstatement.

The functions of the *conclusion* include: (1) reviewing the central idea, (2) reinforcing the belief or action desired, and (3) impressing when appropriate. Pitfalls to avoid include: (1) deprecation of effort, (2) overamplification, and (3) a prolonged close.

Learning Projects

1. See "How to Write a Résumé" on the following pages.

   a. List the main points (I, II, etc.).

   b. Supply the general purpose, specific purpose, and central idea.

   c. Describe its attempts at cohesion: connecting ideas and emphasis.

   d. Describe the method of organization used (chronological, difficulty, spatial, topical, logical, or need-plan).

   e. Evaluate the introduction on the basis of the five functions discussed in this chapter (attention, goodwill, fair hearing, orientation of audience, clarity of purpose). Indicate by line number where each function is served.

2. Using the "functions and requirements" of a good introduction found in the text, write a brief introduction for two of the following specific purposes:

   a. To persuade the class that smoking should be outlawed in all public buildings.

   b. To inform the class about volcanoes.

    c. To persuade the class that the maximum speed limit should be 55 mph everywhere.

    d. To inform the class about hypnosis.

3. Write brief conclusions for two of the topics in project 2 above.

4. Prepare only the introduction to a five- to ten-minute speech that you might use later. Make your general and specific purposes clear, and try to achieve all of the functions of a good introduction: attention, goodwill, fair hearing, orientation, purpose. (See the model outlines in this chapter.)

HOW TO WRITE A RÉSUMÉ

1   If you are about to launch a search for a job, the suggestions I offer here can help you whether or not you have a high school or college diploma, whether you are just starting out, or changing your job or career in midstream.

2   Before you try to find a job opening, you have to answer the hardest question of your working life: "What do I want to do?" Here's a good way.

3   Sit down with a piece of paper and don't get up until you've listed all the things you're proud to have accomplished. Your list might include being head of a fund-raising campaign, or acting a juicy role in the senior play.

4   Study the list. You'll see a pattern emerge of the things you do best and like to do best. You might discover that you're happiest working with people, or maybe with numbers, or words, or well, you'll see it.

5   Once you've decided what job area to go after, read more about it in the reference section of your library. "Talk shop" with any people you know in that field. Then start to get your résumé together.

6   There are many good books that offer sample résumés and describe widely used formats. The one that is still most popular, the *reverse chronological,* emphasizes where you worked and when, and the jobs and titles you held.

7   Next ask, "How do I organize it?"

8   Your name and address go at the top. Also phone number.

9   What job do you want? That's what a prospective employer looks for first. If you know exactly, list that next under *Job Objective.* Otherwise, save it for your cover letter (I describe that later), when you're writing for a specific job to a specific person. In any case, make sure your résumé focuses on the kind of work you can do and want to do.

10   Now comes *Work Experience.* Here's where you list your qualifications. Lead with your most important credentials. If you've had a distinguished work history in an area related to the job you're seeking, lead off with that. If your education will impress the prospective employer more, start with that.

11   Begin with your most recent experience first and work backwards. Include your titles or positions held. And list the years.

12   How should you present yourself?

13   Understand that the most qualified people don't always get the job. It goes to the person who presents himself most persuasively in person and on paper.

14   So don't just list where you were and what you did. This is your chance to tell how well you did. Were you the best salesperson? Did you cut operating costs? Give numbers, statistics, percentages, increases in sales or profits.

15   What if you have no job experience?

16   In that case, list your summer jobs, extracurricular school activities, honors, awards. Choose the activities that will enhance your qualifications for the job.

17   Next list your *Education*—unless you chose to start with that. This should also be in reverse chronological order. List your high school only if you didn't go on to

Reprinted by permission of International Paper Company

college. Include college degree, postgraduate degrees, dates conferred, major and minor courses you took that help qualify you for the job you want.

18   Also, did you pay your own way? Earn scholarships or fellowships? Those are impressive accomplishments.

19   Then tell about your education: special training programs or courses that can qualify you. Describe outside activities that reveal your talents and abilities. Did you sell the most tickets to the annual charity musical? Did you take your motorcycle engine apart and put it back together so it works? These can help.

20   Next list any *Military Service*. This could lead off your résumé if it is your only work experience. Stress skills learned, promotions earned, leadership shown.

21   Now comes *Personal Data*. This is your chance to let the reader get a glimpse of the personal you, and to further the image you've worked to project in the preceding sections. For example, if you're after a job in computer programming, and you enjoy playing chess, mention it. Chess playing requires the ability to think through a problem.

22   Include foreign languages spoken, extensive travel, particular interests or professional memberships *if* they advance your cause.

23   Keep your writing style simple. Be brief. Start sentences with impressive action verbs: "Created," "Designed," "Achieved," "Caused."

24   Make sure your grammar and spelling are correct. And no typos!

25   Use 8 1/2" x 11" bond paper—white or off-white for easy reading. Don't cram things together.

26   Make sure your original is clean and readable. Then have it professionally duplicated. No carbons.

27   Now that your résumé is ready, start to track down job openings. How? Look up business friends, personal friends, neighbors, your minister, your college alumni association, professional services. Keep up with trade publications, and read help-wanted ads.

28   And start your own "direct mail" campaign. First, find out about the companies you are interested in—their size, location, what they make, their competition, their advertising, their prospects. Get their annual report—and read it.

29   Send your résumé, along with a cover letter, to a specific person in the company. The person should be the top person in the area where you want to work. Spell the name properly! The cover letter should appeal to your reader's own needs. What's in it for him or her? Quickly explain why you are approaching *this* company (their product line, their superior training program) and what you can bring to the party. Back up your claims with facts. Then refer to your enclosed résumé and ask for an interview.

30   And now you've got an interview! Be sure to call the day before to confirm it. Meantime, *prepare yourself.* Research the company and the job by reading books and business journals in the library.

31   On the big day, arrive 15 minutes early. Act calm, even though, if you're normal, you're trembling inside at 6.5 on the Richter scale. At every chance, let your interviewer see that your personal skills and qualifications relate to the job at hand. If it's a sales position, for example, go all out to show how articulate and persuasive you are.

32   Afterwards, follow through with a brief thank-you note. This is a fine opportunity to restate your qualifications and add any important points you didn't get a chance to bring up during the interview.

33   Finally, keep a list of prospects. List the dates you contacted them, when they replied, what was said.

34   And remember, someone out there is looking for someone *just like you.* It takes hard work and sometimes luck to find that person. Keep at it and you'll succeed.

(Jerrold G. Simon)

7

OUTLINING
THE SPEECH

CHAPTER
OUTLINE

The outline is to a speech what a blueprint is to a house. A good, clear outline can help you discover mistakes, weaknesses, and unnecessary information *before* you speak, just as the builder or architect can often save costly mistakes by taking a hard look at the plans before starting to build the house.

This chapter begins with practical suggestions for a rough draft outline, then describes basic principles of outlining, and closes with explanations of how to prepare, really, two outlines. The first is a complete sentence outline, the one you will turn in for a grade; the second is your speaking outline, a shorter version of the first.

WHERE TO START

Purpose and Central Idea

Review the assignment. Has your general purpose shifted from *inform* to *persuade* when *inform* was the charge? Then review your *specific* purpose and central idea. If your central idea is clearly stated, it may be a mini-outline. Recall the central idea for the "Role of the Manager" speech in Chapter 5. "Five management functions are planning, organizing, directing, coordinating, and controlling." These five functions can be viewed as the five main points of the speech. As we said in Chapter 6, start with the main points in the body of the speech, make a note of any ideas for the introduction or conclusion, and hold them for the time being. You'll want to review your research notes and ideas to see if they suggest still more main points or perhaps a way to rewrite or combine them.

The examples that follow are informative speeches. Strategic outlining suggestions for the persuasive speech are found in Chapter 11, "Speeches to Persuade." If you are still searching for a subject, see the "Speech Topic Locator" in the Appendix.

Rough Draft

Mark Scott loved his anthropology course and decided to look for his informative speech topic in that general area. The study of human beings was, of course, too broad a topic for a four- to five-minute speech so he thought of two areas of that broad topic that interested him: "The Races of Man" and "The Beginnings of Mankind." Preliminary research in these areas indicated that anthropologists have divided the world's population into three, general racial types—Caucasoid, Mongoloid, and Negroid. Mark also found that *Homo sapiens* (human beings) first appeared in the Pleistocene epoch of the Cenozoic era. The Cenozoic era began about 70 million years ago and humans had mastodons, mammoths, and saber-toothed tigers with which to contend. Mark was fascinated by stories of "Peking man," the oldest discovery. This person may have lived 6 million years ago. Other prehistoric people varied somewhat and were discovered near Neanderthal, Germany, and Les Eyzies, France. The latter were called Cro-Magnon, which is the French word for "great hole" or "cave" in which they were found.

Great materials for a speech, perhaps two or three, but what an overload of confused information. Mark started by listing the more important and interesting points and ideas.

Races of man	Pleistocene epoch
Beginnings of man	Cenozoic era
Anthropology	Peking man
Caucasoid	Java man
Mongoloid	Neanderthal man
Negroid	Cro-Magnon man
Homo sapiens	

Now it was time to combine, subordinate, discard, and generally reduce the list. *Anthropology* covered everything—discard. *Homo sapiens* and human being mean the same thing—discard *Homo sapiens*. *Caucasoid, Mongoloid,* and *Negroid* are all the races of humans—subordinate them.

I. Races of man
   A. Caucasoid
   B. Mongoloid
   C. Negroid

The *Pleistocene* epoch is part of the *Cenozoic* era . . .? *Peking, Java, Neanderthal,* and *Cro-Magnon* are all early, archaeological discoveries that describe the *Beginnings of man.* They can be subordinated.

I. Beginnings of man
   A. Neanderthal man
   B. Cro-Magnon man
   C. Peking man
   D. Java man

Mark wisely decided that he had enough ideas here for two speeches. He selected "Beginnings of Man" because he found it more interesting, and he thought the word "Negroid" might offend some of his classmates. Oh yes, he also had more research material on prehistoric humans.

Because all of these finds referred to prehistoric times, Mark decided that "Prehistoric People" might be a better topic title than "Beginnings of Man." It also occurred to him that the constant use of the word "man" might offend his female classmates. Note also that there is a natural, chronological order to archaeological findings. An outline began to emerge.

PREHISTORIC PEOPLE

INTRODUCTION

BODY

   I. Peking man (6,000,000 to 125,000 years B.C.)

   II. Java man (6,000,000 to 125,000 years B.C.)

   III. Neanderthal man (125,000 to 25,000 years B.C.)

   IV. Cro-Magnon man (25,000 to 8,000 years B.C.)

CONCLUSION

Mark's revised specific purpose and central idea now focused his research on the archaeological findings related to these three periods of early humans and to their inferred characteristics and behavior. His rough outline follows.

ROUGH OUTLINE

      Topic: Prehistoric People

General Purpose: To inform

Specific Purpose: To inform the audience about the characteristics of early humans.

    Central Idea: There are three main periods of early humans based on archaeological finds.

WHENCE HUMAN

INTRODUCTION

Cartoons: *Flintstones, B. C., Alley Oop*

BODY

   I. Peking "Man" (6,000,000 to 125,000 years B.C.) (also Java "Man" and other finds of this period)

   II. Neanderthal people (125,000 years to 25,000 years B.C.) (also other finds of this period)

   III. Cro-Magnon people (25,000 to 8,000 B.C.) (also other finds of this period)

CONCLUSION

A review of characteristics and behaviors

Mark is now ready to develop his complete, finished outline, but first let's review the classic principles of outlining in general.

OUTLINING PRINCIPLES

The *complete-sentence outline* is the most detailed and specific of all the forms. For speech class purposes all main- and first-level subpoints are complete sentences, and second- and third-level subpoints may be explicit phrases or sometimes words. Check with your instructor on this matter. The use of complete sentences helps clarify the relationship between main points and their major subdivisions. Your rough draft is called a *topical outline,* one in which phrases or groups of words carry the essential meanings intended. Its disadvantage as a final working outline is that ideas may be difficult for you to visualize as complete thoughts.

A **key-word outline** is an abbreviated topical outline. In terms of indentation and symbols it looks the same as the complete-sentence outline. The key-word outline is usually easier to remember, and it makes the extemporaneous reordering of ideas much easier when the situation calls for such adaptation.

Combinations of these forms are often advisable when you are speaking on a subject with which you are thoroughly familiar. The main points might be complete sentences, the subpoints phrases, and the subsubpoints key words. We'll describe the *speaking outline* in more detail at the end of this chapter.

Symbolization

Symbolization means that similar symbols (I, 1, A, b, and so on) should represent items of equal importance. The symbol and its indentation should indicate the relative importance of the item that follows. Usually, main points are Roman numerals, major subpoints are capital letters, minor subpoints are Arabic numerals, and so on.

Logical outlining includes (1) divisions of ideas and (2) headings that make these divisions clear. If a topic is divided, there should be two or more parts. In other words, if you're going to have a *1,* you should also have a *2;* if you're going to have an *A,* you should also have a *B.* If your *2* or *B* is not important to your speech, the first point should be incorporated into its superior heading. For example:

    A. Wagon trains.
       1. Role in development of West.

becomes

    A. Wagon trains as factor in development of West.

The numbers and letters used as labels must be consistent. Let your symbols show clearly that the main ideas are relatively equal in importance and that the subpoints are secondary to the main points.

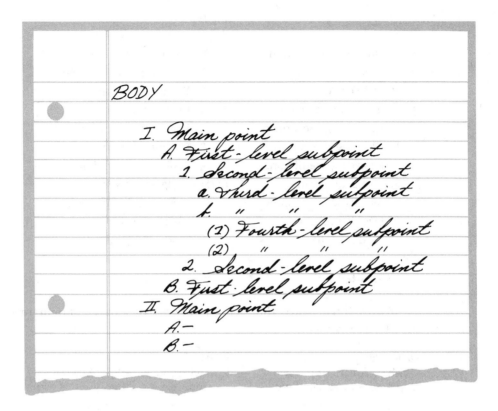

Figure 7.1

The standard system of symbols and indentations is shown in Figure 7.1.

In order to be true main points and not subdivisions, your main points should be of approximately equal importance. Each main point should be worded carefully and completely and should contribute to the central idea of the speech. The order in which you present your main points should aid in the logical development of your speech and strengthen audience motivation, remembering, and understanding.

Subordination

Subordination means that related lesser points supporting a general category or statement should be grouped separately from the category, usually by means of indentation. Items of equal importance should be given equal billing.

WRONG ⊘

A. Learning to type.

   1. Preliminary preparation.

   2. Addressing the keyboard.

   3. Practice exercises.

   4. First-level maintenance.

      a. Unsticking the strikers.

      b. Cleaning the keys.

      c. Replacing the ribbon.

   5. Selecting a typewriter.

      a. Mechanical machines.

      b. Electric machines.

      c. Kinds of type.

RIGHT ©

A. Learning to type.

   1. Preliminary preparation.

   2. Addressing the keyboard.

   3. Practice exercises.

B. First-level maintenance.

   1. Unsticking the strikers.

   2. Cleaning the keys.

   3. Replacing the ribbon.

C. Selecting a typewriter.

   1. Mechanical machines.

   2. Electric machines.

   3. Kinds of type.

Simplicity

Simplicity means that each numbered or lettered statement should contain only one idea.

WRONG ⊘

I. I wish to cover the following major steps in music theory:

  A. The kinds of notes and the musical staff.

  B. Methods of counting and the relation of these to an instrument.

RIGHT ©

I. I wish to cover the following steps in music theory:

  A. The kinds of notes.

  B. The musical staff.

  C. Methods of counting the notes.

  D. The relation of these methods to an instrument.

Discreteness

Discreteness means that each item in an outline should be a distinct point and not overlap other items.

WRONG ⊘

A. Tennis strokes.

   1. The serve.

   2. The forehand.

   3. The backhand.

   4. Various shots.

RIGHT ©

A. Tennis strokes.

   1. The serve.

   2. The forehand.

   3. The backhand.

   4. The volley.

   5. The approach shot.

   6. The overhead.

Coordination

Coordination means that a subordinate list of topics must have a common relationship.

<table>
<tr><td colspan="2">WRONG √</td><td colspan="2">RIGHT ©</td></tr>
<tr><td colspan="2">A. Manufacturing companies in Detroit.</td><td colspan="2">A. Manufacturing companies in Detroit.</td></tr>
<tr><td>1.</td><td>General Motors Corporation.</td><td>1.</td><td>General Motors Corporation.</td></tr>
<tr><td>2.</td><td>Ford Motor Company.</td><td>2.</td><td>Ford Motor Company.</td></tr>
<tr><td>3.</td><td>Chrysler Corporation.</td><td>3.</td><td>Chrysler Corporation.</td></tr>
<tr><td>4.</td><td>American Motors Corporation.</td><td>4.</td><td>American Motors Corporation.</td></tr>
<tr><td>5.</td><td>Campbell Ewald Advertising Company.</td><td colspan="2">B. Service companies in Detroit.</td></tr>
<tr><td>6.</td><td>American Automobile Association.</td><td>1.</td><td>Campbell Ewald Advertising Company.</td></tr>
<tr><td>7.</td><td>Benedict and Moore Insurance.</td><td>2.</td><td>American Automobile Association.</td></tr>
<tr><td></td><td></td><td>3.</td><td>Benedict and Moore Insurance.</td></tr>
</table>

Progression

Progression refers to the arrangement of related items in some sort of natural sequence, such as chronology, time, genre, or space. Keep the items in sequence and don't switch patterns. The following example is based on difficulty and natural sequence.

<table>
<tr><td colspan="2">WRONG √</td><td colspan="2">RIGHT ©</td></tr>
<tr><td colspan="2">A. Courses in mathematics</td><td colspan="2">B. Courses in mathematics</td></tr>
<tr><td>1.</td><td>Algebra</td><td>1.</td><td>Arithmetic</td></tr>
<tr><td>2.</td><td>Arithmetic</td><td>2.</td><td>Algebra</td></tr>
<tr><td>3.</td><td>Calculus</td><td>3.</td><td>Plane Geometry</td></tr>
<tr><td>4.</td><td>Solid Geometry</td><td>4.</td><td>Solid Geometry</td></tr>
<tr><td>5.</td><td>Trigonometry</td><td>5.</td><td>Trigonometry</td></tr>
<tr><td>6.</td><td>Plane Geometry</td><td>6.</td><td>Calculus</td></tr>
</table>

THE COMPLETE OUTLINE

Your rough outline should eventually become a *complete* or *complete-sentence outline* (one in which all main- and first-level subpoints are written out as complete sentences). This form will force you to think your way through the material and help you avoid embarrassing moments on the platform. The sentence outline will also make it easier for your instructor to evaluate and help you with your speech planning. It is the outline that will be graded.

If you intend to use the speech again or if others may have to speak from it, a complete-sentence outline becomes valuable. After this kind of thorough outlining, it is easier to redo the outline in a topical or key-word form for use on the platform.

General Rules

State your topic.

State your general purpose.

State your specific purpose.

State your central idea.

Label the introduction, body, and conclusion.

State main points as complete sentences.

State major subpoints as complete sentences.

In addition to these standard rules, your instructor may ask you to insert transition (connecting) language between main points or between introduction and the body and conclusion. If you are using some special arrangement system (for example, attention, need, satisfaction, visualization, action), use those labels to the left of the standard three divisions.

(Attention)	INTRODUCTION
	I. _____
	II. _____
(Need)	BODY
(Satisfaction)	**I.** _____
	II. _____
	III. _____
(Visualization)	CONCLUSION
(Action)	**I.** _____
	II. _____

Because your *complete* outline reflects your research, attach a bibliography of your major sources of information: books, articles, conversations, interviews, and so forth.

Model Complete Outline

We return to Mark Scott and his interest in prehistoric humans. After more research and thinking, he decided on the title (or topic) of "Cave People." He's been more precise in his statement of specific purpose, and the central idea is more detailed, but still quite limited. Compare what follows to his rough draft on p. 157. Note the kind of natural extension and development of those earlier thoughts.

MODEL COMPLETE OUTLINE

Topic: Prehistoric People
General Purpose: To inform
Specific Purpose: To inform the class about changing human characteristics over the last 6,000,000 years.
Central Idea: There are three periods of prehistoric human development based on archaeological discoveries.

CAVE PEOPLE

INTRODUCTION

(Attention) **I.** You will often see cartoons showing cave people being chased by dino-
(Interest) saurs. This is impossible! You need to know more about your ancestors.

    A. Human bones are from earth 50,000 years old.

    B. Dinosaur bones are from rocks 15,000,000 years old (show cartoons of *Alley Oop* and the *Flintstones*).

(Overview) **II.** I would like to describe briefly the three main periods of prehistoric humankind and explain how they looked and behaved, namely: Peking person, Neanderthal person, and Cro-Magnon person.

BODY

  I. Peking person lived 6,000,000 to 125,000 years B.C.

    A. Archaeological discoveries of the Peking period.

      1. The Peking discovery.

      2. The Java discovery.

      3. The South Africa discovery.

    B. Characteristics and behavior of the Peking period people (show encyclopedia map and magazine pictures).

(Chronological
method)
(Visualization)

      1. They had apelike ridged foreheads and receding chins.

      2. They had 3/4 of modern human's brain capacity.

      3. They made fire and primitive weapons from deer antlers.

  II. Neanderthal person lived 125,000 to 25,000 years B.C.

    A. Archaeological discoveries of the Neanderthal period.

      1. Neanderthal, Germany, was the site of the first discovery.

      2. The Rhodesia discovery.

      3. The Gibraltar discovery.

      4. The Monte Cicero, Italy, discovery.

B. Characteristics and behavior of the Neanderthal people (pictures).

1. They were 5 feet tall with heavy, thick necks.

(Visualization)
2. They had low foreheads, but no ridges.

3. They buried their dead.

4. Scraping tools were found, but no needles or awls were used.

III. Cro-Magnon person lived 25,000 to 8,000 years B.C.

A. Archaeological discoveries of the Cro-Magnon period.

1. The Dordogne, France, discovery.

2. The Moravia, Czechoslovakia, discovery.

3. The Folsom, New Mexico, discovery.

B. Characteristics and behavior of the Cro-Magnon people (pictures).

1. They were nearly 6 feet tall.

2. High forehead, wide cheekbones, big nose and chin were common.

3. Needles and awls were used.

(Visualization)
4. They liked ornaments (carved bone, etc.).

5. They did wall cave paintings of animals.

CONCLUSION

(Transition:
Which cave
people do you
think are your
ancestors?)
I. Three distinctly different cave people walked the earth between 6 million and 8,000 years B.C.

A. The Peking people.

B. The Neanderthal people.

C. The Cro-Magnon people.

(Review)
(Reinforcement)
II. Twentieth-century humankind appears to have changed, but there is much we don't know. Old discoveries are being challenged and refined; new discoveries are still being made.

BIBLIOGRAPHY (SOURCES)

Dr. Leonard Moss, Professor of Anthropology, *Lecture* and *Interview.*

Timothy Severin, *Vanishing Primitive Man* (New York: McGraw-Hill, 1990).

Richard Roe (Publisher), *Anthropology Today* (Del Mar, Calif.: Communication Research Machines, Inc., 1991).

Richard E. Leaky and Roger Lewin, *Origins Reconsidered: In Search of What Makes Us Human* (New York: Doubleday, 1992).

E. Culotta, "Pulling Neandertals Back into Our Family Tree," *Science,* April 19, 1991; E. Delson, ed., *Ancestors* (1985); C. Stringer and C. Gamble, *In Search of the Neanderthals* (New York: Thames and Hudson, 1993); E. Trinkaus, *The Neanderthals and The Slanidar Neanderthals* (New York: Alfred A. Knopf, Inc., 1994).

Author's Comment

Before you speak, check the latest news! As Mark Scott was rehearsing his speech, the news carried a new "find" by anthropologist Susan Antone suggesting that all three cave people may have lived at the same time. More research and rewrite may be in order.

THE SPEAKING OUTLINE

This abridged version of your complete outline functions to help you remember your message and smooth out your delivery. It represents your notes to yourself on how to proceed. It allows for extemporaneous delivery, that is, the ideas flow smoothly but you still have freedom to adapt your language as you speak. Some speakers put the speaker's outline on index cards.

General Rules

Keep it brief. The idea is to keep you from being too dependent on your notes.

Double- or triple-space your entries. This allows you to follow your notes more easily and avoid losing your place. It also allows you room for last-minute additions and notes to yourself (but don't clutter it).

Use phrases and key words unless you have a complex, critical idea that must be stated precisely. In that case write it out as a complete sentence.

Write out complex statistics or long quotations. Either put them on index cards or frame them as cards in your speaker's outline.

Use personal cues for memory joggers and for visual aids. Use a different color type or ink for these.

Model Speaking Outline

Here is Mark Scott's speaking outline based on his complete outline. Note how it uses the same symbolization and subordination (see pages 163–164).

MODEL SPEAKING OUTLINE

CAVE PEOPLE

INTRODUCTION

I. Dinosaurs, Alley-Oop, the Flintstones, and B.C.

use vu-graph slide #1

(Impossible!)

II. Overview: Peking Neanderthal, Cro-Magnon

BODY

I. Peking "Man" (6,000,000–125,000 B.C.)
  A. Archaeological discoveries
  B. How he looked and acted

use world map here "Dig sites"

use vu-graph slide #2

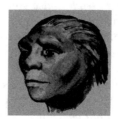

II. Neanderthal people (125,000–25,000 B.C.)
  A. Same as A, B above
  B.

use vu-graph slide #3

III. Cro-Magnon people (25,000–8,000 B.C.)
    A. Same as A, B above
    B.

CONCLUSION
    I. Review three different types.

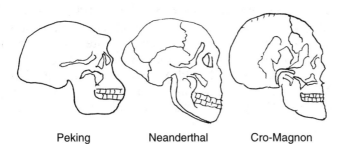

Peking   Neanderthal   Cro-Magnon

    II. This is not the final proof of evolution, but clearly twentieth-century humankind is different and has changed.

EXEMPLAR: OUTLINE DEVELOPMENT

All classroom speeches aren't as academic as Mark Scott's "Cave People" speech on prehistoric humans. Robert, a student at Wayne State University, gave a perfectly delightful speech on the problems and theories associated with being left-handed. It was entertaining as well as informative. Here is how the outlines developed.

ROUGH OUTLINE

Topic: Left-handedness
General Purpose: To inform
Specific Purpose: To inform the class about handedness theories and problems.
Central Idea: Lefties have problems, but society is trying to help.

INTRODUCTION
Humor.
Overview.

BODY
I. Theories of why.
II. Advantages/disadvantages.
III. How many?
IV. Who are they?
V. Help for lefties.

CONCLUSION
Things are improving.
Humor.

After research into some famous left-handers and theories of cerebral dominance, Robert decided to concentrate on problems and what's being done about them. Interviews at a sporting goods store and at the music department were most helpful. He decided that two of his main points could be combined (who and why), one should be divided (advantages/disadvantages), and that the order should be changed from *topical* to more of a *difficulty* order. He sharpened the purpose and central idea and came up with a great title.

COMPLETE OUTLINE

Topic: Left-handedness, "The Left Wing"
General Purpose: To inform
Specific Purpose: To inform the audience about handedness: problems, solutions, theories.
Central Idea: Left-handed people are normal with special problems that society is helping to solve.

THE LEFT WING

INTRODUCTION
I. Left-handed luminaries include:
A. Oprah Winfrey, left-hander of the year.
B. Bill Clinton, top left-hander in politics.

(Attention)　　　**C.** Alan Thicke, top left-handed male entertainer.

　　　　　　　　D. Phil Collins, tops in the music category.

　　　　　　　　E. Even Michelangelo and Leonardo da Vinci.

　　　II. Are you one of those people who have been described as temperamental, unstable, unintelligent, pugnacious, or, in a word, left-handed? Like me!

　　III. Even if you are not, you should know some facts about this sometimes persecuted group.

(Overview)　　　**A.** Their number and famous left-handed people.

　　　　　　　　B. Their advantages and disadvantages.

　　　　　　　　C. Assistance given to lefties.

　　　　　　　　D. Theories as to why they are left-handed.

BODY

(Information)　　**I.** Who are the southpaws?

　　　　　　　　A. Number of them.

　　　　　　　　　　1. 1/4 North Americans originally left-handed.

　　　　　　　　　　2. Schools report an 8% increase.

　　　　　　　　B. Some are famous people.

　　　　　　　　　　1. Present-day lefties.

　　　　　　　　　　2. Historic lefties.

　　　II. Advantages of being left-handed.

　　　　　　　　A. Mirror-writing is easy.

　　　　　　　　B. Sports, in most cases.

　　III. Disadvantages of being left-handed.

　　　　　　　　A. Eating can be embarrassing.

　　　　　　　　B. Musical instruments are mostly right-handed.

　　　　　　　　C. Knitting is difficult.

　　　　　　　　D. Office machines are programmed for righties.

(Visualization)　**IV.** Help for left-handers is on the way.

　　　　　　　　A. The Association for the Protection of Rights of Left-Handers (APRLH).

　　　　　　　　　　1. Oaths for fun and fellowship.

　　　　　　　　　　2. Meetings for some serious issues.

　　　　　　　　　　3. The *Lefthander Magazine*.

　　　　　　　　B. Manufactured goods for lefties are a reality.

　　　　　　　　　　1. Golf clubs.

　　　　　　　　　　2. Musical instruments.

　　　　　　　　　　3. Reversed turnstiles.

　　　V. Theories concerning southpaws are inconclusive.

(Information)　　　**A.** Cerebral dominance theory explanation.

　　　　　　　　B. Heredity theory explanation.

      C. Learning theory explanation.

         1. Surveys.

         2. Tests.

CONCLUSION

  I. If you are left-handed, be comforted in that:

    A. Though your numbers are small, you are not inferior.

(Review)   **B.** Your disadvantages are being reduced.

    C. Society is trying to help.

    D. The theories make you more interesting.

  II. You "righties" should now have a right attitude about the left wing.

  III. Now we know what it is like for a "leftie" to live in a right-handed world.

BIBLIOGRAPHY (SOURCES)

Detroit Free Press, August 3, 1992.

Annual Report, Milwaukee School System, 1992.

Interview, Acme Campus Sporting Goods.

Interview, Harold Arnoldi, Director, Wayne State University School of Music.

Lefthander Magazine, December 1987.

Insight, April 29, 1991.

MODEL SPEAKING OUTLINE

THE LEFT WING

INTRODUCTION

  I. Luminaries: Oprah Winfrey; President Clinton; Alan Thicke; Phil Collins; Michelangelo; Leonardo da Vinci.

  II. Are you called temperamental, unstable, pugnacious? You must be left-handed like me!

  III. Overview of five main points.

BODY

  I. Statistics on southpaws.
(Also list some famous lefties.)

  II. Advantages.

    A. Sports.

    B. Mirror-writing. (*Demonstrate*) *Bring a mirror!*

III. Disadvantages.

    A. Eating. (*Demonstrate*)

    B. Music.

    C. Knitting.

    D. Office machines.

IV. Help is on the way.

    A. APRLH

    B. Manufactured goods. (*Show a left-handed golf club.*)

    C. *Lefthander Magazine* awards.

V. Theories.

    A. Cerebral dominance.

    B. Heredity.

    C. Learned.

CONCLUSION

    I. Review.

    II. You "righties" should now have a right attitude about the left wing.

Robert could also have used the six numbered cards he had prepared. The visual aids served as his memory jogger for the statistics on lefties, the list of famous left-handed people, and the details of the cerebral dominance theory. The cards are shown on pages 171–173.

BODY   2

I. Statistics   USE VISUAL AID (STATS)

II. Advantages
     sports – 1st base, pitch, etc.

     Mirror writing Demonstrate

     (Bring a mirror)

III Disadvantages   3

     Eating (demonstrate)

     Music   role-play?

     Knitting

     Office machinery

IV Help on the way   4

     Assoc. to protect Left-handers

     New products
       – golf clubs (show one)
       – fish reels
       – instruments

     Left-handers awards

I. Theories   5

     A. Cerebral dominance
         USE VISUAL AID (BRAIN)

     B. Heredity

     C. Learning

   (What I think — if time permits)

CONCLUSION   6

I. Review — see card #1
        and stat. slide

II. " You righties should have a
     right attitude about the

   LEFT WING "

Summary

An outline is to a speech what a blueprint is to a house. Start with the main points in the body of the speech, review your research, and refine your most important ideas or points. Prepare a rough draft of your specific purpose, central idea, and main points. This becomes your brief topical outline. A complete outline and a speaking outline will follow.

Basic outlining principles include: (1) symbolization, (2) subordination, (3) simplicity, (4) discreteness, (5) coordination, and (6) progression.

All major- and first-level subpoints are written out as complete sentences in the complete outline. It is the one that will be graded.

The speaking outline is an abridged version of your complete outline. It represents your notes to yourself on how to proceed and allows for extemporaneous delivery. Some speakers put their speaker's outlines on index cards. Use phrases and key words; keep it brief, but write out quotes and statistics. Use personal cues for audiovisual aids and to jog your memory. Use the model outlines in the chapter as guides for your own outline.

Learning Projects

1. Outline the main points and first-level subpoints (A, B, etc.) in the speech "How to Write a Résumé." (Chapter 6, pp. 152–153) Use complete sentences.

    I. _____

        A. _____

        B. _____

    II. _____

2. Make brief, one-page outlines (Introduction, Body, Conclusion) of your classmates' speeches. Key-word the main points and the specific purpose. Give these to your instructor, who will feed them back to the speakers as a means of giving them insight into their organizational effectiveness.

3. Discuss the differences between a rough outline and complete and speaking outlines.

4. Discuss the symbolization errors in the examples in the chapter (pp. 160–161) and explain specifically what is wrong with them.

8

DELIVERING
THE SPEECH

CHAPTER OUTLINE

EFFECTIVE DELIVERY

Your first objective is not to be dull! When told that Calvin Coolidge, the dullest speaker on record, had died, satirical author Dorothy Parker responded, "How could they tell?" In this chapter we are interested in (1) *types* or *ways* of effectively delivering a speech, and (2) the nonverbal signals, especially bodily action and voice, that accompany your message.

When combined with the verbal message, nonverbal signals are quite effective in conveying ideas, particularly emotional concepts such as love and hate. People display quite different nonverbal responses to various emotional situations. Research suggests that some people are more sensitive than others to nonverbal signals and also that young people are less sensitive to nonverbal signals than are older people. No wonder that in some speeches our voices and our actions speak so loudly that our words are often unheard or are not very persuasive.

Speakers should bear in mind that our nonverbal behavior may be unintentionally contrary to our verbal message. We express attitudes through body action, voice and articulation patterns, the objects we wear or own, our use of time and space, as well as our language and verbal messages.[1] There is even good evidence that people rely primarily on nonverbal cues to judge truthfulness.[2]

The *context* and *situation* can radically change the meaning of our nonverbals. One student arrived in class wearing a trenchcoat over a leotard. Lots of nonverbals here, none appropriate for speechmaking, one might presume, but she was giving a demonstration speech on aerobics (and a good one), and her leotard took on a whole different meaning and was suddenly appropriate.

Many characteristics are associated with effective delivery and some are associated with ineffective, even annoying, delivery. Some of the more relevant, positive characteristics include:

1. A well-paced, moving delivery.
2. An alertness of body and mind that indicates enthusiasm.
3. Controlled, yet flexible, body activity that reinforces meaning.
4. A sense of communication indicated by some direct eye contact.
5. A clear, pleasant, conversational voice and articulation.

Various speech studies undertaken to determine what specific aspects of delivery are unpleasant, ineffective, or annoying to audiences help us recognize effective delivery. Those aspects considered annoying include:

1. Stiff body action.
2. Refusal to look at the audience.
3. Excessive nervousness or fidgeting.
4. Monotonous, stiff reading or delivery from a manuscript.

5. Weak, unclear, or monotonous voice.

6. Mumbling of words.

7. Too many mispronunciations and grammatical mistakes.

Gerald Ford was not a gifted speaker but better than silent Cal because of the cues written in the margin of his notes: "Smile," "Pause," "Move." Perennial presidential candidate Pat Paulsen mused, "Whenever I heard Gerald Ford speak on TV, I thought I had lost the color on my set."

It has been observed that President Clinton's nonverbals helped him make "contact" with his audiences and that Senator Dole's did not.

Some habits thought to adversely affect specific perceptions of authoritativeness and sociability include:

1. Use of hedges such as "sort of" or "kind of."

2. Hesitations such as "um" or "er."

3. Meaningless verbalizations such as "oh well" or "you know."

4. Intensifiers such as "quite," "really," or "very."[3]

Displaying a pseudo sense of humility—"In this person's humble opinion . . ."—can also turn off audiences. Golda Meir put it bluntly: "Don't be humble. You're not that great."

Sometimes the right message or word can change even some of these faults. Listen to Dave Powers, an aide of John F. Kennedy.

> I set it up for him to make a speech to the Gold Star Mothers, and you never in your life heard such a speech. He's hemming and hawing and you'd need a pair of pliers to drag the next sentence out of him. The women are all sitting there, waiting to hear him say something, and very little is coming out. Worse than that, it looks like he never learned how to end a speech. It's going on and on and I'm beginning to perspire.

> All of a sudden he says it. The right words come to him and he says it. He says: "Well, I think I know how you ladies feel. My mother, too, lost a son in the war.". . . They broke into applause; some of them started to cry and the mothers rushed forward to grab his hand and hug him. That was his first campaign, and from that minute onward, you could see the tide turn his way.[4]

Probably the best advice comes from a pro like Gerald Gardner. "Be open and easy; treat your audience like old friends . . . be yourself."[5]

TYPES OF DELIVERY

The four principal ways of delivering a speech are: (1) by reading from a manuscript, (2) by memorization, (3) by impromptu delivery, and (4) by speaking extemporaneously. The subject and the occasion are important factors in determining which one or which combination should be used at a given time.

Reading from a Manuscript

Fortunately, the subjects and occasions that demand this method of delivery and preparation are few, for this is probably the most difficult of all the types of delivery. However, such occasions are increasing in number. An important policy speech by the United States Secretary of State may be dissected word by word by foreign governments; therefore, it calls for maximum accuracy in wording and a minimum of opportunity for angry misstatement.

> Speak when you're angry and you'll make the best speech you'll ever regret.
> *Henry Ward Beecher*

The mass media make further demands on a speaker's flexibility. Very often a copy of the manuscript is distributed before the speech is given, and thus the newspapers can print or quote the speech almost before it has been delivered. If the speaker then deviates from the manuscript, he or she invites trouble and confusion. Certain highly complicated and technical subjects demanding absolute accuracy may call for manuscript reading.

The problems of manuscript reading, even for a classroom speech, are apparent. There is little chance for spontaneity or for instant adaptation of the material to the ever-changing demands of the audience. Except for very exceptional readers, the actual delivery is hamstrung by a lack of eye contact and directness. Your eyes are typically glued to your manuscript, except for furtive glances into outer space, which only cause you to lose your place. This embarrassment may cause you to lose emphasis and vocal variety. For some the word is *dull*.

One of the ironies in speech training is that the beginner, apparently in an effort to avoid the inevitable confrontation with the audience, may use the manuscript as something to hide behind. Doing this only delays self-development, because it usually results in an unsuccessful audience experience, which is extremely frustrating for the beginner.

When preparing a manuscript that is to be read aloud to an audience, you have to make some fundamental stylistic changes in the writing. The language of writers, for example, is typically less direct. They use *a person, people, the reader;* a speaker uses *I, you, they,* and the like. The other differences are not as obvious. Although we extemporize in short, simple sentences, we tend to write in longer, more complex ones. When we are engaged in literary writing (material that will be read silently by the receiver), we have less of a problem with this "longer" style, for the receiver can reread and review. In a speech, however, the necessity for shorter, less complex sentences is critical, as is the use of repetition, restatement, and reinforcement. Remember that the listener, unlike the reader, cannot stop and go back over the material or use a dictionary. The spoken words must be instantly clear to the listener. Therefore, they require more illustrations, examples, analogies, contrasts, and vividness than a written essay does. The secret is to write "out loud."

The delivery of a speech from a manuscript is also somewhat different. Normal eye contact and vocal patterns are often disrupted. The manuscript may be hard to see if the lighting is bad or your vision is otherwise reduced. A fan has been known to distract a speaker. The position of the manuscript also creates problems. You may either hold your manuscript in your hand at about waist level or put it on a lectern. In the first case, you inhibit your hand gestures; in the other, you hide most of your body. Either way, the problem is to let your eyes drop to the paper while keeping your head erect.

Most good manuscript reading requires a generous amount of memorization, but *partial* memorization only—that is, of blocks of language that are held together for you by meaning. This permits you more time to look at the audience. When your memory fails, you refer back to the manuscript for the next memorized language group. The problem is trying to find your place. Marginal notes, underlining, and various markings can help. The only real insurance is a thorough understanding of your message and—practice, practice, practice! To achieve successful oral communication, you must learn to spend considerably more time looking at your audience than at your manuscript.

Problems of voice may also be important to manuscript reading. Most people do not read well without practice and training, and this is why we have courses in interpretative reading. Beginners may singsong (speak in a monotonous rhythm of rising and falling tones), use stress and inflection separate from meaning, or project a sleepy monotone. Varying the rate, loudness, pitch, and quality, along with the careful use of pauses, are essential to manuscript reading. It is most important to join these vocal variations to the pertinent meanings. The secret is to try to develop a wide-ranging eye–voice correspondence.

Memorization

Except among actors, who work hard at sounding spontaneous, there is little justification for a completely memorized speech. The effort required for word-for-word memorization is enormous. The delivery, except by professionals, is typically stilted, overly rhythmical, and impersonal. Moreover, memorization does not offer any easy way to adapt the material to the audience. However, just as they will choose to read from a manuscript, many frightened beginners will undertake the enormous task of memorization. This method can result in panic if their memory fails. There is neither a place to go nor a specific thing to do. Grade schoolers repeating a memorized poem are in far better shape than most speakers, because they have a prompter. Moreover, it is only a poem, not a personal message, that is in danger.

This is not to say that you should not memorize *parts* of your speech. A dramatic introduction, a conclusion that includes poetry, a piece of testimony, and a complicated group of statistics (when visual aids are unavailable or awkward) are all likely passages for memorization.

Impromptu Delivery

An **impromptu** speech is one that is delivered on the spur of the moment, without advance notice or time for detailed preparation. Usually you will not be asked to make an impromptu speech unless it pertains to your special knowledge, experience, or training. If you have such expertise that makes you vulnerable to unexpected requests for a "few words," you had better carry at least a mental outline with you at all times. In this way you reduce the risks of being caught completely off guard.

A student from Kenya once observed that even in the most informal gatherings he was routinely asked to explain something about Kenya and his reaction to America. On these occasions, he eventually found himself in a true speaking situation, as more and more people gathered around and as he did more and more of the talking. To improve these presentations, he prepared several highly adaptable speech outlines, committed the outlines to memory, and then tried to anticipate each situation and group in which he was apt to find himself. He explained that he has become so expert at this that he is now disappointed if he *is not* asked to say a few words. People are amazed at his fluent and well-organized "impromptu" remarks!

> It usually takes me more than three weeks to prepare a good impromptu speech.
>
> *Mark Twain*

Your instructor may give you some experience in impromptu speaking by simply stating two or three speech topics and then telling you to choose one topic, to take a minute to collect your wits, and then to start talking. Here are some general rules that may help if you find yourself in this or any other potentially impromptu situation:

1. *Anticipate the situation.* Try to avoid having to present a true impromptu speech. Figure the odds on your being called, and try to determine on what topic you will be asked to speak.

2. *Relate the topic under consideration to your experience.* You will tend to speak more easily and confidently about something with which you have had specific experience.

3. *When in doubt, summarize.* There may be moments when you lose the thread of what you were saying or where you were going. At this moment, a quick review or summary often restores perspective and allows your mind to get back on the right track.

4. *Be brief!* The less time you speak impromptu, the less chance for you to lose track of what you are saying.

5. *Quit when you are ahead!* All too often we make a good impromptu speech and then, either because we feel we have not said enough or because our momentary success has given us false confidence, we continue to ramble on until we eventually ruin whatever communication we had achieved.

6. *If you really have nothing to say, then don't speak!* Better to be thought a fool than to open your mouth and remove all doubt.

There are some who speak one moment before they think.

Jean de LaBruyere

Extemporaneous Delivery

The ***extemporaneous*** method of speaking involves the preparation of a thorough but flexible outline, the cataloguing of much potentially usable material, and the use of a general outline, which is either memorized or carried by the speaker. The language and wording of the speech are adaptable, as is the use of speech materials and details.

In this method the emphasis is on knowing your subject and knowing your audience. This method typically requires collecting a lot more material than you will need. Thus, if one illustration or piece of evidence does not satisfy your audience, you will immediately be able to select another. If one strategy of organization is unclear, you will have a previously determined alternative to adapt to the audience confusion of the moment.

The chief advantage of extemporaneous preparation and delivery is that they give you *flexibility* and *adaptability.* You are able to respond successfully to the communication problems as they develop. You are thinking on your feet in the best sense of that term. These are the essential qualities of good conversation; they should be present in all good speeches as well. The speaker who seeks to inspire need not sound artificial or pompous. A speaker can be eloquent without sounding like divine certainty. On the other hand, adapting conversational qualities to public speaking does not mean employing a matter-of-fact voice, poor preparation, or careless language. Public speaking is more structured, uses more polished language, and more formal body action and delivery.

A famous speech teacher, James A. Winans, once noted, "It is not true that a public speech to be conversational need sound like conversation. Conventional differences may make it sound very different." We are seeking the best qualities and moods of conversation, not a stylized version of conversation.

An extemporaneous speech is most effective when given from a brief but meaningful outline, which is carried in either your head or your hand and which is supported by thorough preparation. This is the type of preparation and delivery expected of you except in those special exercises your instructor may announce.

THE NATURE OF NONVERBALS

Nonverbals of whatever kind—conscious or unconscious—may be characterized as follows:

1. They always communicate something.
2. They are bound to the situation.
3. They are believed.
4. They are seldom isolated.
5. They affect our relationships.

Figure 8.1

Nonverbals Always Communicate Something

Assuming some kind of human interaction, we cannot *not* behave; and because behavior is nonverbal communication, we *cannot not communicate*. A blank stare communicates something to the audience, even it if is just confusion. This fact is not always appreciated by less sensitive personalities. These behaviors may be conveyed consciously or unconsciously, but one way or another they communicate.

Nonverbals Are Bound to the Situation

The context or situation makes a lot of difference. The baby's smile might indicate pleasure in one situation or gas in another. A thumb in the air might mean A-OK on the launch pad or a request for a ride on the highway. When the context or situation is not considered, nonverbals can be confusing indeed. When it is obvious, our nonverbals are most clear. Is there any doubt about what this listener is expressing in Figure 8.2?

Nonverbals Are Believed

Perhaps nonverbals should not be believed, but this tendency exists. Con men have always taken advantage of this fact. Perhaps nonverbals are harder to fake for most of us, but certainly not for good actors. When what you *say* disagrees with how you *look* or *sound*, people tend to believe the nonverbals—"Trust me; you'll love it! Would I lie?" (Figure 8.3).

Figure 8.2   **Figure 8.3**

Nonverbals Are Seldom Isolated

It is very difficult for most of us to be boiling mad and yet control our actions and voice so that we appear calm. A glisten of perspiration, a faster eye-blink, a slight tremble, a dryness in the voice—these and more give us away. Even when you are laughing on the outside and crying on the inside, the character of your laughter probably gives you away. These other nonverbals tend to be related, consistent, and supportive of one another. When they are not, suspicions about your intent are raised. Even in pictures or audiotapes, nonverbals are difficult to isolate.

Nonverbals Affect Our Relationships

We decide three important things about people largely on the basis of nonverbal communication: (1) personal liking or attraction, (2) evaluation of power relationships, and (3) evaluation of the response we get from others. Let's review each of these as nonverbal codes:

1. Sometimes we feel attracted toward another by nonverbal cues alone. That person seems a "likeable sort," "a good guy," and is easy to be with. That the opposite also happens is all too clear.
2. Power assessment is your evaluation of the other person's status, influence, or clout. Nonverbal cues become important, particularly in the absence of verbal information. Several of these will be discussed shortly.
3. Another nonverbal area is your perception of a responsive listener, a person who can and will appreciate your position or your problem.

BODY ACTION COMMUNICATION (KINESICS)

Unconscious Nonverbal Communication

The way a person walks, sits, or stands at a given moment may demonstrate that person's mood more adequately than his or her words do. When we try to avoid looking awkward, we usually communicate even more awkwardness and look unnatural and ridiculous; in addition, such holding back may lead to poor control of our emotions. Lack of action often makes the message less clear. There is no point in trying to avoid body action; there are many good reasons to try to *understand* it, *control* it, and *use* it.

EMPATHY   If your instructor runs his fingernails sharply across the chalkboard, you probably cringe and grit your teeth. If you've ever huddled in the stands, alternately shivering and cheering as your team made a goal-line stand against the Oakland Raiders or the Miami Dolphins, you can understand empathy. If you've ever seen a youngster take a violent and bruising fall, you probably "felt" the pain as you projected yourself into the youngster's situation. Can you empathize with our speaker in Figure 8.4?

Figure 8.4

AP/Wide World Photos.

This type of projection is the basis of empathy. Empathy includes a muscular reaction; to an extent, an audience imitates the actions of the speaker. When a speaker appears mortally afraid and tense, the audience dies a little. When the speaker acts tired, the audience feels tired or bored. When a person paces the floor like a caged lion, the audience usually tires before the speaker does. You should take the audience into account when considering body action and should attempt to use the kind and amount of action that will help achieve the purpose of your speech.

Figure 8.5

EMOTION   Good actors, dancers, and capable speakers appear to communicate emotions effectively. The actor has the script, the set, other actors, and the stylized conceptions of the audience as aids. If the cause of whatever emotion the actor is portraying is also seen (for example, a gun producing fear), the communication is easier to interpret.

In addition to communicating emotion, you can also drain off pent-up tension or emotion through the use of body action. This is why some speakers pace the floor or fidget constantly. Instead of acting in distracting ways, try to use meaningful body action that will help you control your speech fright at the same time that it helps communicate your message.

In this section we shall discuss the patterns of physical behavior that make up total body action. Although these patterns most often occur at the same time, we are separating them here for the purpose of explanation.

Types of Body Action

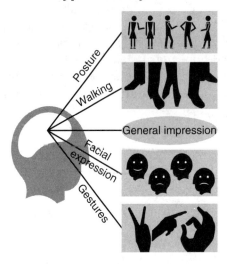

Figure 8.6

GENERAL IMPRESSION   The general impression you create is a combination not only of all the signals that you communicate to your audience, but also of the things in the system over which you may not always have control—for example, the lighting, the building, the platform, and the person who introduces you. However, there are some relatively simple things over which you *do* have some control, things that may contribute much to the general impression you make.

Dress is one of these. In considering what to wear, the watchword is *appropriate.* You don't want to appear conspicuous, yet you do wish to live up to your audience's expectations regarding the dress of its speakers. Your physical and psychological comfort affect your body action. However, there's a lesson to be learned if the audience remembers your leotard instead of your speech.

Another problem is whether to address the audience from a sitting or a standing position. You might feel awkward standing on a platform with only three or four listeners at your feet, and some small, informal audiences may prefer that you sit while speaking to them. However, other small groups are insulted if the speaker sits. The impression they receive, apparently, is that they are not considered important enough for a stand-up speech. Your decision depends a lot upon how well you know the group and how well they know you. As a general rule there is less risk in standing, even before a very small group. If the audience appears uncomfortable, it is much easier to sit down after a speech has started than to stand up. In an Effective Supervision course in which eight to twelve students rated the teachers, the evaluations of the instructors favored those who stood while speaking. Whether you're sitting, standing, or walking, the way you do it is revealing. It can draw people to you or drive them away.

POSTURE   Posture is an important part of the general impression you make. It affects the empathy of the audience and what they conclude from your signals. The way you carry yourself tends to show whether or not you have confidence in yourself. Whether you slouch and cower or whether you stand with military bearing affects your outlook and sense of power and your control over yourself. A slouching posture can tire the audience as quickly as it can the speaker. (See Figure 8.7.)

In general, good posture involves the distribution of your body weight in a comfortable and poised way consistent with the impression you wish to make as a speaker. You should be erect without looking stiff, comfortable without appearing limp. Your bearing should be alert, self-possessed, and communicative. Good posture and poise reflect a kind of cool unconcern. The great danger, as with all stylized body action, is appearing artificial, overly noticeable, or out of place.

A satisfactory standing position should be a balanced one; it should allow you to recover quickly if you were suddenly pushed. Your feet should be fairly close together, one foot slightly ahead of the other. Keep your hips straight, shoulders back, and chin in. Try to find a poised, natural speaking stance. There is not one way that is right for every speech. The stance you finally select will have to be modified to meet changing speech circumstances, such as the size and nature of the audience, the formality of the occasion, and so on.

Figure 8.7 *"What am I doing wrong?* Taking refuge behind the lectern, looking scared to death, shuffling pages, and reading my speech. Relax. Come out in the open, gesture, *talk* to your audience!"

© *International Paper Company*

WALKING   The "femme fatale" actress has a walk that clearly communicates her role; the sneaky villain also has a stylized walk; the child about to be scolded walks quite differently from the child going to the movies.

Walking may serve as a form of physical punctuation. Transitions and pauses may be strengthened by a few steps to the side, emphasis by a step forward. Like the actor, the speaker wishes to appear natural, not awkward. If your walking is ungraceful or mechanical, it will distract rather than accomplish its intended purpose; if it is random, it will detract from the general purpose of your speech. In short, the way you walk tells a lot about you. It can communicate energy, enthusiasm, sloppiness, indifference, fatigue, or any number of other things.

Walking also has empathic value; it can offer physical relief to a suffering audience. On the other hand, too much walking can wear an audience out. The right amount of planned, purposeful walking is an outlet for muscular tension for both the speaker and the audience.

The question of the desirable amount and kind of walking requires the same considerations that apply to all body action: the subject, the speaker, the size of the audience, the formality of the occasion, and so on. In general, the more formal the speech, the less pronounced your walking should be; the larger the audience, the more definite your steps should be. Remember also that walking, like all body action, begins before you actually start to speak. When you leave your chair to approach the speaker's stand, your communication has already begun. You are not finished until you have walked off the platform.

Figure 8.8

FACIAL EXPRESSION Two scholars who have spent a lifetime studying the recognition of emotions from facial expressions insist that there are *universal facial expressions* of emotions. Ekman and Friesen identify them as *happiness, sadness, surprise, fear, anger,* and *disgust.*[6] Others have argued that these expressions should be regarded as cultural artifacts rather than as universals,[7] or that *context* is the overriding variable.[8]

We all have heard of "the face that launched a thousand ships" and been told that "the eyes are the mirror of the soul." The problem is that the speaker may unintentionally use stylized facial expressions unsuitable to the subject. One speech student had a temporary facial disorder that caused one eye to wink uncontrollably about every sixty seconds. Even after the class discovered the real cause of the winking, the signal confusion remained alarming. Once the student learned to blink both eyes, most of the problem was solved. Closing one eye in a wink has a stereotyped meaning. Closing both eyes at the same time in a blink has no stereotyped meaning (unless done in rapid succession) and was, in this case, not confusing or particularly distracting. An emotionally tense person might tighten the jaw and unconsciously take on a crocodile grin. This usually passes as one relaxes, but the first moments of a serious speech by a grinning speaker can be most confusing.

The speaker's eyes, at least for relatively small audiences, are very communicative. Audiences are wary of shifty eyes—"She avoids my eyes" is a frequent classroom criticism. The audience expects to be looked at—not stared at constantly, but looked at occasionally. Directness of delivery is defined by many as being based on eye contact.

The lessons are: (1) avoid unintentional or inappropriate facial stereotypes; (2) make eye contact with the audience; and (3) free your natural and spontaneous facial expressions so that they strengthen your message.

GESTURES U.S. speech education in the nineteenth century suffered from a highly mechanical approach. It was a period of flamboyant language and highly stylized gestures. Delsarte devised a system of gesturing during this time that contained some eighty-one gestures for practically all parts of the body, including specific ones for the nose, eyebrows, and feet. In reaction against this movement, the famous School of Expression of S. S. Curry was born. This view taught that "every action of face or hand . . . is simply an outward effect of an inward condition. Any motion or tone that is otherwise is not expression." In other words, speakers should be so involved in the subject that their expression is always dynamic and spontaneous.

Reinforcing Gestures.   It seems natural to clench our fist or perhaps even pound the lectern when trying to communicate a strong feeling. Such actions emphasize our words. In disagreeing verbally we might routinely turn our palms down or out. In appealing we might naturally turn our palms up or in. These types of gestures reinforce through *emphasis*. Other gestures reinforce through *suggestion*. In communicating a scolding attitude toward the other political party, we might shake a finger in much the same stereotyped way that a scolding parent does. Speakers may emphasize a separation of points by using first one hand ("On the one hand it can be said . . .") and then the other. Or we might only use one hand, suggesting several categories by slicing the air with a vertical palm and moving our hand on a level plane from left to right. No two persons use these reinforcing gestures exactly alike, but the stereotype is usually recognized. These also are called **emblems.** They usually are translated rather directly, as with the hitchhike or A-OK sign.

Descriptive Gestures.   When you are asked to describe the size or shape of something, it is natural to use your hands to indicate the dimensions. If you could not use your hands, it would be difficult to describe a circular staircase to a person who had never seen one. All descriptive gestures are also partly reinforcing. If you really didn't like circular staircases, you might also subconsciously communicate a message of approval or disapproval. Ekman and Friesen refer to these gestures as **illustrators.** Sometimes gestures are part emblem and part illustrator, as shown in Figure 8.9.

Figure 8.9

Detroit News *photos by Edwin C. Lombardo.*

Standards of Good Body Action

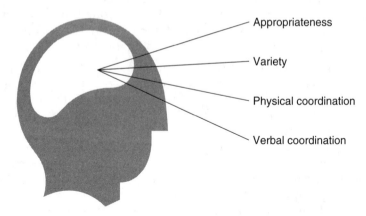

- Appropriateness
- Variety
- Physical coordination
- Verbal coordination

Figure 8.10

APPROPRIATENESS   Your subject, the context, and the size and nature of your audience determine what kind of body action is appropriate. A very formal subject, particularly when combined with a formal occasion and a small, older audience, generally calls for poised but relatively restricted body action. Grand sweeps of the arms and other showy movements would be out of place. Other things being equal, the larger the audience, the more unrestricted your body action may be. Cross-cultural problems abound when it comes to appropriate body actions and gestures.

- The thumbs-up gesture is offensive to Arabs.
- The left-hand gesture is considered unclean in many cultures.
- Waving goodbye is a good way to summon a Filipino.

Figure 8.11

Most speakers use too little body action, whatever the speech occasion. When you are finally free of your inhibitions, remember to match your body actions with the expectations of your audience.

VARIETY　Any body action, but particularly gestures, should be varied occasionally. Otherwise the routineness of the action may call attention to itself and become a distraction. Speakers who pound the table *every* time they make a point, regardless of its importance, soon lose the reinforcing effect.

All of us tend to repeat our favorite gestures. We must periodically ask ourselves if we are overworking some of them, and if our body action really reflects the message we would like to project. If necessary, your instructor will feed this information back to you so that you can correct such distracting habits.

PHYSICAL COORDINATION　Physical coordination refers to the combination of all parts of your body in expressing yourself. You can appear ridiculous by locking your elbows to your sides and moving only your forearms and hands. A "detachment" such as this makes you appear mechanical. The whole body is always involved in any body action.

VERBAL COORDINATION　By verbal coordination we mean timing your words and actions so as to achieve the greatest reinforcement of your message. This includes rehearsed body action. A lack of verbal coordination can be quite humorous. Try saying "Uncle Sam needs *you,*" but instead of pointing on the word *you,* wait three seconds and then point!

VOICE AND ARTICULATION (PARALANGUAGE)

Can we express emotions through the voice alone? You bet we can. Consider a piercing scream—"Help, murder, rape!" Even without the words we get the emotional message of *fear.* "YUCK, what a gruesome sight," we hear as someone observes the picture in Figure 8.12. *Disgust* is in the voice.

Figure 8.12

Voice and Personality

What do you *hear?* Fear, disgust? The voice clearly expresses emotions. It is so effective at conveying attitudes that often we don't need the language. Tone, pitch, and inflection say it all. As a matter of fact, when the voice contradicts the words—"She said *NO,* but there was *YES* in her voice"—we tend to believe the voice. The voice is thought to be a harder signal to fake yet the old radio actors were great fakers. This suggests that voice has a lot to do with self-presentation, and that you can do something about it. As in pantomime, there are certain long-standing stereotypes that we take for granted in the use of the voice. We recognize certain radio roles as voice stereotypes: the mean character, the hero, the coward, the dunce. The very great danger in using voice stereotypes is that one might take on an artificial voice permanently. Of course, we all occasionally fail to match the voice we "put on" with the situation in which we find ourselves. Listen to yourself on occasion. If you sound "arty" when talking about fertilizer, your voice habits may be altering your personality in ways that will seriously affect your communication.

The voice contributes much to the total communication signal. It may be the single most important code we use. Studies of voice and persuasion indicate the importance and the communication potential of this nonverbal code.[9] There is evidence that one's social status can be determined in large part by the signals we receive from the voice alone, apart from language. There is also evidence that Americans tend to downgrade a person who speaks with a foreign accent.

Variable Characteristics of Voice

You have considerable control over certain characteristics of your voice. You can change your *rate* of speaking; you can adjust your *loudness* almost as you would that of a radio; you can speak at different *pitch* levels; you can alter the overtones or partial tones of your voice, which represent a kind of *quality* control often called *timbre* or *vocal color.* Along with *intonation* (sounding the vowels), these characteristics are the nonverbal signals that help a listener determine the structure and meaning of what you say. They are also known as vocal qualifiers.

RATE   Test passages have been devised for measuring verbal speed in wpm (words per minute). In general, a rate of more than 185 wpm is considered too rapid for a normal public speaking situation, and a rate of less than 140 wpm is considered too slow. A poor speaker is more apt to use short, abrupt speech consistently. Really slow talking, young speakers may injure their impressions of competence.[10] Research also indicates that reasonably fast talkers were usually perceived as competent and socially attractive, particularly if their listeners were also known to have fast rates.[11] Unreasonably fast talkers across all contexts and audiences are another matter.

A further problem associated with verbal rate is that words are not really separately formed units but tend to flow from one sound to another; this affects both articulation and pronunciation. Take the phrase, "Did you eat?" If really speeded up, it becomes "Jeet?" This process is called *assimilation.* The length of sounds or tones is also a factor in verbal rate, as are pauses, phrasing, and general rhythm patterns.

The *duration* of sounds and words normally varies with our moods. We generally use tones of relatively short duration when expressing anger and more prolonged tones for expressing love.

Your use of *pauses* and phrases is a factor in your rate of speaking. The "pregnant pause" is no idle jest; it has much to do with our communication. A phrase is a group of words that forms a thought unit. Pauses occur between words and between phrases, and the number and duration of pauses seriously alter the meaning of what you say. The complexity and nature of your speech material should also affect your decisions regarding the use of phrases and pauses. If you were to use a long pause after a phrase for emphasis, fine, but if the phrase were relatively silly you might appear ridiculous. If you were to use long pauses in a random manner not related to meaning (not an uncommon error), you would then *confuse* your listener. Short pauses generally indicate that there is more to come. If you routinely use a rather intermediate-length pause without consistently relating it to what you are saying, you run the added danger of *monotony,* a tiresome lack of variation.

When we increase our rates in normal conversation, that alone carries a message. In addition, our pitch goes up, articulation suffers, and pauses take on less significance or are lost altogether. It becomes, in large part, a question of self-presentation. If your fast rate is done rhetorically with full awareness of the *relationship* risks, that's one thing. If it's done simply as a bad habit, the risk is that it may be construed by others as compensatory or tactless.

LOUDNESS   Loudness is a measure of the total signal. You may think of loudness generally as volume, but speech science indicates that volume is related so intimately to pitch that the term loudness may be misleading. Your volume is easier to raise as your pitch goes up. Furthermore, it is possible to speak with more force or intensity without altering your volume proportionately.

Extreme loudness has strong *relationship* ramifications for most people. We reserve it for emergencies or issues of great concern—and sometimes for conflicts that "get away from us." As Chief illustrates in Figure 8.13, loudness also expresses emotion.

Figure 8.13

There is another side to this loudness question. Sometimes we speak very softly. Among the psychological reasons for a lack of voice projection is a form of avoidance of the speech situation. People tend to *withdraw* from threatening situations. It is almost as if speaking with a soft, barely heard voice is the next best thing to not being in the situation at all. This may cause an audience to infer a lack of competence.[12]

Your receivers will help you adjust your loudness. Look at them for feedback signs. Are they straining to hear? Are they withdrawing?

Much of what we call *vocal variety* is related to loudness. The force with which you utter certain phrases or words is a form of oral punctuation and can add much to another's understanding of what you say. The manner in which you apply force to what you say is also a factor in vocal variety. An audible whisper can be a powerful nonverbal as well as verbal emphasis in some interactions.

PITCH   We can pretty accurately determine sex and, to a point, age through pitch alone.[13] Normal pitch changes as we move from childhood to adolescence to adulthood, and these pitches are generally recognizable as belonging to the appropriate age groups.

Interestingly, men's voices reach their lowest pitch during middle age and then rise slightly with age. It appears that the same may not be true of women; pitch remains more constant during their adult years.

A drop in pitch at the end of a statement frequently indicates that a person is ready to yield the floor. If you are maintaining the floor in part through rapid rate, your pitch rises. When we speak, we use a variety of pitches which are normally distributed in terms of amount of usage. If we were to plot the number of occurrences of the different pitches we use, we would find a central pitch around which the others vary in relatively predictable amounts.

For most people, optimum pitch should be the habitual or central pitch. Often, our optimum pitch is found a little below the habitual or normally used pitch because of tensions that restrict the vocal apparatus.

QUALITY   Voice quality is a product of modification and modulation of the vocal-cord tone by the resonators. It is that attribute of tone and sound waves that enables us to distinguish between two sounds that are alike in pitch, duration, and loudness.

Other things being equal, we can easily distinguish the overly nasal, breathy, or harsh voice. In addition, we are able to make nonverbal distinctions of a much more subtle nature. For example, we recognize the voice of a person who is sincerely touched by a tribute or the voice of a person who is suppressing anger. Emotional moods affect voice quality and may have a profound effect upon emphasis and meaning. In this context, voice quality is often referred to as *timbre*.

Voice quality is considered faulty when an individual's voice contains consistent deviations that detract from the message or its meaning. Certain organic disorders, such as a cleft palate or nasal obstructions, can cause defects in voice quality. Emotional moods may also result in temporary deviations in voice quality. In addition, voice quality may be affected by the strictly temporary physical problems caused by head colds, sore throats, and the like.

An expert in voice and diction training once said, "Bluntly stated, one may have a dull, uninteresting, or unpleasant voice because his voice is defective or improperly used; but he may also have such a voice because he is a dull, uninteresting, or unpleasant person." Vocal training, like all speech training, cannot take place in a vacuum; rather it is intimately related to the whole personality. Just as personality affects voice, voice improvement may affect personality, or at least others' perceptions of one's personality.

Some have argued that President Clinton had an advantage over Senator Dole on voice alone (when the President didn't lose his voice). One critic commented that no matter what Bob Dole said, it always sounded like a raucous, "Get off my grass." Good evidence indicates that when persuasion and social goals are in jeopardy, one's quality of speech rate and vocal intensity tend to be the first to suffer.[14]

Articulation Control

The word ***articulation*** refers in general to a flexible fitting of things together. For example, the bones and cartilages in your elbow are said to articulate. The word is well suited to the action of the speech organs as they *interact* with one another and help join the various sound units into accepted patterns that we call speech.

COMMON ARTICULATORY FAULTS   Some of the more common mechanical causes of careless articulation are (1) locked jaw, (2) slack lips, and (3) muffled mouth.

The ***locked jaw*** problem is caused by a failure to open the mouth wide enough. The jaw is tight and seems locked in position. The speaker talks through his or her teeth and nose because the sound has to escape somehow. Projection is reduced; resonance is increased; vowel quality in particular is injured. This problem may be caused in part by tension and speech fright, but in any case the remedy is the same—unlock your jaw and open your mouth!

In the case of ***slack lips*** the lips are so loose that they do not adequately shape the mouth opening for proper vowel production or for proper articulation of the lip consonants (*p, b, m, w, f,* and *v*). The rule is simple: allow your lips to perform their necessary functions. In addition, an inability to see the speaker's lips move is frustrating to many listeners. Unless you are a ventriloquist, free your lips. Articulation, of course, can also suffer from very tight or tense lips.

The ***muffled mouth*** problem is caused principally by weak or slow tongue activity. Because the tongue is your most important organ of articulation, you may ruin a large part of your speech if you are guilty of this fault. The production of the fine shades of tone that distinguish the vowels from one another is endangered by a muffled mouth, since the tongue position decides in large part the shape and size of the oral cavity. Many consonants also depend upon vigorous and precise tongue action. A *th* sound (*th*ese) easily becomes a *d* sound (*d*ese) if the tongue is lazy and does not move forward far enough to articulate with the teeth. Other consonants, such as *d, l, r,* and *s,* also call for vigorous and specific tongue action. Vigorous and firm articulation of your tongue with your teeth is your best safeguard against muffled quality.

Pronunciation

Pronunciation is the act of expressing the sounds and accents of words so that they conform to accepted standards. In addition to aiding understanding, appropriate pronunciation influences how an audience judges a speaker. Adapting to the varying standards and groups to which you belong again points out the value of using two dialects. In old Milwaukee the word *theater* was typically pronounced "the-*ay*-ter," a compromised carryover from the German pronunciation of "das Theater" (tay-*ah*-ter). In Detroit we hear "thee-*uh*-ter." Some localities may say "drammer" for "drama."

The extremely valuable dictionary is sometimes ambiguous on some pronunciations because there are three generally accepted dialects in the United States (*eastern, southern,* and *standard American*). The most widespread dialect is standard American, and our dictionaries and national mass media are geared to this dialect. Sometimes the use of a second dialect has social and practical advantages.

The problem of showing on paper the desired or different pronunciations of a word is awkward at best. One way is to agree upon and memorize a common code of symbols based strictly upon sound, which is how the International Phonetic Alphabet was born. It has one symbol for every different sound in the language. The news services use a system of *respelling* similar to what was used for the word *theater* two paragraphs above. Dictionaries use *diacritical marks* and relatively stable words as bases of pronunciation. Accent or stress is indicated as primary (´) or secondary (ˌ). A guide to pronunciation and to the diacritical system used in dictionaries is carefully explained in the introduction to any good dictionary and is well worth reading. (See Table 8.1.)

Table 8.1 Examples of Pronouncing Systems

WORD	DIACRITICAL SYSTEM	INTERNATIONAL PHONETIC SYSTEM	RESPELLING SYSTEM
chaotic	/kā-ät-ik/	[keˊatik]	kay-otic
theater	/ˊthē-ət-ər/	[ˊθiətɚ]	thee-uh-ter
nativity	/nə-ˊtiv-ət-ē/	[neˊtivati]	nay-tiv-ity

Some of the more common pronunciation errors are a result of improper stress, errors in spelling-phonetics (pronouncing words as they are spelled), sound substitutions, additions, reversals, and subtractions.

RELATED NONVERBAL BEHAVIORS

Object Language (Clothes and Things)

In one clever study a young woman was dressed and made up attractively for one group of receivers and was then dressed and made up to look unattractive to a similar audience. The young woman was judged to be more believable and was generally found to be more persuasive and more desirable when presented attractively.[15]

Note in Figure 8.14 how meanings become confused when clothes seem out of line with their historical period. It helps if you know that Steve Allen is promoting the classics.

Figure 8.14

© 1981 International Paper Company.

The "times" and context make a difference; sometimes casual dress works as well as more formal attire. At least it did in one study of student perceptions of their instructors.[16] Of course, if you're the only person without a coat at a formal party, you may not come off too well.

One circuit judge was so annoyed with a man who showed up for a court date wearing four gold chains, a gold charm, and six gold rings that he sentenced him to six months on an electronic tether. "It offended me, wearing all of that jewelry," said the judge.

We cannot change everything about our physical appearance through clothing, grooming, and "things" that we put on, hang on, glue on, tie on, or splash on (rings, wigs, eyeglasses, flowers, lipstick, aftershaves). We can do a lot, but it is sometimes a short way from appropriate to inappropriate.

Right or wrong, many stereotypes are associated with clothes and things.

Research helps us define even these. People who wear bizarre clothes are considered more radical and activist. People who wear more conventional dress are associated with everyday jobs and "traditional fun."[17] The problem is in knowing what kind of clothes and things are conventional, in style, or expected of us. Not having this knowledge is a potential problem of *all* communication, whether nonverbal or verbal. The nonverbals of clothes and things make a big difference in the way we are seen totally—that is, socially, vocationally, sexually, and so on. The key word is *appropriate*. We usually do not wish to stand out in a crowd, yet we want to be fashionable and appropriate to what is expected of us at any given time or in any particular situation.

Space and Distance (Proxemics)

Audience arrangement—the physical setting, seating, and so on as discussed in Chapter 4, "Audience Considerations"—are a large part of proxemics. So too is our vocal behavior. We use our voices differently according to distance, message, and mood. Figure 8.15 depicts various speech situations a person might encounter with a description of appropriate volume and style.

Time (Chronemics)

Time is another element over which you have some control. Seldom are you in trouble for being early, but occasionally you may get in trouble for being late!

One famous American general who had risen from the ranks claimed that one of the secrets of his success was always being fifteen minutes early for appointments. Almost every interview form includes an evaluation of the subject's dependability, which often translates into his or her attitude toward being on time. Our culture tends to stress promptness. Television viewers com-

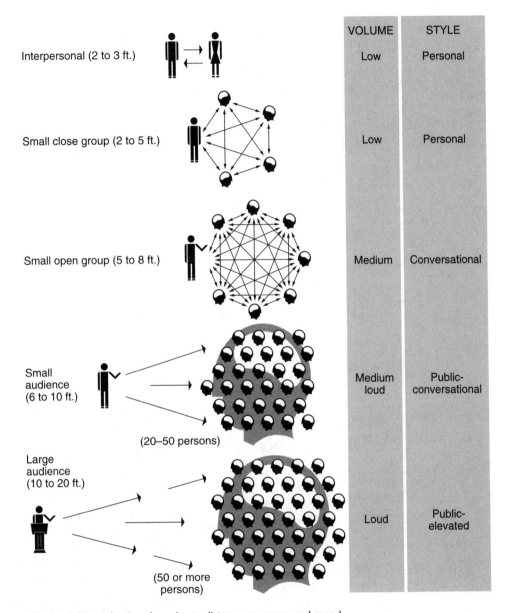

Figure 8.15 Adapting the voice to distance, message, and mood.
© *Raymond S. Ross*

plain by the thousands when a scheduled program is delayed by a news special or a sports event that runs into overtime.

Lateness suggests low regard for the sender, the situation, or the message. We can often save strained relations by giving good reason when we are
late. Knowing when to stop talking is also a *time* consideration (Figure 8.16).

" WELL , I SEE MY TIME IS UP. "

Figure 8.16

Reprinted from the Saturday Evening Post © *The Curtis Publishing Company. Used by permission of Joe Zeis.*

Summary

A well-paced, moving delivery, maintenance of eye contact, and a clear, pleasant, well-articulated voice are associated with effective speaking.

The four principal ways of delivering a speech are: (1) by reading from a manuscript, (2) by memorization, (3) by impromptu delivery, and (4) by speaking extemporaneously.

Our nonverbals may be conscious or unconscious and have five important characteristics: (1) they always communicate something, (2) they are bound to the situation, (3) they are believed, (4) they are seldom isolated, and (5) they affect our relationships.

We decide three important things about people largely on the basis of nonverbal communication: (1) personal liking or attraction, (2) evaluation of power relationships, and (3) the feelings of responsiveness we get from them.

Much unconscious body action accompanies most speeches. A lack of action often makes your message less clear. There is therefore no point in trying to restrain body action, and there are many good reasons for trying to understand it, control it, and use it.

Empathy, the projection of oneself into the situation of another, includes a muscular reaction; the audience imitates, in part, the actions of the speaker. Speakers should adapt their body action to the empathy of the audience. Constant pacing, for example, should be avoided, because it will probably wear out the audience before it does the speaker.

Prolonged restraint on the use of normal body action can result in emotional disintegration. We should use constructive body action to help control our speech fright as well as to communicate our message. The types of body action are: posture, walking, facial expression, and gestures.

Posture is an important part of the general impression you make. It affects the empathy of the audience and what they conclude from your speech. Good posture and poise present a picture of cool unconcern. The great danger is in appearing artificial, overly noticeable, or out of place.

Walking is an important way to express various moods and degrees of emphasis. It serves as a form of physical punctuation for the speaker. Walking also has empathic value; it can offer physical relief to a cramped or suffering audience.

Good facial expression includes (1) the avoidance of unintentional or inappropriate facial stereotypes, (2) eye contact with the audience, and (3) natural and spontaneous expressions that will reinforce your message.

Some gestures are used to emphasize parts of the message. These are reinforcing gestures. Others are used to describe the shape or size of objects and are called descriptive gestures.

In general, speakers should be so involved in their subject and audience that their body action language will be both dynamic and spontaneous. It is evident that we communicate through many learned stereotypes of body action and that a speaker must use these stereotypes.

The standards of good body action are (1) appropriateness, (2) variety, (3) physical coordination, and (4) verbal coordination.

Paralanguage contributes much to your nonverbal signal and thus to your total communication signal; it may be the most important code you use. Voice and articulation are thought to be faulty when they deviate so far from the norm that they call too much attention to themselves. Some common problems of voice are fast rate, wrong pitch, improper level of loudness, and faulty articulation.

There are certain attributes of voice over which you have considerable control. These are rate, loudness, pitch, and quality. Rate is influenced by assimilation, duration, pauses, phrases, and rhythm. Loudness is a product of intensity, volume, and vocal variety. There are central, habitual, and optimum levels of pitch. Your pitch range includes all the pitches you can sing without a complete loss of quality. The most critical problems affecting quality are nasality, breathiness, and harshness.

Articulation is the interacting of the speech organs as they help join the various sound units into accepted patterns that we call speech. Your training of such organs as teeth, tongue, lips, palate, and jaw are of great importance to proper articulation. Some of the more common mechanical faults in articulation are locked jaw, slack lips, and muffled mouth.

Pronunciation is the act of expressing the sounds and accents of words so that they are best adapted to your total communication. There are three general dialects in the United States: eastern, southern, and standard American. Our mass media and dictionaries are geared to the standard American dialect. The problem of showing different pronunciations in print is solved in part through pronouncing systems such as the International Phonetic Association alphabet, the respelling system, and the diacritical-mark system. The last of these is preferred by our dictionaries.

Some of the more common pronunciation errors in the English language are improper stress, errors of spelling-phonetics, sound substitutions, sound additions, sound reversals, and sound subtractions.

Object language uses the influence and display of material things. It includes the clothes you wear, jewelry, cosmetics, and so forth that say something. The key word is appropriate.

Space and distance (proxemics) are the personal space or territory we deem acceptable. Our preferences are culture-bound. Space and distance are closely related to the message, situation, and mood. We adapt our voices in rather set ways to these aspects.

Time as a nonverbal varies with cultures and situations. In our culture we stress promptness. Lateness suggests a low regard for the sender, the situation, or the message.

Learning Projects

1. Write out, word-for-word, a one-minute message in your best oral style. Then rehearse it, visualize it, and prepare to read it from a manuscript.

2. Observe a speaker (live, on radio, or on TV) for at least five minutes. On two separate sheets of paper note the characteristics of good and bad delivery that you observed.

3. Using no props, develop a two-minute pantomime in which you try to communicate an emotion (for instance, fear, love, or rage). Let the class feedback be the measure of your effectiveness.

4. Watch a television show, the first half with only the picture and the second half with only the sound. Describe on one page, for the purpose of class discussion, the effects of having no verbal and no visual signals.

5. Observe the nonverbals of a speaker and be prepared to comment on his or her effectiveness in expressing emotion and conveying attitudes.

6. Observe the nonverbal behavior of a speaker (for example, an instructor, preacher, lecturer, or student) and comment upon his or her effectiveness in terms of appropriateness, variety, verbal coordination, and dynamism.

7. Fill in what these actions indicate to you:

   Slouching _____

   Hands clenched _____

   Unconscious frown _____

   Avoiding your eyes _____

   Key twirling _____

8. Record your voice for five minutes, two and a half while reading and two and a half while speaking impromptu. Complete a written report and inventory of your voice and articulation on the basis of the advice given in this chapter.

9. Record your voice as in Project 8, and then write a report on the personality you think others might associate with it. Record it again, attempting to portray a different personality through voice and articulation alone. Write a brief second report explaining your success or lack of it.

10. Find a piano and, following the advice of this chapter, find your optimum pitch and compare it with your habitual pitch. Report any wide variations to your instructor.

11. Try an experiment in object language. Wear something unusual (for you) and interact with some family or friends. Write a one-page report of what happened to the communication. Discuss it in class.

12. Recall and explain a speech situation in which a person's use of object language, space/distance, or time was seriously out of sync with the intended message.

Notes

1. For a fuller treatment of nonverbal communication see: Judee K. Burgoon, David B. Buller, W. Gill Woodall, *Nonverbal Communication: The Unspoken Dialogue* (New York: Harper & Row, 1989); Mark Knapp, "Nonverbal Communication," in *Human Communication: Theory and Research,* eds., Gordon L. Dahnke and Glen W. Clatterbuck (Belmont, California: Wadsworth, 1990), pp. 50–90.
2. Jerold L. Hale and James B. Stiff, "Nonverbal Primacy in Veracity Judgments," *Communication Reports,* 3, no. 2 (Summer 1990), 75–83.
3. See especially Lawrence A. Hosman, "The Evaluative Consequences of Hedges, Hesitations, and Intensifiers: Powerful and Powerless Speech Styles," *Human Communication Research,* 15, no. 3 (Spring 1989), 383–406.
4. Jim Bishop, *A Day in the Life of President Kennedy* (New York: Random House, 1964), p. 35.
5. Gerald Gardner, *Speech Is Golden* (New York: St. Martin's Press, 1992), p. 107.
6. Paul Ekman and Wallace B. Friesen, *Unmasking the Face,* 2nd ed. (Englewood Cliffs, N.J.: Prentice Hall, 1984), pp. 22–25; also see Paul Ekman, "Facial Expression and Emotion," *American Psychologist* 48, no. 4 (April 1993) 384–92.
7. See Catherine A. Lutz, *Unnatural Emotions: Everyday Sentiments on a Micronesian Atoll and Their Challenge to Western Theory* (Chicago: Chicago University Press, 1988). For more on this debate, see Alan J. Fridlund and Ross Buck, "Reviews and Comments," *Communication Theory,* 5, no. 4 (November 1995), 393–401.
8. Michael T. Motley, "Facial Affect and Verbal Context in Conversation: Facial Expression as Interjection," *Human Communication Research.* 20, no. 1 (September 1993), 3–40.
9. Judee K. Burgoon, Thomas Birk, Michael Pfau, "Nonverbal Behaviors, Persuasion, and Credibility," *Human Communication Research,* 17, no. 1 (Fall 1990), 140–69. See also Stanford Gregory and Stephen Webster, "A Nonverbal Signal in the Voices of Interview Partners Effectively Predicts Communication Accommodation and Social Status Perceptions," *Journal of Personality and Social Psychology,* 70, no. 6 (June 1996), 1231–40.
10. Howard Giles, Karen Henwood, Nikolas Coupland, Jim Harriman, and Justine Coupland, "Language Attitudes and Cognitive Mediation," *Human Communication Research,* 18, no. 4 (June 1992), 500–27.
11. David B. Buller, Beth A. LePoire, R. Kelly Aune, and Sylvie V. Eloy, "Social Perceptions as Mediators of the Effect of Speech Rate Similarity on Compliance," *Human Communication Research,* 19, no. 2 (December 1992), 286–311.
12. Charles E. Kimble and Steven D. Seidel, "Vocal Signs of Confidence," *Journal of Nonverbal Behavior,* 15, no. 2 (Summer 1991), 99–105.

13. N. J. Lass, K. R. Huges, M. D. Bowyer, L. T. Waters, and V. T. Broune, "Speaker Sex Identification from Voiced, Whispered and Filtered Isolated Vowels," *Journal of the Acoustical Society of America,* 59 (1976), 675–78.

14. Charles R. Berger, Steven W. Knowlton, and Matthew E. Abrahams, "The Hierarchy Principle in Strategic Communication," *Communication Theory,* 6, no. 2 (May 1996), 111–42.

15. William I. Gorden, Craig D. Tengler, and Dominic A. Infante, "Women's Clothing Predispositions as Predictors of Dress at Work, Job Satisfaction, and Career Advancement," *Southern Speech Communication Journal,* 47 (Summer 1982), 422–34.

16. T. L. Morris, J. Gorham, S. H. Cohen, and D. Huffman, "Fashion in the Classroom: Effects of Attire on Student Perceptions of Instructors in College Classes,"*Communication Education,* 45, no. 2 (April 1996), 135–48.

17. For more on these matters, see Mark L. Knapp and Judith A. Hall, *Nonverbal Communication in Human Interaction,* 4th ed. (Fort Worth, Texas: HJB College Publishers, 1997).

9

USING AUDIOVISUAL AIDS

CHAPTER OUTLINE

As we learned earlier, audiovisual aids can really enhance feelings of self-confidence, protect your memory, and generally improve the content and quality of your performance.[1] The *thinking about* and *preparation of* the aid may be more valuable than the aid itself. Such research evidence suggests that what follows is well worth your time and application.

CLASSIFYING AUDIOVISUAL AIDS

Functional Levels of Audiovisual Aids

The army sergeant who brings a rifle for each member of his audience and then demonstrates how to fieldstrip a rifle by having each member of the audience *do* it step-by-step with him is providing a hands-on experience. This concrete, excellent teaching method by participation makes the subject clearer and more interesting. When management trainers have students role-play the part of an irate supervisor, a shop steward, or an unhappy foreman, they believe that this contrived situation *involves* the person more actively in the learning process and approaches real-life experience.

This is the *experiential* level of visual aids. There are two other functional levels of visual aids: *representational* and *demonstrational*. You are most apt to use the latter two in your classroom speeches. (See Figure 9.1.)

Figure 9.1   Functional levels of visual aids.

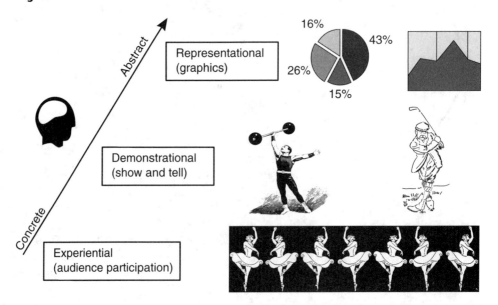

Figure 9.1 describes these levels in terms of function and degree of audience involvement. The most concrete level is learning by *experience,* that is, actually participating in an activity. Our dancers are learning the ballet experientially. Giving everyone a length of rope to learn knot tying is another example. If the speaker is simply *demonstrating* the tying of different knots, the message becomes more abstract but usually less lengthy. If the speaker offers only pictures or diagrams of the knots (you figure out how to tie them), we are at the *representational* or most abstract level. Those that *represent* something, usually through graphics, are the most abstract of the three levels and also the most popular for classroom speeches. Of course, it is possible and, time permitting, often advisable to use two or more of the levels to reinforce one another.

Most visual aids are used to clarify, build interest, reinforce, and sometimes help sell your message. On all counts they are valuable to the speaker, although they are not without some hazards and problems. A knowledge of the types of aid available—and the function for which each kind is best suited—helps one determine what to use in a given situation.

Electronic aids (overhead projectors, slide projectors, audiotapes, etc.) can be used in all three classification levels and will be discussed briefly in a following section.

Selecting the General Level

When making a speech, you are not restricted to just one classification level of visual aids. For instance, the army sergeant had his own rifle for *demonstration* and a large, exploded, *representational* diagram of a rifle for clarity and reinforcement.

Figure 9.2

If your speech topic lends itself to audience participation of even a limited kind, you might choose some part of the *experiential* approach. It often uses too much time in a short classroom speech, but it can work, for example, in a task-comparison speech (pass samples around the classroom) or once again for a knot-tying demonstration (pass out a length of rope for everyone).

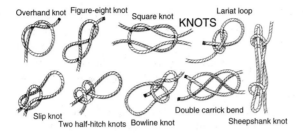

Figure 9.3

Your topic will direct your decision making if you're considering a demonstration speech. Some topics lend themselves to "show and tell" better than others: "Basic Tennis Shots," "Dance Steps," "Folding a Flag," and so on. Others are awkward or impossible because of space, ventilation, or rules. The flag-burning speech in a Pennsylvania classroom survived the legal system, but not the fire marshal.

Figure 9.4

The *representational* type of visual aids—graphs, charts, flat pictures—fit most topical areas but not all. Eulogies, if conducted with great ritual, may call for representational decoration, music, or perhaps a picture, but rarely a diagram on a flip chart.

It is important to consider the occasion as well as the size of your audience and its expectations in planning your audiovisual aids. Physical arrangements play a large part in your decision to use visual aids. A large audience may not be the best for the *experiential* choice. An audience distanced from the podium may not always be conducive to a demonstration. The lighting, wiring, or ceiling height may not permit some electronic visual aids.

Select your general function and level of visual aids in terms of your topic, your specific purpose, the occasion, physical arrangements, and your audience analysis.

REPRESENTATIONAL AIDS

These visual aids *represent* something—a process, some information, an object—in graphic form, occasionally as a three-dimensional model. Standard graphics include charts, tables, maps, drawings, and photographs that are displayed in poster, flip chart, or slide form.

Graphics

Samples of graphics that a speaker might use are shown in Figures 9.5 to 9.11.

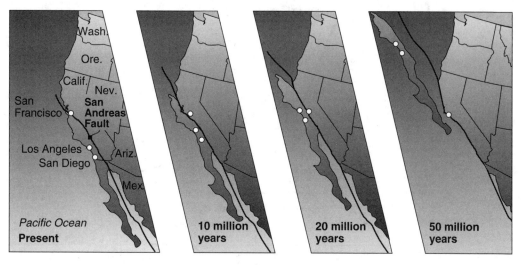

Figure 9.5   Map   Predictions on the earth's shifting crust.

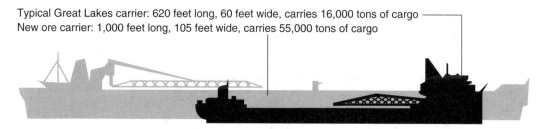

Figure 9.6   Pictogram   Great Lakes ore carriers: the new and the old.

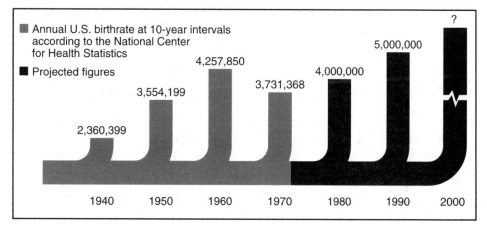

Figure 9.7   A modified bar graph.

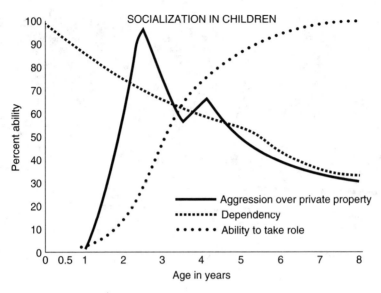

Figure 9.8   A line graph.

From Audio-Visual Products Catalog.

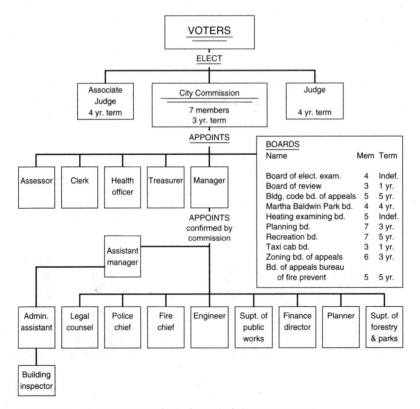

Figure 9.9   An organization chart of a typical city government.

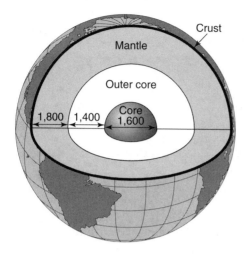

Figure 9.10   An area diagram showing the four zones of the earth's interior.

Special permission granted by My Weekly Reader, *no. 5. Published by Xerox Education Publications. © Xerox Corporation.*

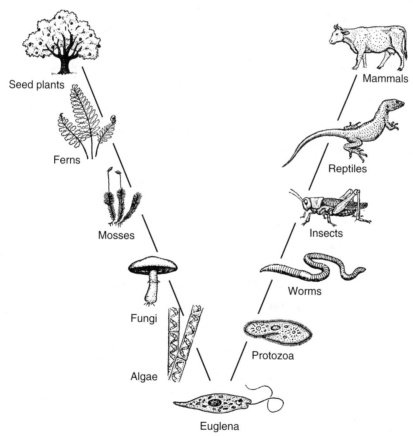

Figure 9.11   A stream or tree chart representing plant life on the left side and animal life on the right.

From Truman J. Moon, Paul B. Mann, and James H. Otto, Modern Biology *(New York: Henry Holt and Company). Reproduced by special permission of Holt, Rinehart & Winston.*

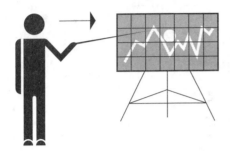

Figure 9.12

Practical Rules

Your instructor may prefer that you not use the chalkboard as a primary aid. Information on the board may be erased or smudged; preparing and protecting your chalk graphics in advance is difficult. There is also the tendency for you to turn your back to the audience.

PREPARING GRAPHICS

1. Start early, rough draft your artwork, and coordinate it with your outline.
2. Label only the significant parts. Restrict details:
   a. One point or relationship per visual.
   b. Maximum of six words per line.
   c. Maximum of six lines per visual.[2]
3. Make a visual aid readily visible. Is it big enough? Are the lines heavy and dark enough (one-eighth to one-half inch thick)?
4. Practice with your final version.

USING PREPARED GRAPHICS

1. Display them where they can be seen by all.
2. Display them only when they are relevant.
3. Talk to the audience. Turn to your visual only to signal the audience to look at it.
4. Orient your audience: for example, "This is a top view."
5. Arrive early and check the display area.

Today, many exciting and effective graphics are possible thanks to electronic copiers and computer-generated graphics packages. These will be discussed shortly under "Using Electronic Assistance."

DEMONSTRATIONS

Demonstrations don't always work as planned. A student once demonstrated a tear-gas pencil in an overheated, poorly ventilated classroom with the temperature outside about zero. Talk about audience involvement! Another student, demonstrating the toughness of unbreakable, bulletproof glass, dropped it on a concrete floor. It did not break—it exploded!—producing one badly shaken speaker. (A glass company spokesman informed us later that the chances of the angle of impact, the temperature, the force, and other factors being perfectly coordinated—which caused the shattering—were about 1 in 10,000.)

The obvious questions are: "What can I do to reduce the probability of things going wrong?" and "If something does go wrong in spite of careful planning, what do I do at that moment of truth?"

The answer to the first question is careful *planning*. Plan exactly *how* you will perform the demonstration. Make sure you have *all* your equipment and have it in the right sequence. Be sure the demonstration *works* in your practice sessions. Emphasize safety precautions. Check for conditions that may vary from the practice session (for example, electric current). Finally, be sure you can do the demonstration. A flight instructor was teaching cadets the principles of airfoil and how an airplane develops lift. To demonstrate, he put a piece of paper between his lower lip and his chin. He then blew over it, creating a partial vacuum on top of the paper, which caused the paper to lift.

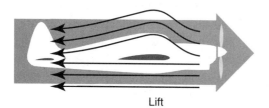

Lift   **Figure 9.13**

A new instructor who had observed this demonstration rushed to the next class with no time for practice. Confident that he could do it, he proceeded to blow—with no movement from the paper and with an audience of well-disciplined cadets trying not to explode with laughter. There are some moments when defeat is very evident.

The answer to the second question, "What if it goes wrong anyway?" is again to be found in planning. More specifically, calculate the extent and nature of the risk and then plan emergency alternative procedures for every disaster you can think of. This is a must. You have no time to change your plans when something does go wrong, and the shock and confusion may cause you to react emotionally rather than rationally.

The student with the "unbreakable" glass had a calculated risk of 1 in 10,000. You can hardly blame him for not being thorough in planning alternate procedures. Those are probably better odds than a pedestrian has on the Los Angeles Freeway. Nevertheless, this student could have had two pieces of glass, just as you should always have two bulbs for your slide or movie projector.

Extra equipment or spare parts are only part of the answer. The real problem is what you will say. Plan your communication strategy very carefully. *When and if the glass breaks I will say, "The odds on that happening were 1 in 10,000. Let me prove it by beating the next piece of glass with this hammer."* If the next piece breaks, you may have to resort to an alternate plan using prayer. You can't win them all!

The value of demonstration is that the audience can see and hear your explanation. It appeals to several senses, reinforces your message, saves time, has dramatic appeal, and is more concrete than just telling. Demonstration also helps speakers remember their material.

EXPERIENTIAL PRESENTATIONS

At this level your audience actually participates, whether it is handling an object, working through a process, or acting out a dramatic presentation in role-playing. These presentations are a must for professional trainers and teachers. They are the most concrete but also the most difficult. You probably will not often use the experiential level in your speech class because of the time, cost, difficulty, surprise, and confusion inherent in most audience participation. Your advanced courses may be smaller in size, and therefore more amenable to this level of presentation.

USING ELECTRONIC ASSISTANCE

The title of this section refers to the use of overhead projectors, 35-mm slide projectors, film, videotapes, television tapes, CD-ROMs or discs, and more. Some beginning speechmaking classes may limit the use of electronic equipment because it involves a complex overload of learning objectives. A speech with simple graphics is challenge enough for most of us. The problems of darkened rooms, visuals that replace the speaker, and the inevitable equipment problems abound. Of all of the electronic options, the overhead projector is by far the least complex and most amenable to public speaking.

> Audiovisuals are not intended to be your presentation. They're intended to support it.
> *Lani Arrendondo, Corporate Trainer*

Computer-Generated Graphics

If you do not have a personal computer with graphics capability, copy stores have them and so does your campus computer lab. Ask about such software programs as Power Point ®, Freelance, and Persuasion ®. These graphics can be printed and enlarged, usually for an extra fee. Some classrooms are now equipped with large screen projectors which allow your graphics to go directly from your laptop to a screen or a TV monitor. If you do have such technology available, take care that the medium doesn't become more important than your message. We'll have more to say about computers in the following section, "Overhead Projection."

Overhead Projection

One advantage of using an overhead projector over other electronic equipment is that it is positioned at the front of a lighted room, allowing the speaker to face the audience and still *see* the visual aid by simply looking down at the transparency (Figure 9.14). If set up properly, every audience member has an unobstructed view of the screen (Figure 9.15).

If you are considering putting your graphics on overhead transparencies (slides), be sure to check with your instructor first. Although there are a growing number of schools that require an "overhead-projector" speech, many are still restricted by time, cost, equipment, and policy.

Some other advantages you should know about for the world beyond this course are:

1. Whatever you can do with charts, you can also do with transparencies and an overhead projector.

2. An overhead projector poses little likelihood of a mechanical failure. There is a much greater possibility of mechanical failure or operator problems with slide, filmstrip, motion picture, or videotape equipment.

Figure 9.14

From Leaders Digest, *published by Audio Visual Division/3M.*

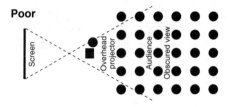

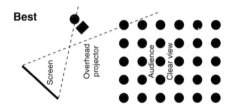

Figure 9.15

3. The overhead projector can be easily turned on and off, directing the attention of the audience from the screen to the speaker.

4. Material can be revealed point by point (a technique known as "revelation"), so that attention is fixed and participants cannot read ahead.

5. The overhead projector does not require expensive and time-consuming technical processing that is involved in slides, filmstrips, and movies.

Making Transparency Graphics

The single factor that is increasing the popularity of overhead projectors is that transparencies can be made easily, quickly, and inexpensively. The 3M Corporation tells us:

> Overhead transparencies are easily made and don't require long processing time. Any document can be converted into a transparency in seconds on a plain-paper copier or infrared transparency maker.[3] (See Figure 9.16)

You can also simply downsize your idea and draw it on a clear transparency. You will need a felt marker or felt-tipped pen. Rub-on or paste-on letters, stripes, and so forth are available at book or art supply stores.

If you have access to a personal computer and the right software, you can generate graphics and then convert them into transparencies for an overhead projector. Computer-generated graphics can also be made poster size if

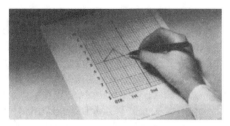

Hand letter, stencil, trace or type your own original on a piece of paper.

To make transparencies on a plain-paper copier, replace the paper in the feed tray with film and follow the instructions which are included with each box of 3M Plain Paper Copier Transparency Film.

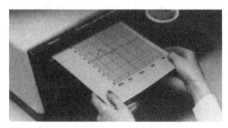

With an infrared copier, set the dial for transparencies and run the film and original through the machine together.

In seconds, your transparency is ready to be framed and projected.

Figure 9.16

From Leaders Digest, *published by Audio Visual Division/3M.*

you have a photocopy machine with this capability. A PosterPrinter is now available which will create in seconds a presentation poster or flip chart page up to eight times the original size, in your choice of seven color combinations.

With modern software, your computer graphics can be transferred directly to an overhead projector through a liquid crystal display (LCD) panel that fits on top of the projector.

High Tech

The versatile CD-ROM (Compact Disk-Read Only Memory) which we found so helpful in library research has now found its way into the world of professional trainers and speakers. With the help of a CD-ROM-equipped computer connected to a large-screen video projector, or the LCD panel discussed under overhead projectors, one can "mouse" excerpts for dramatic illustrations, incorporating everything from pictures to sound bites and music. It is now possible to find personal CD-ROM recorders to "burn" your own disks; these are new and expensive.[4]

At Wayne State University in Detroit, multimedia "Smart Carts" are now available from Media Services. They come fully equipped with projectors, speakers, a VCR, compact disc, laser disc and cassette players, and LCD panels that project images from computer screens. There is also a jack for plugging in a notebook computer. Students should also know that faculty now have software for electronic grade books. After each assignment or test, instructors just plug in the new figure and the overall grade is calculated automatically.

You are probably familiar with high-tech CAD (Computer Assisted Drawing) which replaced mechanical drawing. Enter CAP (Computer Assisted Presentations), not just the computer-generated graphics, CD-ROMs, projection conversions, and so forth, but a full scale program of computer-generated and coordinated equipment and message parts and pieces that constitute a total presentation. In one training session that I observed, the speaker simply introduced the CAP and asked for questions when it was over. Audience involvement was lost. I'm not sure that it was really a "presentation"; certainly, it was not a "speech."

Unless your class is an advanced presentational-speaking course, this high-tech information is useful mostly to prepare you for the communication world "out there." In the words of one high-tech corporate trainer:

> The success of your presentation doesn't lie solely in projecting whiz-bang graphics. It still lies primarily in your relational skills: in how well you relate, and relate your message to people.[5]
>
> *Lani Arrendondo*

Summary

Audiovisual aids are used to help make a subject clearer, to build interest, and to reinforce a message. These aids can be classified in terms of functional level as (1) *representational*, (2) *demonstrational*, and (3) *experiential*. The first is the most abstract and uses visual symbolization in the form of graphics; the second can be described as "show and tell"; the third as audience participation or "doing."

Select the functional level of your aids in terms of topic, purpose, occasion, physical arrangement, and audience analysis.

Representational aids *represent* something typically in graphic form or occasionally as a model. Standard graphics include: charts, maps, diagrams, and bar graphs that are displayed in poster or flip-chart form.

Rules for using prepared graphics include: (1) don't obstruct, (2) let them reinforce not distract, (3) talk to the audience not the chart, and (4) orient your audience to the chart. Rules for preparing charts include: (1) relate them to the topic, (2) make sure they are visible, (3) keep them simple and uncluttered, (4) organize the aid so it helps your memory.

A demonstration speech combines showing with telling. Its purpose is to show how a skill, procedure, process, or device is used. Demonstration appeals to several senses. It reinforces, saves time, and has dramatic appeal. Plan carefully, make sure you can do it, calculate the risks of things going wrong, and plan alternate procedures.

You are least likely to use visual aids at the *experiential* level because of time, cost, surprise, and confusion inherent in audience participation.

Graphics can be computer-generated for nominal fees. Consider software such as Powerpoint, Freelance, and Persuasion. Some classrooms are equipped to project your graphics directly from your laptop computer.

Overhead projectors are advantageous because they allow for full light, speaker visibility, and are less complicated than other electronic aids.

Thanks to photocopy machines, transparencies for overhead projectors are simple to make and can replace the larger charts and graphs. They allow a speaker to face the audience and still see the visual aid. They also allow material to be revealed point by point, and they are relatively inexpensive.

In the high-tech domain of audiovisual aids, CD-ROMs can be computer-connected to large screen and overhead projectors. CAP (Computer Assisted Presentations) may combine all computer functions in such elaborate electronic detail that the speaker may lose relational ability.

Learning Projects

1. What kinds of aids might one use for the following speech topics? Be creative and specific.

    Volcanoes

    Federal deficits

    Networking

    Hypnosis

    Morbid obesity

    Dog training

    Fuel injection

    Spouse abuse

    Statistical significance

    Pari-mutuel betting

    World population

2. Prepare an informal (rough outline) talk on your favorite hobby. Use visual aids (two to three minutes).

3. Observe a speaker (instructor or TV) using audiovisual and/or electronic aids (computer, overhead projector, 35-mm slides, etc.), and evaluate the planning and techniques.

4. Prepare a one- to two-minute demonstration exercise of a simple but interesting process (for example, demonstrating basic tennis shots, a dance step, crewel, basic golf, reading aloud, working a VCR, timing an engine, sketching a landscape, a card trick, shooting dice, solving a puzzle, tying a bow tie, folding a flag, walking like a model).

5. Cut graphics from newspapers or magazines similar to those shown in this text. Identify their function level and evaluate their usefulness. Prepare an oral report.

6. Describe and critique a high-tech communication presentation you have observed or in which you have participated.

Notes

1. See Kent E. Menzel and Lori J. Carrell, "The Relationship between Preparation and Performance in Public Speaking," *Communication Education*, 43, no. 2 (January 1994), 17–26.
2. The 3M Meeting Management Team, *Mastering Meetings* (New York: McGraw-Hill Inc., 1994), p. 142.
3. Ibid., p. 155.
4. For more on these matters, see Joe Elliot and Tim Worsley, eds., *Multimedia: The Complete Guide* (London: DK (Dorling Kindersly Limited, 1996).
5. Lani Arrendondo, *How to Present Like a Pro* (New York: McGraw-Hill, Inc., 1991), p. 101.

10

SPEECHES TO INFORM

CHAPTER
OUTLINE

Figure 10.1
© *International Paper Company.*

TYPES OF INFORMATIVE SPEECHES

You're asked to give a *class report* on "Systems Theory" for your management course. As a student teacher you must *lecture* on "Attribution Theory." You're called upon to give a *book* or *play review* for the Little Theater group. You're required to make a *committee report* to your fraternity or sorority. You're *instructing* Boy or Girl Scouts on the merit badge in ornithology. You're reporting and *explaining* the results of your physics class experiment. You're demonstrating aerobic exercise in your speech class. You're making *announcements* at the local 4-H club. We can report on places where we've been, things we've done, people we've met, and so on. We can instruct and/or demonstrate about everything from dancing and tennis to cooking and magical sleight of hand. We can explain the rationale behind hypnosis, cult behavior, or other concepts from existentialism to Keynesian economics. All these and more are speaking situations where the primary purpose is to inform. Most frequent of these are *reporting, instructing,* and *explaining.* An informative speech may use parts of all of these types.

Reporting

When reporting, one is giving an account or description of events, places, special objects, interesting people, and the like. If you are reporting specifically on the "United Nations Building Floor Plan," you will probably use mostly a spatial order to organize your speech. If you are talking about the "History of the United Nations Building," you will probably use a chronological order. Note how your organizational options change as your specific purpose sharpens. These various, organizational-order options were discussed in Chapter 6, "Organizing the Speech."

- Chronological order
- Difficulty order
- Spatial order
- Logical order
- Topical order

Instructing

Although all informative presentations involve some instruction and explanation, our efforts here concentrate on having our audience learn about and/or understand a process, or perhaps "how to" actually perform a process or special set of actions. The suggestions on demonstration speeches given in Chapter 9, "Using Audiovisual Aids," are very helpful here:

1. Plan it very carefully.
2. Try it. Make sure it works.
3. Check the facilities: power, light, space, and so forth.
4. Calculate the risks.
5. Plan alternative procedures.

Topics are usually concrete and can range from "How to Program a VCR" to "How to Prepare for a Job Interview." The chronological order fits most of these speeches.

Explaining

In this case, we inform and explain ideas and concepts that are more abstract such as theories of persuasion, principles of navigation, transcendental meditation, hermetic philosophy, aesthetics, and so forth. Restrict your speech purpose and central idea in this type of information sharing. One theory of persuasion is very adequate for a short speech. "Shooting an Azimuth" may be enough for navigation. "Modernistic Art" is probably more than enough for aesthetics. The topical order, with considerable definition of the main elements, is primary in this kind of explaining.

Your problems with informative speeches are similar to those a teacher confronts: meaty but not over people's heads; factual but not too technical; theoretical but not obtuse; objective and accurate but not dull and tedious. In the business world this is frequently called *presentational speaking.* How to organize such speeches or presentations and how to make them clear and interesting are primary objectives of this chapter. Visual aids can be of immense help so you may wish to reread Chapter 9. Because learning is involved, let's start there.

LEARNING PRINCIPLES

Not all students and audiences are eagerly waiting to hear what you have to say. Most need to hear some reason, whether it is personal growth and development, making money, saving effort, or simply curiosity. In short, you first need to explain *why* someone should listen to your topic. Geometry seemed stupid to me until the teacher pointed out that I could use it to plot navigation courses for my Power Squadron boating course. Trigonometry was really dull until I relearned it in artillery school. Environmentalists were far-out until I visited Los Angeles during the smog season or found I couldn't eat the fish in Lake St. Clair.

Presenting information is the most common speech purpose. In a sense, you are a teacher. You must motivate your audience to listen. You must present your material not only in a clear and interesting way but also in a way that makes it easy for your audience to learn, remember, and apply the information.

From the Known to the Unknown

In Chapter 1 we learned that people understand a message primarily by applying their previous experience and knowledge to it. It follows that teachers or speakers must select and arrange their material so that they best utilize the knowledge and experience the audience already has. The rule might be stated as follows: *Go from the known to the unknown.* For example, in trying to explain the relationship between wire size and electric current, a speaker compared the wire size to a garden hose (known) and the excess strain put upon the hose when someone restricts the opening with the nozzle. The listeners, having probably once burst a garden hose by turning the nozzle off, understood this explanation. It was clear, interesting, and easy to apply. Similarly, assuming that everybody knows the size of an English sparrow, a robin, and a crow, bird watchers typically relate the size of all unknown or unidentified birds to one of these three. This simple relating of known to unknown has made the communicating and sharing of much information far less frustrating for serious bird watchers.

Use Serial Learning

People tend to learn more readily when things are arranged in some sequence or serial order, especially when they are aware of the order. We teach youngsters addition and subtraction before multiplication and division; we could start with algebra, but we have found that it is more efficient to use a sequence based on difficulty. In history courses we often use a chronological order, but a sequence based on social issues might also be used.

The particular ordering of the material to be learned is determined by the previous knowledge of the audience, the difficulty of the subject, and the specific information the speaker is presenting. The audience is said to be learning serially when it is able to connect each portion of the sequence to the one immediately following it. In learning to drive a car, you must learn a great many details, but you have not really learned to drive until you have connected clutching, braking, steering, and other operations in such a way that one action is followed automatically by the next appropriate action.

Use Reinforcement and Emphasis

Perhaps in an education or psychology course you have heard the expression **SRX.** In discussing the subject of learning, theorists use S to stand for **stimulus,** R for **response,** and X for **reinforcement.** This X may be a reward for responding in the desired way, a punishment, some form of known association, or perhaps some form of repetition. The teacher who "feeds back" criticism by a smile, a frown, or a high grade is practicing reinforcement. So is the drill sergeant with a really loud voice. This enhancement of a desired response is an application of reinforcement, whether it be by repetition, loud voice, or some other form of emphasis.

In an experiment, a fifteen-minute informative speech was given to student audiences in a relatively neutral or emphasis-free mode. Then experimental speeches, each loaded with various amounts of repetition and verbal emphasis, were given to similar audiences. Retention of material was significantly better when the following reinforcers were used.[1]

Rank	Form of Emphasis
1	For example, "Now get this" (verbal emphasis preceding a remark)
2	Three distributed repetitions
3	Repetition (early in speech)
4	Speaking slowly (half normal rate)
5	Repetition (late in speech)
6	Pause
7	Gesture

These results are strong evidence of the value of emphasis—whether verbal, vocal, gestural, organizational, or some combination of the above.

The evidence also contains some serious warnings for speakers.

1. Although three repetitions were a significant factor in retention, four repetitions were much less of a factor, and two repetitions appeared to cause no effect. Although the results of one limited experiment in no way suggest that three repetitions are a magic number, they do imply that too much repetition is as bad as too little. All of us have grown weary of certain

TV commercials that continually repeat a product name. On the other hand, we all appreciate the teacher who repeats and reviews course work, making it easier to understand and recall the important items. Optimal repetitions offer more opportunities for cognitive processing.[2]

    2. It was found that voice, especially volume, made a difference. In the case of a loud, almost bombastic voice used for emphasis, the difference was negative. It hurt retention. A really soft voice for emphasis didn't seem to make much difference. Although the results do not mean that we should never use a loud voice, they do demonstrate that in certain communication circumstances a loud voice may interfere with recall of information.

    In sum, take care not to overdo a good thing or to draw overly specific rules from limited experiences. Reinforcement in the form of verbal, vocal, gestural, and organizational emphasis can be a real asset to speakers presenting information—as long as they are careful to adapt the amount and kind of reinforcement to the particular subject, situation, and audience. "Now get this" might be a little strong for some audiences!

CLARITY AND INTEREST

In seeking *clarity* we utilize what we know about learning to make understanding easier. Perhaps not quite so evident is the fact that an audience's *interest* or *motivation* to learn may have an important effect on how much they remember.

    Your speech topic should be chosen with your own interests in mind, but you should also be considering audience interests and topic orientation at the same time. The key questions to consider are:

1. How important is the subject to the audience?
2. What does the audience know about the subject?
3. How do they know what they know?
4. What is their attitude toward the subject?
5. How do they assess my topical credibility?

Achieving Clarity

    The *scope* of your purpose (the amount of information you wish to cover in a given period of time) is a vital factor in clarity as is the organization of the material.

    The philosopher H. P. Grice offers nine maxims that communicators share which make understanding possible. Good speakers apply them to achieve clarity and understanding.

1. Make your speech as informative as is required considering purpose and time restraints.
2. Do not make your contributions more informative than is necessary.
3. Do not say what you believe to be false.
4. Do not say that for which you lack adequate evidence.
5. Be relevant to your topic and your listeners.
6. Avoid obscurity of expression.
7. Avoid ambiguity.
8. Avoid unnecessary prolixity (wordiness).
9. Be well organized.[3]

The use of audiovisual aids is still another method of improving clarity (Chapter 9). Clarity is also enhanced by the use of the forms of support discussed in Chapter 5: illustrations, examples, analogies, statistics, testimony, restatement, and, of course, effective organization.

Developing Interest

Interest, the second primary objective in a speech to inform, refers to the motivation of the audience to want to listen or learn. The problem is to hold the attention of your audience while you are practicing all of the suggestions for clarity. What are the categories of things that tend to interest all of us? How can they be applied to your subject in such a way as to motivate the audience to pay attention and want to learn? Much of a speaker's interest depends upon his or her style of delivery and use of vocal variety; however, we are concerned here mainly with speech *content.* Some of the more useful qualities of speech content that stimulate interest are specificity, conflict, novelty, curiosity, immediacy, vital concerns, and humor.

Figure 10.2 Animal Crackers.

SPECIFICITY   When a speaker says, "Let me give you an example of what I mean by dog-tired," you probably pay closer attention than if he or she were simply to give you some general, academic explanation. Suppose the speaker used this example:

> The men of Hurricane Hugo's Red Cross rescue group thought after two days of forced march through wreckage-strewn coastal areas that they were dog-tired. Then they saw the remote victims of the storm, who seemed to be moving on sheer instinct and determination alone. They staggered through their broken homes with drooping shoulders, so physically drained that it seemed to take every last ounce of strength to put one foot in front of the other.

Specificity, reality, or *concreteness* are more interesting than clichés, vague generalities, or abstractions. Instead of saying, "A boy was run over," be specific. Call him by name; indicate his age; identify the car: "Mark Scott, age 6, ran into the street to greet his mother approaching from the other side and was dashed to the pavement by a 1997 Explorer traveling in excess of the 30-mile speed limit."

CONFLICT   TV stories always seem to pit "bad guys" against "good guys." This conflict and fighting pay off in viewer interest. Can you imagine *NYPD Blue* or a daytime soap opera without conflict or uncertainty?

Sports contests create interest for most people. Disagreement and opposition have elected and destroyed many a politician, but almost always in an interesting way! If you can use conflict in your examples, illustrations, and explanations without seeming to set up nonexistent battles, your speech should have added interest for the audience.

Figure 10.3

Figure 10.4

NOVELTY   Something that is novel is *different, unusual, contrasting,* or *strange.* Of course, if the subject is so exotic that listeners cannot relate it to their previous knowledge and experience, interest may be lost rather than gained.

Novelty is not limited to the exotic. Relatively average things become novel if the world about them is in contrast. At one time a bikini would have been a novelty, mostly because of its contrast to more conservative swimsuits. In our time a man or woman would probably gain more attention wearing one of the old-fashioned neck-to-ankle suits of the early 1900s. New Yorkers find nothing unusual or novel about their skyscrapers, but visitors are entranced by the Empire State Building or World Trade Towers. However, the tower of Pisa is a novelty even to New Yorkers.

The unusual, the contrasting, the exotic, the strange, the rare, and the generally different things in life are more interesting than the run-of-the-mill. Let your examples, analogies, and explanations be novel for added audience interest.

CURIOSITY   One of the more marvelous and exasperating aspects of young children is the seemingly endless series of questions they ask. Grown-up children (men and women) are not really much different, except that they may become a little more precise about the subjects they want to know about and the questions they ask. Humans seem to have to find out what lies around the corner or beyond the stars. Each new discovery in space leads to added suspense about what the universe is really like and to the big question, "Is there life out there?"

Unanswered questions, uncertainty, suspense—these are the ingredients of curiosity that may be used effectively by speakers to arouse interest.

IMMEDIACY   By immediacy we mean the use of *issues of the moment* or of the specific occasion that will quickly arouse and maintain attention and interest when related to a speaker's subject. A company training director had the rare ability to memorize names of individuals along with other relevant facts after just one informal meeting. She once startled a group of forty executives on the second day of a course by randomly calling them by name throughout a two-hour period: "Mr. John Kolon, what do you think of . . .?" Needless to say, interest was high. Her listeners never knew when she would call their name, cite their job description, or ask their opinion.

A reference to a recent incident that is known to the audience may also heighten interest. In a speech to a business audience in Flint, Michigan, a speaker was interrupted by two window-rattling sonic booms. The audience stirred nervously. The speaker walked to the window and said, "Just a couple of young jet jockeys from the air base. I'll want to talk to them at the next briefing!" The audience quickly returned its attention. Not only had the distraction been acknowledged, but the audience felt closer to the speaker.

Learning about the occasion, the audience, last-minute headlines, the community (proximity of the air base), and all other matters of the moment is time well spent in helping to make your speech interesting.

VITAL CONCERNS   If, while reading this book you had the FM radio playing and the announcer suddenly broke in to say, "Alert! Alert! Please turn to your emergency frequencies at the civilian-defense white triangles on your radio dial," you would undoubtedly stop reading and turn the dial as instructed. The reason is obvious. Staying alive, protecting your loved ones, defending your home—all these are *vital concerns* to you, and you are interested because you have to be.

Vital concerns, if truly vital, will gain attention because of personal involvement. Create interest in your speeches by using arguments, examples, and illustrations that affect your audience's self-preservation, reputation, property, sources of livelihood, and freedoms. More will be said about the role of these factors in Chapter 11, "Speeches to Persuade."

HUMOR   If you feel you do not tell a joke well or you find it difficult to be a humorous speaker, perhaps you need not be too concerned. Long-standing research on the impact of humor on an audience seems to indicate mixed results. A series of more recent studies produced similar mixed results, except that humor did seem to improve the character ratings of the speaker and better student retention of humorous informative lectures was demonstrated.

Remember that humor, when offensive, can work against you; so too if it confuses the mood or is in some other way a distractor of the message.

Related, funny anecdotes (if told well and in good taste) have probably helped hold attention and increased retention.

If you do decide to try humor, make it as professional as possible. There is no feeling quite as desperate as viewing a poker-faced audience after you have told your best joke. Make sure that the material is related to either the subject or the occasion; make sure you can tell it fluently; make sure you remember the punch line; and make sure that it will not offend your audience. The best advice of all—try it out on a small group of friends first. In other words, *practice* and *polish!* More will be said about humor in Chapter 13 under "After-Dinner Speeches."

> When you set out to be *instantly* funny about some relevant subject, bend a critical eye on what you say. If you aren't almost certain that it will bring laughter and good-will, forget it and stick to your regular speech.
>
> *Gerald Gardner, Professional Speaker and Speech Writer*[4]

ORGANIZING EFFECTIVELY

When Chauncey Depew, a gifted speaker and state senator from New York, was asked to reveal the secret of his oratorical success, he replied:

"First, tell them what you are going to tell them; second, tell them; and third, tell them you have told them." I'm sure Mr. Depew would allow another step involving *why* someone needs to know what someone is about to say. Mr. Depew didn't need that additional step as much as the rest of us because his audiences were usually eagerly awaiting what he had to say.

1. Tell 'em *what* you're going to tell 'em.

2. Tell 'em *why.*

3. Tell 'em.

4. Tell 'em you've told 'em.   **Figure 10.5**

Let's revise this language to facilitate outlining. Here is what we end up with: *attention, overview* (what and why), *information,* and *review.*

The learning principles discussed in this chapter should assist in organizing information. What does it tell us? It tells us of the need to grab listeners' attention early and to motivate them to listen; it tells us of the value of serially ordered material; and it tells us of the need for reinforcement and for preparing states of readiness to learn or listen.

1. Attention
2. Overview
    What you're going to say.
    Why they should listen.
3. Information
4. Review

Figure 10.6

Your immediate purpose is to create a desire in the listeners to hear more about the information you have to offer. If the audience is already highly motivated, your *attention* step and part of the *overview* becomes proportionately less important. When interest is a serious problem you may wish to move the *why* up to the *attention* step.

If you have some natural credibility about your topic, it usually motivates the audience to listen—an athlete talking about her sport, a pilot explaining flying, a premed student discussing health care, and so on.

In a student speech "to inform the class about some of the sociological problems facing India," the speaker first explained that he had lived in India for three years. (Your introducer can also help here.) He then opened with the following (*attention* and *interest*): "Did you know that half of the world's population is illiterate and that one-third of this half lives in India? Did you know that over three hundred languages are spoken in India? That fourteen thousand babies a day are born in India? That Indians feel Americans are uncaring? Americans do care—they are just poorly informed."

The speaker used startling statistics and curiosity for attention. Notice the suggestion on why the audience needs to know—because we are perceived as uncaring. The student overviewed and then discussed each of four points in order. He gave us the detailed *information.* At the close of the speech, he repeated the four points, but in addition he briefly summarized some of the important details from the information step. In other words, he *reviewed* the speech, or "told 'em what he told 'em." The completeness or amount of detail you put into your summary or review will depend upon the complexity of the subject, the time allotted, and your purpose. In some speeches you may prefer to deliver a brief summary of the points you have tried to make; in others, perhaps detailed conclusions that sum up your speech.

The *reinforcement value* of this four-part development is obvious. Once more, remember that a listener cannot go back and reread or review. Therefore, an occasional internal summary, review, or preview in the information step may help.

If your instructor agrees you might wish to reverse the labeling procedure as shown in the student *speaking outline* that follows. The specific purpose was "To inform the audience about the fundamental concepts of music theory."

MUSIC SMARTS

ATTENTION

Introduction A

   I. Play a few bars of music on the violin. (demonstration)

  II. Recognize the music majors in the class.

 III. Restate the specific purpose.

 IV. Explain why music majors are weird but lovable.

OVERVIEW

   I. The kinds of notes.

  II. The musical staff.

 III. Methods of counting the notes.

 IV. Relation of these three points to an instrument.

INFORMATION

   I. The kinds of notes.

     A. Neutral notes: A, B, C, D, E, F, G.

     B. Sharp notes: a half tone up.

     C. Flat notes: a half tone down.

  II. Explanation of the musical staff.

     A. The treble clef and melody.

       1. Contains 5 lines: E, G, B, D, F.

       2. Contains 4 spaces: F, A, C, E.

     B. The bass clef and rhythm.

       1. Contains 5 lines: G, B, D, F A.

       2. Contains 4 spaces: A, C, E, G.

Visual aid

Body B

 III. Methods of counting the notes.

     A. Whole note gets 4 beats.

     B. Half note gets 2 beats.

     C. Quarter note gets 1 beat.

     D. Eighth note gets half a beat.

 IV. Relation of these points to a musical keyboard.

     A. The notes (whether neutral, sharp, or flat) correspond to the lines and spaces in the staff.

     B. The position of the notes on the staff determines what note or key is to be played on the musical instrument.

     C. The number of beats the note receives tells how long the note is to be played on the instrument.

REVIEW

Conclusion C

   I. I have tried to make clear the following four factors of musical theory:

     A. The kinds of notes.

     B. The musical staff.

Conclusion C (continued) {

  C. Methods of counting the notes.

  D. Relating the theory to an instrument. Play a few bars. (demonstration)

  II. Now you can start writing your own music and better understand the music majors.

The speech on management functions discussed in Chapter 6 was given by a management major student which added interest and credibility to her message. She had a *speaking outline* labeled as follows:

THE ROLE OF THE MANAGER

INTRODUCTION

Attention   **I.** In a well-run organization, confusion pertains 25 percent of the time.

  A. Visual aid with data and another with list of functions.

  B. Studies show that communication breakdowns occur foolishly.

Overview   **II.** Management is getting work done through others.

  A. That makes communication the heart of all management functions.

  B. That takes a knowledge of the other basic functions.

  1. Planning.

  2. Organizing.

  3. Directing.

  4. Coordinating.

  5. Controlling.

> 1. Planning.
> 2. Organizing.
> 3. Directing.
> 4. Coordinating.
> 5. Controlling.

Visual aid

BODY

Information   **I.** The planning function.

  A. Determine objective.

  B. Consider tools available.

  1. Time.

  2. Space.

  3. Personnel.

  4. Material available.

  C. Consider possible lines of action.

  D. Select the best line of action.

  E. Determine the actual process.

  1. Who?

  2. When?

  3. What?

  4. Where?

  5. How?

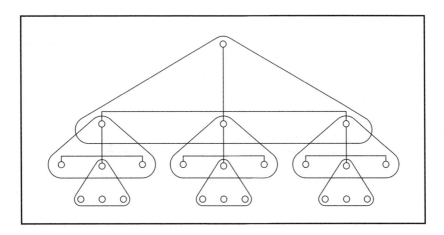

Visual aid

II. The organizing function.
   A. Line of authority.
   B. Span of Control.
      1. Number of personnel.
         a. Nature of job.
         b. Ratios (1–20, 3, 7).
      2. Distance.
      3. Time.
   C. Homogeneous assignment.
      1. Like functions grouped together.
      2. Avoid several unrelated responsibilities.
   D. Delegation of authority.
      1. Cannot delegate responsibility.
      2. Clearly define limits of delegated authority.
III. The directing function.
   A. Communication.
   B. Understanding people.
IV. The coordinating function.
   A. Relating to lateral organizations.
   B. Relating to the parent organization.
V. The controlling function.
   A. Reporting.
   B. Inspecting and evaluating.

III, IV, V

Human relations and
communication area

Visual aid

CONCLUSION

Review **I.** I have tried to make clear the five basic management functions.

    A. Planning.

    B. Organizing.

    C. Directing.

    D. Coordinating.

    E. Controlling.

  II. Communication is the heart of all management functions! It has to be—management is getting work done *through* people—and that takes communication.

SAMPLE SPEECH

"COIK" which stands for "Clear Only If Known" is the title of a speech by Edgar Dale, a former professor of education at Ohio State University. It is a classic illustration showing how to apply the principles covered in this chapter: learning, motivation, clarity, interest, and even humor. Dale grabs your attention quickly with an illustration with which most people can easily identify (paragraphs 1 and 2). Paragraph 4 clarifies what he's trying to say. He makes good use of relevant humor in paragraphs 5, 13, and 14). All of the paragraphs contain lessons which can help you as you plan and prepare your informative speech.

Attention 1   For years I have puzzled over the inept communication of simple directions, especially those given me when touring. I ask such seemingly easy questions as : "Where do I turn off Route 40 for the by-pass around St. Louis? How do I get to the planetarium? Is this the way to the Federal Security Building?" The individual whom I hail for directions either replies "I'm a stranger here myself," or gives you in kindly fashion the directions you request. He finishes by saying pleasantly, "You can't miss it."

Attention 2   But about half the time you do miss it. You turn at High Street instead of Ohio Street. It was six blocks to the turn, not seven. Many persons who give directions tell you to turn right when they mean left. You carefully count the indicated five stoplights before the turn and discover that your guide meant that blinkers should be counted as stoplights. Some of the directions exactly followed turn out to be inaccurate. Your guide himself didn't know how to get there.

    3   Now education is the problem of getting our bearings, of developing orientation, of discovering in what direction to go and how to get there. An inquiry into the problem of giving and receiving directions may help us discover something important about the educational process itself. Why do people give directions poorly and sometimes follow excellent directions inadequately?

Clarification [4]   First of all, people who give directions do not always understand the complexity of what they are communicating. They think it a simple matter to get to the Hayden Planetarium because it is simple for them. When someone says, "You can't miss it," he really means, "*I* can't miss it." He is suffering from what has been called the COIK fallacy—Clear Only If Known. It's easy to get to the place you are inquiring about if you already know how to get there.

Humor [5]   We all suffer from the COIK fallacy. For example, during a World Series game a recording was made of a conversation between a rabid New York baseball fan and an Englishman seeing a baseball game for the first time.

The Englishman asked, "What is a pitcher?"

"He's the man down there pitching the ball to the catcher."

"But," said the Englishman, "all of the players pitch the ball and all of them catch the ball. There aren't just two persons who pitch and catch."

Later the Englishman asked, "How many strikes do you get before you are out?"

The Brooklyn fan said, "Three."

"But," replied the Englishman, "that man struck at the ball five times before he was out."

These directions about baseball, when given to the uninitiated, are clear only if known.

6   Try the experiment sometime of handing a person a coat and ask him to explain how to put it on. He must assume that you have lived in the tropics, have never seen a coat worn or put on, and that he is to tell you *verbally* how to do it. For example, he may say, "Pick it up by the collar." This you cannot do, since you do not know what a collar is. He may tell you to put your arm in the sleeve or to button up the coat. But you can't follow these directions because you have no previous experience with either a sleeve or a button.

7   The communication of teachers to pupils suffers from the COIK fallacy. An uninitiated person may think that the decimal system is easy to understand. It is—if you already know it. Some idea of the complexity of the decimal system can be gained by students who are asked by an instructor to understand his explanation of the duodecimal system—a system which some mathematicians will say is even simpler than the decimal system. It is not easy to understand with just one verbal explanation, I assure you.

8   A teacher of my acquaintance once presented a group of parents of first-grade children with the shorthand equivalents of the first-grade reader and asked them to read this material. It was a frustrating experience. But these parents no longer thought it was such a simple matter to learn how to read in the first grade. Reading, of course, is easy if you already know how to do it.

9   Sometimes our directions are overcomplex and introduce unnecessary elements. They do not follow the law of parsimony. Any unnecessary elements mentioned when giving directions may prove to be a distraction. Think of the directions given for solving problems in arithmetic or for making a piece of furniture or for operating

a camera. Have all unrelated and unnecessary items been eliminated? Every unnecessary step or statement is likely to increase the difficulty of reading and understanding the directions. There is no need to overelaborate or labor the obvious.

10   In giving directions it is also easy to overestimate the experience of our questioner. It is hard indeed for a Philadelphian to understand that anyone doesn't know where the City Hall is. Certainly if you go down Broad Street, you can't miss it. We know where it is: why doesn't our questioner?

11   It is easy, for example, to overestimate the historical experience of a student. The instructor often forgets that his students were toddling infants when Jimmy Carter was President. Events that the instructor has immediately experienced have only been read or heard about by the student. What was immediate knowledge to the instructor is mediated knowledge to the student.

12   We are surprised to discover that many college freshmen do not know such words as *abrogate, abscond, accrue, effigy, enigma, epitome, exigency, hierarchy, lucrative, pernicious, ruminate, fallacious, salient, codify, coerce,* and *cognizance.* College professors are surprised to discover that even their abler students do not know such words as *protean, shard, ad hoc, restrictive covenant,* and *prorogue.*

Joke   13   Another frequent reason for failure in the communication of directions is that explanations are more technical then necessary. Thus a plumber once wrote to a research bureau pointing out that he had used hydrochloric acid to clean out sewer pipes and inquired, "Was there any possible harm?" The first reply was as follows: "The efficacy of hydrochloric acid is indisputable, but the corrosive residue is incompatible with metallic permanence." The plumber then thanked them for the information approving his procedure. The dismayed research bureau tried again, saying, "We cannot assume responsibility for the production of toxic and noxious residue with hydrochloric acid and suggest you use an alternative procedure." Once more the plumber thanked them for their approval. Finally, the bureau, worried about the New York sewers, called in a third scientist who wrote: "Don't use hydrochloric acid. It eats hell out of the pipes."

Joke   14   Some words are not understood and others are misunderstood. For example, a woman confided to a friend that the doctor told her that she had "very close veins." A patient was puzzled as to how she could take two pills three times a day. A little girl told her mother that the superintendent of the Sunday school said he would drop them into the furnace if they missed three Sundays in succession. He had said that he would drop them from the register.

15   We know the vast difference between knowing how to do something and being able to communicate that knowledge to others, of being able to verbalize it. We know how to tie a bow knot but have trouble telling others how to do it.

16   Another difficulty in communicating directions lies in the unwillingness of a person to say that he doesn't know. Someone drives up and asks you where Oxford Road is. You realize that Oxford Road is somewhere in the vicinity and feel a sense of guilt about not even knowing the streets in your own town. So you tend to give poor directions instead of admitting that you don't know.

17   Sometimes we use the wrong medium for communicating our directions. We make them entirely verbal, and the person is thus

required to keep them in mind until he has followed out each of the parts of the directions. Think, for example, how hard it is to remember 426-7249 merely long enough to dial it after looking it up.

18   A crudely drawn map, of course, would serve the purpose. Some indication of distance would also help, although many people seem unable to give adequate estimates of distances in terms of miles. A chart or a graph can often give us an idea in a glance that is communicated verbally only with great difficulty.

19   But we must not put too much of the blame for inadequate directions on those who give them. Sometimes the persons who ask for help are also at fault. Communication, we must remember, is a two-way process.

20   Sometimes an individual doesn't understand directions, but thinks he does. Only when he has lost his way does he realize that he wasn't careful enough to make sure that he really did understand. How often we let a speaker or instructor get by with such mouth-filling expressions as "emotional security," "audio-visual materials," "self-realization," without asking the questions which might clear them up for us. Even apparently simple terms like "needs" or "interests" have hidden many confusions. Our desire not to appear dumb, to be presumed "in the know," prevents us from really understanding what has been said.

21   We are often in too much of a hurry when we ask for directions. Like many tourists, we want to get to our destination quickly so that we can hurry back home. We don't bother to savor the trip or the scenery. So we impatiently rush off before our informant has really had time to catch his breath and make sure that we understand.

22   Similarly, we hurry through school subjects, getting a bird's-eye view of everything and a closeup of nothing. We aim to cover the ground when we should be uncovering it, looking for what is underneath the surface.

23   It is not easy to give directions for finding one's way around in a world whose values and directions are changing. Ancient landmarks have disappeared. What appears to be a lighthouse on the horizon turns out to be a mirage. But those who do have genuine expertness, those who possess tested, authoritative data, have an obligation to be clear in their explanations. Whether the issue is that of atomic energy, UNESCO, the UN, or conservation of human and natural resources, clarity in the presentation of ideas is a necessity.

24   We must neither overestimate nor underestimate the knowledge of the inquiring traveler. We must avoid the COIK fallacy and realize that many of our communications are clear only if already known.[5]

Summary

The most frequent types of informative speeches involve reporting, instructing, and explaining. Useful learning principles related to communicating information include: (1) relating new information to what an audience already knows, (2) ordering the material in some serial progression that makes it easier for people to follow and relate the significant points, and (3) reinforcing the message and the response through a sensible amount of repetition, verbal emphasis, organization, and voice—all of which communicate importance, reward, punishment, or some other meaning. The final lesson to be gained from learning theory is that there appears to be a point of diminishing returns with all these devices; too much repetition can be as harmful as too little. This point of diminishing returns depends upon the specific and total communication circumstance.

The primary goals in informative speaking are achieving clarity and interest. Methods of achieving clarity include illustration or example, analogy or comparison, statistics, testimony, and restatement. The factors that create or add interest are specificity, conflict, novelty, curiosity, immediacy, vital concerns of the audience, and humor. Maxims that promote understanding are: present an appropriate amount of information, avoid false statements, use evidence for what you say, be relevant to your audience as well as your topic, avoid obscurity, ambiguity and prolixity, and be well organized.

Psychologically sound organization requires (1) gaining *attention,* (2) preparing the audience through a preview or *overview,* (3) presenting the detailed *information,* and (4) *reviewing* the significant points for added reinforcement. Establishing credibility helps motivate your audience to listen to you. Visual aids are a big help in making your information clear and interesting.

The "COIK" model speech is an excellent illustration of how to apply the principles covered in this chapter.

Learning Projects

1. Pick a topic for each of the speech types described (reporting, instructing, explaining) and write a specific purpose statement for each. See the appendix for topic ideas.

2. Analyze a student speech:

   a. Find an example of the speaker applying a learning principle described in the text: (1) going from the known to the unknown, (2) using serial order, and (3) using reinforcement.

   b. Find one example of two of the following: specificity, conflict, novelty, curiosity, immediacy, vital concerns, humor.

3. Consider the speech topics that follow and write three different specific purposes (to inform) for any two of them.

Diamonds	High schools	Cuba	Iraq
Weather	Dating	Dolphins	Thanksgiving
Travel	Rock music	Earthquakes	Aesthetics

   EXAMPLE

   TOPIC: YF–22 TACTICAL FIGHTER PLANE   (Possible purposes)

   Specific purpose: (1) To inform my audience about my first flight in a YF-22 fighter.

Specific purpose: (2) To inform the class about the political travail associated with the YF-22 fighter.

Specific purpose: (3) To inform the class about the engineering development of the YF-22 fighter.

4. Analyze the speech "Clear Only If Known" by Edgar Dale (pp. 236-239).

  a. Is it reporting, instructing, or explaining? Explain.

  b. Identify two paragraphs that motivate you to listen (or read on in this case).

  c. Find one or more paragraphs that illustrate each of the learning principles: known to unknown, serial order, reinforcement, and emphasis.

  d. Find paragraphs that illustrate the principles of clarity and interest.

  e. Identify two examples of humor and evaluate their impact.

Notes

1. Raymond Ehrensberger, "An Experimental Study of the Relative Effectiveness of Certain Forms of Emphasis in Public Speaking," *Speech Monographs*, 12, no. 2 (1945), 94–111.

2. J. T. Cacioppo and R. E. Petty, "Effects of Message Repetition and Position on Cognitive Responses, Recall, and Persuasion," *Journal of Personality and Social Psychology*, 37 (1979), 97–109.

3. Adapted from H. P. Grice, *Studies in the Way of Words* (Cambridge, Mass.: Harvard University Press, 1984), pp. 26–27.

4. Gerald Gardner, *Speech Is Golden* (New York: St. Martin's Press, 1992), p. 73.

5. Reprinted by permission of Edgar Dale.

11

SPEECHES TO PERSUADE

CHAPTER
OUTLINE

TYPES OF PERSUASIVE SPEECHES

All speeches to persuade involve efforts to get receivers to: (1) accept your interpretation of *disputed facts,* or (2) align their *beliefs, attitudes,* and *values* more closely with yours, and/or (3) move them to *action* on your proposition. Some speeches may involve efforts in all three areas.

> When Isocrates taught rhetoric to his Greek schoolboys he empowered them; he helped them see avenues for making their minds count in the affairs of society.
>
> *Roderick P. Hart*

The more closely you can define the type of speech and audience with which you're dealing, the more efficiently you can seek out information and arrange it into an effective strategy. As we shall see shortly, if your audience thinks differently than you do about these critical dimensions, you'd better find that out as quickly as you can.

Disputed Facts Speech

". . . facts are actions, events, or conditions which have been *properly* observed, described, classified, and reported." Space travel is now a *fact* since it meets the definition above, but what of flying saucers (UFOs)? The saucers fail for most people on the word *properly* but clearly not for all. UFOs become (for believers) a persuasive speech using their version of the disputed facts.

Of course, people may not agree with the definition of fact given above. One dictionary definition allows for "information presented as having objective reality." An argument over the Koran or the Bible might be a question of disputed fact for one person and a question of belief or value for another. All questions are not as complex as these, but they may involve inconclusive facts. "Is there life out there in space?" "What causes Alzheimer's disease?" "Why can't Johnny read?" "Is the defendant guilty of the crime?" These are all questions where persuasive efforts are possible, sometimes difficult, sometimes frustrating.

Some facts really aren't worth arguing about—"Which is higher, the Andes, the Alps, or the Rockies?" An encyclopedia or PC can solve that one. Do your audience analysis even when you think things are obvious. There are still many people who do not accept the "fact" that Neil Armstrong set foot on the moon.

Belief and Value Speeches

Beliefs are constructs we hold about the world; they give rise to related attitudes. A strong belief in protecting the environment can affect one's attitudes about a wide range of things from political candidates to spotted owls. Values, as we learned in Chapter 4, "Audience Considerations," are still larger, more important frames of reference which hold our belief and attitude systems together.

These speeches do not necessarily ask audiences to take action, although it is often implied. One can argue the case (pro or con) for assisted suicide in an effort to change people's beliefs without detailing what they should do. The same is true of other controversial topics which typically engage people's belief and value systems: capital punishment, abortion, birth control, life supports, and so forth. Your speeches should include many facts and much information if you are to give responsible and effective belief speeches. Some real-world speeches on questions of strong values sometimes rely on overly emotional efforts.

Action and Policy Speeches

These are speeches to *actuate,* or move people to action. For example:

Sign this petition.
Vote for Senator Foghorn.
Enlist in the Marines.
Buy this Chevrolet.
Give blood.

Beliefs and attitudes may also be involved but the bottom line is some kind of action, even if it is only a "yes" response indicating a strong intention to ultimately take the action you are suggesting.

When we deal with more involved and specific courses of action, we're talking about policy. Facts, beliefs, values, attitudes—all are involved here, but now we're talking about what *should* or *should not* be done over time.

What should be our school system's position on funding public education?

How should the USA deal with the proliferation of nuclear arms?

What should be our policy regarding national health care?

Most policy questions involve some controversy. For some audiences on some topics the mood can be downright hostile: abortion, feminism, secular humanism, AIDS, gays in the military, church and state, and so forth. There are special strategies for antagonistic groups that sometimes work. These will be discussed later in this chapter.

In these speeches, from a sales talk to one of controversial policy, you will have to demonstrate a need or a problem which calls for a solution. You will then have to provide a solution or plan that meets the need you've hopefully made clear. This is usually the more difficult part because not only must you show that your solution is practical, but also that it is more sensible than other practical solutions that may be available. Our need for health care reform seems obvious to most citizens, but the precise nature of the specific needs is open to argument. Certainly the range of solutions from rationing to socialized medicine is daunting.

Audience analysis is very important for these speeches because even a few people who take severe issue with your stand or are seriously offended by it can be disruptive. "You can't win 'em all" but you don't always have to. Attitudes, as we shall see shortly, are usually changed incrementally.

THE NATURE OF PERSUASION

Persuasion is but a part of very large systems of influence and motivation, but its emphasis on reasoned, intentional messages and its insistence on ethical choice for receivers makes it a very special part indeed.

Influence, Motivation, and Persuasion

Influence, the most general of these terms, refers to a power that affects a person or a course of events, usually indirectly. It can be positive or negative, human or nonhuman, intentional or unintentional, ethical or unethical. Influence includes mood setters like lighting, music, and pictures as well as the actions or presence of other people.

Motivation pertains to *any* stimulation or inducement that leads to an act or belief. It could be caused by drives to reduce tension, achieve goals, or grow as a person, or by a need for self-understanding. These various causes suggest that we are motivated both by need and by plenty. Success and satisfaction usually foster motivation. So frequently do failure and dissatisfaction. We are often motivated through argument or social compliance and laws. We have avoidance needs as well as growth needs. Human motives have been defined by Krech and Crutchfield as *survival, security, satisfaction,* and *stimulation.*[1] These are grouped into deficiency motives (survival and security) and abundancy motives (satisfaction and stimulation). **Deficiency motivation** is characterized by needs to avoid danger, threat, disruption, and discomfort. **Abundancy motivation** is characterized by desire to grow, discover, create, enjoy, and achieve. The various motivations are both *verbal* and *nonverbal, logical* and *emotional.*

Motivation need not be intentional; it can be accidental. Furthermore, it is essentially **amoral**—that is, not particularly concerned with notions of right or wrong, fair or unfair. The King's incentive in Figure 11.1 may be influential and motivational, but it is not persuasion in the sense that communication scholars view it.

Figure 11.1   The Wizard of Id.
By permission of Johnny Hart and News America Syndicate.

Persuasion is certainly concerned with social influence and human motivation but in a very special way. Persuasion is a change process resulting mostly from shared, symbolic-thinking activity. Whereas this text is concerned mostly with spoken messages, the effects of persuasion are in the thoughts and behaviors, the sociology, of the receivers. This fact suggests that receivers have some bias and also some choice in these matters. Persuasive messages attempt to influence *how* receivers choose or decide which information to process and respond to.

A persuader has an *ethical responsibility* for the strategies and for their social consequences. Techniques and strategies are ethical unless they are dishonest, unfair to the facts, or so subtle that they give no clue to the receiver. The clue is important. It protects the receiver's fundamental right of choice. There is no lasting persuasion without honesty, pressure free of violence, receiver choice, tolerance for strategy, fair hearing, and a willingness to comply with persuasion from legitimate authority. In a democracy, ethical persuasion is the major means of social influence.

In this context persuasion is a nonviolent means of ethically influencing and motivating others through messages. It is an instrument for obtaining reasoned adherence to rational propositions. By these definitions, persuasive influence must clearly protect a receiver's right to choice. "Your money or your life" may involve influence and motivation, but it does not afford a viable choice.

The Concept of Attitude

Persuasive efforts are directed in large part at changing or maintaining the attitudes of others. These efforts are usually directed at producing some related behavior: a vote, the sale of a product, some compliant action. Does oral argument (speech) affect attitudes? For centuries we have answered yes on the basis of subjective observations. Objective observations and research as early as 1931 have also clearly indicated that persuasive speaking can make a difference.[2] Logical arguments work but so do the psychological and more emotional speeches.

Attitude refers to the thinking, feeling, and behavioral intentions that govern our predispositions toward people, situations, and things. Attitude has also been defined as a tendency to respond in a given way. This response may be *cognitive* (how one thinks), *affective* (how one feels), or *behavioral* (how one behaves, or intends to behave). The altering of attitudes is for some the altering of a receiver's cognitive, schematic structures as well as behaviors as a result of message processing.

We are also persuaded by *logical appeals* as well as by *emotional appeals.* When we are persuaded to buy a product, take a position, or join a cause, how much of our behavior is based on reasoned discourse? How much on appeals to our emotions? There is strong evidence that people are multi-motivated.

Many of our attitudes are expressions of our experience and our values. They maintain and promote our value systems and our *self-identity.* For example, if we value our health and clean air highly, we will probably have unfavorable attitudes toward smoking and fluorocarbons.

All of us are somewhat directed by *self-interest.* Egoism is thought by some to be a major motivator of all human conduct. We defend our own egos, our own welfare and advancement. Take care of Number One! This self-interest has been called an *ego defensive* function. It is often difficult to change and is frequently destructive.

Some theorists view attitudes as being underlaid by *belief systems.* *Beliefs are sets of inferences* we make about the world. *Beliefs are nonevaluative.* They are probability statements we hold about the world.

Consider the following belief statement: Smoking and heart disease are related. This statement is a belief because it makes a probability inference between smoking and heart disease. Now consider the following attitude statement that might grow out of that belief: Smoking is bad. The statement is an attitude because it makes an evaluation of one of the objects (smoking) in the belief statement. The significant point is that our *attitudes are evaluative and grow out of our belief systems.*

But attitudes cannot always be represented adequately by a single point on a scale. They represent different strengths and different ranges or latitudes of acceptance. Consider Figure 11.2.

This person would be difficult to persuade to support the statement as the range of objection (or rejection 3–7) is so large. Suppose, however, that the data looked like Figure 11.3.

The more acceptable (√) or noncommitted positions one observes, the wider the latitude of acceptance and therefore the greater likelihood of attitude change.

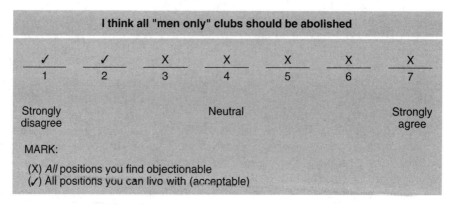

Figure 11.2

Figure 11.3

Research on how we make judgments about physical objects also gives us insights into our social judgments. If you put your hand in a pail of hot water for a minute or so and then put it in a pail of lukewarm water, you tend to judge the water *colder* than it is. If you go from cold to a pail of warm water, you tend to judge it *warmer* than it is. The hot pail (or cold) serves as a **referent point** or anchor for our succeeding judgments. When the temperature is sharply contrasted from that of the anchor, you tend to perceive it as farther from the anchor or colder than it really is; when temperatures are close to that of the anchor, you tend to assimilate it, to perceive it as warmer than it really is.

This tendency for assimilation and contrast has been applied to attitude change. A receiver's *initial* attitude toward the persuasion serves as a referent point or anchor for making judgments about the message. In general, the more extreme the initial attitude (anchor), the less attitude change you can expect. The less extreme the anchor, the more change you can expect.[3]

Intrapersonal Responses to Persuasion

Successful persuasion evokes favorable thoughts or internal responses from receivers. These thoughts may then affect favorable behaviors, feelings, or ideas (cognitions). This familiar notion of communication as a process suggests that listeners, in their decoding, sort, select, and elicit from their storehouse of knowledge those things they feel relate best to the message elements.

Cognitive-response theory helps show how people may evoke persuasive materials (thoughts) from their storehouses that may not be contained in the message sent. If these "cognitive responses" (thoughts) agree with the persuader's purpose, they should promote attitude change in the desired direction. If, on the other hand, the message somehow backfires and evokes unfavorable or disagreeing thoughts, the sender's purpose may be defeated or at least inhibited attitudinally.

The Elaboration Likelihood Method (ELM) of persuasion is based on this approach, namely, that the more elaborately a receiver responds cognitively, the greater the likelihood of attitude change.[4]

Cognitive-response theory suggests that just as personal growth and development are often considered to be really *self*-growth and *self*-development (or that learning is in the final analysis self-generated), we really persuade ourselves through these cognitive reevaluations.[5] This theory helps explain why the receivers of highly polarized attitudes are sometimes so busy processing, repeating, and rehearsing their own thoughts and views that they really do not hear the message. Highly polarized audiences may have quite different constructions of reality than yours based on different experiences and a different sociology of knowledge. Analyzing an audience's cognitive responses from *their* view of reality should help us better decide the kind, the length, and the ordering of arguments that will promote favorable "self-generated" responses.

Enthymematic persuasion seems to be a logical extension of the strategy implicit in cognitive-response theory. *Enthymemes* are syllogistic arguments with unstated premises. Their rhetorical function is to let the audience correctly supply the desired missing premises. Like cognitive-response theory, enthymematic persuasion assumes that thoughts are often more influential if they are our *own* rather than if they were explicitly stated in the message by others.

Cognitive-response researchers Richard Petty and John Cacioppo suggest two components or "routes" to persuasion: *central* and *peripheral*.[6] *Central* is characterized by more "elaborative" reasoning about issue-relevant matters; *peripheral* refers to the more affective, nonissue-relevant, contextual cues. Of the two routes, the more thoughtful *central* resulted in more enduring and resistant persuasion than did the peripheral.[7] This is not to say that the affective domain is unimportant. Advertising research suggests that the affective and the more cognitive central are both important indicants of overall message effectiveness.[8]

Aristotle's explanation of the enthymeme and his routes to persuasion make clear that he too was most interested in a receiver's intrapersonal responses. He called them *modes:*

> Of the modes of persuasion furnished by the spoken word there are three kinds. The first kind depends on the personal characteristics of the speaker, ETHOS; the second on putting the audience into a certain frame of mind, PATHOS; the third on the proof or apparent proof provided by the words of the speech itself, LOGOS.[9]

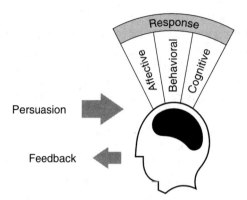

Figure 11.4 Intrapersonal response

These are strikingly similar to the dimensions of attitude discussed earlier: cognitive (*Logos*), affective (*Pathos*), and behavioral (*Ethos*). By *ethos*, Aristotle meant speaker credibility or persuasion based on a person's behavior, past and present. We'll have more to say about credibility in the next section.

There are, then, three basic intrapersonal responses to persuasion and, therefore, three related methods or modes a speaker should consider.

In the model shown in Figure 11.4, *cognitive* refers to logical thoughts, to thinking, to the mental process (cognition) by which knowledge is acquired, constructed, and elaborated. *Affective* refers to feelings, thoughts, and things more emotional. *Behavioral* can be an action, an action intention, or a thought response to the past behavior of the speaker (credibility) or the current speaking behavior (ethical proof).

Persuasion, in this context, is a process of skillfully and ethically using logical thoughts, affective appeals, credibility, and ethical proof to influence and motivate others to respond as you wish them to. Persuasive methods or *modes* can then be described as logical, affective, and behavioral. The *logical* mode (cognitive component) includes reasoning, evidence, argument, and logical consistency. The *affective* mode (affective component) includes the feelings induced by emotional appeals, personal involvement, and needs reduction.[10] The *behavioral* mode is concerned with (1) credibility and ethical proof, that is, speaker behavior, past and present, and (2) a receiver's personal involvement (behavior or behavioral intention) with the message, speaker, or situation.

Your first goal as an ethical speaker is to support your specific purpose with logical, consistent reasoning and argument. However, the affective and behavioral modes are not unethical as long as they reasonably relate to your logical argument and are fair to the facts.

Persuasion is like an arrow. The shaft is evidence and reasoning; the feathers are ethics and credibility which provide direction; the arrowhead is attention and emotional appeal which promote target response. The arrow must be properly assembled, balanced, and then skillfully aimed. If the flight of such an arrow of persuasion is true, and its target a rightful one, then its prospects are favorable.

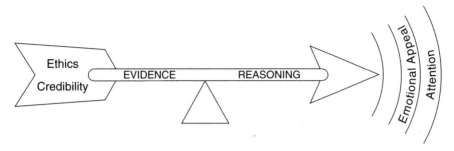

Figure 11.5

This chapter mostly concerns the feathers and the arrowhead, that is, the more psychological, the more peripheral route to successful persuasion. The more logical, more central route will be discussed in Chapter 12, "Logical Reasoning and Argument."

Most persuasive speeches use a combination of logical, affective, and behavioral elements. It is, of course, possible to have a speech based almost entirely on evidence and closely reasoned argument. On the other hand, many of our radio and television commercials make it abundantly clear that some efforts are based almost entirely on affective appeals. Some of these elements, such as source credibility, ethical proof, and personal involvement, embody both affective and cognitive dimensions and are difficult to divide. How much of one's perception of intent, trust, expertise, or status is based on affect? How much on evidence and logical deduction?

Most persuasive efforts are mixed mode and complex—sometimes very subtle, sometimes blatant. Consider the persuasion efforts of political campaigns. How much is logical persuasion? How much is affective? How much is based on source credibility?

ROUTES TO EFFECTIVE PERSUASION

Getting an audience to think or, more specifically, to *rethink* a proposition is the goal of most persuasive efforts. However, internal reevaluation, as we just learned, is triggered by affective as well as cognitive arguments.

Improving Perceptions of Credibility

Credibility refers to a receiver's acceptance of or disposition toward the source. Aristotle used the term *ethos* to designate the audience's perception of the speaker. In regard to ethical proof, Aristotle set forth the general rule that "there is no proof so effective as that of the character." It may be more fact than fiction that "what you are speaks so loudly I can't hear what you're saying." Perhaps it's also true for some that "if you're not part of my group (or party), I *won't* hear what you're saying." "My perception of reality is right and yours is wrong."

SOURCE CREDIBILITY   ***Source credibility*** is related to Aristotle's concepts of goodwill, good moral character, and good sense, as these are perceived by receivers. In modern times, source credibility has been discussed as good intentions, trustworthiness, and competence or expertise. Source credibility includes our perceptions and attitudes of trust and confidence, which are based in part on our beliefs about the intent, position or status in society, knowledge, and sincerity of the speaker. High source credibility generally produces more attitude change in the receiver.

Both reason and research tell us that an obviously untrustworthy speaker, regardless of his or her other qualities, will be viewed as a questionable message source. However, many special aspects and conditions also affect people's perceptions of credibility. Although a convicted, hard-core, experienced car thief may not meet the classical tests of credibility (goodwill, good moral character, good sense), if he were to speak (or write) about the secrets of his trade, he might indeed be perceived as having a special credibility. After all, he is an expert!

Characteristics that we infer about a source may cancel all or some credibility. Jesse Delia hypothesizes that "many persons hearing a militant speaker openly and explicitly advocate an abhorrent position on an issue important to them would make with equal certainty the attributions that the speaker is honest and forthright, but also very misguided and unsafe.[11]

The receiver's perception of a sender's intent appears to influence credibility. A persuasive message was prepared on the topic of raising the minimum driving age, and the same speech was given to two groups of teenagers. One group of subjects was told that the purpose of the program was to study the speaker's personality. The other group was told that the speaker considered teenage drivers a menace. In the first group the speaker's intent to persuade was made less clear; in the second it was made abundantly clear. The second group saw the communicator as more biased, as might be expected; the first group made a greater attitude change in the direction advocated.[12]

In a study designed to persuade eighth graders to take a more conservative attitude about drugs, a law enforcement officer was less successful than others.[13] Perhaps his intent was perceived in a way that injured his credibility. His presentation may have been too threatening for his audience. Or perhaps his status as a law officer didn't carry over to his expertise (if he had any) about drugs.

People's status may also vary with the issue. We may have high status in one role and low in another. George Patton had high status as a combat general but low status as a diplomat.

Apparently people form their general impressions of a sender's credibility on the basis of a wide array of variables: Intent, trust, and competence are only the beginning. We should view credibility as an interactive process among sources, messages, and receivers. It is no wonder that research evidence on credibility is sometimes inconsistent. However, when high source credibility is *perceived,* and when it is *relevant* to the message and the situation, it generally produces more favorable attitude change in the receivers.

There is also a practical credibility or likability that can be established or reinforced by the speaker's characteristics (as perceived by the audience) and behavior during the sending of the message. These speaker behaviors have been referred to as "ethical proofs" and are thought to be closely related to an audience's impressions of the honesty, character, wisdom, and goodwill of the speaker.

ETHICAL PROOF AND SELF-PRESENTATION   Other things being equal, persuaders may be most influential when they are perceived by receivers as having attitudes *similar to their own. Ethical proofs* also include the speaker's *self-presentation* in terms of voice, language, humor, information, and evidence.

Studies have found that excess verbalizations and signals indicating disorganization detract from a speaker's credibility.[14] Recall that even social status may be inferred.

The use of humor may enhance speakers' pragmatic ethical proof, if not their persuasion, as measured by attitude shifts among the audience. Humor and satire, when used with a professional touch, can affect audience interest and attention and thereby retention. That they can boomerang when not used properly is very clear from research and common experience.

Can we manage these impressions? One sociologist thinks so. According to Erving Goffman, **impression management** is a doable part of how you present yourself to receivers.[15] Impression management suggests that in our efforts to present our best and most persuasive self, we try to give appropriate performances on the stage of life. Let us consider a college student presenting his senior thesis before the faculty or a potential employer. He may attempt an impression of maturity, self-confidence, knowledgeability, and dependability. According to Goffman, this can be done in the following general ways:

1. *An appropriate front.*   This is general behavior that is designed (or natural) to better define (persuasively, we hope) who you are. Your personal front includes such things as appearance and manner. It also includes things over which you have only limited control, such as sex, age, and size. Clothes, posture, gestures, facial expressions, and language patterns are more modifiable dimensions of your front. Should our college student appear in dirty shorts, needing a shave, and using the English language profanely, would that front offend or reassure his audience?

2. *Dramatic realization.*   According to Goffman, we must clearly realize the role expected of us and work it into the performance. We may have to put on an act to hide our lack of confidence. If the role calls for attentiveness, we had better give such an impression; we may be paying attention, but if we are not perceived that way, then we have

done a poor job of impression management. A flip physician who writes a fast prescription, however accurate the quick diagnosis, may be viewed suspiciously by a patient.

3. *Mystification.* This aspect of impression management refers to perceptions of *social distance* between the actor and the audience. Our physician above is more apt to be concerned with this kind of impression than is our student presenter. That is, the physician must not become too folksy lest he or she lose some of the mystery of the medical role. Our college student, however, must accommodate the real or fancied social-distance factors of the theater in which he finds himself.

The point of those various examples is that we *do* present ourselves to others, and others *do* form impressions—good, bad, and indifferent. If, as a student of persuasion, you understand this dramaturgical model, you should be better equipped to deal with impression management. The important lesson is that credibility and ethical proof also involve impressions of trust and confidence based on the perceived intent, position, knowledge, and sincerity of the source.

Appeals to Human Needs

To a great extent, the sources of affective persuasion are found in an understanding of human needs and behavior. Some are learned; some are thought to be innate. Ever since ancient times, humankind has tried to find simple explanations of what motivates people to do what they do. If you could discover these explanations and determine universal systems of human motivation, you could theoretically control the behaviors of others in many ways. In modern times we speak of reducing internal tensions, but are wary of surefire manipulations of those tensions. We're not only interested in the message sent but also the message received. In a systems view there is an interaction—something mutual about persuasion.

To some philosophers, most notably Aristotle, "the proper study of man is man himself." The assumption is that all humans, at least in a general sense, are much alike. At the physiological level this assumption presents few problems, for despite obvious individual differences in height, weight, color, and other physical attributes, all people exhibit a striking physical similarity. We could hardly have a science of medicine were this not true. In the nonphysiological realm the problem is more complicated. Plato argued that to study humans one must investigate their environment; for Plato, "man" was but a reflection of his own society, a view not unlike the social constructionist theories of today. Both Plato and Aristotle make sense. We can learn much from studying the similarities among all of us; perhaps even more by studying the social environments that produce many of our differences.

Any attempt to classify similar human needs must begin with biological needs. Such a system has been supplied by A. H. Maslow.[16] His notions synthesize much of the tension-reduction theorizing and also extend our understanding by suggesting that human needs are arranged hierarchically.

These five general categories of needs, in the order of their importance, are *physiological, safety, love, esteem,* and *self-actualization.* As each need in the sequence is satisfied, a person seeks out the next highest level. This hierarchy of needs may be thought of as a ladder or steps shown in Figure 11.6.

If members of your audience cannot climb to even the first rung of the ladder, they theoretically are not as likely to be persuaded by the higher rungs. Starving people are thought to be almost blind to all appeals except those promising food and drink. However, once fat and full, they become concerned with safety. After achieving a feeling of safety, they can be more appealed to by the higher rungs of the ladder. In simple terms, individuals are

Figure 11.6

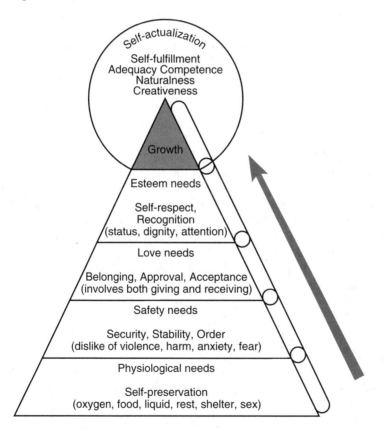

no longer motivated by needs (however basic) that are pretty much satisfied. These needs can all be operating at one time but with varying strengths.

Certain prerequisites in the Maslow system are so important that they themselves become strong motivators when denied or endangered.[17] The environmental prerequisites include such things as free speech, intellectual freedom, the right to self-defense, and a desire for justice, honesty, and orderliness.

In Chapter 1 we pointed out that receivers decode according to their past experiences, emotions, and attitudes. More specifically, they decode in terms of their interacting needs. At one time the need for love may predominate, coloring the meaning listeners attach to a communication; at another time the need for esteem may be foremost, and their openness to persuasion is altered accordingly.

Specific needs, motives, appeals, and so forth can be roughly sorted under the five basic needs as shown in Figure 11.7; Napoleon headed toward the self-esteem needs and internal-tension reduction.

Engaging the Consistency Principle

Our thought systems seek an agreeable, balanced set of relationships between our view of the world and our latest information. This search for consistency suggests that speakers can persuade by using reasoning that causes an audience feelings of dissonance with their own point of view. The word *dissonance* refers to these ill-fitting, inconsistent thoughts. Sources of such dissonance range from logical argument to emotion and mixed feelings.

COGNITIVE DISSONANCE   Leon Festinger, chief architect of cognitive-dissonance theory, points out that we could substitute the words *frustration* and *disequilibrium,* among others, for *dissonance.*[18] Whatever the label, the word refers to ill-fitting, inconsistent relationships among our thoughts and beliefs. *Logical* inconsistency is a typical source of dissonance. There are, of course, other sources of dissonance between beliefs based, for example, on past experience and cultural norms.

The basic hypotheses of cognitive-dissonance theory are:

1. The existence of dissonance, being psychologically uncomfortable, will motivate the person to try to reduce the dissonance and achieve consonance.

2. When dissonance is present, in addition to trying to reduce it, the person will actively avoid situations and information which would likely increase the dissonance.[19]

The theory of cognitive dissonance clearly states that *behavior can cause persuasion.* Many very creative research projects support this point and provide suggestions for involvement and self-persuasion.[20] For example, in argu-

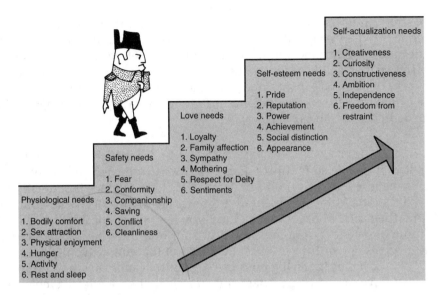

Self-actualization needs

1. Creativeness
2. Curiosity
3. Constructiveness
4. Ambition
5. Independence
6. Freedom from restraint

Self-esteem needs

1. Pride
2. Reputation
3. Power
4. Achievement
5. Social distinction
6. Appearance

Love needs

1. Loyalty
2. Family affection
3. Sympathy
4. Mothering
5. Respect for Deity
6. Sentiments

Safety needs

1. Fear
2. Conformity
3. Companionship
4. Saving
5. Conflict
6. Cleanliness

Physiological needs

1. Bodily comfort
2. Sex attraction
3. Physical enjoyment
4. Hunger
5. Activity
6. Rest and sleep

Figure 11.7 Motive terms and the basic needs.

ing against one's own point of view, as college debaters must often do, it was found that the speakers changed their attitudes more than the listeners. This kind of logical inconsistency apparently creates intrapersonal dissonance and, often as a result, self-persuasion.

The practical suggestions stemming from cognitive consistency indicate that a persuader may need to create dissonance through argument (a need) and then show how to achieve consonance (a plan). Audience analysis is needed to see how much need may already exist. The second hypothesis suggests that *too many* dissonance-provoking arguments might induce avoidance. How many are too many? That is not easily answered because an audience's *personal involvement* or commitment, especially a public one, to an issue or its source (pro or con) can make a real difference in how a receiver is apt to respond.[21] A superficial opinion on the number of beans in a jar doesn't represent much personal involvement; a lightly held belief or attitude, such as a preference for one brand of coffee over another, suggests only a modest personal involvement. A public commitment to a religion, family, country, or lifestyle is quite another matter. Here we are dealing with values and serious social constructions of reality. Values were defined earlier as *frameworks that hold attitudes together.* Values involve us very personally. They help define our self-concept. They are ego-centered.

Recent research suggests that when receivers perceive your message as having high personal relevance for them, three really strong arguments are better standing alone than adding another two or three weak ones. Interestingly, when listeners had low personal involvement with the issue, the combination of strong and weak arguments was more persuasive than the strong arguments alone.[22] When people don't see much personal relevance in an issue but *like* the speaker, one good strong argument is often sufficient. It was found more effective than a *disliked* speaker using even as many as five strong arguments.[23]

It seems clear that one is well-advised to adapt one's message to the personal interests of the audience. Clarify early why your message is relevant to audience members.

AFFECTIVE/COGNITIVE DISSONANCE   Both research and experience suggest that people suffer dissonance when what they feel (affective) and what they believe (cognitive) do not agree.[24] If clear evidence is suddenly discovered that long-time Representative Smith is receiving kickbacks from his staff after their salaries have been padded, you may suffer considerable dissonance (or inconsistency) in supporting him. Your new information (he's dishonest) is inconsistent with your longtime affection for Smith, the man.

Scandals involving politicians, political candidates, and even televangelists have caused many Americans to suffer pangs of affective/cognitive dissonance. How does one reduce such tensions and achieve consistency in such dilemmas? Affective/cognitive theory suggests three things that one can do. All have implications for speakers who would use this merged-mode of persuasion.

Upon hearing the evidence regarding Representative Smith a receiver might (1) *reject* the data and communication that brought about the difficulty: "I simply don't believe it"; (2) *fragment* the original attitude by trying to isolate the affective and cognitive elements: "Others do it. He just got caught," or "The good he's done outweighs the bad"; or (3) *change* your attitude by accommodating the dilemma in such a way that your feelings and beliefs are consistent: "I'll not vote for him. My feelings have changed. I don't believe in dishonesty." Presumably you could also escape by trying not to think about the inconsistency.

As we learned earlier, the amount of your *involvement* with or *commitment* to Representative Smith could make a difference. A heavily involved person might simply stop at choice 1, that is, reject the news of Representative Smith's dishonesty as preposterous. A lightly involved person might briefly test choices 1 and 2 and then decide on choice 3 and change his or her attitude. Indeed, a hierarchical sequence is suggested here. One's first tendency is to reject, then fragment, then change one's attitude.

Using Both-Sides Persuasion

When you feel that you have good, solid arguments to support your position but also know that your audience clearly doesn't agree, is it better to stick with just your one-sided arguments? Or is it better to acknowledge opposing arguments as well?

The advertisement by Seagram Distillers not only acknowledges, but also concedes the disrupting effects of too much alcohol. The handwriting in the Seagram ad (Figure 11.8) is also a clear and interesting use of the logical supports of persuasion.

Both-sides persuasion presents arguments both pro and con to the point you are making. This method of organization typically opens with the "other" side, that is, a conceding of some of the obvious arguments against (con) your position. It is a particularly good method when there is obvious antagonism or opposition toward your point of view or when the audience has been *inoculated* against your position.

The Gerber baby food ads which are opposed by some pediatric societies (who want mothers to breast-feed) start out with the clear concession that "Mother's milk is best." They then suggest that "If mother's milk is not

Figure 11.8

From "Moderation Messages," Seagram Distillers Co.

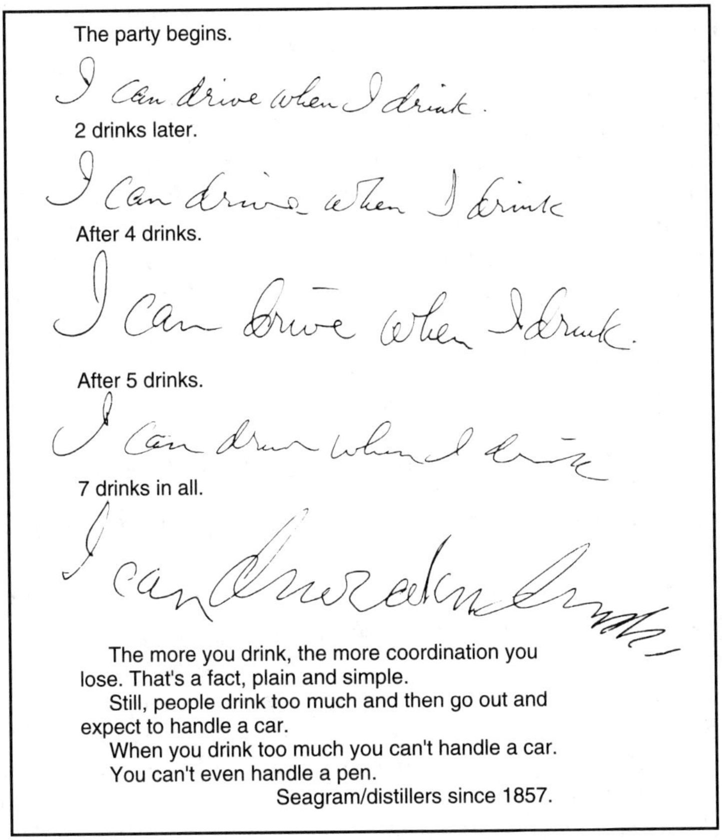

The party begins.

I can drive when I drink.

2 drinks later.

I can drive when I drink

After 4 drinks.

I can drive when I drunk.

After 5 drinks.

I can drun when I drin

7 drinks in all.

I can drverdrin drm

The more you drink, the more coordination you lose. That's a fact, plain and simple.
Still, people drink too much and then go out and expect to handle a car.
When you drink too much you can't handle a car.
You can't even handle a pen.
Seagram/distillers since 1857.

available, we should use Gerbers." Reasons to do so follow. Note that those opposed to *any* and all advertising of baby foods may not be impressed, of course, and will probably not be persuaded by any argument, whatever its organization. "You can't win them all!"

The effects of argument arrangement on antagonistic receivers when their initial attitudes are known have been generalized as follows:

1. Presenting arguments on both sides of an issue is more effective than giving only the arguments supporting the point being made.

2. Audiences previously persuaded by both-sides argumentation are more resistant to counterpersuasion than those persuaded with one-sided argumentation.

The supporting research concludes that a two-sided presentation is more effective in the long run than a one-sided one (1) when, regardless of initial opinion, the audience is exposed to subsequent counterpersuasion, or (2) when, regardless of subsequent exposure to counterpersuasion, the audience initially disagrees with the speaker's position.[25]

Both-sides persuasion has the appeal of objective, rational evaluation. It is a subtle yet honest call for fair play. Opposing arguments are not omitted; therefore, opposed listeners are less antagonized. Listening should be more favorable because the listener will not be rehearsing as many counterarguments during the positive persuasion. Both-sides persuasion not only helps insulate or inoculate audiences against counterarguments but also forces speakers to be more audience oriented. Successful both-sides speakers are more sensitive to their audience's attitudes and to all the relevant arguments and issues. One student speaker, after much research on both sides of his speech topic, reported that he was now convinced of the other side.

> He who knows only his side of the story doesn't know that—
>
> *J. S. Mill*

Some specific characteristics of a both-sides persuasive speaker are:

1. *Objectivity:* is fair; bases bias on evidence; concedes the obvious; refutes equitably.

2. *Suspended judgment:* avoids superpositive statements; creates doubt; frequently uses the hypothesis form.

3. *Nonspecific opponents:* does not stress audience opposition; seeks common ground.

4. *Critical willingness:* promotes common reevaluation; motivates receiver to reconsider the other side.

5. *Qualified language:* avoids overgeneralized statements; avoids harsh criticism.

6. *Audience sensitivity:* adapts the presentation to feedback signs; considers alternative actions before making the speech.

7. *Ethical conduct:* above all, is honest; acknowledges or concedes significant opposing arguments in an objective manner.

If the opposition to the topic bleeds over to include you, the speaker, you should try in some way to establish common ground. The experience of professional speakers pretty much agrees with the more academic suggestions:

1. Be friendly and modest. (Avoid "I think . . .")
2. Refer to common experiences.
3. Compliment tactfully.
4. Use tasteful humor (especially at your own expense).
5. Point out agreements with their beliefs and attitudes.
6. Commit reasonable time for opposing arguments.[26]
7. Make sure your facts are absolutely correct and supported.
8. Let your introducer help establish your credibility.

> The best argument is that which seems merely an explanation.
>
> *Dale Carnegie*

In its simplest form the both-sides strategy appears as follows:

Thesis or Claim: (Unless obvious, this is typically withheld until the transition.)

INTRODUCTION

BODY
   I. Acknowledgments (con side)
      A. Arguments against your claim
      B. Concessions when obvious
   II. Transition (An appeal for a fair hearing of your side of the issue)
   III. Pro side arguments and appeals
      A.
      B. } (Pro)
      C.
      D. Meeting objections

CONCLUSION

More detailed organizational methods and illustrations will follow shortly.

Using Evidence and Logical Reasoning

The intrapersonal and cognitive response models discussed earlier argued that when receivers could be induced to think or elaborate about issue-relevant arguments they were most likely to be persuaded. This was the more central versus the peripheral route to effective persuasion. Clearly a responsible and ethical persuader needs intelligent arguments supported by valid evidence, logical reasoning, and critical thinking. This route to effective persuasion is important enough to warrant its own chapter, "Logical Reasoning and Argument," following this chapter.

ORGANIZING THE PERSUASIVE SPEECH

Natural-Order Method

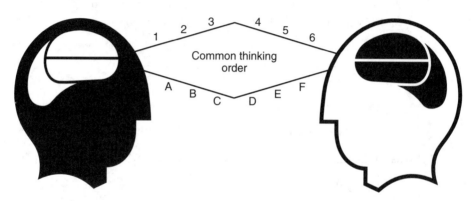

Figure 11.9

The most famous natural-order or common thinking system is what John Dewey called *reflective thinking.* This pattern is used frequently in group problem solving and is discussed further in Chapter 14. It includes:

1. Attention and awareness of felt difficulty.
2. Recognition of a problem or need.
3. Sorting of objections and counterplans in search of the best solution.
4. Working out and visualizing the proposed solution.
5. Evaluation of the solution, leading to its acceptance or rejection.

Persuaders and speech scholars have made many adaptations. One suggests that the fundamental tasks of a speaker are attention, interest, impression, conviction, and direction. Some other popular organization systems based on natural order follow:

Table 11.1   A Comparison of Natural-Order Systems

	HOLLINGWORTH	McGEE[27]	MONROE	ROSS
Introduction	Attention	Attention	Attention	Attention
	Interest	Problem	Need	Need
Body	Impression	Solution	Satisfaction	Plan
	Conviction	Visualization	Visualization	Reinforcement
Conclusion	Direction	Action	Action	Direction

Alan H. Monroe called his popular method the *motivated sequence,* the sequence of ideas which by following the normal process of thinking motivates the audience to respond to the speaker's purpose.[28] The key steps are (1) attention, (2) need, (3) satisfaction, (4) visualization, and (5) action. This system argues that, first, our attention must be caught; second, we must be made to feel a definite need; third, we must be shown a way to satisfy this need; fourth, we must be made to see how the proposal applies to us personally; finally, we must be shown how we should act. This system is really a need-plan or need-solution system, as explained in Chapter 6. Most of our TV commercials follow this format.

Natural-order systems for organizing persuasion make much of the **attention concept.** William James once said, "What holds attention determines action . . ." This readiness to respond does not, of course, follow every good attention step, but the research on emphasis and its use in successful advertising does suggest its importance. Attention is also selective and often fleeting. It is necessary to concentrate on keeping an audience attentive and interested throughout the steps in the organizing process.

In its full form the *need* step involves a fourfold development: (1) a *statement* of the specific problem; (2) an *illustration* of the need; (3) the *ramification* or reinforcement of the need through the enumeration of additional examples and evidence; and (4) a *pointing out* of the direct relationship of the need to the receivers.

The "satisfaction" step, when fully developed, consists of a fivefold procedure: (1) a clear *statement* of the belief or action you wish the receivers to adopt; (2) an *explanation* for further clarity; (3) a *theoretical demonstration* of how the solution specifically meets the need step; (4) the use of *practical experience*—that is, examples and evidence that prove the efficacy of your solution; and (5) the *meeting of objections*—that is, the forestalling of opposition to probable counterarguments.

In Chapter 10 we discussed the forms of emphasis useful in transferring information to the audience. Audiences were better able to remember things that they had been told with emphasis. Granted, an improvement in an audience's remembering or interest does not necessarily mean that their attitudes have been changed, or even that they are more open to change. However, if attention and interest do help determine action and a readiness to respond, as James says, then the suggestions for presenting information fit here also.

Whatever specific organization adaptation you decide upon, the following *psychological order* is used, at least theoretically, in all persuasion speeches:

1. Creation of attention and location or establishment of need.
2. Arousal of interest and problem awareness by relating the need to the specific audience.
3. Explanation of the solution in terms of the problem, need, previous experience, knowledge, and personality of the audience.
4. Evaluation, when necessary, of all important objections, counterarguments, or alternative solutions.
5. Reinforcement of your message throughout your speech, particularly toward the end of it, through verbal reminders, reviews, summaries, and visualizations.

Any message-arrangement prescription is a simplification of a very complex persuasion system. Nevertheless, the popular practices shown in Table 11.1 are very useful in showing the relationship of message, receiver, sender, and how one begins to organize the parts of a message.

A speaker's outline on the subject of "Dutch Treating" follows. He used the motivated sequence arrangement method and labeled his motive appeals.

MODEL OUTLINE

Topic: Dutch-Style Dating

General Purpose: To persuade.

Specific Purpose: To persuade the audience that both men and women reap benefits by "Dutch Treating."

Central Idea: Male treating engenders fears of unequal date obligations.

DUTCH IT UP A LITTLE

ATTENTION

I. Women, have you ever dated men whom you really never got to know that well?

(Conflict)

   A. Have you ever experienced an odd feeling of indebtedness after or even during a first or second date?

   B. Have you ever found yourself pushing to enjoy yourself rather than simply *being* yourself?

Introduction

II. Men, have you been discouraged by costly dates?

(Conflict)

   A. Since you're paying, do you ever feel chauvinistic?

(Conflict)

   B. Have you ever thought that your mixed feelings had stopped the *real* you from shining through?

NEED

I. Our Student Council survey on dating had two main conclusions.

    A. Many women feel unnecessarily indebted to men who insist on treating them on the first few dates.

(Self-esteem)   **B.** Many men take pride in their being able to afford a nice evening for two but feel that it's simply taken for granted.

Body   **II.** To pay or not to pay is a real fear.

(Conflict)   **A.** Women may appear pushy or pushover.

    B. Men may appear stupid or chauvinistic.

  III. Whether male or female, students are not usually independently wealthy.

(Safety)   **A.** Why does one pay the whole bill and the other nothing?

    B. Is this simply the way it is or is there a sound basis?

SATISFACTION

Body

(Safety)   **I.** Only through the practice of the "Dutch Treat" can these fears be alleviated.

    A. Women need not feel uneasy or dependent in any way on men they hardly know.

(Love)   **B.** Men are able to say, in a special way, "I'd like to treat you tonight because I enjoy your company."

      1. Contrast to our taken for granted, "He always treats."

      2. A way of saying something special we all like to hear.

  II. Both men and women benefit from "Dutch"-style dating.

(Self-actualization)   **A.** Only when two people are equal in a relationship can they really reach for the sky together.

    B. Neither men nor women feel an unnecessary indebtedness with "Dutch"-style dating.

(Love need)   **1.** They are thus able to concentrate on how they really interact with each other.

(Self-actualization)   **2.** Fulfilling relationships can develop under these conditions.

VISUALIZATION

  I. The "He always pays" way of dating has gone too far.

    A. If a woman wishes to pay her own bill, her date often feels that her action is a form of rejection.

(Safety)   **1.** Why shouldn't she have this right to independency?

      2. Couldn't her gesture mean she cares for him and his financial situation?

  II. Personal illustration.

    A. Mabel misunderstood.

    B. I had not been forthright.

ACTION

Conclusion

(Fear)

    I. Try dating "Dutch" next time, but heed two warnings:

      A. Warnings to men.

        1. Misunderstanding may result due to assumed status quo.

        2. Misunderstanding may result from a lack of forthrightness.

      B. Warnings to women.

        1.

          same as above

        2.

    II. Make your dates as enjoyable as my second one with Mabel!

The next speaker outline followed the more standard introduction-body-conclusion format for the outline and labeled the persuasive modes "logical" and "affective."

MODEL OUTLINE

Topic: Ozone
General Purpose: To persuade.
Specific Purpose: To persuade the audience not to buy a car with air conditioning.
Central Idea: Dangerous ozone depletion is caused by leaking chlorofluorocarbons (CFCs) from 100 million automotive air conditioners.

BE COOL WITHOUT CFCs

INTRODUCTION

    I. Ozone, the Jekyll and Hyde of chemicals.

Logical Mode

      A. O_3 occurs as a gaseous layer seven miles above the earth.

      B. It is a shield that absorbs intense ultraviolet radiation.

    II. In the lower atmosphere "ground ozone" is a major pollutant.

      A. It contributes to smog.

Affective Mode

      B. It damages crops and forests.

      C. It endangers human health.

BODY

    I. Chlorofluorocarbons (CFCs) drift upward and destroy the natural ozone layer.

      A. This causes excessive ultraviolet radiation.

Affective Mode

      B. This can cause skin cancer and cataracts.

      C. This is deleterious to animals and plants.

II. Sources of chlorofluorocarbons (CFCs).

  A. Blow-in and polystyrene insulation is a source.

  B. Propellants in aerosols are a source.

Logical Mode   **C.** Certain cleaners used in electronics.

  D. Coolants (freon) used in refrigerators and automotive air conditioners are a major source.

III. Don't let your car contribute to natural ozone depletion.

  A. 100 million American cars used CFCs in their air conditioners.

Logical Mode   **B.** Each unit springs a leak every three years.

  C. Quick fixes only contribute more CFCs that last 150 years.

CONCLUSION

I. Keep your air conditioner in good repair.

Logical Mode   **A.** Run your AC at least 10 minutes every month to protect the seals.

  B. Seek out service that uses a CFC recycling machine.

II. Don't buy a car with air conditioning built before 1995.

Logical Mode   **A.** Alternate coolants solved the CFCs problem by then.

  B. Use shades, windshields, sun barriers, and fans.

Merged Mode   **III.** Do your part to protect the ozone layer and to prevent ground ozone pollution. Be cool without CFCs.

Both-Sides Method

There are three general ways to organize two-sided messages: (1) acknowledge and concede first (con); (2) present your side first (pro); and (3) repeat the con-pro order with each issue (con/pro, con/pro, and so forth).

The research evidence discussed earlier generally supports the *con-pro* order, that is, acknowledge and concede first, then refute and explain your side. This is an especially good choice when audiences are antagonistic, ill-humored, or hostile. When audiences are not unusually troubled with your position, it may be enough to simply discuss and meet objections to your case at the end of the speech. If your speech involves multiple issues each of which is in contention, it may be advisable to interweave the con-pro strategy as you take up each new issue.

A useful format for the con-pro order follows. First, acknowledge or concede opposing arguments and then refute and support your own claim.

Topic:
General Purpose: Persuade (both-sides persuasion)
Specific Purpose:
Thesis or Claim:

INTRODUCTION

    Attention

    Orientation

BODY (CON)

    Acknowledge con arguments

    Concede con arguments

TRANSITION

    The bridge between the con and pro;
    an appeal for fair hearing
    and reciprocity

BODY (PRO)

    Refutation and arguments supporting your claim

CONCLUSION

    Review and/or visualization

    Final pro-side appeal

If your speech has two or three major arguments or contentious issues that pretty much stand alone, the "con-pro-repeat" organization might be preferable:

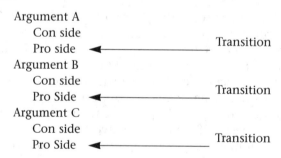

INTRODUCTION

BODY

    Argument A
      Con side
      Pro side   Transition
    Argument B
      Con side
      Pro Side   Transition
    Argument C
      Con side
      Pro Side   Transition

CONCLUSION

A sample student outline showing both-sides organization follows. Note that it opens with a concession and the critical arguments *against* (con) the position. The state of Michigan has a deposit law on beer and soft drink containers. A campaign to repeal the deposit law was under way, supported by both the Can Manufacturing Institute and some consumers who objected to the extra cost. Many in the audience supported the repeal and all would be exposed to media counterpersuasion—a good time for both-sides persuasion.

MODEL BOTH-SIDES OUTLINE

Topic: Repeal of deposit law

General Purpose: To persuade (both-sides persuasion).

Specific Purpose: To persuade the audience to retain the deposit law.

Central Idea: We should resist the campaign to repeal the deposit law because the law protects the environment at a reasonable cost.

MANY HAPPY RETURNS

INTRODUCTION

(Attention)

I. Are these a familiar sight to you? (Exhibits: several bottles and cans).

    A. As you know, last December 3rd the deposit law went into effect.

        1. It requires a deposit on all beer and soft drink containers.

        2. Deposits are then repaid when consumers return the containers for reuse or recycling.

    B. Since most of you probably drink soft drinks or beer, this law affects you directly.

BODY (con side)

I. And you as consumers know this law does affect your pocketbook.

(Acknowledgments and Concessions)

    A. The Can Manufacturing Institute's recent survey of shelf prices indicates that beer and soft drinks cost about one dollar a case more in Michigan than in states that don't have deposit laws.

    B. The Stroh Brewing Company and Coca-Cola of Detroit concede: "Unfortunately the cost of doing business has to be passed on."

II. Industry representatives show that the price increases are due to the extra handling which the law creates.

    A. When the consumer returns the bottles and cans, the retailer has to store them until the bottler picks them up.

    B. Many retailers and bottlers are complaining about storage problems and sanitation problems which increase costs.

        1. They need more warehouse space to store empties.

        2. They need bottle washers.

        3. They need additional delivery trucks to transport the empties.

        4. They also need to hire more drivers.

III. There are other complaints about the law.

    A. It eliminates some jobs in glassmaking (bottles are reused).

    B. The law probably wastes energy by forcing trucks to make additional trips with empty containers.

BODY (PRO SIDE)

    I. But if you really think about it, what are we supposed to do?

      A. Repeal the law like the Associated Food Dealers want to do.

(Transition to Pro Side)

      B. Then go back to all the cans, bottles, and broken glass on our streets, highways, and landscaping.

      C. I think not; listen to the reasons for supporting our deposit law.

    II. Volunteers have recently staged a cleanup throughout the state.

      A. Of 9,000 items picked up, only 9 were returnables.

(Evidence)

      B. Look at the differences in our roadsides and our neighborhoods (before and after pictures).

      C. Our penalty litter fines obviously were not doing the job.

    III. Five other states now have deposit laws.

      A. A survey in Oregon (which has a long-standing deposit law) says that 95% of the people still favor the law.

      B. Oregon's deposit return rate is 94%.

      C. In Vermont (which also has a deposit law) a study shows:

        1. A 76% decline in beverage litter.

        2. A 35% reduction in total litter volume.

(Evidence)

        3. A 31% decline in state costs for litter pick-up.

        4. The law has created about 400 new jobs in sorting, storing, and truck driving.

        5. Vermont figures that the container manufacturers save 708 million BTU's in energy annually as a result of recycling and reuse. (That's enough energy to heat the homes of 15,000 people.)

(Meeting Objections)

    IV. The increase in the prices of beer and soft drinks may also be caused by other factors.

      A. The Michigan United Conservation Clubs recently asked the Attorney General to investigate the increases in prices. They found:

        1. Many bottlers changed their product designs.

        2. Bottlers switched to metric volumes. (Display ½ liter Coke bottle.)

        3. Bottlers installed new equipment.

      B. These are new and mostly one-time costs.

      C. Once these costs are assimilated, bottle and can prices should drop.

        1. The average bottle is used over and over (about 15 times).

        2. The aluminum cans are recycled over and over and over, which reduces the cost of aluminum and saves our natural resources.

        3. A Faygo spokesman said that the deposit law will result in some reduced prices after the new equipment is paid for.

CONCLUSION

    I. The deposit law is a way to deal with the problem of litter from beverage containers.

      A. Isn't it nice to see the Michigan streets cleaner again?

      B. Wouldn't it be even nicer to see the whole country cleaner?

(Visualization)

    C. Because people have to pay a deposit on a container, it's more than likely they will return it rather than throw it around.

    D. As we have seen, the deposit law is not solely responsible for our current price increases.

    E. It may be inconvenient returning the containers but isn't it worth the trouble?

  II. This law is a major step in cleaning up this country. Support the deposit law—resist the repeal campaign.

    A. If someone asks you to sign a petition to repeal the law, DON'T DO IT.

(Final appeal)

    B. If, by some chance, it comes on the ballot in 1998, vote to keep our deposit law.

    C. There is talk of a nationwide deposit law to clean up the whole country. I urge your support.

  III. The benefits greatly outweigh the inconvenience.

    A. Help keep Michigan and the Nation clean.

    B. "Many Happy Returns."

Summary

All speeches to persuade involve efforts to get receivers to: (1) accept your interpretation of *disputed facts;* or (2) align their *beliefs, attitudes,* and *values* more closely with yours; and/or (3) move them to *action* on your proposition. When we deal with more involved courses of action, we are talking about policy—speeches on what *should* or *should not* be done over time. In action speeches one must demonstrate a need or problem and then provide a practical plan or solution. Most attitudes are changed incrementally.

Influence refers to any power that affects a person or course of events. Motivation pertains to any stimulation or inducement that leads to an act or belief. Motivation need not be intentional and is essentially amoral. Persuasion is an ethical, nonviolent means of influencing and motivating others through messages. It is an instrument for obtaining reasoned adherence to rational propositions.

Attitudes refer to the thinking, feeling, and behavioral intentions that govern our predispositions toward people, situations, and things. An attitude may also be defined as a tendency to respond in a given way. The dimensions of attitude have been described as cognitive, affective, and behavioral. Attitudes are underlaid by belief systems, which have vertical and horizontal structures; that is, they can be engaged by us at different levels. Attitudes cannot always be represented adequately by a single point on a scale. They have different ranges or latitudes of acceptance. There is also a tendency for attitude response to have an assimilation or contrast effect depending on how discrepant one's initial attitude is.

The *Elaboration Likelihood Method* (ELM) of persuasion suggests that the more elaborately a receiver responds cognitively, the greater the likelihood of attitude change. Cognitive-response theory suggests that people really persuade themselves through cognitive reevaluations. The basic speaker strategy is to develop messages that (1) evoke favorable thoughts and (2) induce people to rehearse and remember these thoughts.

In the intrapersonal-response model, these responses may be affective and behavioral as well as cognitive. *Persuasion,* in this context, *is a process of skillfully and ethically using logical thoughts, affective appeals, credibility, and ethical proof to influence and motivate others to respond as you wish them to.*

Five routes to effective persuasion include: credibility, human needs, consistency theory, both-sides persuasion, and logical reasoning.

Credibility refers to the audience's acceptance of or disposition toward the source. It is related to Aristotle's notions of goodwill, good moral character, and good sense—in modern times, good intentions, trustworthiness, and competence or expertise. High source credibility generally produces more attitude change. Ethical proof includes attitude similarity, language, humor, voice, evidence, and general impression.

Impression management includes practical facts on how you present yourself to receivers. *Front* is your appearance and manner. *Dramatic realization* is the role you play on the stage of life. *Mystification* refers to the social distance between you and the audience.

Maslow's theory provides us with a useful classification of human needs. In order of their importance, these needs are physiological, safety, love, esteem, and self-actualization. A satisfied need is no longer a motivator according to this theory. Motive appeals are useful triggers of human needs.

Cognitive-dissonance theory assumes that when new information is contradictory to or inconsistent with a person's ideas and attitudes, some psychological confusion and tension will result. This tension motivates people to adjust their attitudes or behavior in order to reduce this inconsistency. (A persuader needs to create enough dissonance [or need] and then show how to achieve consonance [a plan].) However, too many dissonance-provoking arguments might induce avoidance. Other variables that may intrude are speaker likability and the personal involvement of the audience.

An audience's personal involvement or commitment to an issue or its source makes a difference in how they are apt to respond. The number and strength of arguments used by a sender should vary with the personal relevance perceived by receivers.

Affective/cognitive consistency theory suggests that when our beliefs are in conflict with our feelings, the resulting dissonance can be relieved by: (1) rejecting the data, (2) fragmenting the original attitude, or (3) changing our attitude.

Both-sides persuasion has been shown to be superior to one-sided persuasion when the audience is initially opposed to the point of view being presented or when, regardless of initial attitude, the audience is exposed to counterargument. A rational form of persuasion, the both-sides approach is characterized by objectivity, suspended judgment, nonspecific opponents, critical willingness, qualified language, audience sensitivity, and ethical conduct.

A natural thinking order suggests the following procedure for organizing persuasive messages:

1. Creation of attention and location or establishment of need.

2. Arousal of interest and problem awareness by relating the need to the specific audience.

3. Explanation of the solution in terms of the problem, need, previous experience, knowledge, and personality of the audience.

4. Evaluation, when necessary, of all important objections, counterarguments, or alternative solutions.

5. Reinforcement of the message throughout the speech, particularly toward the end, through verbal reminders, reviews, summaries, and visualizations.

There are many plans similar to this one. Hollingworth suggests that the fundamental tasks of a speaker are attention, interest, impression, conviction, and direction.

Alan H. Monroe calls his system the motivated sequence, "the sequence of ideas which, by following the normal process of thinking, motivates the audience to respond to the speaker's purpose." The key steps are (1) attention, (2) need, (3) satisfaction, (4) visualization, and (5) action.

There are three ways to organize two-sided messages: (1) acknowledge and concede first (con); (2) your side first (pro); and (3) repeat the con-pro order with each argument (con-pro, con-pro, and so forth). The con-pro order works best when audiences are antagonistic or ill-humored. When audiences are not unusually troubled it is often enough to state your case and meet objections to it at the close. In multiple argument or issue speeches, the interwoven con-pro strategy may work best.

Learning Projects

1. Find or invent topics for each of the persuasive speech types: (1) disputed facts, (2) belief and values, and (3) action and policy. Explain your reasoning.

2. Describe two situations where you have experienced primarily influence and motivation as differentiated from persuasion.

3. Prepare to discuss an attitude you hold that is based on conflicting belief systems. Explain how the conflict affects the strength of your attitude, or perhaps your behavior.

4. Find two print advertisements that used mostly credibility as a route to persuasion.

5. Research either a really good or really bad example of impression management. In a short speech describe how the person or organization developed a front, attempted dramatic realization, and used social distance or mystification. (Possible examples are: a doctor's office, the dean's office, a fancy party, a police officer, a rock group or singer, a teacher.)

6. In an editorial or advertisement, find appeals to any of the following human needs: physiological, safety, love, esteem, self-actualization. Take the specific audience into account.

7. Find two print advertisements that employed cognitive-dissonance theory. Explain.

8. Describe a time when your attitude components were in conflict (for example, affective-cognitive). How did you resolve the inconsistency?

9. Report and illustrate a radio or television commercial or other appeal (whether for antagonistic groups or not) that made use of both-sides persuasion. Create one of your own. (See pp. 258–261.)

10. Consider and prepare to report your feelings about the advice from professional speakers on how to deal with antagonistic, ill-tempered audiences (p. 261).

11. Analyze a print advertisement, and find the following natural-order steps: attention, need, satisfaction, visualization, and action.

12. Assume antagonistic receivers and *rough*-outline a both-sides strategy for one of the following:

a. U.S. Olympic athletes should not be subsidized by the federal government.

b. Sex education should be required in all public schools.

c. College students should hold a part-time job while in school.

d. Dual air bags should be required in all automobiles.

e. The federal government should enact a law to require the sterilization of the mentally deficient and the insane.

f. One of your own choice.

Notes

1. David Krech, Richard S. Crutchfield, Norman Livson, William A. Wilson, Jr., and Allen Parducci, *Elements of Psychology,* 4th ed. (New York: Alfred A Knopf, 1982), p. 435.

2. See Raymond S. Ross, *Understanding Persuasion,* 4th ed. (Englewood Cliffs, N. J.: Prentice Hall, 1994), pp. 65–68.

3. For more on this theory, see Ross, *Understanding Persuasion,* pp. 79–83; also see Carolyn Sherif, Muzafer Sherif, and Roger Nebergall, *Attitude and Attitude Change* (Philadelphia: Saunders, 1965; reprint 1982), p. 226.

4. See Richard E. Petty and John T. Cacioppo, "The Elaboration Likelihood Model of Persuasion," *Advances in Experimental Social Psychology,* vol. 19 (New York: Academic Press, 1986), p. 175.

5. Richard M. Perloff and Timothy C. Brock, ". . .'And Thinking Makes It So': Cognitive Responses to Persuasion," in *Persuasion: New Directions in Theory and Research,* ed. Michael E. Roloff and Gerald R. Miller (Beverly Hills, Calif.: Sage Publications, Inc., 1980), p. 90. For a modified view, see Daniel J. Bretl and James Price Dillard, "Persuasion and the Internality Dimension of Cognitive Responses," *Communication Studies,* 42, no. 2 (Summer 1991), 103–13.

6. John T. Cacioppo and Richard E. Petty, "Central and Peripheral Routes to Persuasion: The Role of Message Repetition," in *Psychological Processes and Advertising Effects,* eds. Linda F. Alwitt and Andrew A. Mitchell (Hillsdale, N.J.: Erlbaum, 1985), pp. 91–111.

7. Petty and Cacioppo, "Elaboration Likelihood Model."

8. Richard J. Lutz, "Affective and Cognitive Antecedents of Attitude Toward the Ad: A Conceptual Framework," in Alwitt and Mitchell, *Psychological Processes and Advertising Effects,* pp. 45–63; also see R. P. Bagozzi, "An Examination of the Validity of Two Models of Attitude," *Multivariate Behavioral Research,* 16 (1981), 323–59; and R. P. Bagozzi, A. M. Tybout, C. S. Craig, and B. Sternthal, "The Construct Validity of the Tripartite Classification of Attitudes," *Journal of Marketing Research,* 16 (1979), 88–95.

9. See Lane Cooper, *The Rhetoric of Aristotle* (New York: Appleton-Century-Crofts, 1932), pp. 24–25.

10. See Rajeev Batra and Michael L. Ray, "How Advertising Works," in Alwitt and Mitchell, *Psychological Processes and Advertising Effects,* pp. 13–43.

11. Jesse G. Delia, "A Constructivist Analysis of the Concept of Credibility," *The Quarterly Journal of Speech,* 62, no. 4 (December 1976), 361–75.

12. Jane Allyn and Leon Festinger, "The Effectiveness of Unanticipated Persuasive Communications," *Journal of Abnormal and Social Psychology,* 62 (1961), 35–40.

13. James E. McCLeaf and Margaret A. Colby, "The Effects of Students' Perceptions of a Speaker's Role on Their Recall of Drug Facts and Their Opinions and Attitudes about Drugs," *Journal of Educational Research,* 68 (July 1975), 382–86.

14. James J. Bradac, Catherine W. Konsky, and Robert A. Davies, "Two Studies of the Efforts of Linguistic Diversity upon the Judgments of Communicator Attributes and Message Effectiveness," *Communication Monographs,* 43 (March 1976), 70–79.

15. Erving Goffman, *The Presentation of Self in Everyday Life* (Garden City, N.Y.: Doubleday & Company, 1959; New York: Overlook Press, 1974), p. 208.

16. Abraham H. Maslow, "A Theory of Human Motivation," *Psychological Review,* 50 (1943), 370–96.

17. Abraham H. Maslow, *Toward a Psychology of Being,* (New York: Van Nostrand Reinhold Company, 1968), p. 25.

18. Leon Festinger, *A Theory of Cognitive Dissonance* (Stanford, Calif.: Stanford University Press, 1957), p. 14; also see Tori DeAngelis, "Cognitive Dissonance Alive and Well," *APA Monitor,* August, 1990, p. 10.

19. Ibid., p. 3.

20. Ross, *Understanding Persuasion,* pp. 76–79.

21. See Chris A. Dickerson, Ruth Thibodeau, Elliot Aronson, and Dayna Miller, "Using Cognitive Dissonance to Encourage Water Conservation," *Journal of Applied Social Psychology,* 22, no. 11 (June 1992), 841–54.

22. R. E. Petty and J. T. Cacioppo, "The Effects of Involvement on Responses to Argument Quantity and Quality: Central and Peripheral Routes to Persuasion," *Journal of Personality and Social Psychology,* 46 (1984), 69–81.

23. S. Chaiken, "Heuristic Versus Systematic Information Processing and the Use of Source Versus Message Cues in Persuasion," *Journal of Personality and Social Psychology,* 39 (1980), 752–66.

24. Milton Rosenberg and Robert Abelson, "An Analysis of Cognitive Balancing," in *Attitude Organization and Change,* eds. Carl Hovland and Milton Rosenberg (New Haven: Yale University Press, 1960; Westport, Conn.: Greenwood Press, Inc., 1980), pp. 112–63; see also M. Rosenberg, "An Analysis of Affective-Cognitive Consistency," in *Attitude Organization and Change,* pp. 15–64.

25. For a review of the classic Yale studies, see Ross, *Understanding Persuasion,* pp. 189–96; also see Mike Allen, Jerold Hale, Paul Mongeau, Sandra Berkowitz-Stafford, Shane Stafford, William Shanahan, Philip Agee, Kelly Dillon, Robert Jackson, and Cynthia Ray, "Testing a Model of Message Sidedness: Three Replications," *Communication Monographs,* 57, no. 4 (December 1990), 275–91.

26. See Mike Allen, "Meta-Analysis Comparing the Persuasiveness of One-sided and Two-sided Messages," *Western Journal of Speech Communication,* 55, no. 4, (Fall 1991), 390–404.

27. John A. McGee, *Persuasive Speaking* (New York: Charles Scribner's Sons, 1929).

28. B. E. Gronbeck, R. E. McKerrow, D. Ehninger, and A. H. Monroe, *Principles and Types of Speech Communication,* 13th ed. (New York: Addison Wesley Longman Publishers, 1996), p. 175.

12

LOGICAL REASONING AND ARGUMENT

COGNITIVE PERSUASION

The "Mostly" Central Route

In this, the cognitive or more "central route" of the persuasion process, we are concerned primarily with evidence, rational reasoning, critical thinking, and argument—that is, with the logical rather than the psychological and emotive modes of persuasion.

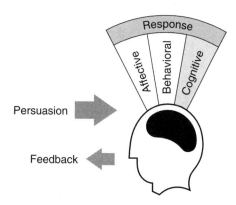

Figure 12.1

We are speaking of *making* arguments rather than having them, but the same intrapersonal thinking process is involved in both types. These internal efforts to evaluate reasons, evidence, and argument, if elaborated positively by receivers, lead to persuasion.

Humans are clearly different from animals in that they have the capacity to reason at higher levels of abstraction. They are, as a result, vulnerable to unethical or confused appeals that only *sound* logical. Those who intentionally muddle their arguments or befuddle their receivers are perhaps the most unethical persuaders of all. Those who don't analyze their audiences and check their assumptions are not far behind.

The new student in the first grade in Traverse City, Michigan was put on the spot by Ms. Clocko who asked, "Scott, when do the robins come to your home?" An uncomfortable six-year-old seemed evasive and confused. "Come, come Scott, you know the answer. Think hard." In a tentative, trembling voice, Scott answered, "Fall." "No, no, no. You think for a moment. " "Mark, can you answer the question?" "Yes, Ms. Clocko—spring." The sad part of this story is that Ms. Clocko was reasoning only from *her* view of the situation. Scott had recently moved from New Orleans, his home of birth, where the robins indeed do come in the fall.

The discussions that follow should help us avoid Ms. Clocko's problems (and Scott's) and also protect us from those who would intentionally use deceptive reasoning and argument.

We should be aware of unethical or confused arguments and the overlapping nature of emotive and rational appeals as we study the *primarily* logical, central modes of persuasion. Other things being equal, good, clear evidence, reasoning, and argument are critical to the quality and stature of your persuasion.

Sources of Evidence

The sources of evidence are objects or things that are observable, or reliable reports about such things. For our purposes, the most useful sources of evidence are (1) statements by authorities, (2) examples, and (3) statistics. These were discussed in detail in Chapter 5 under "Forms of Support."

In quick review, *authority* evidence is usually in the form of quoted *testimony* from a person better qualified than the speaker to give a considered opinion about something.

An **example** is a specific illustration, incident, or instance that supports a point you are trying to make.

To prove that a person can operate normally in a state of weightlessness, you can cite one example of an astronaut who has done so successfully. However, in some situations *one* factual example, though proving its own case, may be so exceptional that it does not truly support a generalization. If you were arguing that Volkswagens are assembled poorly and carelessly, and you supported this statement with only one example of a car that was defective, then your proof would become suspect. The question in the latter case becomes, "How many specific examples do I need?" This involves the question of inductive proof, which we'll discuss shortly.

"Figures don't lie, but liars figure." This old saw is a bit strong, but when used as evidence, *statistics* are sometimes confused, distorted, or misinterpreted. Divorce statistics are a case in point. The dramatic statistics—sometimes cited as high as one in two marriages ending in divorce—are generated by a one-year sample. For example, if your city showed records of 100,000 marriages and 33,000 divorces, you might say that the divorce rate was $33\frac{1}{3}$ percent or "one in three." However, if you judge the statistics *over time,* perhaps there will be one million marriages in the city. The divorce rate then becomes 3 percent! The statistics on the average duration of marriage are something like 6.9 years: however, the median duration is 43 years.

It is clear that statistics can quickly become complicated and capable of many applications. The lessons are (1) select the most appropriate statistics for your claim or thesis, and (2) make sure your audience will understand them.

A speaker's use of good *evidence* may significantly increase immediate attitude change and credibility when the message is delivered well, and particularly when the audience has little or no prior familiarity with the evidence. Evidence also appears to make listeners less easily persuaded by future counterargument. Assuming a message has information of some essential worth, the delivery of it and its accompanying ethical proof are also important to how the audience finally evaluates the evidence.[1]

FORMS OF REASONING

From Generalization

Reasoning from generalization involves inducting from fair and sufficient samples or examples. "*Induction* is a type of reasoning that begins with specific instances and through the process of synthesis arrives at conclusions that are probable."[2]

"HELLO, FDA?... I'D LIKE TO REPORT RESEARCH THAT DIRECTLY LINKS CHEESE WITH DEATH IN RATS."

Figure 12.2 Some generalizations are better than others.

© 1977 Wayne Stayskal, Chicago Tribune.

Generalization rests on the assumption of regularity of a characteristic within a class. If a new Mazda automobile shows up with a defective motor mount, we may have an atypical or special case. If fifty of the identical models show up with the same defect, it is probably time to argue for a recall. The argument is based on the assumption that if defective mounts are found in these known cases, then they will probably show up in the unknown cases.

Here are some tests for good generalizing from specific cases:

1. Are there a reasonable number of cases?
2. Are the cases typical?
3. Are the negative cases accounted for?

Whenever you argue from "accepted" to particular cases, you are reasoning *deductively*. If we agree on the generalization or first premise that "all birds have wings," then our deduction appears as follows:

Premise 1:	All birds have wings.
Premise 2:	All ostriches are birds.
Conclusion:	Therefore, all ostriches have wings.

The preceding example is called a categorical syllogism. A syllogism may only have three terms, and the middle term may not appear in the conclusion. *Wings* is the major term, *birds* the middle term, and *ostriches* the minor term.

Most of your speeches that use deductive argument will not follow such a strict syllogistic form. However, the testing of your deduction, and perhaps your entire speech purpose, may be aided by utilizing the syllogistic form.

Suppose your specific purpose is to persuade the audience that *smoking should be made illegal.* The general premises you are considering are:

> *Actions that cause cancer are evil.*
> *Smoking is an action that causes cancer.*

Your conclusion is:

> *Therefore, smoking is evil.*

The conclusion now becomes a premise in another syllogism.

> *That which is evil should be made illegal.*
> *Smoking is evil.*
> *Therefore, smoking should be made illegal.*

More likely your deductive argument would appear in the form of an *enthymeme,* that is, an abbreviated syllogism.

> *Any action that causes cancer is evil, and therefore smoking should be made illegal.*

Note that you have also logically tested your central idea (or discovered it).

Of course your premises may not always be accepted at face value, and you may have to establish their validity with valid evidence and critical thinking efforts.

To reason correctly from a false principle is the perfection of sophistry.

Emmons

From Analogy

Analogies can make things clear, vivid, and interesting. Some analogies are figurative or emotive, others more literal. All offer support, but the literal are thought to be the more logical.

A **literal** analogy is open to less argument but is nevertheless always imperfect proof. Its effectiveness depends on how close the comparison really is. In arguing for gun control, Senator Edward Kennedy tried a *literal* analogy:

Opponents of firearms laws insist that gun licenses and record-keeping requirements are burdensome and inconvenient. Yet they don't object to licensing automobile drivers, hunters, or those who enjoy fishing. If the only price of gun licensing or record-keeping requirements is the inconvenience to gun users, then the public will have received a special bargain. Certainly sportsmen will gladly tolerate minor inconvenience in order to protect the lives of their families, friends, and neighbors.

George Ziegelmueller and Jack Kay analyzed this analogy as follows: "Senator Kennedy asserts that gun licensing is like automobile, hunting, and fishing licensing in an essential characteristic (inconvenience), and he suggests that it will be like the other forms of licensing with regard to the characteristic (tolerance) known in the other forms but not known in the instance of guns."[3]

Figurative analogy is often persuasive but not always very logical! (See Figure 12.3.)

Some tests of argument by analogy follow:

1. Are the compared cases essentially similar?
2. Are the compared cases accurately described?
3. Are there other analogous cases?[4]

"The parallel you drew between the rewards awaiting the pure of heart and an unending supply of Sanders' tin-roof sundaes was beautiful."

Figure 12.3 Cliff Wirth, cartoonist. *The Detroit News.*

From Cause

Suppose you found a dead man (the effect of something) with a bullet in his heart. Can we conclude absolutely that the bullet is the cause? This is reasoning from effect to cause—*a posteriori* reasoning. The bullet is certainly a possible cause, but as any *Law and Order* fan knows, the man might have been killed by arsenic poisoning, then shot after his death as a means of hiding the real cause. We should expect causes to be complex and interrelated. Coincidence is frequently mistaken for cause.

Your car battery is weak, you observe that it's ten degrees below zero, and you conclude that your car isn't going to start. This is before-the-fact, or *a priori*, reasoning. The conclusion is based upon circumstances you observed before the disputed fact. You are reasoning from *cause to effect.*

If when you get up tomorrow morning you say, "It's ten below zero; my car won't start; I'll be late for school," you are reasoning from *effect to effect.* Both your faltering battery and your tardiness (as well as the thermometer reading) are the effects of a common cause—low temperature. In arguing from effect to effect, you must first sort out the effect-to-cause and cause-to-effect elements and then apply the general requirements for arguments based on causal relations. These are as follows

1. Is there a consistent association between alleged causes and attributed effects?
2. Is the association strong and dependable across different circumstances?
3. Do the alleged causes and effects appear in logical order over a reasonable time frame?
4. Does the relationship hold up in the light of other known data?

From Signs

We reason from circumstances or clues that act as signs. We use *sign* reasoning every day, often without applying proper tests.

> He drives a Porsche; he must be wealthy.
> She is wet; it must be raining.

Wrong! The man is a car thief, and "she" fell in the swimming pool! However, all sign reasoning isn't confused. A trained auto mechanic knows how to interpret the growl signs in the front end of your car and quickly deduces that it is a wheel bearing. Medical diagnosis is another example of sign reasoning. In both cases sign reasoning is strengthened if there are multiple signs available. The mechanic also reads signs from alignment, wheel shimmy, and the absence of other growl sounds. The doctor finds special pain signs, elevated white blood cell count, and others that lead to the suspicion of appendicitis.

A really good detective has to be an expert at sign reasoning. His or her minimal list includes:

Are the signs reliable? (that is, not accidental or coincidental)
Are they in sufficient number?
Do any contradict one another?

ELEMENTS OF ARGUMENT

If reasoning is how we go about generating and testing ideas that support a position we are taking, or a claim we are making, then argument is the scheme by which we link and demonstrate the logic of our claims.

The Toulmin Pattern

This is a system of logic and critical thinking devised by Stephen Toulmin,[5] which gets one from evidence to inference and avoids symbolic relationships seen in the more syllogistic models. For some, it may be easier to relate to everyday argument, and most importantly, it tries to avoid the "allness" problem often associated with formal syllogisms.

According to this model, we reason from a presumed, or at least stated, piece of evidence or fact (the *Data*) to a statement of an inferential nature (the *Claim*). The two are connected or made reasonable by a more general bridging statement. Toulmin calls these bridges *Warrants*. The last element is the *Qualifier,* which allows for exceptions, qualifications, or reservations. Toulmin symbolizes the relationship between the data and the claim in support of which they are produced by an arrow, and indicates the authority for taking the step from one to the other by writing the warrant below the arrow.

Figure 12.4

To allow for exceptions, special conditions, or qualifications, Toulmin uses the symbol "Q" for such Qualifiers. "R" stands for rebuttal.

Figure 12.5

For example:

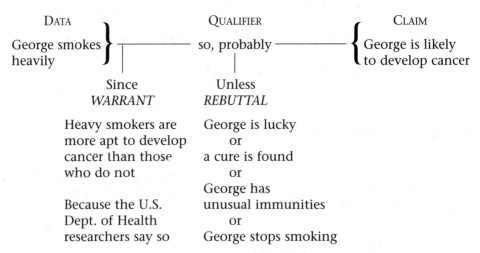

DATA   QUALIFIER   CLAIM

George smokes } ———— so, probably ———— { George is likely
heavily   to develop cancer

                  Since   Unless
                  WARRANT   *REBUTTAL*

              Heavy smokers are   George is lucky
              more apt to develop   or
              cancer than those   a cure is found
              who do not   or
                                       George has
              Because the U.S.   unusual immunities
              Dept. of Health   or
              researchers say so   George stops smoking

Figure 12.6

This system stresses the reservations (qualifiers) and should suggest caution to both speakers and listeners in making claims. It also puts a priority on *warrants* (Is your claim warranted?), that is, the explicit justification of the reasoning between Data and Claim.

Some good ground rules for logical reasoning and argument follow. These are the kinds of questions to ask yourself before you advance your thinking in a formal speech.

Figure 12.7   Testing your arguments

CRITICAL THINKING ERRORS

> Most people would rather die than think; indeed most of them do.
>
> *Bertrand Russell*

Common Reasoning Errors

FALSE ASSUMPTIONS   Galileo's claim that earth was not the center of the solar system put him under house arrest for the last eight years of his life.

Clearly the assumptions of otherwise good thinkers were in error. That the earth was the center was absolutely obvious and they were supported in that false assumption by another—"God would not have had it any other way." Galileo has, of course, been vindicated but perhaps, more importantly, forgiven. Close-minded, false assumptions have been changed and a lesson in critical thinking learned. Be vigilant about your beliefs and do be objectively *skeptical* of new or strange ideas but do *not* be close-minded about either. The famous counselor and therapist Carl Rogers advised, "Always allow a one- to five-percent chance that you're wrong." In other words, maybe the patient is sane and "I'm losing it." This is not to say that we shouldn't hold strong beliefs, attitudes, and values, but it does mean that they should be based on evidence, logical reasoning, and a willingness to update and reevaluate. Unfortunately, Galileo's early critics would not even look at his evidence and his reasoning. Modern scientists and the U.S. Air Force are very skeptical about the presence of UFOs but they are eternally looking "out there."

> As dysfunctional as they may be on occasion, our theories, preconceptions, and biases are what make us smart.
>
> *Thomas Gilovich*

DEFINITIONAL CONFUSION   If you define *sound* as "free from error," how does it affect your answer to the question, "When a big tree falls in isolation in a distant forest, does it make a sound?" Not a very helpful definition you say. Try this one: "Acoustic sensation perceived by the sense of hearing." If no one was around to hear it, then there was no sound. Hold on. It must have sounded like thunder! Try the scientific definition: "Mechanical radient energy that is transmitted by longitudinal pressure waves in a material medium (as air)." *Now* the tree has made a sound. Nothing really changed in the forest, only the reasoning from different and yet "sound" definitions.

It gets worse. "When does life begin?" At birth? When brain life begins? At conception? When survival outside the womb is possible? Clearly there are strong differences of opinion here, and also some people who haven't considered any definition but their own.

We even have definitional questions about *death*. Some states are still debating that definition because of the problem of organ transplants. "Brain function" defines death in many states, breath or heart function in others.

You can save yourself and your audience considerable confusion if you carefully consider your definition of terms. An example often helps. "By the Federal Government, I mean the Federal Trade Commission." Explanations of what you *don't* mean often help. "By intervention, I do not include military operations." One can also find definitional help from authority. "Poverty as defined by the *Statistical Abstract of the United States*." "Tax-sharing as defined by Rush Limbaugh." Here all authorities are not created equal. On topics involving religion, it may be a church leader, the Koran, the Bible, or a distinguished theologian; for some, it may be a secular humanist.

Terms and words, even definitions, do not mean the same thing in all senses and in all situations. If you think they do, you are guilty of the fallacy of equivocation.

MISATTRIBUTIONS   One weather-weary backwoods Michigander called the popular local meteorologist and told him that he'd had enough and that if the ice was not off the bay by April 15th, he was coming after him with a chain saw. A real case of misattribution; in this case, guilt by association. Did our backwoodsman really think that the weather forecaster was causal? Thank goodness the ice went out on April 14th.

All misattributions aren't as harmless (?) as the one above. Accidental physical association alone may lead to more serious false attributions or accusations of guilt. You are seated in a fancy restaurant one table behind a table of known gangsters. The aggressive reporters capture you as background in all of their videotape. How easy it is to infer false notions of guilt by association.

As we learned in the language chapter, much confusion is caused by loose word association. For some, a humanist, a secular humanist, a social psychologist, a Darwinian, an empiricist, a behavioralist are all identical bad people who do not believe in God. They attribute the beliefs and traits of some to all. For the record, Edison, Einstein, and even Darwin made it very clear that they believed in God. Critical thinking demands some effort to distinguish fact from judgment and belief from knowledge.

The suggestions given to listeners in Chapter 3, "Critical Listening," also apply to persuaders seeking logical supports of their claims.

Beware of misinterpreting chance events, second-hand information, wishful thinking, conventional wisdom, and language confusion.

SINGLE PERSPECTIVE

For every complex problem there is an easy answer, and it is wrong.

H. L. Mencken

Single perspectives usually produce simplistic, singular answers to most questions. They are sometimes viable, rarely wise, and almost always undemocratic.

Single perspectives are attractive to some people who find they allow one to eliminate much of the dissonance caused by having to think critically or, in some cases, to think at all. Surely the followers of self-appointed Messiah David Koresh and the Branch Davidians found it so.

All single perspective errors are not as far-reaching and as dangerous. Some are applied more gently to single issues where one may have had a traumatic experience. Phobias apply here, but so do issues where one has simply a sincere concern: the spotted owl, wetlands, ozone layer, and so forth.

Critical thinkers, for example, will consider the perspectives of the logging and lumber industries as well as those of the environmentalists. Considering more than one perspective, however, may not, perhaps should not always lead to compromise. The plea is not to accept; the plea is to *consider*.

There are ways to expand our perspectives and improve our critical thinking. One is called playing *devil's advocate*. The early Roman Catholic Church used this device to make sure they heard arguments from a different perspective in making canonization or beatification decisions. It is, in this case, the appointing of someone to use arguments and perspectives with which they did not personally agree—a role play. In individual cases, it is prevailing upon yourself to search out and seriously consider the best relevant arguments of perspectives other than your own.

Another way to avoid the single perspective error is double checking your *facts* or what you presume to be the facts. We prefer to believe what we prefer to be true. A second, more dispassionate look at the facts is often a real eye opener. You studied *Romeo and Juliet* in high school and you are startled to hear someone say that you really did not—that is, your version was considerably different from Shakespeare's original version. A close examination of high school anthologies shows that over 300 lines have indeed been dropped. All sexual material was removed—even words like *bosom* and *maidenhood*. The love story was mostly lost as were most lines that in any way associated religion with violence.[6]

Verify your facts. Are yours the only facts? Are your sources reliable? Are they up-to-date? Are you blinded by your beliefs? When absolutely sure, look again.

A third way of expanding a single perspective is to seek out the opinions of people holding more neutral views or broader perspectives than your own on the issue at hand. An uncensored library is another source of second opinions and multiple perspectives.

Common Argument Errors

These behaviors represent reasoning too far removed from the facts or often a tangle of generalizations based on inadequate facts. The unscrupulous may deliberately use fallacious errors hoping that they will not be detected. Our cognitive systems are sometimes easily deceived by fallacious messages. To complicate matters even more, fallacies are very often unintentional or accidental. They are usually plausible-sounding arguments using false, inadequate, or invalid evidence. Once detected by an audience, a careless or unethical speaker is in for a difficult time.

Aristotle devised a classification of fallacies that has been the springboard for all classification systems to this day. He divided fallacies into two principal types: those in the *language* of the argument and those in the *content* or matter of the argument. Fallacies of language were discussed in Chapter 2. There are seven fallacies of matter, or "beyond the language." Aristotle himself admitted that there were problems in his system, so we may presume to rearrange his list. For our purposes we shall examine four major types of fallacies, together with their respective subtypes. The four are **overgeneralization** ("They're all dumb."), **false cause** ("The dance caused the rain."), **begging the question** ("Everybody knows they're crooks"), and **ignoring or ducking the issue** ("What discrimination?").

OVERGENERALIZATION

"They're all dumb."

Snap judgments or generalizations based on insufficient evidence or experience belong in the category of overgeneralization. We are not talking here about language and the dangers of the word *all,* but rather the concept of *allness* itself. This fallacy results in our going from the general case to a specific case or vice versa. It is similar to the problems of induction and deduction.

It is in the *exceptions* to generally accepted rules that overgeneralization causes the most trouble. We would all agree that it is wrong to kill a person. However, a specific case of killing in self-defense can be an exception to this rule. To take another example, there could be exceptions to the rule, "Alcohol is harmful." Not if it's used for fuel.

Sampling.   A group of star high school football players was being oriented to a certain Big Ten campus when they observed a dozen devastatingly chic females coming out of a campus building. To a man, the generalization was, "Wow! What coeds this place has!" The coach did not bother to tell them that these women were all professional fashion models who had just come from a faculty spouses' program.

Consider the size and representativeness of your sample before generalizing. A rash of teenage delinquencies may cause some people to conclude that all teenagers are juvenile delinquents, but this would be an unfair generalization. The most treacherous part of this fallacy is that it does start with facts. There *were* twelve stylish females on a given campus; teenage delinquency *has been* recorded. It is the lack of objective analysis of the sample of experiences or subjects that causes the trouble.

Extrapolation.   This "thin entering wedge" is also known as the "camel's nose in the tent." It too is a form of sampling trouble (as are all overgeneralizations), except that this one is keyed to *prediction* and *probability.*

Stuart Chase put it well: "You chart two or three points, draw a curve through them, and then extend it indefinitely!" Space scientists extrapolate or they do not predict at all. This is also true of economists and the weather forecasters. Scientists usually know the dangers of extrapolation; to offset these dangers, they generally phrase their predictions in terms of *statistical chance* or confidence. Scientists draw predictive curves only when they have found enough points to make a qualified prediction. We are well advised to do the same.

FALSE CAUSE

"The dance caused the rain."

This is the fallacy of assigning a wrong or false cause to a certain happening or effect. It also is refutation with irrelevant arguments. Superstitions belong here. If you blow on the dice and win, was it the blowing that brought you luck? Rabbits' feet are still being sold; and most hotels still have no thirteenth floor. Debaters call it *nonsequitur* (it does not follow).

After This, Therefore Because of This.   Superstitions fit here. In our saner moments we are aware of this fallacy. It arises from the subtle misuse of time sequence. For example, if a new city government comes into power after a particularly rough winter and is faced with badly damaged roads, you may hold them responsible as you survey one ruined $70 tire: "We didn't have roads like this until after their election." The great Roman Empire fell after the introduction of Christianity—care to try that one? You will hear it in Latin as *post hoc ergo propter hoc:* after this, therefore because of this.

Thou Also.   This fallacy consists of making a similar, but essentially irrelevant, attack upon an accuser. A discussion between a Brazilian student and several Americans about Communist infiltration in Latin America became quite heated. Suddenly, the Brazilian said, "Communists? How about segregation in your country?" The retort was equally brilliant: "How about Nazis in Argentina?"

Consequent.   This fallacy simply is the corruption of the reasoning or inferential process used in conditional syllogisms. The problem in conditional syllogisms is with possible, partial, or even probable truths. If he lies, he will be expelled from school; he was expelled; therefore, he lied. (In actuality, he may have been expelled for poor grades.) When we use conditional reasoning and argue from the truth of the consequent (what happened: he was expelled) to the truth of the antecedent (what preceded: he lied), or when we argue from the falsity of the antecedent to the falsity of the consequent, we are committing the fallacy of the *consequent.*

Either/Or.   Certainly, there are things in this world that are either one way or another? You are either living or dead; the lake is frozen or it is not. There is no such thing as being slightly pregnant. Even these can be argued in terms of definitions. "Certainly, when a statement or problem with more than two possible solutions is put in an either/or context, we have a fallacy. "The fight is either Jan's or Jim's fault." It may be neither's fault, or it may be the fault of both. There are shades of gray in most things. All too often, we hear either/or arguments that only slow real solutions: science versus religion, capitalism versus socialism, suburban versus city living, and so forth.

Loaded Question.   This trick assumes something has already happened; it usually asks two questions as if they were one. You're in trouble no matter how you answer. In a speech it may take the form of a great many questions, the combination of answers leading to fallacious reasoning. The answers sought are *yes* or *no*. "Have you stopped drinking? *Yes* or *No?*" If you answer *no,* you are an admitted drinker. If you answer *yes,* you are an admitted former drinker. Either way, the loaded question stacks the deck against you. "Heads I win, tails you lose."

BEGGING THE QUESTION

"Everybody knows they're crooks."

This fallacy assumes the truth or falsity of a statement *without proof.* A common form is the use of two or more unproved propositions to establish the validity of one another. Other forms are simple, unwarranted assumptions or statements. It is related to loaded questions.

Arguing in a Circle.   This is the classic form of using two or more unproved propositions to prove one another. "Professional boxing should be outlawed because it is inhumane; we know it is inhumane because it is a practice that should be outlawed." "Detroit is to blame for the smog in Los Angeles since they make the cars we drive." This assumes cars are the major source of pollution, and that all the cars are made in Detroit—a vicious circle. We might just as easily accuse the Japanese car makers.

Direct Assumption.   In this form of question begging, language is carefully selected to conceal unsupported assumptions. Many statements may be used, or perhaps just a word or two are subtly inserted. In a discussion of big-time college football, an opposition speaker started with the words, "It is my purpose to show that buying professional players is not in the best interest of college football." This statement begged the whole proposition by assuming at the outset that colleges buy professional players. Unless the statement is proved, it remains an assertion.

IGNORING OR DUCKING THE ISSUE

"What discrimination?"

 This fallacy can be a subtle, treacherous, and often vicious process. It almost always uses apparently relevant but objectively irrelevant arguments to cloud or duck the real issue of argument. This fallacy has several types, and each is worthy of a word of warning to the listener and unsophisticated speaker.

Attacking Personalities. This fallacy is also known as *ad hominem*. When a speaker attacks the personal character of an opponent rather than the issue at hand, that person is guilty of *ad hominem* argument. The purpose of *ad hominem* is to change the issue from an argument on the proposition to one of personalities. To argue the stage and screen abilities of Burt Reynolds by referring to him as "that self-centered woman-chasing louse" is a good example of *ad hominem*. Mr. Reynolds's stage and screen *abilities* have no direct logical connection to his alleged off-stage pursuits. This is not to say that every personal attack is unfair or illogical. If Mr Reynolds were being evaluated on his public relations abilities, it might be a different matter.

Appeals to Prejudice. This is an appeal to the people through their biases and passions. The symbols of motherhood, the flag, race, and sin are typical themes. Vicious and often unsupported attacks have been made against liberal Americans in the name of un-Americanism, Romanism, Zionism, racism. The "ist" words—sexist, racist, feminist, abortionist, socialist—are often misused in this type of appeal. *Ad populum* appeals should become less successful as the general population becomes better educated and more sophisticated.

False Appeal to Authority. This type of fallacy is an appeal to authority and dignity. When the authority is legitimately connected to the subject, as Aristotle is to logic, we have no problem. However, if in our reverence of Aristotle we use him to oppose modern probability theory, we are guilty of false appeal. Michael Jordan and John Elway are highly paid experts in their specialized fields. They are probably not authorities on laser theory or even beer or breakfast cereal. If you are impressed because Dr. Whosis says that alcohol causes cancer, find out if Whosis is an M.D. or an English professor.

Appeals to Ignorance. This is a mean trick, hiding weak arguments by overwhelming an audience with impressive materials about which they know little. A twelve-cylinder vocabulary can screen many a feeble argument. Improper use of statistics (or even proper use) for people ignorant of the theory or the numbers involved is a good example of an appeal to ignorance. This is not to say that vocabulary and statistics are the problem; it is the intent with which the speaker adapts them to the audience that is the problem.

Summary

In this, the cognitive or more "central route" of the persuasion process, we are concerned primarily with evidence, rational reasoning, critical thinking, and argument.

Useful sources of evidence are (1) statements by authorities, (2) examples, and (3) statistics.

Four basic forms of reasoning are derived from (1) generalization, (2) analogy, (3) cause, and (4) sign. The Toulmin pattern of argument includes the following elements of argument: claims, grounds, warrants, backing, qualifiers, and rebuttals. One is advised to first determine the underlying purpose of the argument and then to evaluate as follows: (1) the *grounds* must be sufficient to support the *claim;* (2) the *warrant* must be applicable and based on solid *backing;* and (3) exceptions and possible *rebuttals* must be considered.

Some good questions for testing your arguments are:

1. How good is my evidence?
2. Does the evidence support my *specific* claim?
3. Is there contradictory evidence?
4. Have I accounted for variable circumstances?

Critical thinking errors include four *reasoning* errors: (1) false assumption, (2) definitional confusion, (3) misattributions, and (4) single perspective; and four argument errors: (1) overgeneralization, (2) false cause, (3) begging the question, and (4) ducking the issue.

Learning Projects

1. Search a newspaper or magazine and find one good use of evidence and one use that is less persuasive, if not invalid.

2. Find or create an example of each of the four forms of reasoning: (1) from generalization, (2) from analogy, (3) from cause, (4) from sign.

3. Set up a proposition or claim and diagram your argument using the elements of argument discussed.

4. Critically evaluate the logic of your classmates' speeches; especially watch for weak reasoning. Write out your critique and be prepared to cross-examine the speaker. See the four test questions in the summary above.

5. Check your thinking habits on the following items:

   a. An archaeologist found a coin marked 45 B.C. How old was it?

   b. If you divided 30 by $\frac{1}{2}$ plus 10, how much would you have?

   c. Which side of a horse has more hair?

   d. How far can a dog walk into the woods?

e. If you went to bed at 8:00 and set the alarm to ring at 9:00 in the morning, how many hours of sleep would you get?

f. Does England have a Fourth of July?

6. What critical thinking errors lead some people to answer the above questions incorrectly?

7. Can we agree on definitions and still have honest differences of opinion on related issues? Explain.

8. Read your editorial pages and find an example of the *misattribution* error.

9. Consider an issue where you tend to apply a single perspective. Compare it to a different perspective and demonstrate that you understand both.

10. Prepare a two-(or more) perspective speech on a controversial topic using the both-sides strategy discussed in Chapter 11.

11. Define the word "fact" and give three examples of "facts" that meet your definition.

12. Search the media and find two examples of fallacious messages as defined by any of the following: (1) overgeneralization, (2) false cause, (3) begging the question, or (4) ignoring or ducking the issue.

13. Consider this actual exchange between a researcher and a non-literate Central Asian peasant. Report your observations and conclusions in class.

(Syllogism) In the Far North, where there is snow, all bears are white. Novaya Zemlya is in the Far North and there is always snow there. What color are the bears there?

. . ."We always speak only of what we see; we don't talk about what we haven't seen."

(E:) But what do my words imply? The syllogism is repeated.

"Well, it's like this: our tsar isn't like yours, and yours isn't like ours. Your words can be answered only by someone who was there, and if a person wasn't there he can't say anything on the basis of your words."

(E:) . . . But on the basis of my words—in the North, where there is always snow, the bears are white, can you gather what kind of bears there are in Novaya Zemlya?

"If a man was sixty or eighty and had seen a white bear and had told about it, he could be believed, but I've never seen one and hence I can't say. That's my last word. Those who saw can tell, and those who didn't see can't say anything!" (At this point a younger man volunteered, "From your words it means that bears there are white.")

(E:) Well, which of you is right?

"What the cock knows how to do, he does. What I know, I say, and nothing beyond that."

From A. R. Luria, *Cognitive Development: Its Cultural and Social Foundations* (Cambridge, MA: Harvard University Press, 1976), pp. 108–109.

Notes

1. See Raymond S. Ross, *Understanding Persuasion,* 4th ed. (Englewood Cliffs, N.J.: Prentice Hall, 1994), p. 113.

2. George W. Ziegelmueller and Jack Kay, *Argumentation: Inquiry and Advocacy.* 3rd ed. (Boston: Allyn and Bacon, 1997), p. 349.

3. Ziegelmueller and Kay, *Argumentation,* p. 105.

4. See Austin J. Freeley, *Argumentation and Debate,* 9th ed. (Belmont, Calif.: Wadsworth, 1996), pp. 172–74.

5. S. Toulmin, *The Uses of Argument* (Cambridge, England: Cambridge University Press, 1958); see also Barbara Warnick and Edward S. Inch, *Critical Thinking and Communication: The Use of Reason in Argument* (New York: Macmillan, 1994), pp. 179–88.

6. Joan Del Fattore, *What Johnny Shouldn't Read* (New Haven: Yale University Press, 1992), Chap. 1.

13

UNIQUE FORMATS AND OCCASIONS

CHAPTER OUTLINE

AUDIENCE PARTICIPATION OCCASIONS

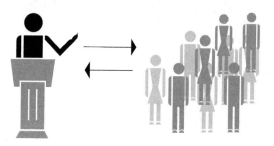

Figure 13.1

In a sense, every speech situation in a democracy represents potential audience participation, if not a formal open forum. Questions, comments, and objections from the audience may come at any time. You should always calculate the risk of being interrupted or even heckled. Some speakers ask for trouble by pleading with the audience to interrupt for any reason whatsoever. A very large audience of perhaps hundreds can be a real nightmare if there is no pre-arranged system of handling questions.

The Economic Club of Detroit has the audience of 800 to 1,000 people turn in written questions that are screened for duplication and relevance while the speaker is still on the platform. Of course, there are situations, such as certain discussion groups or small classes, in which you seek immediate audience participation. Although formal speakers should be democratic and focus on the audience, they must also cover their subject and stay within their allotted time. Unreasonable questions and interruptions have ruined many an otherwise good speech and have shaken even experienced speakers.

> The way a question is asked limits and disposes the ways in which any answer to it—right or wrong—may be given.
>
> *Susanne K. Langer*

The solution to the general problem is in the word *control*. Speakers must stay in control of the communication situation. They must control audience participation in such a way as to do justice to the *audience,* the *material* to be covered, and the *time* restrictions placed on their speech.

Most **business communication and training programs** use a great deal of audience participation. This is as it should be, for educational psychology teaches us that *people learn faster and better when they have a feeling of participation and involvement.* The audience, particularly in training programs, is usually invited to interrupt the speaker or teacher. However, the speaker who chases after every question, relevant or not, will soon be in serious trouble. One inexperienced speaker pleaded sincerely for interruptions and he *got* them—some good, some bad, some ridiculous. He tried to react, answer, or comment on each equally. The result was that he covered only one-fourth of his material, and even this part was confused because of the free-for-all participation.

Another situation in which you may find yourself is the more typical **open forum** after a speech. The problems indicated above apply here, but perhaps to a lesser degree, because you have much better control of your time, and you have probably covered the points you set out to cover.

The third typical audience situation is the **symposium forum.** A symposium forum usually allows one-third of the total time for questions from the general audience. Many convention programs are run this way. Once again, the rules and problems are similar to those of the two situations discussed above, except that a decision must often be made as to which of the panelists should respond to each question. The respondent must consider both the audience and fellow panel members. The size of the audience is again a key factor. If the audience is larger than was expected (say, one hundred instead of thirty-five), the moderator might have the panelists ask one another questions first, thereby ensuring some relevant questions. Furthermore, audience size alone may discourage members of the audience from asking questions.

General Rules

The *first* rule regards your audience.

1. *Know your occasion, subject, and audience.*

You are now in a position to apply the *second* rule:

2. *Second-guess the questions.*

Try to guess what areas of your subject are most vulnerable to questions, and try to predict what questions this particular audience will ask. *Third:*

3. *Try sincerely to answer or at least react to all questions.*

Consider and react courteously to even the irrelevant questions, and attempt, if necessary, to clarify or postpone the question. The *fourth* rule, and one that is very easy to overlook in your eagerness to meet the question asked, is:

4. *Consider the rest of the audience.*

You must try to satisfy not only the person asking the question, but the total audience as well. Otherwise, you might satisfy the statistician, for example, while thoroughly confusing everybody else. *Fifth:*

5. *Do not feel or act as if you have to know everything or win every argument.*

Finally:

> **6.** *When the situation calls for an open forum, encourage good questions and audience participation.*

It is very easy to discourage questions by a slightly overbearing attitude. However, it is possible to be so overbearing that the audience decides to interrogate you. People who assume leadership have to be constantly on guard not to intimidate others simply because of their position or rank. The sergeant who loosely followed the manual's advice to always ask, "Are there any *dumb* questions?" did not get many. That was why he said it! However, when such an attitude is *not* intended, the situation is even more unfortunate.

Rules for Answering Questions

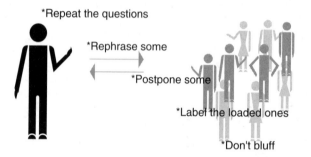

*Repeat the questions

*Rephrase some

*Postpone some

*Label the loaded ones

*Don't bluff   **Figure 13.2**

An audience of about 400 students was listening to a famous philosopher speak. At the close of the speech the chairman asked for questions from the audience. Most of the hands raised were in the first row, where the Philosophy Club had gathered. The speaker pointed to a hand in the first row. To those near the middle of the audience the question sounded like, "I should zzum ug ask hrump zud Hegel?" The speaker moved to the lectern, stroked his chin, and then, speaking to the front row, said, "A very good question." He then proceeded to give what was probably a very good answer. The problem was that most of the audience did not know what the question was because they had not *heard* it. The speaker handled three or four more questions in the same manner, the audience becoming frustrated, then restless, and finally rude, as they started to leave.

One of the most elementary mistakes a speaker or panelist can make is to assume that everyone in the audience has heard and understood a question that is asked. Listening to misdirected answers without knowing the question is the height of frustration for most listeners. Speakers should communicate with the whole room, not just the questioner.

REPEAT   *Repeat the question* is the first rule. This is a good idea even with small audiences, for although the members are in a position to hear, they may not be listening. Another serious aspect of the all-too-common error illustrated above is that people will attempt to reconstruct what the question must have been in terms of the answer. Counterquestions based on inaccurately reconstructed questions can really raise confusion to a high level.

Sometimes a question may be asked in a loud, clear voice but the wording is awkward or unclear. A famous army general was giving a speech at my university at the time of a Middle East crisis. In the large audience were foreign students from all of the countries involved, including Egypt, Iran, Kuwait, Iraq, and Israel. One of these students took the general to task in perfectly clear and audible English, except that the question was long and complicated. The general said, "I know what you're getting at," and proceeded to answer for about ten minutes. As the general completed his answer, the foreign student leaped to his feet and proceeded to give another short speech, which said, in effect, "But that's not what I asked." The general tried again, for five minutes this time, but still with no success. After one more unsuccessful attempt, the desperate general finally held up his hand and said, "Let's see if we can agree on what the question is."

REPHRASE   Sometimes it is necessary not only to repeat but also to *rephrase the question.* When rephrasing, you should gain the approval of the questioner. Ask the questioner if your phrasing is a fair statement of the question to see if the person objects verbally. You do not always have to rephrase questions; do so only when it is necessary for clarity, and then always seek approval.

Some long, complicated questions deserve careful attention if they are relevant to the issue and if you are capable of giving some kind of answer in the time available. When, however, you receive questions that are irrelevant, that demand a highly technical or complex answer, or that would consume all the open-forum time, you have a different kind of problem. Such questions can ruin an otherwise good speech. Though in principle you do not want to avoid questions, you also owe it to the rest of your audience to stay on the subject and to give more than one person a chance to ask a question.

POSTPONE   Let us therefore formulate a third rule: *Postpone the irrelevant, overly technical, or time-consuming questions.* Postpone such questions until after the official open-forum period, or until the end of the period if you have time remaining. For interruptions this rule becomes more complex, for a person may ask a question that you intend to cover later in the speech. In this situation you should delay the answer until you arrive at that point: For example, you might say, "Could I hold the answer to that for a few minutes? I will cover the issue a little later." The problem is to remember the questions you may have postponed. One solution is to suggest that the person ask the question again, but after you have covered the point at hand.

LABEL LOADED QUESTIONS   Even the experienced and unflappable Gary Hart was jolted when he was asked, "Have you ever committed adultery?" People sometimes deliberately ask the "Are you still beating your dog?" kind of question but equally difficult are the questions that are unintentionally loaded. These are difficult to detect because they are often both subtle and naive at the same time, and they are sometimes asked by people who are not troublemakers by reputation. "Why is it that writers have such insatiable egos?" an author was once asked. If you are a writer, try to answer that without condemning yourself!

Thus, rule four is, *label a loaded question.* There are several ways to do this, if you are lucky enough to detect such a question in time. The most effective way is to pause long enough for the audience to label it for you. An audience is often quick to chuckle if they see the speaker faced with a "heads I win, tails you lose" situation. Or you could say frankly, "That's a loaded question." A more tactful way might be, "It looks like I'm in trouble no matter how I answer this." Another method is to ask the questioner to repeat the question. The audience will listen more closely and may label the loaded question for you, or the questioner may "unload" it. After you have successfully labeled or unloaded the question as courteously as possible, you should then attempt to answer. With the proper labels applied, the audience is not apt to be prejudiced by the question.

DON'T BLUFF   The surest way to get in trouble in an open-forum period is to try to bluff your way through a question for which you honestly do not have a satisfactory answer. Once an audience senses that you are bluffing, you can expect them to ask more questions on this bluff point. The solution is to know your subject thoroughly—but if you do not have an answer, say so right away and save yourself the embarrassment of being trapped later on. No speaker is expected to have all the answers to all the questions in the world. This rule, then, might simply be called the *"I don't know"* rule.

However, you cannot escape all the hard questions by simply saying, "I don't know." In some question-answer situations you may wish to say, "I don't know, but I have an opinion," or "I don't know, but I can answer in terms of my specialty." The point is that you should answer any question you are capable of answering and yet be honest enough to admit it when you cannot supply an answer.

Corollaries to "don't bluff" are "don't get belligerent" and "don't get defensive." Acknowledge honest differences of opinion and get on with the open forum.

It will be a sad day for man when nobody is allowed to ask questions that do not have any answers.

Kenneth Boulding

Generating Participation

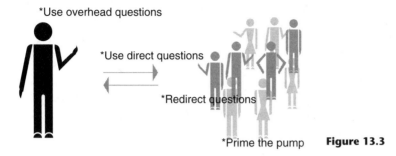

Figure 13.3

In some situations audiences just seem to spring into action; in other cases they must be given the proper stimulus for participation. Here are several techniques that might be useful for you.

THE OVERHEAD QUESTION   This is a direct question from the speaker or discussion leader to the entire audience. If no questions arise from the audience (or even if they do), you might say, "Let me ask this question in order to get some feedback. Given one million dollars, how would you use it to improve this university?" The problem is to make sure you choose a question that will cause a reaction, for if there is silence, you may be worse off than before. Sometimes you can react to your own question in such a way as to promote participation. "OK, then react to what I'd do with it." Consider a few, carefully worded overhead questions as a method of fostering participation.

THE DIRECT QUESTION   This technique consists of choosing a specific member of the audience and asking that person a direct question. This is often very effective if the individual is known to the rest of the audience or is in some special way qualified to answer. The size of your audience may present a problem in that the audience may have difficulty seeing or otherwise determining who has been singled out. Classroom audiences or larger groups that meet regularly respond well to this technique. Try not to call on the same person all the time, but do pick individuals who are most apt to get participation started. Try to tailor the question directly to the individual chosen. The question should be relatively short and clear and should demand more than a simple yes or no answer. If the situation is really desperate, however, you may have to settle for yes or no.

THE REDIRECTED QUESTION   This technique may also be called the ***reverse method*** or the ***relay method.*** In using the reverse technique, you simply redirect a question to the person who asked it: "That's a very good question. How would you answer it?" In using the relay method, you redirect the question to some other person: "A good question. Let's see how Mrs. Wright would answer it." A third approach is to overhead the question to the whole audience.

As a general rule, do not redirect a question unless you yourself know at least a partial answer to it. An exception to this rule is a simple question of fact upon which you can freely admit ignorance. Take heed of the story of the beginning teacher who redirected a tough question to which he did not have the answer to each individual of the class, only to find that it came right back to embarrass him.

PRIMING THE PUMP   This is the all-important technique of building questions into your speech. In the main, your questions or implied questions should develop your point, stimulate audience thinking, and attract interest and attention.

SPEAKING WITH HUMOR

Humor

Other things being equal, a little showmanship is better than dull, hedged, powerless language and delivery. At the University of Arkansas business school, the final speaking assignment is a stand-up comedy routine. According to Professor Tabott, "If you can do that you can master any form of speaking."[1] However, some people are better at humor than others. They do have an advantage if they can discern when their humor may be *inappropriate*.[2] All "humorous" people do not tell jokes equally well.[3] If you're a poor jokester, perhaps you need not be too concerned. Long-standing research on the impact of such humor on audiences seems to indicate that at least in persuasive speeches for some people it may make little difference. Humor and showmanship include more than just jokes. A funny story if told well helps; so does relating an amusing experience you've had or someone else has had.

Comparing humorous and nonhumorous *information* lectures did show significantly better student retention of the humorous lecture over a period of six weeks.[4]

Remember that humor when offensive or tendentious[5] can work against you; so too, if it confuses the mood or is in some other way a distractor of the message. Related, funny anecdotes (if told well and in good taste) have probably helped hold attention for many an otherwise dull speaker. The professional writers of humorous lines certainly think so. They received $300 per minute of delivery time for the following:

(Roast of a successful clothing manufacturer)

Well, Tom, we managed to get all your friends together under one roof . . . they're outside in the car.

Actually Tom adores his wife and four children. He always wanted a big family . . . it saves on manikins.

(Introduction of a famous plastic surgeon)

Dr. Stevens has integrity. In fact, he's so honest he returns your old parts.

The head of this agency (Comedy Unlimited) describes how he goes about his work, and it makes for good advice.

> A lot of research goes behind just one line. We do a thorough analysis of the client's needs before sitting down to the typewriter.

> We look for lines that are perfectly appropriate for both the client and the audience. What might be hilariously funny and quite effective for a sales manager might be disastrous for the chairman of the board.

> Practice is critical and this is where most speakers including some naturally humorous people fall down—the polishing.

The wit used by Comedy Unlimited was at least mildly disparaging. Research on deprecating and self-deprecating humor has been mixed. However, the last word seems to be that such humor if used sparingly and in good taste may help a speaker without damage to the traditional factors of ethos.[6] So much depends on the occasion, and on the people—the entire system must be considered. Research indicates that people differ on contexts perceived as appropriate for humor as well as on its type and spontaneity.[7] Audiences seemed to find the self-deprecating humor of some of our presidents endearing: Kennedy mocked his wealth and his youth; Ford mocked his clumsiness; Reagan mocked his age; and Clinton his addiction to Big Macs. Even Lincoln was able to make fun of his homeliness. When during a debate Douglas accused him of being two-faced, without hesitation Lincoln calmly replied, "I leave it to my audience—if I had two faces, would I be wearing this one?"

The person has a lot to do with how an audience views appropriateness. A Jewish student evoked an appreciative response in a speech class with a joke about a bumblebee wearing a yarmulke. "The bee didn't want to be taken for a wasp." One must wonder if the story would have been as funny told by anyone else. Ethnic, racial, and sexual jokes are tricky and double-edged for speakers, yet research indicates that they are prevalent and, for some, popular.[8] No matter how popular the sexist jokes were rated, at least one rater was always turned off. The rule is "Sexism is just not funny." Racist jokes are no longer acceptable anywhere. One must marvel at what people will or will not laugh at when humor is involved. Joke A below was considered sexist by the majority surveyed. Joke B was a winner but still had at least one rater label it sexist.

A	**B**
"Is this the Salvation Army?" "Yes." "Do you save bad women?" "Yes." "Well, save me three for Saturday night."	The young husband was waiting outside a hospital room when the doctor emerged from his thorough examination of the wife to explain the sudden pain in her shoulders. The doctor said gravely to the husband, "I must tell you that your wife has acute angina." "Yes, yes, I know. But what's wrong with her?"

We laugh at unexpected deviations from scripted behavior. That's why bloopers or *spoonerisms* are funny for most people. We laugh at pratfalls if they happen to people in the public eye whether we like them or not. Try some of these *bloopers*.

> Tonight's sermon: "What is hell?" Come early and listen to our choir practice.
>
> This week's youth discussion will be on teen suicide in the church basement.
>
> "This being Easter Sunday, we will ask Mrs. White to come forward and lay an egg on the altar."
>
> Wednesday the Ladies Liturgy Society will meet. Mrs. Jones will sing, "Put Me in My Little Bed," accompanied by the pastor.
>
> And from a newspaper, the headline CROWDS RUSHING TO SEE POPE TRAMPLE 6 TO DEATH.

If you're going to use humor, and especially jokes, take one more look at your audience. One person's belly laugh is another's yawn, or worse, a turnoff.

After-Dinner Speeches

Figure 13.4

Today's after-dinner speeches are not what they used to be. For one thing they might be given after breakfast or after a luncheon banquet. Although a banquet may indeed be the setting for a very serious and profound speech to persuade or inform, there is a tradition of so-called "after-dinner" speaking that is rather special in our society. This is the good-humored, lighthearted, genial situation whose major purposes are a sociable meal and some relaxed enjoyment. This is the type of speech situation with which we are concerned here. The audience has been made content with good food and is tolerant and benevolent. It is not in a mood for argumentation, moral reevaluation, or complex issues. Such speeches are typically brief, light, and humorous. They are not easy speeches to deliver; for some, they appear almost impossible. You need not be a professional jokester; indeed, unless you tell a good relevant joke especially well, you are better advised to use your humor in another vein. Four general principles to guide you are:

1. *Select suitable topics.* "Great Snafus of the Civil War" was a delightful after-dinner speech at a history buff's banquet recently. The group was, of course, interested in the deeper aspects of the war, but not at this particular moment. Look on the lighter side of issues for your subject. If you are going to talk about teachers, concentrate on their eccentricities, not their educational philosophies.

2. *Be clear and brief.* Avoid complex organization; stick to one or two obvious main points. Do not use complicated forms of support. Use examples and entertaining illustrations. Above all, be brief. Plan several cutoff points in your speech should the whole program take more time than expected, or should the audience seem unusually restless or quiet (asleep).

3. *Be good-humored.* The diners are full of food and full of goodwill. Heighten the fellowship. Avoid bitter argument.

4. *Adapt to the audience.* Make sure you *really* know the audience, the occasion, and the program. Capitalize on this information. Tie your good humor appropriately and directly to your specific audience.

United States statesman Adlai Stevenson had an unflagging sense of humor and was a great after-dinner speaker. We can sympathize and laugh with him as he relates his experiences while campaigning for the presidency.

THE CAMPAIGN SPEECH

You must emerge, bright and bubbling with wisdom and well-being, every morning at 8 o'clock, just in time for a charming and profound breakfast talk, shake hands with hundreds, often literally thousands, of people, make several inspiring, newsworthy speeches during the day, and ride through city after city on the back of an open car, smiling until your mouth is dehydrated by the wind, waving until the blood runs out of your arm.

Then, you bounce gaily, confidently, masterfully into great howling halls, shaved and all made up for television with the right color shirt and tie—I always forgot—and a manuscript so defaced with chicken tracks and last minute jottings that you couldn't follow it, even if the spotlights weren't blinding and even if the still photographers didn't shoot you in the eye every time you looked at them. Then all you have to do is make a great, imperishable speech, get out through the pressing crowds with a few score autographs, your clothes intact, your hand bruised, and back to the hotel—in time to see a few important people.

And, too, there is mirth mingled with the misery all along the way. They shout, "Good old Adlie." If you run for office and have a slightly unusual name, let me advise you to change it before you start, or be prepared to take other people's word for it. And I shall not soon forget about the woman in the crowd in San Francisco who reached into the car to shake hands with me, and not long after discovered that she had lost her diamond ring. Nor will I forget the warm welcome I received on a whistle stop in Bethlehem, Pa., and my thanks to "the people of Allentown."[9]

If you do decide to try humor to create interest, make the humor as professional as possible. There is no feeling quite as desperate as viewing a poker-faced audience after you have told your best joke. Make sure that the material is related to either the subject or the occasion; make sure you can tell it fluently; make sure you remember the punch line; and make sure that it will not offend your audience. The best advice of all—try it out on a small group of friends first. In other words, *practice* and *polish!*

INTRODUCTIONS AND SPECIAL OCCASIONS

Weddings, funerals, graduations, award ceremonies, retirements—all call for special remarks from somebody. Sensitivity and appropriateness are among the most important watchwords. Speeches of introduction occur often enough and are so frequently unsuccessful that they will open our discussion. Mark Twain lost his patience with awkward introductions and for a while he insisted that he not be introduced at all.

Speeches of Introduction

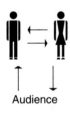

Audience

Figure 13.5

"I just now met our speaker, who is a buddy of our president and a speaker on human relations. He teaches speech and should be a good example for all of you to follow. It gives me great pleasure to introduce Mr. Edwin J. Forsythe."

How would you like to speak to a strange audience after that introduction? It sounded as if the speaker were being foisted upon the group by a "buddy" in the organization. It was evident that the introducer in this case did not know anything about the speaker (not even that his name was Edward not Edwin!) and that he was not particularly interested in "human relations." Attention was called to the speaker's oratory instead of his subject and his credibility. The only good point about the introduction was its brevity.

Equally awkward is the overly dramatic, lavish praise introduction that overstates your credentials and piles on embarrassing flattery. A former Governor of Michigan was guilty of all of the above in introducing President Lyndon B. Johnson. The unflappable Johnson responded in a way that cut through the smoke and let him rejoin the human race. "Ah wish my parents were alive to hear that introduction. My father would have enjoyed it . . . and my mother would have believed it."

Even more devastating as a speech of introduction is a twenty-minute nightmare of poor jokes, trite language, and oral essays. This is especially cruel when the speaker intends to speak for only thirty minutes. What makes the situation really unfortunate is that the introducer is usually a well-intentioned, sincere person who is simply not skilled at introducing people. It is very difficult for speakers in this situation to undo the damage without appearing unkind. On one occasion a young instructor was introducing a distinguished professor to a group of university personnel who knew the professor. The instructor proceeded to give a speech that explained every entry on his bibliography. To make matters worse, he proceeded to give an oral essay on the very topic on which the guest was supposed to speak. After some prodding from the chairperson, the introducer stopped abruptly and said, "Professor Monroe will now give his address." After a long pause, Professor Monroe rose and calmly said, "1714 Norfolk Drive, Lafayette, Indiana." He then sat down!

Remember that the major purpose of the speech of introduction is to *create harmony between the speaker and the audience,* which in turn creates a desire for the audience to want to hear the speaker's subject. You want the audience to like and respect the speaker and be inclined to listen attentively. Toward this end, follow these rules:

1. *Be brief but adequate.* Make sure that enough is said about the speaker and the subject to achieve harmony and advance the speaker's credibility. Do not overplay your role, for you are not the main speaker. Remember that your job is to focus attention on the speaker and the subject. You might introduce our president simply and adequately with "Ladies and gentlemen: the President of the United States." Seldom should a speech of introduction run more than three or four minutes.

2. *Stress the importance and appropriateness of the speaker's subject.* However, take care not to give the main speech! Do not explain the speaker's subject to the point of stifling curiosity and attention to the topic.

3. *Make sure you know something about the speaker and the subject.* Consult the speaker before the meeting; see if there are some things the speaker prefers to be said or not said; and get his or her name right!

4. *Consider the audience.* The length, language, and style of your speech should be carefully adapted to the audience. How well does the audience know the person? Are they friends, foes, or undecided? What do they already know about the speaker's topic?

5. *Speak with sincerity and enthusiasm.* If you are not familiar with the speaker or the subject or are simply not interested, have someone else make the introduction. Do not stress the speaker's "oratorical" skills. Do not use trite language. In general, speak about accomplishments rather than about virtues.

6. *Pay attention to the speaker.* After you have finished your speech of introduction, be a model listener. This suggests that the audience should also be good listeners. A gabby or hyperactive introducer can ruin audience concentration.

The introduction of a distinguished professor might be quite different for the following different audiences: (1) faculty colleagues, (2) graduating seniors, or (3) a local American Legion post.

FACULTY COLLEAGUES

"Chance favors the prepared mind." This statement by Louis Pasteur characterizes our distinguished colleague and seminar speaker. Professor Raymond is no stranger to any of us nor is most of his research, but how he bends lady luck to get these huge grants and research supports is a mystery to most of us. Friends, here's Mark Raymond to tell all, and perhaps explain what Pasteur was talking about, and whom he knows at the Ford Foundation.

GRADUATING SENIORS

"Chance favors the prepared mind." This statement by Louis Pasteur characterizes our commencement speaker. His research success in advertising and public relations effects was no more accidental than his winning the *Croix de Guerre*. His training has been arduous and thorough, with a bachelor's degree from the Annenberg School of Communication and master's and doctor's degrees in psychology from Yale University. Dr. Mark Raymond is currently a full professor of communication and psychology at the University of Michigan where he is a member of the Institute of Social Research, the Group Dynamics Research Center, and the Institute of Industrial Relations. Dr. Raymond has served as a research consultant to many government, business, and industrial organizations. He is the author of six textbooks and thirty-seven research monographs; he is listed in *Who's Who in America* and every other lexicon of important people in the world.

Dr. Raymond is not going to speak to you this evening on his latest research into cognitive-response persuasion, but rather about how post-commencement career preparation can help you bend fortune in your direction. Dr. Mark G. Raymond.

AMERICAN LEGION POST

"Chance favors the prepared mind." This statement by Louis Pasteur characterizes our speaker this afternoon. B.A., M.A., Ph.D., a half-dozen books are only half the story. How about the *Croix de Guerre,* the Silver Star, and two Purple Hearts? Here is a man who knows about chance and preparation as well as advertising and public relations. This man who rose from the ranks to lieutenant-colonel has our best interests at heart, and is here to criticize constructively our public relations efforts. His research on our current image is thorough, revealing, and a bit of a shocker—he wants to help change that for the better. And why not; he's a fellow legionnaire—Colonel Mark Raymond from the University of Michigan.

The commencement introduction to graduating seniors meets all of the rules and is longer and more formal than the other versions. The version for Dr. Raymond's colleagues is much shorter and even uses some humor; after all, they know the speaker. The American Legion audience calls for more adaptation. The speaker's military background is given more emphasis and, because criticism is forthcoming, pains are taken to make clear that he is a friend.

Speeches of Presentation and Acceptance

Figure 13.6

"Thanks for holding down the other end of the log" was engraved on a simple brass plaque and signed by four appreciative students. The students presented this award by simply placing it on the center of a professor's desk and saying "Thanks," as he retired from the University. With this close little group, a speech, a banquet, a formal meeting between professor and students was unnecessary. The recipient was honored and felt that his efforts were appreciated and recognized. The presentation was both sensitive and appropriate. Most often, however, a speech is called for when an award is given. The major purpose of such a speech should be to show honor, appreciation, and recognition.

Goodwill and appreciation can be transmitted under considerably different circumstances. A five-minute formal speech read from a manuscript before a banquet audience of 300 people concluded: "For these and his many other achievements, it was unanimously agreed by the Executive Faculty of the Marquette University of Speech that Dr. James W. Cleary was richly deserving of our Distinguished Alumni Award in the field of Speech Education."

The point is that presentations vary widely. The size of the group, the nature of the award, and the occasion all determine how much is said and how formally it is said. There are two general principles for most speeches of presentation:

1. *The speech should sincerely communicate honor, appreciation, and recognition.* It should not stray from the facts; if so, it becomes insincere. Do not overpraise, overstate, or overemotionalize. Review the recipient's accomplishments honestly.

2. *Adapt your speech to the occasion and the award.* For annual and routine service awards, only a short, straightforward word of congratulation may be necessary, even on a formal occasion. When many

similar awards are given, as with contest winners, one short speech can often show honor and recognition for the entire group, each of whom might then step forward individually to receive a medal. This is not to say that a brief speech should be a less sincere speech. Make sure the speaker selected to present an award is thoroughly familiar with the kind of effort and achievement involved.

On some award occasions the speaker may also have to consider the donor of the gift. A university giving an honorary degree or a distinguished alumni award deserves some recognition and reflected glory. This is also true of business and industrial concerns who honor long-time employees. In situations in which the award may have a history or be unusual in some other way, a short description of these facts may be in order.

An acceptance speech should measure up to the total communication situation, and especially to the expectations of those making the award. If you are representing a group or organization, make this clear and explain briefly why the award is appreciated by the others as well as yourself. If appropriate, you may wish to mention individuals and their specific efforts or merits related to the award. If the award is a personal gift, your response might vary from a simple but sincere "thank you" to a short statement of gratitude. So much depends on the nature of the award, the expectations of those honoring you, the total communication climate—and, of course, your own feelings.

Below is a sample speech of presentation followed by its corresponding acceptance speech. Mr. Hope's speech is shortened slightly. While not all of us can or should accept with as much humor, Bob Hope is a special case. So too is the presenter, Ronald Reagan.

TELEVISION PRESENTATION BY PRESIDENT REAGAN:

This award honors a lifetime of service and achievement. It is appropriate that the first award should go to a gentleman who has practiced the liveliest of arts—comedy—for over six happy decades. Bob Hope has given generously of his valuable time and talent in support of worthy causes, perhaps more than any human being alive today. Bob recently returned from the Persian Gulf where he let some of our finest young people know how much we love them and how proud we are of the job they're doing.

So you see this award is not only in recognition of accomplishments past but is also an incentive to future generations to be inspired to carry on the traditions established by Bob Hope. It is my pleasure now to present this award to the man whose name is a description of life—Where there is life, there is Hope.

ACCEPTANCE BY BOB HOPE:

Thank you very much, Mr. President. You know you've done some nice things around this neighborhood. You've done many wonderful things out here (Palm Springs, California) and we like you around here, and I think that after you've finished your term you ought to come here and do a stage version of *King's Row.* No, I appreciate the nice things he said about me even if I'm not Russian (referring to the Gorbachev meetings).

Naming a culture center for me is like naming a monastery for Gary Hart. (More political jokes followed). I bumped into former President Gerald Ford this afternoon. I said, "Pardon me," and he said, "I don't do that anymore."

As you know Mr. President, no one who gets this kind of recognition can ever claim solo credit for his career, and the list of people who have come into my life and allowed me to reach this point is long and impressive. Some of them are here this evening, and some of them appeared on that video we just saw. Some have been content to make their invaluable contributions from behind the scenes. I owe them all my deepest "thanks for the memories" and for the love and support they have shown me over the years. Once again, my thanks to all who are responsible for my receiving this impressive award, and I shall treasure it and try to live up to its meaning. Thank you, Mr. President and thank you, ladies and gentlemen.

Speeches of Tribute and Commemoration

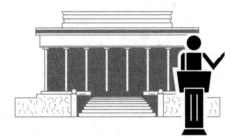

Figure 13.7

This form of special-occasion speaking includes *eulogies, anniversary addresses, dedicatory speeches,* and some *nominating speeches.* The eulogy is typically a speech of tribute upon the death of a person or shortly thereafter. It may also apply to the anniversary of the birth or great moments in the life of a historical figure, such as Lincoln or Washington. Anniversary speeches celebrate an event, a person, or an institution. Dedicatory speeches are usually tributes; buildings, monuments, ships, libraries, and other things are generally dedicated in honor of some outstanding personality, institution, or group of people. In some nominating speeches, it is the practice to pay tribute to the nominee as a way of proving his or her qualifications for office. As most organizations now use nominating committees, nominations are made with less oral flourish.

All commemorative speeches are tributes. Their purpose is to gain or increase respect, emulation, and appreciation for the people or institutions being honored and their impact upon society.

You can organize your speech according to the history of the person or institution being commemorated. Or, if time is short and the history is generally well known, you can concentrate on selected aspects of personality, achievement, or impact on society. Here are three general rules for most tributes and commemorative speeches:

1. *Develop a sensitive understanding of the subject.* To deliver a funeral oration about a stranger would be awkward and embarrassing, if not disrespectful. Make sure you have more than just the immediate facts about the person, occasion, memorial, or building being commemorated. Try to capture the personality of the subject in both large and small incidents that typify the person's virtues or outlook on life. Know the outstanding achievements well, but do not lose sight of the personality.

2. *Be objective and fair to the facts.* Perhaps we should not speak ill of the dead, but neither should we be totally dishonest. To eulogize a lazy, intemperate, hardheaded old lady as "this kind, generous model of moral simplicity" is apt to incite outright laughter and do a disservice to whatever virtues and respect the woman did have. No person is perfect in every way. Washington was not a model tactician at Valley Forge; young Lincoln was defeated so many times at the polls that his political future was in real danger. You will want to magnify and concentrate on the subject's virtues and achievements, but let the person be human.

3. *Use a style of language and delivery that is in keeping with the occasion.* Commemorative occasions often demand a style that is slightly more elevated than the style generally prescribed in this book. The expectations audiences have of a speaker in a church or cemetery are somehow special. In paying tribute to someone tragically killed, the speaker's voice and measured cadence help express the grief, reverence, and solemnity of the occasion. On the other hand, there are many happy anniversaries, dedications, and tributes, and these call for a different style. Most commemorative speeches demand an elevated style at some point during the speech.

THE SPEECH OF COMMEMORATION

The abridged model that follows helps illustrate this point. It was delivered on the floor of the United States Senate by Senator Everett Dirksen after President Kennedy's assassination. A formal resolution was read, and Senator Dirksen was then recognized:

MR. DIRKSEN: Mr. President, the memory of John Fitzgerald Kennedy lingers in this forum of the people. Here we knew his vigorous tread, his flashing smile, his ready wit, his keen mind, his zest for adventure. Here with quiet grief we mourn his departure. Here we shall remember him best as a colleague whose star of public service is indelibly inscribed on the roll of the U.S. Senate.

And here the eternal question confronts and confounds us. Why must it be? Why must the life of an amiable, friendly, aggressive young man, moved only by high motives, lighted on his way by high hopes, guided by broad plans, impelled by understanding and vision, be brought to an untimely end with his labors unfinished? And why, in a free land, untouched by the heel of dictatorship and oppression, where the humblest citizen may freely utter his grievances, must that life be cut short by an evil instrument, moved by malice, frustration, and hate? This is the incredible thing which leaves us bewildered and perplexed.

On the tables of memory, we who knew him well as a friend and colleague can well inscribe this sentiment:

"Senator John Fitzgerald Kennedy, who became the 35th President of the United States—young, vigorous, aggressive, and scholarly—one who estimated the need of his country and the world and sought to fulfill that need—one who was wedded to peace and vigorously sought this greatest of all goals of mankind—one who sensed how catastrophic nuclear conflict could be and sought a realistic course to avert it—one who sensed the danger that lurked in a continuing inequality in our land and sought a rational and durable solution—one to whom the phrase 'the national interest' was more than a string of words—one who could disagree without vindictiveness—one who believed that the expansion of the enjoyment of living by all people was an achievable goal—one who believed that each generation must contribute its best to the fulfillment of the American dream."

The *te deums* which will be sung this day may be wafted away by the evening breeze which caresses the last resting place of those who served the Republic, but here in this Chamber where he served and prepared for higher responsibility, the memory of John Fitzgerald Kennedy will long linger to nourish the faith of all who serve that same great land.[10]

THE EULOGY

The combination of appreciation and eulogy is illustrated by the touching speech that Tom Hughes gave in tribute to his brother, football player Chuck Hughes, who died of a heart attack on the field while playing for the Detroit Lions. All of the Lions were at the funeral in San Antonio. Tom gathered the Lions around him and spoke.

Words cannot express the gratitude for you that I now hold in my heart. Sunday you were names. Today you are and always will be in my heart and the hearts of all of those that I hold dear. The love we have for Chuck, I now feel, was shown by you, the Detroit Lions.

This to me is the finest tribute you could ever bestow on him. I have on numerous occasions heard that the Lions are a team of class. These past three days have shown it. Please try to continue this. You strike me, an outsider really, as being a tightly knit family. My personal family is this way too.

Please don't let this tragedy spoil the things that make you stand out so prominently. Chuck died doing the one thing he wanted to do for such a long time. It was his life.

I'd prefer it, and so would he, that he died on the field, rather than in some other tragic way. Forget the tragedy of Sunday and remember him as the man you knew personally. He'd like that. He gave his all and I know that if he had to die he would tell you, losing is the tragedy. Play it to win.[11]

"IT'S IKE HIMSELF. PASS THE WORD."

Figure 13.8   *Willie and Joe* cartoon by Bill Mauldin.
By permission of The Detroit Free Press.

Some tributes are brief, some almost cryptic. No old soldier missed the touching message in Bill Mauldin's cartoon or in his "Willie and Joe" eulogy on the death of General Dwight David Eisenhower, Supreme Allied Commander in Europe (World War II) and thirty-fourth president of the United States (Figure 13.8).

GOODBYE FROM WILLIE AND JOE

They met in the mud a long way from home, when Ike was a five-star general and Willie and Joe were GIs.

Willie and Joe had no use for generals. They were pen-and-ink people, cartoon characters dreamed up by an upstart Army artist named Bill Mauldin, and they did their talking from the pages of *Stars and Stripes,* the GI newspaper. They weren't happy about the war.

Always, Willie and Joe were hungry, filthy and fed-up. They never had clean socks or a decent meal; they smoked cigaret butts and never got their mail; their feet hurt, their bones ached and the rain always rained on them. In time, they were famous—the absolutely perfect prototypes of American soldiers everywhere.

The brass didn't like Willie and Joe much and Gen. George Patton once threatened to ban them from the newspaper. It was Ike who came to their rescue, the only time an officer ever did anything for Joe and Willie. Ike arranged a meeting between Mauldin and Patton. They talked things over and Willie and Joe stayed.

When the war was over, Ike came home and so did Mauldin, but Willie and Joe stayed behind. Some said they were just too tired to climb out of the foxhole they had shared so long; others figured Willie and Joe just decided to stay with their friends. There were 300,000 dead in the fields of France and the jungles of the Pacific and so Willie and Joe stayed on.

They met once again, when Ike was a president and Willie and Joe were in Korea, but the years passed and the friendship dimmed. Only in the battlefields now quiet and green, the crosses marching white to the horizon, was there time to remember the history they shared.

He was the only general they ever learned to like.[12]

All eulogies should strike an emotional nerve and be in a special style that captures what the person meant to those assembled. It doesn't have to be a person. Consider this touching tribute by Steve Rubenstein who lost his dog.

A VERY GOOD DOG IS WHAT SHE WAS

Annie was a good dog. This might surprise anyone who knew her, but newspapermen are not allowed to bend facts. The truth is that Annie was the best dog around. I loved her and that's true, too.

Annie died on Wednesday on an operating table in Corte Madera, and I suppose this is her obituary. If you don't want to hear an obituary about a yellow Labrador retriever, you might wish to leave, because that's what this is.

In obituaries you are supposed to mention how many years old the subject was when she died. Annie was 0. She had yet to reach her first birthday. She was 11 months and 3 days old when her gentle heart stopped beating. It's not a long time to live unless you lived life like my dog did, which was pleasurably if not particularly honorably.

Annie enjoyed her 0 years. She spent them on Ocean Beach, chasing tennis balls. She spent them in the lake behind Stern Grove, swimming for sticks. She spent them in a house in Miraloma Park, chewing sofa cushions.

Annie had her own way of doing things, and it was rarely the right way.

She knew how to heel well enough to know she didn't care for it. She could fetch the newspaper, only to drop it halfway up the steps. She learned to stop chewing phonograph records about the time she learned to start chewing compact discs.

In her 0 years, she attended three weddings. One of them was mine. She was the ring bearer, a duty she performed with her customary enthusiasm and absentmindedness. The moment the parcel was fastened to her collar, she took off down the beach in pursuit of a spaniel.

My dog was just getting the hang of things. She could catch a Frisbee, sometimes. She could roll over, if nudged. She was developing a taste for bananas. When you die at the age of 0, you leave a lot of bananas uneaten and many of them are in a bowl by the sink. She left many uneaten Milk Bones, too, one of which I just pulled out of my windbreaker pocket.

Annie liked ice cubes, especially the way they slid like hockey pucks across the kitchen floor. We called them water bones. She especially liked kicking them under the stove and watching me crawl around and fish them out.

And she like to travel. In her 0 years, she climbed to the top of Multnomah Falls in Oregon, swam in the Rogue River, romped through a snowstorm near Truckee and ate a barbecue beef sandwich in San Luis Obispo. She visited Los Angeles, too, because she was in the back of my car and had no choice. She forgave me, in exchange for a Milk Bone.

On her last day we visited the dog run in Mill Valley. It was a favorite place, located enticingly close to the sewage plant. We played fetch with a tennis ball and then it was time to drop her off for her ankle operation. I kissed her on the top of her head before the man led her away. I was always kissing her on the top of her soft, fuzzy head. People said I kissed my dog too much, but it's not really any of their business, being as the practice was conducted between consenting parties.

A few hours later, the call came from the surgeon. The anesthesia reaction that had stopped Annie's heart was a 10,000-to-1 occurrence. And the bone chip in her ankle, which necessitated the operation, was a 100-to-1 chance.

You can work it out for yourself. You multiply 10,000 by 100 and you find that Annie was one dog in a million. That's what she was, officially certified. She was a good dog, too, but that's not official. You only have my word on it.[13]

Summary

General rules for handling audience participation speeches include: (1) know your occasion, subject, and question format, (2) second-guess the questions, (3) answer or react to all questions, (4) consider the rest of the audience, (5) don't act as if you must know everything or win every argument, and (6) encourage participation in open forums. Rules for answering questions include: (1) repeat, (2) rephrase when necessary, (3) postpone the irrelevant or time-consuming, (4) label loaded questions, and (5) don't bluff. To help generate participation use: (1) overhead questions, (2) direct questions, (3) redirected questions, and (4) prime the pump by building questions into your speech.

Other things being equal, a little showmanship is better than dull, hedged, powerless language and delivery. Some people are better at humor than others. All humorous people do not tell jokes well. Humor is more than jokes and is helpful when appropriate. Research also indicates that people differ on contexts perceived as appropriate for humor as well as on its type and spontaneity.

The after-dinner speeches with which we are concerned take place in a good-humored, lighthearted, genial situation whose major purpose is a sociable dinner and relaxed enjoyment. These speeches should be brief, light, and humorous. Some principles to follow are: (1) select suitable topics; look on the lighter side of issues; (2) be clear and brief; stick to one or two obvious main points; (3) be genuinely good-humored; avoid bitter argument; (4) adapt to the specific audience; tie your message and humor directly to the audience at hand. Beware of jokes that injure people. Practice and polish all attempts at humor. The major purpose of a speech of introduction is to create harmony between speaker and audience, which makes the audience want to hear about the speaker's subject. Toward this end, (1) be brief but adequate, (2) stress the importance and appropriateness of the speaker's subject, (3) make sure that you know something about the speaker and the subject, (4) consider the audience, (5) speak with sincerity and enthusiasm, and (6) pay attention to the speaker after he or she starts to speak.

Two general principles for speeches of presentation are: (1) the speech should sincerely communicate honor, appreciation, and recognition, and (2) the speech should be adapted to the specific occasion and to the award. An acceptance speech should measure up to the total communication situation and especially to the expectations of those making the award.

Speeches of tribute and commemoration include eulogies, anniversary addresses, dedicatory speeches, and some nominating speeches. The purpose of all commemorative speeches is to gain or increase respect, emulation, and appreciation for the people being honored and their impact upon society and its institutions. The key topics on which to concentrate are the subject's personality, achievement, and impact on society. Three general rules are: (1) develop a sensitive understanding of the subject, (2) be objective and fair to the facts, and (3) utilize a style of language and delivery in keeping with the occasion.

Learning Projects

1. Observe an open forum or interrupted speech episode in person or on radio or television. Evaluate how well the participants follow the principles and rules described in this chapter. Be especially alert to the five rules for answering questions.

2. Assume you have just spoken to your classmates on a topic that is currently in the news. Now prepare for a two- to three-minute open forum. Anticipate the key questions, and give some thought to answers. Remember to follow the five basic rules for answering questions.

3. Rehearse a joke or humorous anecdote; try it out on several people (groups if possible). Evaluate your success. What would you do or say differently?

4. Describe the best or worst after-dinner speech you have ever heard. Explain.

5. Attend a convocation or other event on or off campus and evaluate the *introduction* speeches. If there are awards or tributes, make note of how well they meet the speech criteria suggested in this chapter.

6. Watch TV awards programs such as the Oscars, Grammy, Tony, etc., and evaluate the effectiveness of the special speeches, especially those of acceptance.

7. Find an example of a tribute or commemorative speech that was not ideal. Explain why.

Notes

1. Edith Paal, "Communication Skills Lauded," *The San Diego Union-Tribune,* November 25, 1996, C, 2. Also see Craig Johnson and Larry Vinson, "Placement and Frequency of Powerless Talk and Impression Formation," *Communication Quarterly,* 38, no. 4 (Fall 1990), 325–33.
2. Melissa Wanzer, Melanie Booth-Butterfield, and Steven Booth-Butterfield, "The Funny People: A Source Orientation to the Communication of Humor," *Communication Quarterly,* 43, no. 2 (Spring 1995), 142–54.
3. Ibid.
4. R. M. Kaplan and G. C. Pascoe, "Humorous Lectures and Humorous Examples: Some Effects upon Comprehension and Retention," *Journal of Educational Psychology,* 69 (1977), 61–65.
5. Joan Gorham and Diane M. Christophel, "The Relationship of Teachers' Use of Humor in the Classroom to Immediacy and Student Learning," *Communication Education,* 39, no. 1 (January 1990), 46–62.
6. Charles R. Gruner, "Self- and Other-Disparaging Wit/Humor and Speaker Ethos: Three Experiments," paper delivered at the Fourth International Conference on Humor, Tel Aviv, Israel, June 1984.
7. Steven Booth-Butterfield and Melanie Booth-Butterfield, "Individual Differences in the Communication of Humorous Messages," *Southern Communication Journal,* 56, no. 3 (Spring 1991), 205–18.
8. James Hassett and John Houlihan, "Different Jokes for Different Folks," *Psychology Today,* January 1979, 64–71.
9. Bill Adler, "Adlai Stevenson's Wit," *This Week Magazine,* September 12, 1965, p. 5. Copyrighted 1965 by the United Newspaper Corporation. Reprinted with the permission of the author and his agents, Scott Meredith Literary Agency, Inc., 580 Fifth Ave., New York, New York 10036.
10. *Congressional Record,* 1964, pp. 21, 596–97.
11. Quoted by Jerry Green, *Detroit News,* October 28, 1971, p. 5D.
12. By permission of *The Detroit Free Press.*
13. Steve Rubenstein, "A Very Good Dog Is What She Was," © *The San Francisco Chronicle.* Reprinted with permission.

14

SPEAKING IN GROUP SETTINGS

CHAPTER
OUTLINE

THE NATURE OF MEETINGS AND GROUPS

(Phone rings) "Hello. Larry Logan here."

"Larry, this is Ed Brock, your old biology teacher at Groves High School."

"Yes, Mr. Brock. What can I do for you?"

"Well, Larry, you know that the PTA, the school board, and the community are considering the merits of sex education. Since you're in premed and were an honored graduate, I'd like your input at a discussion we're holding on Thursday night at the school."

"Sounds interesting. What time?"

"Seven thirty. Will you do it?"

"Sure, and thanks for thinking of me."

Good luck to Larry Logan! He never asked what he was really getting into, or how, or even *if,* he should prepare.

So Larry arrives promptly at 7:30 on Thursday. That's his second mistake. He has no time to adjust to what he finds. He thought a discussion was a few people informally kicking an idea around; sometimes it is, but not tonight.

The meeting is in the auditorium, which is already half full. The stage is set with seven chairs in a semicircle. It looks like a discussion set-up, but if it's a *panel,* it's also a *panel forum.* Why else are there microphones in the aisle?

Mr. Brock points to a chair and says, "Larry, you're third. Try to limit your opening remarks to three or four minutes."

"Yikes," says Larry to himself, "I've got to give a speech." Right, Larry, and welcome to a *symposium forum.* A symposium, he discovers, calls for short, uninterrupted speeches.

After the speeches have been given the moderator (Brock) invites the participants to question one another. This is a panel format, but hardly a cohesive, unified, small group. Larry is challenged sharply on his words "human sexuality."

"What does that have to do with sex education?" demands Mrs. Himmler.

"Well, let me better define sex education," Larry replies.

Himmler interrupts. "Don't define sex education for me, young man. I know what it means."

Larry is no longer in a discussion (if he ever was). This is a debate, and a rough one at that. "Shouldn't we at least define what we're talking about?" mutters Larry. It is not one of Larry Logan's better nights.

"Thanks for coming to our roundtable discussion, Larry," says Brock.

Larry sneaks out as quickly as possible, thinking "Roundtable? What in thunder is a roundtable? Wasn't there a *Roundtable of the Air* on the radio years and years ago?"

The point of this horror story is that many people don't really know the differences between the various forms of discussion. As a leader, Mr. Brock was better at biology than at communication.

If you find yourself in Larry's place, check out the purpose, setting, audience, and agenda. Also be prepared for the possibility of a speech. At the very least, ask Brock what he means by "a discussion" and what the setting will be. Is it to be a single-form discussion? Or a panel perhaps? Is it apt to combine several forms? A multiform? Be prepared for him not to know that he was talking about a symposium forum rather than a panel discussion. (We'll review these definitions, and leadership functions shortly.)

Small Coacting Groups

Coacting groups are more than just small, casual gatherings. There must be some common purpose, intent, or problem that requires interaction. Members share a kind of mutual identification that binds them together.[1] They are sensitive to their own behavior as well as to the behavior of others. Feedback is often swift and to the point in small groups; large audiences are sometimes slower to respond and more formal in their patterns of response. (Larry might argue that!)

An audience is sometimes passive; a good group is usually active and dynamic. The group's small size permits active and instant participation by all. Some members may, of course, have a greater desire to take charge than others do. If Larry Logan were a member of the local YMCA or CYO board, he might find himself involved in friendly problem solving at one meeting and rather stiff debate at another. Some boards are very large and only their executive committee meets as a coactive group. Their report to the whole board might very well be in the form of symposium speeches.

All small groups are *not* coacting groups; several characteristics help define coacting groups:

1. They have a common purpose or goal.
2. Members have interdependent, interactive communication.
3. Members experience pressure to conform.
4. Members decide and take action as a unit.

Some generalizations based on observation and research of coacting groups are:

1. Group discussion can change attitudes and behavior.
2. Group judgment is frequently better than individual judgment.
3. Group communication can be improved through training.

This kind of small-group discussion has also been defined as ". . . a few people engaged in communication interaction over time, usually in face-to-face settings, who have common goals and norms, and have developed a communication pattern for meeting their goals in an interdependent manner.[2]

Assuming, then, that we have a real, interacting, face-to-face group—persons with some common goal, not just a loose collection of individuals—we might say that at its best *small-group discussion is cooperative thinking.* However, healthy argument and debate short of verbal aggression is also part of the definition.

To enhance cooperation group members should:

1. Use tact when arguing.
2. Be enthusiastic and friendly.
3. Interact democratically and actively.
4. Seek agreement on procedures.
5. Share leadership.
6. Research the topic objectively.

Discussion/Debate Continuum

Groups may generate little discussion on one issue and vigorous argument or debate on another. Some discussion/debate distinctions are helpful.

The term **discussion** is derived from the Latin *discussus*—to strike asunder, to pull apart, to separate and subordinate the elements and ideas that make up a question or topic. Discussion is many-sided. **Debate** is two-sided and more competitive. If decision is impossible through systematic discussion, then discussion may very well lead to useful debate. Debate may then lead to resolution. If it does not, the group very possibly will return to discussion. Premature, verbally aggressive, or unnecessary debate impedes problem solving. A discussion/debate continuum is illustrated in Figure 14.1.

Frequently a speaker goes from easygoing participant to an advocate. You may need to review Chapters 11 and 12 on persuasion and logic for certain situations. In some organizational settings you may also need to review parliamentary law. We will explore problem solving and agendas after we describe the basic forms of discussion.

Figure 14.1

CONTEMPORARY FORMS OF DISCUSSION

The basic forms of group discussion are dialogue, panel, and symposium. Three techniques that may be used with any of these forms are the buzz group, role-playing, and brainstorming. A *forum* is simply that part of a discussion in which the audience may speak. It can be and often is included in any of the discussion forms. Rules for open-forum participation were discussed in Chapter 13, "Unique Formats and Occasions."

A *dialogue* is a two-person interaction, such as conversation, an interview, or counseling. If a dialogue is held before an audience and the audience is invited to participate, the interaction becomes a *dialogue forum.* (See Figure 14.2.)

The *panel discussion* is most often three to seven persons pursuing a common goal in an informal climate that promotes interaction. An audience may or may not be present. A panel discussion generally calls for a procedural leader, one who plans, starts, and ends the meeting. A simple program, or an *agenda* might be called for. (See Figure 14.3.)

A *symposium* is a small group (three to five) that has special knowledge of different aspects of a broad topic. Each individual makes uninterrupted speeches before an audience. A procedural leader controls the order of speakers and the time limits. A forum usually follows, except when an audience is

Figure 14.2   Dialogue forums.

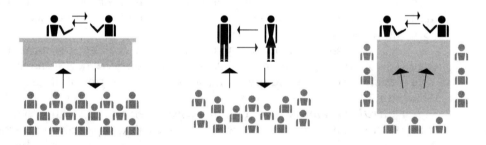

Figure 14.3   Panel forums.

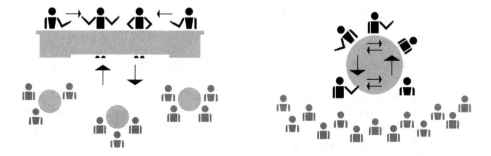

not physically present (as with radio or TV broadcasts). Frequently, the symposium speakers then relate to one another more informally in a panel discussion. (See Figure 14.4.)

These forms of discussion can be used for information sharing, problem solving, or decision making, as well as for instructional purposes. Examples of *information-sharing groups* are staff meetings, study groups, and workshops. The overlap among these groups is evident and probably unavoidable. A workshop, for example, may be thought of as a study group that has concentrated its work into a couple of days or even a few hours.

Problem-solving groups include committees, conferences, and governing boards or councils. These discussion groups have the power of decision, or at least the power to recommend action. Their group discussions are usually closed to nonmembers.

Instructional formats include case conferences, role-playing, and, to some extent, all the forms and techniques of discussion. A *case conference* is a discussion of a real or hypothetical incident that has a learning objective. It may or may not be conducted with an audience present. It can be evaluated according to the quality of the interaction, leadership, agenda setting, or solution.

Large groups in which wider individual participation is desired may be divided into subgroups of four to six persons for more intimate, informal discussion. This technique is known as a *buzz session* or "Phillips 66." The numbers refer to subgroups of six, which discuss a carefully worded question. The results of the individual buzz sessions are reported to the larger group by a spokesperson. The number of people in the subgroups seems to be important. A person is more apt to speak up in a group of six than of six hundred. (See Figure 14.5.)

The extemporaneous acting out of assigned roles or dramatic parts in a group—often a case conference—is known as *role-playing.* As a technique, role playing is often a good preliminary to the other forms of discussion. (See Figure 14.6.)

Brainstorming is a technique used when a group wants to generate a lot of ideas in a short period of time. This technique operates in an arbitrary psychological climate complete with penalties, the purpose of which is to prohibit immediate criticism of ideas. Its rules include:

1. No criticism or discussion of ideas.
2. No evaluation of any kind.
3. The wilder the ideas, the better.
4. "Hitchhiking" or combining ideas is encouraged.

Take the question, "What should this class use as a topic for a project discussion?" Under brainstorming rules, this question regularly produces sixty or seventy topics in ten minutes. No evaluative discussion of the topics is allowed until later. Using buzz groups to screen the list more systematically is a good follow-up (Figure 14.7).

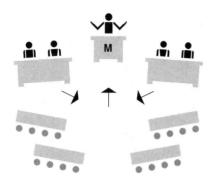
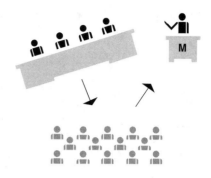

Figure 14.4   Symposium forums.

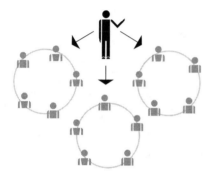
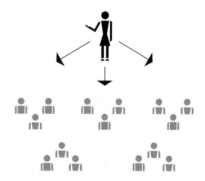

Figure 14.5   Buzz groups.

Figure 14.6   Role-playing.

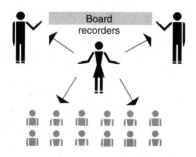
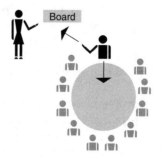

Figure 14.7   Brainstorming.

GROUP PROBLEM SOLVING AND DECISION MAKING

Patterns and Procedures

It has been shown that "successful" groups tend to *analyze* the problem *before* seeking a solution and that "unsuccessful" groups tend to start with solutions. Further, that open communication which focuses on the task and related issues facilitates successful problem solving and decision making.[3]

Good problem-solving patterns tend to resemble the reflective thinking pattern discussed in Chapter 12. A useful one follows:

A FOUR-STEP PROBLEM-SOLVING PROCEDURE

1. Define the problem.
   - **A.** State the felt difficulty, problem, or goal.
   - **B.** Limit and phrase the question.
2. Analyze the problem.
   - **A.** Separate and subordinate the elements and ideas (facts, policies, values).
   - **B.** Review the history of the problem.
   - **C.** Describe possible causes of the problem.
3. Establish criteria for solutions.
   - **A.** Minimum-maximum limits.
   - **B.** Order of importance (weighting).
4. Generate and test solutions.
   - **A.** Consider potential solutions.
   - **B.** Test solutions against criteria.
   - **C.** Arrive at decision and plan implementation or report.

A discussion of the four steps follows:

STEP 1   DEFINE THE PROBLEM   Most problem-solving discussions start by establishing rapport, or at least trying to. This is usually followed by "Why are we here?" "What is the felt difficulty?" This preliminary ventilation helps remove any emotional heat and usually helps a group determine goals and move toward a more formal defining of the problem.

The *critical thinking* errors discussed in Chapter 12 are all applicable to assessing the felt difficulty: false assumptions, definitional confusion, misattributions, and single perspective.

The definition step consists of the *definition* and the *limitation* of the problem. For example, a group may talk about unemployment and limit the problem to unemployment in Chicago. If a group defines a problem in several different ways and, worse, is not aware of the differences, confusion and irritation are sure to follow. Time spent here in phrasing the question will make life less confused later on. Most of your problems will be stated as questions of policy or value rather than fact. "What should the federal government do to help citizens contend with the cost of medical care?"

If your felt difficulty had to do with *textbooks,* consider the following guidelines as you develop the idea into a reasonable question for discussion:

1. *Phrase it as a single question.*

   NOT: What should the college do about the cost of textbooks and laboratory fees?

2. *Avoid loaded questions.*

   NOT: How can we keep publishers from textbook price gouging?

3. *Limit through specificity.*

   NOT: What can be done about textbooks?

   BETTER: What college policies, if any, are needed to control the prices of textbooks?

The main purposes of the definition step are to explore the nature of the problem, limit the problem, and agree on the phrasing of the specific question for discussion.

STEP 2   ANALYZE THE PROBLEM   Stick to your plan. Sometimes after a spirited definition step, group members are tempted to start arguing solutions.

The three procedure suggestions under Step 2, *Analyze* (see previous page) should usually be taken up in that order. This is especially true if you have formulated your own question for discussion. If you are discussing a case or critical incident (e.g., Desert Survival, Moon Survival, etc.) and are given fact sheets, implied or stated policies, and other data, then suggestion A, "Separate and subordinate the elements and ideas (facts, policies, values)," should be given more time.

Start by seeking a consensus on the *facts.* The meaning of fact is complicated and only appears to be obvious. For the most part, facts are actions, events, or conditions that have been properly observed, described, classified, and reported. Can the phenomenon under discussion be verified by facts to the satisfaction of group members?

The listening lessons from Chapter 3 apply here: beware of misinterpreting chance events, beware of secondhand information and wishful thinking.

Take up *policies* next. First, consider policies already in place that are likely to remain so. Then briefly consider what new policies or changes to existing policies may have to be implemented. This part of the discussion may sometimes have to be limited and/or postponed to the criteria or solution step.

A consensus on the facts and policies already in place often leads to solutions without struggling with the dimension of *value.* Value is concerned chiefly with judgments about attitudes, beliefs, and feelings—very often the things most difficult on which to agree. Leave it until last unless the whole question is primarily one of values.

The next step is to analyze the history and causes of the problem, looking carefully for criteria by which to evaluate possible solutions.

STEP 3   ESTABLISH CRITERIA FOR SOLUTIONS   A ***criterion*** is a standard or yardstick by which we measure or evaluate something. In the case of group discussion, it refers to an ***agreed-upon standard.*** If a group has a reasonably clear and agreed-upon criterion in mind, the evaluation or testing of suggested solutions is a lot easier.

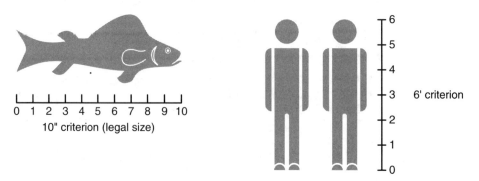

Figure 14.8

If, for example, a group were discussing the problem of a clubhouse for their organization, it would want to clearly establish the criteria of *cost, size, location, new or old,* and so on. The concept of limits can help a group at this point. If we are talking about cost in terms of $100,000, what do we really mean? Is that the minimum or the maximum? If the group really meant $75,000 to $110,000, it should state this, at least to itself. The same could be said for size and location. Criteria can also be negative. The group could, for example, name locations that it would not consider under any conditions.

The concept of ***weighting*** your criteria in terms of importance should also be considered. If size is the single most important criterion, then the group should agree on that point. Say, for example, that the old clubhouse is crowded; unless the next place is X amount larger, however beautiful a bargain, it won't solve the problem. If location is next most important (the facilities must be close to where the members live), followed by cost, parking, architecture, and so on, then you have the beginnings of a subagenda for evaluating solutions. Your list of criteria should then appear in some kind of *rank* in terms of importance. Weighting may be used profitably by a group if some of the criteria are close together in importance. Assuming a 100-point weighting scale and the determination that both size and location are very important, the group might assign to size, 90 points, to location 80 points, to cost 50 points, to architecture 20 points, and so on, along with specific upper and lower limits for each criterion (see Figure 14.9). Such a scale gives the group considerably more insight into its criteria, and a more logical, systematic approach to the solution step.

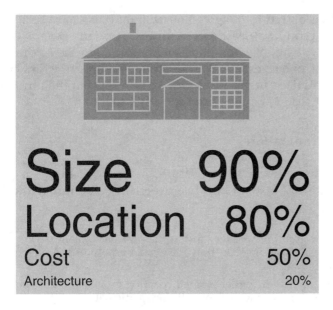

Size 90%
Location 80%
Cost   50%
Architecture   20%

Figure 14.9

STEP 4   GENERATE AND TEST SOLUTIONS   To continue the illustration of the clubhouse, the group next considers solutions. If Steve A. offers real estate data on a building he's found, but the building fails the criterion of size because it doesn't meet the lower limit and no plan for enlargement is provided by the contributor, then the group is quickly ready to go on to the next possible solution. It is possible that a group may come up with several solutions that meet the major criteria; the discussion may then focus on the less heavily weighted criteria. This is progress, and the group is aware of it. Without stated criteria to follow, the group might engage in lengthy argument over minor aspects of a problem while virtually ignoring the major aspects.

> Off-the-rack solutions, like bargain basement dresses, never fit anyone.
>
> *Francoise Giroud*

Discussion is sometimes called upon to solve inappropriate questions. Discussion is not needed to solve most questions of fact or even some questions of probability; the library, the computer, the map—these solve such problems without group discussion. Nor does discussion solve the unsolvable; some questions of value belong here. Once past the educational value of defining the differences, we sometimes may be well advised to adjourn. We should, of course, always look for viable solutions of the moment, if not for all time.

Remember the earlier critical thinking lessons: (1) sometimes we are victims of our own emotions and wishful thinking, and (2) single perspectives are frequently wrong.

Once a decision has been agreed on, you may also have to agree on a plan of implementation or at least a plan for reporting the general decision. In the case of costly textbooks, the implementation might be in the form of a letter to publishers or suggestions to bookstores. In some of your classroom discussions, your solutions might be reported to the class in the form of symposium speeches or through a delegated spokesperson.

Personal Preparation

Recall the case of Larry Logan, "Merits of Sex Education," (page 320). He learned the hard way. To avoid his bad experience, you might ask the following questions:

1. Who is in the group of speakers and in the possible audience? Do they have flexible or rigid positions? Do they view the purpose of the meeting differently than you do?
2. Is it a large group meeting, or a small coacting group? What is the physical setup? Is there an audience? If so, will they participate?
3. Is the format to be dialogue, panel, or symposium? If it's a symposium, you know you'll have to prepare a formal speech. Find out if you have been assigned to a specific aspect of the topic.
4. Is there an "order of business"? a prepared agenda of items to be covered? a formal statement of the problem?

As with formal speaking, researching the topic presumes you have a purpose, goal, or question in mind. Let's assume you are dealing with the question: *How, if at all, should we educate public school children about sex?*

Consider the agenda system. It suggests that you first *define* and *limit*. The language "*if at all*" suggests that consideration of a straight negative position has not been ruled out. The *terms* of the question help further define and limit. "*Public school*" suggests that private schools are not at issue here. "*Children*" may limit us to age 17 (or does it?), but it leaves open the question of children in elementary, middle, or secondary schools. "*Educate*" suggests some formal school program; most important, is the program to be voluntary or compulsory? "*Sex*" *appears* to be unrestricted semantically. But is it? Does it include Larry Logan's human sexuality? Does it include or exclude birth control, abortion, homosexuality, dysfunction, venereal disease, and so forth? Generally, what isn't clearly excluded is possible agenda or topical fare.

After this preliminary soul searching, you may find that your first meeting with the group (assuming there will be more) will be an attempt to further limit and clarify—a kind of brink-of-analysis situation. The group is trying to avoid detailed and lengthy discussions or speeches *before* the participants know what they are about.

Before the first formal meeting, however, you now have enough direction to at least start your research. A discussion outline or impartial brief is a good way to begin your preparation. A ***brief*** usually includes a documented record of judgments of the moment and the evidence and argument to support them. A law firm may prepare a common brief that looks both ways at a case; more likely, they will be building a case in terms of their initial judgment. You will probably be better served by the more impartial *discussion outline*. It can serve as a source of information as the discussion proceeds, or can provide the content for short, extemporaneous speeches. Symposium speeches would follow the organizational advice given earlier. Your outline can follow the agenda steps.

LEADERSHIP COMMUNICATION

> What I wanted to be when I grew up—was in charge.
>
> *Brigadier General Wilma Vaught*

Sources of Leadership

In general, ***leadership*** should be thought of as any significant action by any discussant that influences group achievement. A group may have an *assigned* leader, whose duties may range from a modest regulation of participation to strong goal control. It is possible to be in a leaderless group (that is, with no appointed leader) and still have considerable leadership, should this leadership emerge in some way from the group. By the same token, you could be in a group with a poor assigned leader; if no good leader(s) emerged, this group would really have no leadership. All group members have a stake and often a part in leadership. Thus, what follows applies to all group speakers, whether they be an assigned group leader, chairperson, moderator, or whatever.

Leadership, however temporary, may fall upon a person in a group simply because he or she was appointed moderator. It may be assigned to a person only on certain issues because that person happens to be the best informed on those issues. It may befall a person by reason of *role, position,* or *status* in the group (for example, she happens to be the boss, or he is an expert).

Particularly in leaderless groups, leadership may fall to a person who happens to perform communication skills exceptionally well—who knows how to speak, how to assess people, how to build and apply agendas, how to keep the lines of communication open.

Functions of Leadership

Leadership, whatever its source, should help a group move toward its goal or help it find its goal. Leadership should also promote a healthy, democratic communication climate within the group.

If your perceived leadership role does not happen to agree with most of your receivers' expectations, you may not exert much influence. In relatively informal, short-lived groups, such as committees or subcommittees, it usually helps all concerned if there is some concordance about role expectations. If your role is strictly procedural and is a random appointment, don't emerge as a George Patton; not many will be expecting that of you. If, on the other hand, you have been hand-picked because of your experience and expertise, you can look for different role expectations, but not always! Sometimes your qualifications are not known to members, and sometimes they don't bother to do their homework. You may need to explain and assess your role in these situations. You may risk some embarrassment in so doing, but not to do so is to risk charges of entrapping or embarrassing the others in the group.

Even when people agree upon position descriptions (chairperson, president, supervisor, lawyer), they may not agree upon role expectations. Some people express antipathy toward formal leadership, but even such behavior is predictable if it shows up in your preliminary search for ***concordance*** (agreement between actual and expected role). To complicate things further, people change; their roles and their expectations change; not very long ago most formal leadership was gendered—male.

The major functions of leadership are goal achievement, procedural matters, and effective interpersonal relations (communication climate).

Figure 14.10 Leadership Functions

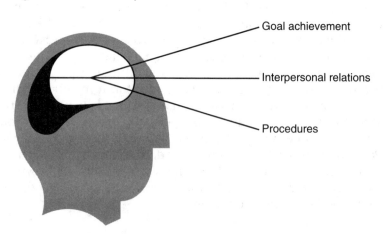

Goal achievement

Interpersonal relations

Procedures

GOAL ACHIEVEMENT   This is leadership related primarily to *content* or *task*. It includes such things as contributing and evaluating ideas, locating issues and consensus, synthesizing and cross-relating the ideas of others, and generally seeking specific contributions toward a goal. It helps if you are enthusiastic about and personally committed to the task at hand.

PROCEDURAL MATTERS   Leaders, particularly when assigned or designated, must also attend to the more practical functions, such as starting the meeting, drafting an order of business, clarifying statements, summarizing, and ending the meeting. Procedural functions may also include advance planning and physical arrangements.

As a procedural leader, you must review the purposes of the meeting. You should consider the members individually and decide the *degree of formality* necessary and the specific way you wish to open the discussion. You should consider group goals according to the time available. As a procedural leader you are also responsible for *participation*—that is, for preserving order, seeing that only one person speaks at a time, and gatekeeping—fairly distributing the right to speak. You may find it necessary on occasion to clarify what has been said as well as to remind the group of the agreed-upon items of business. The agenda of items should be agreed upon by the members unless it has already been designated.

INTERPERSONAL RELATIONS   Qualities of leadership in this area include such things as establishing rapport, controlling emotions, establishing the communication and psychological climate, resolving conflict, regulating the too-talkative and the silent, and generally promoting and facilitating those actions concerned with members' human or social problems.[4]

Leaders as well as participants have a responsibility to help the group whenever the situations shown in Figure 14.11 arise.

Styles of Leadership

Style refers in part to method and in part to philosophy. Many times style is determined by the type of organization in which you are operating. For example, a Marine Corps drill instructor (D.I.) understands full well the autocratic-style expectations of the Corps, and the recruits put up with this highly directive style because, after all, that was what they expected.

Styles of leadership are variously described as *laissez-faire, nondirective, permissive, democratic, supervisory, authoritarian,* and *autocratic*. These styles may be ordered on a continuum according to degree of control, as shown in Figure 14.12.

Experience advises that a democratic style is generally superior to an absolute or nonresponsible style. Which leadership style we may occasionally use depends in part on the group's expectations, in part on the task, and in large part on the situation of the moment.

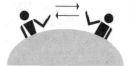
One or two members dominate.

Some members will not talk.

Some apparently lack interest.

Discussion drifts to irrelevant matters.

Conflict occurs between members.

Discussion "techniques" backfire.

Figure 14.11

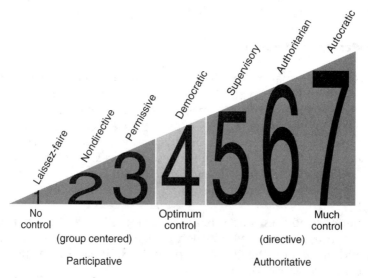

Figure 14.12

Summary

Many people tend to confuse the various forms of discussion, and do not understand coacting groups.

Characteristics of coactive groups are: (1) common purpose or goal, (2) interdependent, interactive communication, (3) pressure to conform, and (4) unitary decisions and actions. Other generalizations about small groups are: (1) discussion can change attitudes and behavior, (2) group judgment tends to be better than that of individuals alone, and (3) group communications can be improved through training.

Assuming a group with a common goal, we can define group-discussion speaking as cooperative thinking. If decision is impossible through discussion, discussion may very well lead to debate. Discussion is cooperative and many-sided. Debate is two-sided.

The basic forms of group discussion are dialogue, panel, and symposium. Three techniques that may be used with any of these forms are the buzz group, role-playing, and brainstorming. A forum is simply that part of a discussion in which the audience may speak.

These forms of discussion may be used for information sharing, problem solving, and instruction. Information-sharing groups include staff meetings, study groups, and workshops. Problem-solving groups include committees, conferences, and boards or councils. Instructional formats include case conferences, role-playing, and, to some extent, all the forms and techniques of discussion.

Successful groups analyze before seeking solutions. Open communication which focuses on the task and related issues facilitates problem solving and decision making.

Good problem-solving procedures tend to follow reflective thinking patterns. The four-step procedure includes (1) definition, (2) analysis, (3) criteria, and (4) solution.

Guidelines for phrasing a discussion question include: (1) phrase it as a single question, (2) avoid loaded questions, and (3) limit through specificity.

Leadership can be considered as any significant action by any discussant that influences group achievement. It is possible to have no assigned leader and still have leadership; it is also possible to have an assigned leader and no leadership. All group members have a stake and often a role in leadership.

Leadership may fall upon a person through designation or as a result of that person's superior information, role, position, or special ability to perform vital group functions.

The major functions of leadership are goal achievement and effective interpersonal relations. Leadership, particularly when designated, also has procedural functions. These functions may be planning, physical arrangements, purposes, degree of formality, goal setting, and the business agenda. The procedural leader is also responsible for general control of participation and for preserving order.

Styles of leadership may be described as autocratic, authoritarian, supervisory, democratic, permissive, nondirective, and laissez-faire. A leader's style is dependent upon group expectations, contingencies that arise, and participant behavior. A democratic style is generally preferred.

Learning Projects

1. Consider the similarities and differences between preparing for a discussion and preparing for a more formal speech. What is the same? What is different? Which is easier? Be prepared to discuss the issue in class.

2. Observe a problem-solving group in action. It may be formal or informal. Evaluate how well they did on the following criteria:

   goal achievement   personal skills of participants
   procedural functions   leadership
   interpersonal functions   problem-solving procedures

3. Review the critical thinking suggestions in Chapters 3 and 12. Select two of them (e.g., chance events, second-hand information, single perspective, and so on) and explain how their misuse might lead to poor group problem solving.

4. List all the groups of which you are a member. Rank them in terms of their level of formality, personal importance to you, and by the amount of time you have been a member. Write a short paper describing your speaking role in each group.

5. With an assigned group of four to six, determine a suitable topic for a 20- to 25-minute symposium/panel discussion. Each member makes a one- to three-minute position statement in symposium-speaking style. A panel discussion follows in the time remaining. A designated leader is at your option (or your instructor's).

6. Consider the following general topics and write a problem-solving discussion question for each. Make sure you phrase it in concordance with the criteria suggested in this chapter.

   Crime   Mars
   Middle East   Witchcraft
   Health Care   Drugs

Notes

1. Raymond S. Ross, *Small Groups in Organizational Settings* (Englewood Cliffs, N.J.: Prentice-Hall, 1989), p. 33.
2. John F. Cragan and David W. Wright, *Communication in Small Group Discussions*, 4th ed. (St. Paul, Minn.: West Publishing Co., 1995), p. 7.
3. Abran J. Salazar, Randy Y. Hirokawa, Kathleen M. Propp, Kelly M. Julian, and Geof B. Leatham, "In Search of True Causes: Examination of the Effect of Group Potential and Group Interaction on Decision Performance," *Human Communication Research*, 20, no. 4 (June 1994), 529–59.
4. For more on group facilitation techniques, see L. R. Frey, ed., *Innovations in Group Facilitation: Applications in Natural Settings* (Cresskill, NJ: Hampton Press, 1995).

Appendix A

RESEARCHING THROUGH THE INTERNET

WHAT IS THE INTERNET?

World Wide Web—A series of multimedia "pages" housed on separate computers around the world linked together through the phone lines of the Internet. There are various ways to search for information on the WWW.

Browser—A software program needed to "surf the net," such as Netscape or Internet Explorer.

E-mail—A way of sending electronic messages to people on the Internet. A special software program is needed to send and receive e-mail.

The Internet was born more than twenty years ago because the Department of Defense needed a way to keep lines of communication open between government officials during a foreign invasion. Today, the Internet refers to the vast network of computers connected to one another. The network links everyone from college students to scientific researchers to businesses to news organizations. Everyone from the Pope to *Playboy* magazine has a site on the Internet.

However, no one agency or individual owns the Internet and no one individual is in control of what information is put on the Internet or who may access that information. In fact, many argue that the Internet has thrived because no one controls it. Students, researchers, and novice computer buffs

By Jack Kay, Wayne State University and Timothy A. Borchers, Moorhead State University have been allowed to let their creative energies develop software, hardware, and protocols that allow computers to talk to each other in many interesting and exciting ways. It is unclear how many people use the Internet. Some estimates say that 30 to 40 million people in 160 countries have e-mail accounts. By some counts, the number of net users has grown more than 1,000 percent during the past three years.

There are several components of the Internet, each of which offers unique types of information. The most popular feature of the Internet is e-mail. *E-mail,* short for electronic mail, allows connected users to send a message to each other without using the telephone or "snail mail." The advantages are that users pay no long-distance charges and the respondents may read the message and respond at their leisure. Additionally, e-mail allows users to subscribe to "mailing lists" or other on-line discussion groups. By subscribing to an on-line discussion group (which is usually free), users can read and respond to messages posted by other members of the group from all around the world.

Another aspect of the Internet is Gopher. Originated at the University of Minnesota, Gopher is a menu-based display of textual information. Users are presented with a menu of options and choose whichever menu contains the information they are looking for. Many government agencies use the Gopher system. It is easy to administer and the simplest way of providing information.

For the most part, however, Gopher has given way to the most exciting component of the Internet—the World Wide Web. The "Web" or WWW is a graphically-oriented system of displaying text, graphics, movies, and sounds. The WWW is composed of "pages"—which resemble newspaper or newsletter pages—which contain "hypertext" links. The hypertext links are often words or pictures that are underlined. Clicking the computer's mouse on the word, phrase, or picture allows the user to access the information alluded to by the highlighted link. Many businesses, college students, and even some departments of communication have set up WWW pages. A special, but easily mastered, language—hypertext markup language (HTML)—is used to write the pages.

Another aspect of the Internet are Newsgroups. Newsgroups are similar to e-mail discussion groups, but they do not require a subscription and users can drop in and out to read and respond to messages. Usenet is the name of the primary list of newsgroups. There are nearly 11,000 Usenet groups discussing everything from television shows to college football to politics. The software that is used to access the World Wide Web is usually able to access newsgroups as well.

ACCESSING THE INTERNET

For many college students, access to the Internet is relatively simple and affordable. Many colleges and universities are already wired to the Internet. Consequently, many buildings, including dormitories, on those campuses may already have the hardware in place to gain access. Usually a call to the computing support center on campus will provide you with the information necessary to get connected. If that is not possible, the school will more than likely have a computer lab which offers access to students and instructors. College libraries may offer access as well. Check with the computer center on your campus for information.

It is also possible to gain Internet access from a wide variety of commercial providers. The largest providers include America On-Line, CompuServe, Prodigy, and Delphi. There are many local service providers that can connect you to the Internet as well. Most providers also have local phone numbers for dial-in access, in which case you are not charged long-distance or toll rates for your access. You pay only for "on-line" time, and many companies now provide unlimited access for a fixed monthly fee. You can find information about the larger service providers in many computer magazines or other publications. Local service providers can be found by looking in your phone book. In any case, gaining access is not difficult.

WHAT WILL I FIND?

The practical benefits of using the Internet are potentially limitless. The Internet is like a library with no limits on size or resources. The library of the Internet holds as much information as people are willing to provide. The government, commercial organizations, and private individuals and scholars "serve" information for the Internet. The federal government has made available a great deal of information. Information about virtually every matter before Congress and the President is available on-line. Congress has set up an extensive WWW location which describes bills it is considering and provides background on the proposed legislation. Full text of the Congressional Record is also available and it is searchable by keyword. President Clinton has established a comprehensive on-line presence. Many of Clinton's speeches, press conferences, and position papers are available, as is information about many executive branch agencies. The judicial branch has court opinions and case histories available as well. Finally, many state and local governments have documents of local interest on-line too. For persuasive speeches, the government information available on the WWW is a virtual gold mine. Government information may be found at these locations:

- http://thomas.loc.gov/
- http://www.whitehouse.gov
- http://www.uark.edu/depts/comminfo/www/political.comm.html

To access these locations on the World Wide Web you need to enter the URL address (for example, http://www.whitehouse.gov) using a browser program such as Netscape or Internet Explorer on your computer.

Increasingly, commercial news organizations are putting full texts of their publications on-line. Many of these sources have search features which allow the user to access articles in previous publications. Some of these sources include *Time* magazine, the Associated Press, Reuters, CNN, National Public Radio, the Voice of America, *Sports Illustrated,* and *People.*

In addition to news information, diverse information about many subjects exists as well. Between commercial organizations, university researchers, and private individuals, there exist many articles, publications, and technical documents. In addition, many think tank groups or other special interest organizations have posted information. Information comes not only from sources in the United States, but from most countries throughout the world. You will find information about virtually any topic on the Internet, and from many different political, social, and cultural viewpoints!

However, much of the information on the Internet is often poorly organized and difficult to find. The Internet can be thought of as a big library with no single card catalog or index. Each organization that has a site on the web uses its own indexing system. The key, then, is mastering the art of navigating the Internet. Just as the best way of learning to use a library requires you to visit the building, you will find that accessing the Internet and exploring what is there is the best way to become an effective researcher. Don't worry—you can't break the World Wide Web, so go on-line and explore!

HOW DO I FIND INFORMATION FOR SPEECHES?

The World Wide Web is a vast collection of information. Finding specific information on the Web, however, is somewhat difficult. The key is to be able to use the various "search engines." Some of the more popular search engines are Yahoo! (http://www.yahoo.com), Lycos (http://lycos.com), and AltaVista (http://www.altavista.digital.com). There are many more search engines with new ones appearing quite frequently. Most search engines function in two ways. First, they work as a "search" tool. You simply type in the word or words that you are looking for and the site lists on your computer screen links to sites that may or may not be related to what you are looking for. Try to be as specific as possible when entering key words. For example, instead of typing "President," type "President Clinton." You then scroll through the links the search engine provides in order to find specific information. A search using "President Clinton" would return thousands of links. Some addresses would refer to news articles about the President, some to WWW sites devoted to Clinton, and some to official government locations. Using key words would make the search more precise. For example, type "Clinton Whitewater" to obtain those sites only about Clinton and the Whitewater financial scandal.

Second, the search tools function as an index, or a directory. You would follow the menus to find information. For example, you could follow the "Government" listing on the page to find the site for the White House.

From there, you could follow links relating to Clinton and public statements he has made. In other words, the search engines function as a phone book with a long list of categories, subcategories, etc.

Allyn and Bacon, the publisher of this text, provides an excellent site on the World Wide Web to help you develop skills in Internet research. To access the information point your browser to the following address: http://www.abacon.com/compsite/research/search.html

The various search tools of the Internet can help you narrow your topic and locate specific and useful information. For example, you may wish to do a speech on "racism." There are many different aspects of racism so you would be wise to focus the topic. You could turn to one of the Internet's search engines and enter the term "racism." You could then sift through the numerous files that would be returned about racism until a more specific aspect of racism catches your attention. For example, you could find information about discrimination in housing and use that as the more focused topic of your speech. Then, you could return to the search engine and type "housing discrimination" and find a great deal of information about discrimination in housing that could be used as support material for your speech. Thus, the Internet can help you narrow a speech topic.

In addition to using search engines to find particular information, the Internet contains a vast array of reference sources, ranging from dictionaries to fact books, newspapers to government documents. Many publishers, university libraries, and academic organizations have sites on the World Wide Web which provide links to important reference sources. The Allyn and Bacon CompSite page (http://www.abacon.com/compsite), for example, provides a tutorial that helps students find reference sources on the Internet. The home page of the Department of Communication at Wayne State University (http://www.comm.wayne.edu/comm/links.html) provides links to a variety of newspapers, electronic news organizations, and academic sources of information. The American Communication Association (http://www.cavern.uark.edu/comminfo/www/ACA.html) provides links to resources particularly useful to those interested in human communication. Organizations such as the Commission on Presidential debates (http://www.debates96.org) provide extensive material on the history of political debates, and have on-line searchable transcripts of past presidential debates. One of the best sites for finding presidential documents and reports from the executive branch of the U.S. government is the White House site (http://www.whitehouse.gov).

USING INTERNET INFORMATION IN SPEECHES

Information, whether from Internet sources or from conventional sources, must be documented. As of yet there is not one standard way of citing information retrieved from the Internet. Style books such as the *MLA Handbook for Writers of Research Papers* and the *Publication Manual of the American Psychological*

Association provide useful guidelines for documenting material obtained on the World Wide Web. The user of Internet information should strive to determine which person or organization is responsible for placing the information on the Internet and record enough information to allow others to track down the information. A useful approach for citing information which is published for the first time on a WWW site is to include the following:

* Author
* Title of the article
* Date and time at which the information was retrieved
* URL address (http://www.XXX.XXX)
* Individual or organization that sponsors the WWW site

To cite information that originated in another source and is republished on the Internet, include the following:

* Author of the original material
* Author of the site on which the material is placed
* Title of the article
* Date and time at which the information was retrieved
* URL address (http://www.XXX.XXX)
* Source in which the material originally appeared
* Date on which the material originally appeared
* Individual or organization that sponsors the WWW site

Most Internet browsers have a "preferences" or "page setup" function that allows the user to print much of this information on their Internet print-out. See any help files that came with the browser application for more information. More detailed suggestions for documenting and citing Internet sources may be found at the following on-line locations:

* MLA-Style Citations of Electronic Sources (http://www.cas.usf.edu/english/walker/mla.html)
* The MLA and APA Information at Purdue (http://owl.trc.purdue.edu/files/110.html)
* Citation Guides for Electronic Documents (http://www.nlc-bnc.ca/ifla/l/training/citation/citing.htm)

An excellent discussion of on-line documentation is provided at the Allyn and Bacon CompSite at http://www.abacon.com/compsite/research/citation.html.

QUALITY OF RESEARCH

There is certainly a great deal of information on the Internet. However, there are several cautions you should exercise when using the Internet. First, the

Internet is no substitute for the library. While you may find a great deal of timely information about your topic, you may miss some of the most important information if you do not also search the library. Most books and many periodicals are not yet included on the Internet. Make sure that you don't miss these valuable sources of information.

Second, the information found on the Internet may not always be of the best quality. Information to be used as supporting material in speeches should be tested and reviewed by qualified individuals. This textbook, for example, was subjected to a lengthy review process before it was made available to students and faculty. Most journalists, as well, use very strict guidelines to insure that what they print is verifiable. Much of what is found on the Internet has been subjected to a review process of some sort. For example, using an article from the *New York Times* would be just as credible if it were taken from the newspaper, from a microfilm copy of the newspaper, or if it were received via the Internet. However, people who place information on the Internet are not always as careful or rigorous as they should be. Many individuals can establish Internet sites without any review of or expertise in their subject. Virtually anyone can create a World Wide Web home page and place almost anything they want to place on the page, including false information. Take great care when selecting Internet research so that your credibility as a speaker is not compromised.

ACTIVITIES

Activity One: Finding Search Engines

The purpose of this activity is to locate various search engines.

1. Use your browser to access the following URL: (http://home.mcom.com/home/internet-search.html)
2. Record the URL names for ten of the search engines identified at this site.

Activity Two: Using Search Engines

The purpose of this activity is to learn how to use various search engines to find material for a speech.

1. Use three different search engines to find information about public speaking.
2. Experiment with different ways of entering the key words "public speaking." Try, for example, entering the key words "public and speaking" as well as entering "public speaking." Try, for example, entering the words "public speaking" in quotation marks. Note that some search engines allow you to use the minus (–) symbol to conduct a "not" search—you could enter the words "school -public" to find "school" when it appears without "private." The Lycos search engine allows you to use a period (.) after a keyword to look for an exact match—you would enter "school." to find "school" and not "schools"

and "schooling." Several search engines allow you to use the dollar sign ($) to enter a word fragment. Entering "air$" would retrieve "airport," "airplane," and "airbus."

3. Can you find instructions on-line to help you better use the search engines? Hint: look for help and search help buttons on the page where you start your search. To find help for the Lycos search engine, go to: http://www.lycos. com/search-help.html

Activity Three: Discovering Differences between Search Engines

The purpose of this activity is to discover how searching for the same word produces different results depending upon the search engine that is used.

1. Using three different search engines enter the same key word.

2. Record the number of different "hits" each search engine reports.

3. Describe the difference in results between the three search engines.

Activity Four: Learning How to Conduct Advanced Searches.

The purpose of this activity is to learn where to find information on conducting advanced searches using search engines.

1. Use a search engine to discover on-line reference material that helps you learn how to more effectively use that search engine.

Activity Five: Accessing Newsgroups.

The purpose of this activity is to learn how to obtain information from a newsgroup.

1. Using software that allows you access to newsgroups, browse through a list of newsgroups available through your server.

2. Look at the messages contained in several of the newsgroups.

3. Briefly describe the messages.

4. Describe the typical user of the newsgroups you viewed.

Activity Six: Establishing the Credibility of WWW Sites

The purpose of this activity is to assess the credibility of various sites on the World Wide Web.

1. Select a topic such as "global warming" or "presidential debates." Conduct a search of one of the search engines (Yahoo!, Lycos, AltaVista, or any other search engine) for information about this topic. Then, visit a number of the sites listed by the search engine.

2. Determine what type of site you are visiting. Is the site a news organization? A special interest group? An academic research paper? Someone's personal home page?

3. Write a short paper comparing five of the sites you visit. Which of the sites was the most credible? Which was the least credible? How do you determine which information should be used in your speech?

Activity Seven: Basic Audience Analysis in Newsgroup Communities

The purpose of this activity is to discover differences between communities in the way they use evidence, values, and arguments.

1. Select three different news groups that focus on related subject matter and follow their messages for a three-day period. You might, for example, select a Newt Gingrich fan club discussion group, a President Clinton support group, and an alternative politics white-power newsgroup.

2. Select one representative thread from each group and print out that thread.

3. Analyze each thread to provide answers to the following:

   a. What values are emphasized in the thread?

   b. What constitutes evidence for the group?

   c. What type of supporting material is needed to prove an argument?

4. In two typed pages discuss the differences in the way each community uses evidence, values, and arguments.

Activity Eight: Visiting WWW Sites of Socio-Political Groups

The purpose of this activity is to identify source material that group members would find credible and persuasive and to identify arguments which group members would believe without any external supporting material.

1. Visit WWW sites provided by five different political organizations (e.g., The White House Home Page, the Militia of Montana Page, the Abortion Rights Home Page, the People for the Ethical Treatment of Animals Home Page, etc.). Print out the home page.

2. In a short paper do the following:

   a. List two articles/sources each group considers credible.

   b. Identify one argument for each group that members would accept as a premise (without additional supporting material).

   c. Identify one argument that each group would accept only if credible external evidence was provided.

3. Compare and contrast the different standards used by the groups.

Activity Nine: Examining
Unacceptable Information

The purpose of this activity is to find World Wide Web sites which contain what you consider to be "outrageous" or "unacceptable" positions.

1. Find two WWW sites which you feel take positions that run contrary to your own views and to the views of most members of our society. These sites might, for example, advocate white supremacy, complete racial separation, or even slavery.

2. Analyze the sites to determine the strategies used to convince people to adopt the group's views.

3. In a short page paper discuss the strategies used. Evaluate these strategies from an ethical point of view.

Appendix B

SPEECH TOPIC LOCATOR

The *Idea Starters* (A) may be all you need to trigger a creative and manageable topic for your next speech. The *Idea Elaborators* (B) are meant to help you narrow your general topic and to suggest ways of dividing it into main points.

If you are still struggling to find a topic, consult the *Topic Inventory* (C) for help in finding a general topical area that interests you. Apply the *Idea Elaborators* to the topic chosen and proceed to narrow and refine it.

Shown are only 13 of the most obvious elaborators, but multiplied by the 500 topics in the inventory gives you a total of 6,500 ideas for speeches. There is plenty to talk about!

A. IDEA STARTERS

People	Objects	Events	Problems	Issues
Policies	Definitions	Theories	Hobbies	Structures
Processes	Places	Concepts	Plans	Jobs
Your interests	Natural phenomena	Computers	Incredible phenomena	

B. IDEA ELABORATORS

History of	Influence of	Current practices	Classic examples
Importance of	Differing views	How to do it	How it works
How to make it	Where it is located		Why it is done
Implications of	Dangers of		

C. TOPIC INVENTORY

Falconry	Hand guns	ROTC	Aggression
Law clerks	Pregnancy	Acupuncture	Adoption
Auto repairs	Senior citizens	Aliens	Kibbutzim
Scuba diving	Iran	Boat navigation	Koran
Archery	Gun control	Dance	Ku Klux Klan
Acid rain	UFOs	Advertising	Knighthood
Drunk drivers	Marilyn Monroe	Pollution	AIDS
Leadership	Pyramids	Bottle laws	Fly tying
Capital punishment	Sleep research	Architecture	Chemical warfare
Mummification	Earthquakes	Islam	Old Faithful
Lasers	Ozone layer	Birth control	Word processing
Beijing	Cable cars	Writers	Existentialism
Bar Mitzvah	Solar energy	Automobiles	Epistemology
Bas Mitzvah	Dog training	Copyrights	Fidel Castro
Astrology	Filmmaking	Floods	Furniture refinishing
Witchcraft	Umpiring	FBI	South Africa
Cheating	Kite flying	Hinduism	Fairness doctrine
Biological warfare	World Series	Infant mortality	Smoking
Martin Luther King	Drugs	S & L's	Crime
Peace Corps	Music	Banks	Day care centers
Internships	Amnesia	Macrame	Pornography
Working out	Kuwait today	War games	Marines
Sailboarding	Dog breeding	Mammoth Cave	Robotics
Birding	Hypnotism	Kremlin	Ageism
Child abuse	Violence	United Nations	Statue of Liberty
Teen violence	Beatles	Stock market	Rose Parade
Dutch treating	Volcanoes	Labor unions	Affirmative action
Dinosaurs	Handwriting	Military tactics	Zone defense
Iraq	Ghosts	Washington, D.C.	Superdome
Organ donating	Books	Expressionism	World wonders
Cancer signs	Missiles	Phenomenology	IRS
Computers	Karate	Word processing	Urban League
Home brew	Tai chi	Sailing	Numerology
Marxism	Metaphysics	Nelson Mandela	PLO
ESP	Hypnotherapy	Public relations	Psychic phenomena
College athletics	Jazz	Sex discrimination	Racism
Nuclear energy	Camping	Diets	Transcendental meditation
Laser disks	Politics	Leisure	
Soul food	FCC	Buddhism	Supreme Court
Used cars	Alcoholism	Body building	Surrogates
Pee-Wee hockey	Investments	Awards	Weight lifting
Ballooning	Divorce	Aerospace	White House
Ski racing	Censorship	Amnesty	Unknown soldier

C. TOPIC INVENTORY (cont.)

Artists	Cloning	Zero population growth	West Point
Bermuda Triangle	Funerals	Future wonders	Aborigines
Counterfeiting	ERA	Psychics	Basilicas
Ecology	Gay rights	Arbitration	Apocalypse
CIA	Retirement	Ethics	Taj Mahal
Health care	IQ	America's Cup	Rocket planes
Inflation	NAACP	Art deco	Speed
Esperanto	Olympics	Biofeedback	Panama
NOW	Pulitzer Prize	Bullfighting	Mermaids
Nutrition	Scientology	Forensic medicine	Mayflower
Papacy	Suicide	Persuasibility	Harvard
Royalty	Whales	Titanic	Everglades
Telepathy	Tatooing	Stamps	Holocaust
Transplants	Submarines	Pygmies	Tar pits
Zen	Satellites	Mound builders	Erosion
Wind	Illusions	Jacques Cousteau	Creationism
Telescopes	Noah's Ark	Magna Carta	Pigeon racing
Boxing	Mormons	Native Americans	Eclipses
Credit	Ghostwriting	Comets	Alchemy
Economics	Knighthood	Glaciers	Black death
KGB	Hot springs	Fingerprints	Naval Academy
Nursing homes	Rain forests	Eskimos	Alfred Nobel
Health insurance	Voiceprints	Etiquette	H.M.S. Beagle
Maoism	Evolution	Galileo	Casey Jones
Nielsen ratings	Fencing	Curling	Great Lakes
Obscenity	Abstract art	Fossils	Fallacies
Population	Babe Ruth	Flags	Riots
Psychoanalysis	Aesthetics	Death Valley	Kaizen
Saints	C.I.O.	Dead Sea	Apartheid
Slavery	Indian art	Cave people	Rape
Zodiac	Bicycling	Castles	Terrorism
Waves	Cholesterol	P. T. Barnum	Torture today
Recession	Semantics	Aztecs	Famines
Chauvinism	Self-presentation	Pompeii	Poisonous plants
Cults	Collective behavior	Abolitionists	Unusual monuments
Gambling	Propaganda	Railroads	Boxing
Acting	Altruism	Henry Ford	Baseball cards
Census	Family violence	Camouflage	Great imposters
Test-tube babies	Substance abuse	Wankel engine	Mediation
Vitamins	Desktop publishing	Eiffel Tower	Agnosticism
Zoos	Herbs	Dead Sea Scrolls	Aptitude testing
Ventriloquism	Endangered species	Cannibals	Atlantis
NASA			Blood pressure

C. TOPIC INVENTORY (cont.)

Gardening
Free trade
Campaigns
Journalism codes
Teambuilding
Karaoke
Brainwashing
Roots
A.F.L.
Cave art
T-groups
Cybernetics
Androgyny
Seals
Dolphins
4-wheeling
Helmets
ATVs
Draft
Sexism
Hall of Fame
Colorization
Lotteries
Mafia
Gangs
Aerobics
OSHA
Snowboarding
World Cup
PGA
NRA
Right to die
Air bags
Consumerism
Deeds of valor
Heroes
Stamp collecting
Video games
MADD
Fashion
Skydiving
Saddam Hussein
Nintendo

Star gazing
Camcorders
Photography
Wine
Wildflowers
Passover
Body language
Malcolm X
Mt. Everest
Compressed speech
Animal magnetism
Artificial intelligence
Betting behavior
ACLU
Prisons
Taboo phenomena
Icebergs
Maternity
Lake levels
Honor system
Computer dating
Self-disclosure
Dress codes
Codes of conduct
Facial expressions
Parkinson's law
Photojournalism
Proxemics
Hawthorne effect
Self-concept
D day
Pearl Harbor
Storytelling
Classic cars
"Goat Ropes"
    (rumors)
Invitro fertilization
Hiroshima
P-51 Mustang
Tanks
Jogging
"Politically Corrects"
McCarthyism

Deconstructionism
Secret Service
Libel
SLAPP's
Iacocca
Subliminal
    communication
Psychokinesis
Suez Canal
Civil liberties
Color
Deficit
Comics
Verbal aggression
Jupiter
Saturn
Meteors
Ramadan
Zeppelins
Mars
Amelia Earhart
Robots
Amish
Loch Ness Monster
Heimlich Maneuver
Wonder drugs
Rock music
Dietary laws
Management
    functions
Fraternities
Sororities
Movie code ratings
Feuds
Rosa Parks
Alarm systems
Miracle sites
Williamsburg
Riding
Sleep research
Listening
Best forgers
Clairvoyance

Adolescence
Animal
    communication
Interpersonal
    attraction
Cognitive complexity
Dream analysis
Chronemics
Ice age
Medal of Honor
Competitive skiing
Black Sox
Hollywood scandals
Harlem Globetrotters
Hoaxes
CPR
EPCOT
Antiquing
Tidal waves
Heisman Award
Cy Young Award
Albinism
Defensive driving
Loon preservation
Couponing
Nudity
Nudists
Self-esteem
Dangerous pets
Bankruptcies
M1A1 Tank
Indy 500
Sports scholarships
Special museums
Crafts
Hypertension
War powers
Animal rights
Family communica-
    tion
Greenhouse effect
Poultry science
4H Club

C. TOPIC INVENTORY (cont.)

FFA
Grieving
Grievance procedure
Board membership
Child custody
Slang
Recycling
Waste disposal
Super tankers
Toxic substances
Noninvasive surgery
Hi-definition TV
Exceptional children
Firearms
Bonsai
Rug hooking
Colors
Early radio
Puppetry
Infrared
Ergonomics
Time management
Study skills
Genealogy
Body massage
Family boating
Volunteerism
Student government
Financial aid
Extracurricular
   activities
Commercial art
Criminal justice
Hospitality
   management
Law enforcement
Maritime academies
Pilot training
Travel agents
Fitness labs
Container gardening
Correctional
   institutions

Card weaving
Calligraphy
Databases
Happiness
Magic
Wildlife rescue
Edible flowers
Graphoanalysis
Kuntaw
Law aptitudes (LSAT)
Shamanism
Human sexuality
Pottery
Sign language
Dowsing
Clowning
Assertiveness
Aikido
Yoga
Loom weaving
Judo
Blacksmithing
Basketry
Flower arrangement
Shiatsu
Citizenship
Hurricanes
Social Security
Norplant
Centenarians
Eagle Scouts
U.S. acquisitions
Acropolis
Nature trails
Lyme disease
Camping
Glasnost
Parochiad
Police brutality
Stonehenge
Population
Alzheimer's disease
Canning/freezing

Microfilms
   International
James Baldwin
Prostitution
ADC
Ecumenicism
Open housing
Rapid transit
Inner cities
States' rights
"As one"
DT/DCC
Boxing
Pentagon
Headstart
Cost of living
Blight
Budgeting
Terrariums
Circus
Shakespeare
Ergology
Phobias
Diabetes
Welfare
Parachuting
Frostbite
Bridges
Churches
Grand Canyon
Graffiti
Posters
Instant replays
Lightning
Esalen
Tiananmen Square
Archivy
Communal living
Gerontology
Poverty
Marijuana
Tuition costs
Forest fires

Avalanches
Bonding
Salvation
Systems theory
Mushrooms
Auto safety
E.T.V.
Common law
   marriage
Foreign imports
Multimedia
Shintoism
Branch Davidians
Yugoslavia
Somalia
Fundamentalism
Feminism
Haiti
Breast cancer
Prostate cancer
Cuba
Panama Canal
NAFTA
Health care
Taxes
Movies
Power pianos
Flash cooking
Fuel cells
Virtual vision
Virtual reality
Bio-lite
Madonna
Gold
Floods
Landfills
Fires
Charter schools
Custody battles
Sports salaries
Privacy act
Credit cards
Homelessness

C. TOPIC INVENTORY (cont.)

Solar energy
Casinos
New age
Genetic engineering
Sunset law
Obesity
Distance learning
Militias

Zaire/Ruwanda
Christian coalition
Microprocessors
Internet
World Wide Web
CD-ROM
Chat rooms

Fiber optics
Gulf syndrome
Mars
Bible
Koran
Torah
Diets

Bike trails
Snowmobiling
Afghanistan
Taliban
Rhodes scholars
Boeing 737 jet
Kwanza

NAME INDEX

SUBJECT INDEX